Fire in the Plaça

Fire in the Plaça

Catalan Festival Politics After Franco

Dorothy Noyes

PENN

UNIVERSITY OF PENNSYLVANIA PRESS

Philadelphia

Publication of this volume was assisted by grants from the College of Humanities of The Ohio State University and from the Program for Cultural Cooperation between Spain's Ministry of Education and Culture and United States Universities.

10 9 8 7 6 5 4 3 2 1

Published by
University of Pennsylvania Press
Philadelphia, Pennsylvania 19104-4011

Library of Congress Cataloging-in-Publication Data

Noyes, Dorothy.
    Fire in the plaça : Catalan festival politics after Franco / Dorothy Noyes.
       p.   cm.
    Includes bibliographical references and index.
    ISBN 0-8122-3729-3 (cloth : alk. paper) — ISBN 0-8122-1849-3 (pbk. : alk. paper)
    1. Corpus Christi Festival—Spain—Berga. 2. Festivals—Political aspects—Spain—Berga.
3. Berga (Spain)—Social life and customs. 4. Spain—Social conditions—1975–. 5. Spain—
Politics and government—1975–. I. Title.

GT4995.C6N68 2003
394.26'0946'72—dc21   2003051232

*To the people of Berga, with love and thanks, and
in special memory of Ricard Cuadra and Pepito Tañá*

Contents

A Note on Catalonia and the Catalan Language

ALTHOUGH BERGA IS WITHIN THE BORDERS of the state called Spain, it is linguistically and culturally part of Catalonia, which I am going to call a nation because the Berguedans do: it is an experiential unity felt as "home" of which a political expression is generally desired. The language of Catalonia is Catalan, a Romance language with a long literary tradition. Dialects of Catalan are spoken in Catalonia, the region of Valencia, the Balearic Islands, a fringe of Aragon along the Catalan border, the co-principality of Andorra, the Department of the Pyrénées-Orientales in France (where more effective centralization has largely degraded the language to a patois), and the city of Alghero (Alguer) in Sardinia. These regions are collectively known as the Països Catalans. Catalonia proper—a triangle with the Pyrenees as one side, the Mediterranean as another, the Noguera Ribagorçana and Ebre rivers approximately marking the third, and Barcelona, the capital, in the middle—is now an autonomous region of the Spanish state. Catalan is its co-official language.

Catalonia has been fortunate in its native and foreign scholars, particularly in history and anthropology. Although I will cite several of them, I cannot do justice to the wealth of the scholarly tradition on which my own work depends. Readers interested in pursuing the subject have several fine collections in English with which to begin: McDonogh (1986), Llobera (1990), Azevedo (1991), and, in a more literary vein, Sobrer (1992).

I ask the reader's patience with the Catalan words and phrases I have included. Many Berguedan things and practices do not translate gracefully into English—the *plens*, for example—and I imagine that the reader with some knowledge of Romance languages will like to see the real names and portions of original texts. I should note for readers of Catalan that I am following the Berguedan vernacular rather than the norms of Fabra: hence the presence of dialectal words such as *àliga* and Castilianisms such as *petardos* or *Pepito*.

Readers who are familiar with the much-documented sociolinguistic situation of Barcelona should be aware that the Catalan interior tends far more to monolingualism in Catalan. All of the current local media in Berga use Catalan; the language of administration is Catalan; the language of the street and of the home is Catalan. Castilian Spanish serves as a domestic language among first-generation immigrants, the language of literacy for working-class people educated under the dictatorship, and the primary language of access to the world outside Catalonia. All conversations reported or translated in this book are in Catalan; for the original language of translated texts, see the citations.

Introduction

THERE IS NOTHING ELSE IN THE WORLD, they insisted, and by the end of my stay I believed them, almost enough to stay for good. Inside the whirling mass in the burning *plaça*, there is nothing else: the crowd has shaped the *axis mundi* there on the hard stones, a wheel of smoke and sweating bodies rubbing against the crumbling facades of a provincial capital in the Pyrenees, where most of the factories have closed.

Performed annually for nearly four hundred years, the Patum of Berga has simultaneously celebrated and refused the political order at every turn. Its dancing effigies—giants and dwarfs, Turks and Christian knights, devils and angels, a crowned eagle and two flaming mule-dragons—serve as vehicles for a multitude of allegories. But the festival obscures its own apparent messages through techniques of the body cultivated with special intensity since the last years of the Franco regime: strong rhythms and constant motion, vertigo, heavy drinking, sleep deprivation, and the smoke and dense falling sparks of firecrackers at close range. After five days, symbolic combat ends in physical consensus and the incorporation of both individuals and social categories into a felt totality: metaphorically, a social body. In the 1970s, this body was a proposed democratic Catalonia, and the festival served as rehearsal for the massive demonstrations in Barcelona. In the 1980s, industrial decline and factionalism in this small mountain capital turned the festival into an end in itself, a passionate creation of an immanent unity recognized as ephemeral from the outset. This book, an ethnography based on several periods of fieldwork since 1989 as well as historical research, explores festival as a primary instrument and framework of action—social, political, economic, religious, and intellectual—for a community with limited resources.

The first half of the book describes the synchronic experience of Patum participants, taking as its ethnographic present the years from 1989 to 1992, the main period of my fieldwork and perhaps the zenith of Berguedan public life in the early years of democracy. The second half historicizes that powerful moment, examining how it emerged from the Franco regime on one side and how the liberalism resulting from European integration and globalization is dissolving it on the other.

In Part I, I present the community's takeover of my field research as a way of opening up the tensions between representation and presence in the festival. These tensions take shape in a factionalized community with a history of civil war and a present of economic threat—a story that the community tells itself in the festival and then refuses to hear. Today, as I will illustrate, the incorporation of individuals into active community membership is the primary goal of the Patum, and the history that militates against that incorporation must be overtly silenced and covertly transformed. The second chapter briefly lays out the Patum's condensation of this history, and shows how the festival elements articulate Berga's body politic in the present.

Part II examines social interaction in the Patum, showing how social distance is both semiotically and physically compressed in order to transform an experience of individuation and interpretation into one of incorporation and immanence. Chapter 3 presents the Berguedan model of everyday social interactions as structured along a continuum of respect and solidarity, personhood and belonging. Chapter 4 shows how the festival effigies are, through interaction with participants, brought to life as sacred persons who epitomize the two polarities of the everyday continuum. In Chapter 5, I describe the Patum's manipulations of participant bodies, including crowding, strong rhythms, repetition, drink, continuous dancing, centripetal movement, and intense pyrotechnics, as well as a gradual acceleration toward vertigo during the course of the five days of the festival. These techniques of incorporation disable everyday critical faculties and transform the festival from a representation of social divisions into a forcible communion between them.

Parts III and IV describe the recent history of the Patum, in which Berguedans of all classes treated the event as a deliberate instrument of community reproduction, despite intense disagreement about the nature of the community in question. Part III examines the shift in key metaphors under the Franco regime from the social body to the Oedipal family, a more suitable vehicle for negotiating conflict and change over time. Chapter 6 describes the metaphors of maternity used in the past thirty years to characterize the Patum's role in the local community. These metaphors are related in chapter 7 to the patriarchal discourses of the Franco regime, and the constraints these discourses placed upon local cultural reproduction. All factions associated the Patum with a vernacular sacrality and especially with the local Madonna, whereas the Franco regime resurrected the disembodied, hieratic religion of the Corpus Christi procession. Chapter 8 describes how the Patum became a national focus of resistance and a school of Catalanist democratic mobilization, in which the language of origins was used to reconstruct the primal scene of the new generation. The Patum's nonverbal techniques of incorporation provided a means both of reconciling Catalanists across ideological differences and enabling the participation of the immigrant population: the Patum became a much-copied template and was appropriated not only into other festivals but into all genres of Catalan collective performance. It offered, I argue, the experiential basis for the now hegemonic Catalan theory of identity as the embodied memory of performance.

In Part IV, the consequences for the Patum itself emerge: it became a festival of mass physical participation, both intensifying and extensifying in performance, and exceeding the control of its local mobilizers, who increasingly define it as a kind of "addiction." Chapter 9 describes the transformation of the Patum when Berga's primary relationship with the outside world became one of consumption rather than production. Chapter 10 explores the contemporary Berguedan debate between "networkers" and *integristes*. Networkers are proponents of economic, political, and cultural linkages with the outside world: they therefore favor preserving distinctions between persons as individuals, but dissolving the member/outsider boundary. The skeptical *integristes* cite a history as old as the Patum in which such linkages have produced nothing but political domination, economic exploitation, and local division. They are ready to make members of outsiders, but tolerate neither spectators nor relations at a distance: for them, you are either incorporated or nonexistent. This contest of survival strategies is conducted largely through divergent styles of reproducing and appropriating the Patum. Chapter 11 draws back to give a more general account of the fate of local culture between transition and globalization, showing how the forms of compromise that provided a model for accommodation in the democratic transition leave the community vulnerable in less equal negotiations with global capital. At the same time, they continue to sustain Berga's and Catalonia's refusal of violent separatism.

Organic Solidarity in the Provinces

Like the people of Berga in the Patum, I attempt to construct in this book a coherent totality out of heterogeneous and resistant matter. The Berguedans have the advantage of me by four hundred years and several thousand more minds on the job, yet even they have not been able to master their social experience by modeling it. Naturally, I have not come close, but a principal object of this book is to show the parallels between their project and mine. The compressed theoretical introduction that follows should not alarm the reader, though it may initially bewilder. I simply want to show with a synoptic glance how much is packed into traditional collective performance. The book that follows will unpack a good deal of it; no scholar knows enough to unpack all of it.

Festival has been an important topic in folklore, history, and anthropology for some years, and what it accomplishes at the symbolic and discursive levels is now beginning to be understood. It dramatizes actual or proposed social arrangements, especially collective identities and hierarchies, in order to win consent, force acquiescence, or destabilize other such representations. However, a view of collective performance as an arena of contesting utterances in the present fails to take seriously the widespread native insistence that some identities are not constructed, but real, that some performances are "imposed" and some are "in the blood." Attending to the diachronic experience of bodies in the festival, this book shows that such distinctions are neither the false consciousness resulting from successful naturalization nor interest-based allegiance disguising itself as attachment. Rather, they point to a sophisticated native awareness of how repeated performance, grounded in everyday material relations, can gradually transmute experience into something like essence.

I will describe the "techniques of incorporation" exercised upon me as a potential new Berguedan, and the first-person voice sheds light not merely on this ethnographic encounter, but on the general process of socializing outsiders and creating local loyalties in a world of transnational individuals and global forces. Poor communities cannot afford to ignore outsiders, high or low: outsiders must be converted into social persons and thus made useful. Concluding from historical experience that even the autonomy of personhood poses risks to the general good, Berguedans go further. Through the Patum's aggressive communion, they force newcomers as well as themselves to become members of a single social body. They acknowledge, however, the costs thus imposed on individuals, and the Patum's constraints are both desired and resented by all concerned.

During the 1970s, the Patum became a means of mobilizing a larger Catalan social body and a widely appropriated model for collective action. Its controlled violence to individual selves enabled viable collective action to emerge from the aftermath of civil war, dictatorship, and mass immigration. The emotional impact of participation in the Patum suggested a formulation of Catalan identity that could overcome those historical divisions: identity is not found in ethnic or ideological lineage, but in the embodied memory of performance. This performative model has profoundly influenced the practice of the regional government since 1979. It is not free of ambivalence. My informants fear the consequences of a strong collective identity even as they cultivate it, and sometimes when they sing their own music they hear the echo of the Francoist anthem.

This book sets the period of democratic transition into a longer history of the Patum's use by Berguedans as a model for articulating the relationship of individuals, the community, and the larger world. When the Patum emerged from the church feast of Corpus Christi, the hierarchy of members in the sacralized body politic was contested, but the local linkages to larger social and cosmic orders were clear. Later, as Catalonia experienced violent industrial and nationalist conflict, the Oedipal family became a more productive metaphor than the social body, and the Patum became at once maternal refuge and primal scene. Democratization and European integration raised the fear of a mass with no center or edges, figured in a Patum ever longer, more crowded, and more intense. Most recently, Berguedans have responded to the challenge of reproducing the community in a global economy by attempting to impose two new models. Many make a virtue of necessity by reconceiving Berga as a nexus in a constantly refigured network and the Patum as an object of exchange. Those unwilling to surrender sacrality and stability revert to the idea of the Patum as Berga's Corpus Mysticum, now a more literal social body no longer capable of shifting between microcosm and macrocosm. Standing for nothing but itself, the Patum of these skeptics, who have been "burned" once too often, declares the end of representation.

Through all of these variations, dating from early modernity to modernity's apparent end, Berguedans have used the Patum to address the quintessentially modern task of constructing a totality out of diverse social elements. Their reliance on the social body as metaphor for this purpose is of course common to a long tradition of European social theories as well as the collective performances influencing them and influenced by them: the medieval theology of the Corpus Mysticum, nationalism's construction of the nation-state as an organic individual, Fascist corporatism, and the neocorporatism of the welfare state and the new Europe.[1] But the strategies of Berguedans and their immediate situation—the industrial community—resonate most strongly with Durkheim and his concept of "organic solidarity." As defined by Durkheim, this is the form of integration proper to societies with a strong division of labor, a valuing of complementarity as a result of mutual dependence; it stands in opposition to the "mechanical solidarity" of simple societies in which all members are animated by a common consciousness ([1893]1984).

In practice, as even Durkheim was compelled to admit, the division of labor fosters conflict, and where forms of organic solidarity exist, they have generally been engineered by social elites as mitigation. The Patum offers the "folk" or grassroots equivalent of such elite engineering, typical of small communities in which it is generally accepted that difference and inequality must be lived with, because both radical social change and individual exit are impractical (cf. Hirschman 1970). Several European festival genres, indeed, address this problem. Perhaps most familiar to scholars is Carnival, a space of licence and inversion in which criticism may take place, resentment may be vented, and alternatives may be imagined.[2] The Patum participates in a rather less well-examined class of performances: folk dramas of encounter and combat ending in some mode of reconciliation.[3] These performances theatricalize social divisions in ways indirect enough to be denied if necessary, but legible enough to be understood by community members. Integrating social struggles into founding narratives, they show difference as the base of community. They acknowledge the pains of coexistence and supersede them, in part, through the shared experience of participation.

This latter effect is intensified in the Patum by the presence of other ritual forms—those of communion and those of civic display.[4] In this way, many of Durkheim's contradictions find potential resolution. In practice, the only alleviation Durkheim could suggest for the pains of a class society was the cultivation of mechanical solidarity in subgroups or crosscutting identifications.[5] The Patum, however, cultivates both organic and mechanical solidarity by differential use of two levels of the festival, which Durkheim later distinguished as "representative ritual" and "collective recreation" ([1912]1960, 543). The former lays out the differences and groupings in Berguedan life for all to examine. Not only does it construct them as complementary parts of a whole, it presents each element as an object of desire, promising and in some cases delivering attainment. Here the Patum recalls Durkheim's suggestion that heterosexual desire provides the deep model for organic solidarity.[6] The lower level of the festival, intense and uncontrolled bodily performance in which difference is lost, relieves the concentration on symbols and creates the "collective effervescence" that is the corporeal basis for mechanical solidarity.

I refer often to Durkheim and Freud in this book, not as explanatory frameworks but as high-theory analogues of the "sensuous thought" of the Patum.[7] The theories and the festival share not only core concerns and metaphors, but core ambivalences and contradictions in their attempts to address modernity.[8] One justification for the Durkheimian parallel is genealogical: Durkheim's organic solidarity ultimately derives from the same theology of the Corpus Mysticum that gave birth to the Patum.[9] Further, like Durkheim and his school, Berguedans are highly sensitive to the cognitive and emotional power of bodily experience and recognize the importance of "natural symbols" (Douglas [1973]1982) for creating social facts. Finally, like Durkheim, Berguedans are willful functionalists in an unpropitious historical situation, insisting against all the evidence on the foundational, normal, and systemic character of collective expressions that are in fact visibly reactive, compensatory, and maintained by powerful social controls (cf. Lukes 1985, 173–74; Coser 1984, xxiii). This last similarity is not unrelated to the others. Durkheim declared sociology the historical successor to religion: both are efforts to conceptualize society (Lukes 1985, 467, 476). Given Catholic Europe as our context, we might suggest that both festival participants and social theorists partake of a sacramental habit of thought in which representations are credited with a direct relationship to reality, and to act on one is to act on the other. In this way, for example, the body as metaphor suggests the body as instrument. Berguedans manipulate the Patum—and themselves in it—in the hope of transforming Berga. Scholars are sometimes given to similar confidence that the refinement of their models will enable them to reshape society.[10]

The Patum is a genuine "collective representation," incorporating Berguedan diversity both in symbol and in performance. Generated out of everyday social interactions, it has become the matrix through which all social relations are understood. But having created this powerful "total social fact" (Mauss 1967, 1), Berguedans find themselves trapped in it. A language as all-encompassing as the Patum allows only the partial freedoms of revoicing, revision, or parody; no statements make sense outside of it. Drawing everything into itself, the Patum also serves to maintain all the social memory on which it has fed: nothing in Berga ever goes away. In this sense, Berguedans feel themselves primordially determined. And here they find themselves in company with Freud. Though his determinism is different, they share his language of the sexual body: ostensibly literal for him, metaphorical for them. Like Freud's subjects and Freud himself, Berguedans obsessively elaborate and rework this body metaphor, using it both to speak and to deny speech. Although they resist direct exegesis of the sacred they have made, metacommentaries at a distance from the Patum spell out its implications, endlessly demystifying what will once again be mystified in next year's performance. Berguedans share Freud's pessimism and his ambivalence about symbolic processes, ultimately seeing them as offering the only freedom of maneuver in a closed system.

Here we come to a third great theorist of modernity, for the symbolic determinism with which the Patum is generally credited is acknowledged by Berguedans to be a mask for a different kind of determinism. The cardboard-and-plaster figures of the festival dance on the hard ground of political economy. Berguedans are practical Durkheimians, because history has left them disenchanted with revolutions and (they say) without the courage to undertake one. But when pressed, they agree with Marx instead (and of course this industrial region has a long familiarity with socialist thought). Marx is particularly resonant today in the post-Transition Patum. Whereas Durkheim writes inside the moment when collective representations emerge, Marx writes of their decay, when the social facts have come unmoored from the structures that generated them and taken on an autonomous and increasingly automatic life.

I am at once a sympathetic Durkheimian participant, a self-doubting Freudian, and a skeptical Marxist outsider. Although this triple identification has made for confusion in my text as well as my sense of self, it is better acknowledged than evaded.[11] Trained as a folklorist, I am obliged to take my Berguedan interlocutors at least as seriously as I do the theorists and to carry out a "hermeneutics of completion" as the basis for any later "hermeneutics of suspicion" (Ricoeur 1970, 20–36). I begin, then, by attempting to enter and recreate the Patum from within, drawing on my own experience of participation and on community metacommentaries. My first task is to reconstruct the world the Patum makes in a more systematic and explicit language than participants require. More than that, I am reproducing as well as representing the Berguedan project: I try to create at the textual level the same kind of integrated whole that the Patum makes out of Berga. For this work, the tools of symbolic anthropology are apt: they are essentially Durkheimian.[12]

But the ethnographer's work does not end in translating from a re-stricted to an elaborated code (Bernstein 1971) or in creating a scholarly equivalent to folk poiesis. The next task is to draw back and, in dialogue with the Berguedans, contextualize the construction they have made, look-ing at the materials they had to work with, the goals they sought, and the environment they hoped to transform. At this distance, both the Bergue-dans and I have mixed feelings about the power of symbolic communica-tion and, in particular, of performance: the setting into motion of symbols by bodies (cf. Fernandez 1986). Like Bakhtin, I am enthralled by the ca-pacity of repetition to modify but also to perpetuate older messages (1981); Berguedans are similarly preoccupied with certain inertias in their performance forms. Like James Scott, I see symbolic performance as the space of maneuver in which those who cannot speak freely conduct their politics (1990). But Berguedans continue to use the Patum even after de-mocracy has been restored and a Habermasian public sphere of rational-instrumental communication has been made available (Habermas 1989). They worry about this: are they "folklorizing" themselves, and would they do better to spend their time on "serious" things? They worry, too, about the toll taken by performance. In the Patum, the "natural symbol" of the body is the primary expressive resource (Douglas [1973]1982), and this en-tails an expenditure of the self not demanded by more alienated codes. The intensity of bodily performance in many subaltern settings suggests that the power subjects cannot exercise on their surroundings is turned back on the self, the only domain they may control. Repressed aggression can turn performance into outright self-destruction.[13]

To be sure, Berguedans cannot be called subaltern from any global perspective: the proper adjective is *provincial*. But in this setting, the Pa-tum's physical intensity is unexpected. The festival is a public assault on the clothes and skins and backs and livers of people who in everyday life are greatly concerned with appearances and respectability. We might ask whether this visibly self-damaging performance is not itself metaphori-cal. Berguedans characterize these aspects of the Patum as "primitive" and "of the poor," sometimes even as wasteful and degrading. This peri-odic self-abjection dramatizes their strong sense of "relative deprivation": inferiority to the Barcelonans and, a fortiori, the Europeans with whom they compare themselves (Runciman [1966]1971). More, it suggests a deep ambivalence toward performance that we might see as characteristically provincial.

Scholars have not theorized the provincial very much: our best ap-proximation is found in Bourdieu, whose work takes for granted the ho-mologies between the field of social class and the field of the nation-state (1984, 1990a). The provincial occupies the same uneasy middle ground in the latter that the petit bourgeois occupies in the former. Both are socially ambiguous, and both aspire to incorporation in higher status categories. We can therefore extend to the provincial Bourdieu's characterization of the petit bourgeois. Investing extraordinary effort in a performance of self that is intended to win external recognition and consequent reward, he is ultimately "haunted by appearances" (1984, 253) and the uncertain reality of his achievement.

The real anatomy of the provincial condition is found in the nine-teenth-century novel, and there we can clearly see its radical ambivalence, torn between local attachments and metropolitan ambitions. The ideal subjects of organic solidarity, provincials feel their own lack and seek com-pletion in contact with the outside world. The provincial novel thus re-produces the fairy tale plot, with the hero leaving home to seek his fortune in a world of wider possibilities. But in the novel, the hero may or may not succeed.[14] One who does win sexual and economic incorpora-tion pays for it affectively with the loss of home and community. How-ever, the ambitious provincial who stays in place receives, at best, token metropolitan encouragement, at a high cost to others and with no eleva-tion for the province as a whole.[15]

The provincial is the maker of the modern.[16] In part, it is a question of energy: the provincial is at once well-fed enough and hungry enough for the struggle. But more importantly, whether they fail or succeed, whether they leave or stay, provincials are "*committed* to the symbolic" (Bourdieu 1984, 253): they are performers, dreamers, and theorists. Unsat-isfied with their position in a world which, if ideal, would see them better placed, they aspire to more perfect unions. The sacramental consciousness of a Berguedan is open to transmutation into the engineer's faith in her blueprint.[17]

Berguedans have occasionally nurtured such aspirations, imagining the Patum as the foundation of a native modernity. But just as the provin-cial novels repeatedly show us characters whose imaginings are destructive of others and the self, so Berguedans have innumerable instances in their collective memory of provincial projects going awry. [18] The three Carlist Wars of the nineteenth century provide local examples. More recently they have experienced the high human costs of Francoism (quintessentially provincial in its resentful oscillations between autarky and emulation); and since the Transition they have had the negative exemplar of the terrorist group ETA in the Basque country, now more than ever relentless in its assault on the ideological center as well as the local infrastructure. These disasters and more modest failures of local administration and personal ambition have fostered a certain humility among Berguedans, along with a feeling that the half-acknowledged, willful self-delusion of sacramental thinking is not so dangerous as the modern's conviction of his ability to control reality. The Patum offers at least the compensation of communion in exchange for its renunciation of mastery.

The Patum's giants, dwarfs, and mules dance out an eternal debate between irreconcilable postures toward the central power of the moment: aspiration to inclusion, self-mockery of pretensions to inclusion, and rejection of the terms by which inclusion can be won. And the Patum as a whole is a reluctant obsession in local conversation, standing for all Berguedan self-fashioning: endlessly celebrated as the capital by which Berga's fortune will be made, endlessly dismissed as a self-destructive waste of time and resources.

I will argue in the conclusion that globalization makes us all provincials, and this is certainly true of our relation to the symbolic. The proliferation of the sign in postmodernity coincides with the end of faith in representation and a loss of confidence in the ability to operate on reality directly: hence both our fantasies and our fears of the performativity of the sign. In Berga, as in many enclaves with special resources for performance, the response has been a cultivation of immanence through which body and community become their own referents. Some Berguedans have made the ontological shift, granting "firstness" to the Patum (Peirce 1991, 188–89), and dismissing all external relations and representations as inherently alienated from that core reality. There is, they insist, nothing else in the world.

There is, at any rate, nothing else going: provincial regions increasingly need to live off their symbols. Today Catalan festivals are attracting growing attention among a global public, owing primarily to the rise in tourism resulting from the 1992 Summer Olympics (which featured Patum-derived devils in the closing ceremonies). In the ensuing years, the Patum itself appeared internationally in several television travel programs and numerous guidebooks internationally, along with a growing number of scholarly works in English (Harris 2003 and 2000; Gilmore 2002; Warner 1998). Exoticized and dehistoricized, it provides the setting for an erotic encounter in Colm Tóibín's novel *The South* (1991). In 2004, it will be Spain's candidate for the UNESCO designation of Masterpiece of the Oral and Intangible Patrimony of Humanity. As Berguedans and their fellows in peripheral communities around the world await the tour buses and resign themselves to the loss of such control as they have had over their own representation, it becomes important for an English-speaking audience to see that today's passionate, participatory festivals are neither simple drunken revels nor mystical survivals of ancestral rites but resonant forms of collective action in response to a global crisis of local communities. More urgently, since the Spanish transition to democracy has been proposed as an answer to "Balkanization" and a model for other plural societies around the Mediterranean (cf. Linz, Stepan, Gunther 1995, 77; Morán 1991, 243–41), the long-term integrative power of that transition's mobilizing devices is of more than local interest. Finally, when cultural representation is increasingly proffered around the world as a response to inequality, it is vital to understand both the power and the limitations of performance in modifying social arrangements.

The Setting: Berga in Catalonia

Berga is a city of roughly fifteen thousand inhabitants in the foothills of the Spanish Catalan Pyrenees, about eighty kilometers north-northwest of Barcelona (Map 1). It sits on a rocky shelf below the Serra de Queralt, a little to the west of the valley of the Llobregat River, which descends from Castellar de n'Hug, close to the French border, to meet the sea just south of Barcelona.

The Llobregat bifurcates the *comarca* or county of the Berguedà, of which Berga is the capital (Map 2). Above Berga is the mountainous and heavily wooded Upper Berguedà, full of almost abandoned villages and a few small towns: Bagà, seat of the old barony of Pinós; La Pobla de Lillet, in the eighteenth century an industrial rival to Berga; Castellar de n'Hug, a beautifully reconstructed tourist trap with a remaining shepherd or two. In the northwest of the *comarca* is the impressive twin-peaked massif Pedraforca, well known to Catalan mountaineers, with a barely functioning coal mine at its foot and mining and cattle towns on its skirts. The Berguedà is topped by the high Pyrenean ranges of Cadí and Moixeró, which were crossed mostly by smugglers, bandits, and shepherds until the opening of the Túnel del Cadí in 1984. On the other side

FRANCE

ARAGON

Olot

BERGA

Solsona   Vic

Girona

Manresa
Montserrat▲   Granollers

Lleida

Barcelona

Tarragona

M E D I T E R R A N E A N

VALENCIA

Map 1. Catalonia

is the plain of the Cerdanya, a *comarca* divided between French and Spanish Catalonia in the 1659 Treaty of the Pyrenees and now subsisting on
tourism.

Below Berga is the Lower Berguedà, hilly and calcareous but considered part of the Catalan central plain. Along the winding narrow high-
ways to Ripoll and Vic in the east and the diocesan seat of Solsona in
the west lie municipalities of dispersed farms: animal fodder is the chief
crop of the rocky land, and cows and pigs are raised in fairly significant
numbers. The central axis of population is the Llobregat, whose meager
water supply furnished power for dozens of textile factories from the

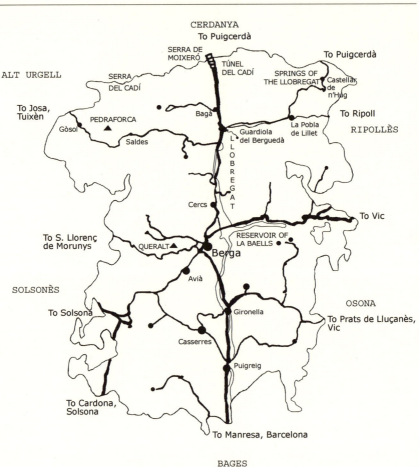

CERDANYA
To Puigcerdà
SERRA DE
MOIXERÓ
TÚNEL
DEL CADÍ
To Puigcerdà
ALT URGELL
SERRA
DEL CADÍ
SPRINGS OF
THE LLOBREGAT
Castellar
de
n'Hug
To Josa,
Tuixèn
PEDRAFORCA
Bagà
To Ripoll
Gòsol
La Pobla
de Lillet
RIPOLLÈS
Saldes
Guardiola
del Berguedà
L
L
O
B
R
E
G
A
T
Cercs
To Vic
To S. Llorenç
de Morunys
QUERALT
RESERVOIR OF
LA BAELLS
Berga
Avià
SOLSONÈS
OSONA
To Solsona
Gironella
To Prats de Lluçanès,
Vic
Casserres
Puigreig
To Cardona,
Solsona
To Manresa, Barcelona
BAGES

Map 2. Berga and its hinterland

mid-nineteenth century on. The towns of Gironella and Puigreig serve
as municipal centers to the industrial colonies, factories surrounded by
worker housing, the owner's summer house, a school, and a church. The
great majority of these factories have closed in the past twenty years.
These factories go all the way down the increasingly murky Llobregat,
past the large industrial city of Manresa (ca. 100,000 inhabitants) and the
strange fingery peaks of Montserrat to the delta below Barcelona—once
the richest agricultural land in Catalonia, now industrial suburbs. The river's

Figure 1. The city of Berga below the Queralt range. Photo by Luigi, Berga.

trajectory has long directed economic flows: it is also the route followed by Berguedans for bureaucratic obligations and, increasingly, for education, leisure, and employment.

The city of Berga (Figure 1) offers a microcosm of its *comarca*: mountains behind it and plain beneath it, coal mines to the north, textile factories within the town, and a largely hypothetical tourist industry. The people, too, are set between two worlds—one eye toward the mountains' peace and isolation, one toward Barcelona's dynamism.

The early industrial modernization of Catalonia was not accompanied by a liberal belief in free trade: Catalonia's traditional industries prospered best under protectionist legislation or in times of diminished foreign competition (as in the case of the World War I boom). In the Berguedà, the autarkist policies of early Francoism were in part economically beneficial (apart from the new impetus they gave to smuggling, an important local occupation): the 1940s and 1950s saw the expansion of both lignite coal mining and textile manufacture, the *comarca*'s principal industries (Pedrals 1990, 76). The economic expansion of the 1960s provided further stimulus to expansion, but almost immediately the invasion of international competition precipitated a long decline. Employees in the textile industry numbered 10,937 in 1962; 2,154 in 1987 (Miralles i Guasch et al. 1990, 83); and many fewer today—the few factories remaining open are heavily mechanized. The mines had nearly 3500 employees in 1960, and 900 in 1986 (87–88). The principal mine at Fígols closed entirely in 1990, and the smaller Saldes mine reduced its operations in 1991. The agricultural sector, long plagued by low prices and small, undercapitalized farms, is beginning to develop small-production specialties, such as goat cheese, natural veal, and truffles, for metropolitan connoisseurs.

An expansion of services, public employment, and construction has offset industrial decline in the city of Berga at the expense of the rest of the *comarca*, which suffers the intense depopulation characteristic of the Catalan interior. Because Berga is the only large town within a wide area, families that once only shopped there are now moving there for the sake of the schools or the convenience. But Berguedan commerce relies heavily on pensioned miners and state employees, neither of whom are likely to sustain the general burden much longer, and must compete with that of much larger and now easily reached Manresa and Barcelona. Attempts to develop tourism face the challenges of deficient infrastructure, recent fierce forest fires, and more spectacular offerings on the other side of the Túnel del Cadí.

The Berguedà is *la Catalunya pobra*, both by objective measures and in their own self-estimation. Catalonia, of course, is rich, and the absolute poverty of the Berguedà is nothing to that of, say, Extremadura in southern Spain. But Catalans look largely to Europe, not Spain, as their model, and in this framework, Berguedans consider themselves disadvantaged.

Berga is part of Old Catalonia, the northeastern region that was fully reconquered from the Saracens by the ninth century: it belongs to what is in many respects the most conservative part of the country. It is part of the traditionalist area that fought for God, king, and local rule in the Carlist Wars of the nineteenth century; that collaborated with Barcelona industrialists to create the turn-of-the-century Lliga Regionalista, a right-wing Catalanist party that tried to model the new order upon the old; and that now gives Convergència i Unió, the center-right Catalanist coalition that has governed Catalonia since the restoration of autonomy in 1979, the bulwark of its power. In everyday practice, Berguedans are almost monolingual in Catalan, and middle-class townspeople as well as the farmers go to Mass on Sundays; they hold fast to their festivals and to tradition for tradition's sake. There is a substantial working-class socialist vote (local socialists are strongly Catalanist), a respectable minority supporting Catalan independentist parties, and, through the 1980s and 1990s, a growing level of political disaffection. In each case, localism—seen as realistic self-limitation to achievable or at least necessary goals—tends to override faith in any larger political entity.

Architecturally, Berga is a typical Old Catalan city (Map 3), with a medieval core and nineteenth- and twentieth-century additions. The Casc Antic, or old city, is narrow and irregular, with small *places* dotting tangled streets and no buildings of special distinction. The top of the town has a stream flowing through it which provided power to several factories. Below, the long Carrer Major (Main Street) stretches between the Plaça Sant Joan, with the palace of the old lords of Peguera and the templar's church of Saint John, and the Plaça Sant Pere, the site of the parish church of Santa Eulàlia and the city hall. Above and to the east of this *plaça* is the oldest part of the city and the last surviving medieval gate, the Portal de Santa Magdalena.

The first *eixample* (broadening) of Berga dates from the mid-nineteenth century: it is the long Plaça Viladomat, popularly known as the Vall, which extends into an avenue leading to factories, the cemetery, the high school, and the twentieth-century *xalets* (detached houses with gardens) on the little Serra de Casampons. The Vall and its extension are below and to the east of the Plaça Sant Pere.

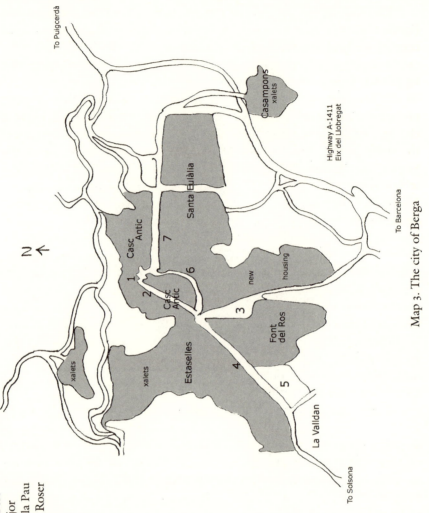

1. The Plaça Sant Pere
2. The Carrer Major
3. The Passeig de la Pau
4. The Carrer del Roser
5. The *caserna*
6. La Canya
7. The Vall

To Puigcerdà

Casampons
xalets

Highway A-1411
Eix del Llobregat

Santa Eulàlia

Casc
Antic

7

1

6

2

Casc
Antic

new

housing

To Barcelona

3

Font
del Ros

xalets

Estaselles

4

5

La Valldan

To Queralt

xalets

N

To Solsona

Map 3. The city of Berga

The second *eixample* is the Carrer del Roser, the beginning of the highway to the episcopal seat of Solsona, built up in the late nineteenth century with the villas of Berga's upper class. *Xalets* were built above it in the twentieth century, and the Plaça de la Creu was expanded into the long Passeig de la Pau, lined with banks and modern apartment blocks, which descends to the main highway. Past the Carrer del Roser and the old park is the municipal annex of La Valldan, with its Romanesque church and its old roadside inn. The boundary is marked by the *caserna*, the Spanish army post built after the Civil War on land used during the Second Republic as a fresh-air school for poor Barcelona children. Resented as the army has been, much of the population regrets that the Ministry of Defense decided to shut down the *caserna* in the early 1990s: soldiers spent money in restaurants and bars.

The Casc Antic is the scene of the Patum, and the present route of the *passades* is close to that of the processional route documented in the early eighteenth century. The narrow gray stone streets and constricted squares give the Patum its brightness and the bang of the *fuets* its resonance. The Plaça Sant Pere, center of the action (Map 4), has all its features exploited.

The Plaça Sant Pere was long known as the Plassa Cremada, the Burned Square, a name taken from a 1655 French visitation that was to be repeated by Napoleon's troops, the Carlists, and the liberals during the course of the nineteenth century. It is an indefinable polygon; in 1929 its remodelers tried to turn it into a triangle with paving stones patterned to lead to the apex of city hall, but failed to impose perfect regularity. The church is on the north side, at a rough right angle to the wall of houses on one side of the Ajuntament, with the Carrer Major opening between them. Beyond the church, the Carrer Buxadé rises along the north side of the *plaça*, with the stone *barana* to delineate it. The part of the crowd that prefers to look on or likes to fight with the Guita Grossa stands behind the *barana*. A space between the end of the *barana* and the block of houses jutting into the *plaça* on the east is used for scaffolds of seating in the Patum—mostly used by older people and young children; behind it, the Berruga, a wooden-beamed avenue beneath the houses, leads into more medieval streets.

The city hall is at roughly the southwest corner of the *plaça*; the architects of its 1929 renovation adapted the building to the corner site by covering the unassuming portal with a huge convex balcony supported by four Doric columns, suitable for presiding over the Patum and anything

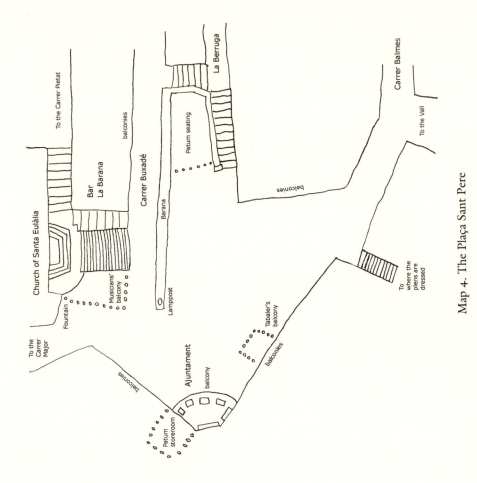

Map 4. The Plaça Sant Pere

Church of Santa Eulàlia

To the Carrer Pietat

Bar
La Barana

balconies

Carrer Buxadé

La Berruga

Patum seating

Barana

Lamppost

Fountain

Musicians' balcony

Carrer Balmes

To the Vall

balconies

To the Carrer Major

balconies

Ajuntament

Tabaler's balcony

balconies

balcony

Patum storeroom

To where the
plens are
dressed

else. The effigies of the Patum are stored in a warehouse space on the ground floor below the balcony, and it is here that most *comparses* and their families tend to congregate during the Patum.

The south wall of the *plaça* comprises more houses, formerly of the wealthiest citizens. The balconies are a favored site for viewing the Patum, and these families are obliged to entertain every day of the festival.

The southeast part of the *plaça* gives way to a smaller *placeta*, site of the old hospital and now of the Ateneu Berguedà (an old working-class Republican club), the museum, and the municipal police station. A narrow stair to the south at the entry to this *plaça* descends to the back of City Hall; it is there that the *plens* are dressed, so this stair is much transited. The *placeta* itself receives the overflow of the Patum. Below it is the Vall; to the east are the streets of the old Jewish quarter.

"We know the *plaça* with our feet," one *patumaire* said affectionately of its dingy, irregular stones and its rises and falls in unexpected places. Since my first fieldwork, the *plaça* has been restored, its facades cleaned up and strengthened, the *barana* rebuilt, the crumbling church steps replaced and given a handicapped-access ramp, and the pavement redone (to erase its former "fascistic" tendencies, according to the architects). The architects of the Catalan Generalitat were prevented by Berguedan traditionalists from making any major changes, much to their annoyance ("why should four days have to prevent the *plaça* from working the rest of the year?"), but still, the texture of the Patum has been changed.

PART I

REPRESENTING
THE FESTIVAL

I

Between Representation and Presence: The Onlooker Problem

T'HI FICARÀS O NO? they demanded. Are you going in there or not?

I was surprised at the insistence of this question in the weeks before the feast of Corpus Christi. Earlier, I had been given lots of advice on how to protect myself at the Patum of Berga. "The first time you have to watch from a balcony. Don't go into the *plaça* until you know what it's about." "Always move counterclockwise in the *plaça* or you'll be trampled." "Tie up that hair under a good hat or you're going to lose it!" "Don't try to do the Patum in those shoes! Get some heavy boots." "Don't wear synthetics, only wool or cotton; they don't burn as easily." I am not brave and they easily convinced me that I had to be careful. "If you lose your wallet, if you lose your shoes, if you lose your pants, don't stop for anything!" an old man warned me. "Once the *plens* have started, not even God enters!"

Suddenly my willingness to get burned was the test of my seriousness. If I really wanted to know what people in Berga were like, I had to enter the crush of the Plaça Sant Pere during the *salt de plens*, the final unleashing of fiery devils that is the culmination of the Patum. I had come to Berga to live for six months, of which I had been there three. I had earnestly read in the library and combed the municipal archives; I had talked to old people and requested interviews of *patumaires*—until I realized that the Patum comes up in half the conversations in Berga anyway and the interviews just made people self-conscious. My welcome had been enthusiastic, and so far most people in Berga seemed to approve of me, interpreting my speaking Catalan, singing with the Easter carolers, and lunching in the "popular" bars as marks of my willingness to play by their rules. But I had not expected to be invited into this particular game: I had planned to be a spectator.

La Patum s'ha de viure, they said over and over as I asked for analyses, anecdotes, and personal histories. It's no use my trying to put it in words; the Patum has to be lived. And when the Patum came, I found that Berguedan goodwill was intent on making me live it properly. "I saw you up on that balcony!" said one woman after I'd retreated to get a better view and to rest my unaccustomed feet. "What do you think this is, theater? You can't understand the Patum by looking at it." During the evening *passacarrers*, the nightlong passage of Patum effigies through the streets, they made sure I did more than look. A bar owner I knew was jumping the *maça*, a club with firecrackers affixed to the top. As it burned lower, she thrust it into my hands, and I had no choice but to start skipping, bouncing the pebble-filled *maça* up and down to keep it lit, showering myself with sparks until my turn was over. The Guita Xica, the smaller and more mobile of the two fire-breathing mules, chased me into a corner every time it set eyes on me: I cowered with my hands over my head until it tired of shaking the flame over me and went after someone else. Agustí, the guide at the head of the beast, was unabashed when I later taxed him with his pursuit. "Daughter," he said, "this is the baptism by fire we all have to suffer." Through the five days of the festival, I opened my mouth to fierce alcoholic mixtures in leather flasks and glass *porrons*; I let children take up my arms and dance me across the *plaça*; I ducked inside the Eagle and the Black Giant; I was given a ride on the back of the Guita Grossa and exulted over the black waves of the crowd beneath me; I put a shoulder under the Guita Xica when the *guitaires'* girlfriends carried it up the Carrer Major and shouted with the rest of them as we lowered the neck to charge; I went out to eat supper every night at five in the morning, drank champagne and sang until eight, and rose three hours later in an unsuccessful effort to get myself to Mass—so as properly to document the complete event. My much-ridiculed little notebooks became progressively less legible. I began to lose sight of the symbolic oppositions that had seemed so obvious in the written accounts and at last to attain a glimmering of what they'd been trying to tell me: the Patum is not a mere spectacle of traditional dances but a force that runs through you.

Et surt de dintre, ran their third refrain. It comes up from inside you. The Patum, with all its antiquity, all its complexity, is not fundamentally a part of the external world: it lives in the body of each Berguedan, who has heard the beat of the Tabal since infancy, danced along with the giants as a toddler, "sucked in the Patum with the mother's milk," as more than one person has told me. The Patum bursts out of Berguedan bodies on joyous occasions—an out-of-town reunion of Berguedans, a victory of the Barcelona Football Club—and is simply bottled up the rest of the time. Agustí Ferrer, then mayor of Berga, wrote: "At Corpus, the Patum which beats inside you all year explodes all at once" (Ferrer i Gàsol 1989, 2).

The Patum had to beat inside of me before I would be qualified to talk about it. To open myself up to this went against my whole history as a person and a scholar. I am not brave: this was the challenge of my field-work. The Patum brought me face to face with a reality that could not be known by reading.

I had learned Catalan in my senior year in college because there was no course in Provençal that year, and I was interested in the troubadours. In graduate school, after too many years of reading nothing written after 1914, I had studied folklore as a way of reconnecting myself with the world I lived in. However, my disinclination to engage myself with the guilt and pain of contemporary America persisted, and I looked for research projects at a certain distance. Not in Africa or Asia or Latin America, where my well-meaning liberalism, trying to forget its ancestry, again interfered with my ability to concentrate, but in continental Europe, where my retrograde cultural preferences were less out of place than at home and where people's problems were not my fault. (I am making no generalizations here about ethnography and ethnographers: it simply happened that I approximated more closely than most a certain stereotype of the ethnographer as E. M. Forster heroine.)

I came upon a book, *La Patum de Berga*, by Josep Armengou i Feliu, a priest of Berga ([1968]1994). It described a Corpus Christi festival in a small city in the Pyrenees. "La Patum" was a sequence of dances by fabulous creatures in plaster and papier-mâché: giants dressed as kings, little knights in horse-shaped skirts, a green monster called a mule that breathed fire like a dragon, devils covered in firecrackers that set themselves alight. The event had evidently obsessed the town for centuries, and the commentaries amassed by Mossèn Armengou included a range of contradictory origin narratives clearly shaped by the exigencies of the historical moment of narration. Elite accounts shaped a civil-religious ceremony of order and decorum. Underneath, rising in the flames of the devils and the green monster, was the threat of revolution.

What really drew me to Berga for my fieldwork was that green thing, the *guita*. As a child I had been much attached to a fifteenth-century painting in the Art Institute of Chicago, a Saint George and the Dragon by Bernat Martorell—who, as it turned out, was a Catalan. In my junior year abroad I collected reproductions of dragon-slayer images: Uccello, Donatello, Piero di Cosimo. In graduate school I read many versions of that most famous of folktales, Aarne-Thompson type 300, as I learned to identify it, and the related founding myths in which the conquered dragon is nature tamed by civilization. But nature's submission, as we know, cannot be counted on for long, and the paintings make it clear that the princess, once returned to her palace and her father, must have yearned for the dragon and the cave. As for me, you can draw your own conclusions.

Of course I had my theoretical reasons too. The festival was proving resistant to the ethnography-of-communication approach then dominant in folklore studies, not only because so many actors were involved but also because of its continuity over time: though the context of the moment affected it, it tended rather to make its own context, subduing participants to its own rules instead of vice-versa. The creative individual agent, beloved of folklorists since the 1960s, here submitted shamelessly to tradition, the collective, and the inarticulate, reckless of all the trouble we had taken to dismantle survivalist and superorganic assumptions.

In designing my field research I hadn't yet gotten that far: I intended only to get beyond semiotic approaches locating meaning in the fixed program of the festival and was confident of finding self-conscious, heterogeneous actors if I looked hard enough. To begin with, I was preoccupied with the problem of observation. The ethnographer can attain a kind of omniscience through collecting and collating data from many sources: a good seat in the balcony, local documentation, and multiple reports of what is happening elsewhere. But we had become more interested in the "aura" of proximity to the center: what it's like to be up close, what the participant is feeling. How do people understand their cultural performances? How do symbols convince their makers and beholders? In short, how do cultural forms and the mind of the native work upon each other?

We cannot get inside the native's head, said the symbolic anthropologists I had been reading. We are no longer so naive or ethnocentric as to suppose that they think like we do; we are not so presumptuous as to claim to understand. What we can do is hermeneutics: we can read the texts they have made. The "stories they tell themselves about themselves"—to use a key phrase of the school—are framed performances of which the outsider may quietly join the audience (Geertz 1973).

Having come to folklore from literary studies, I was reassured by this "interpretive turn." But my department at the University of Pennsylvania, having a strong sociolinguistic bent, had also discovered practice. Our teachers never let us forget that our informants were not just culturally constructed intellects reflecting on themselves for the pleasure of it: they were constrained by the struggle to sustain bodily existence in more or less difficult material and political conditions. Moreover, they were individuals with whom we engaged in real relationships, implying mutual obligations and real-world consequences.

I had two concerns, then, in my project of reading texts. The first was to remember that texts have authors and readers with purposes (folklore had to assert this before it could begin to deconstruct it). The second was to spare myself and my informants as far as possible the dreadful weight of mutual obligations and real-world consequences.

The Patum itself could not be treated as a text, I decided. It had no author—although many nineteenth-century commentators had attempted to create one for it. It had no puppeteer pulling the strings from above and coordinating the action; there was no one consciousness that could perceive, much less direct, the whole. It was a genuinely collective and emergent creation, too shifting and evanescent to pin down. Each participating individual would not merely interpret the whole from his or her own position—on a balcony, inside an effigy, and so on—but would have to imagine the whole as well: interpretation would entail the creation of a text.

So I devised a study of the multiple "texts" of the Patum that exist in public and semipublic space. From Mossèn Armengou's book and other readings, I knew about festival programs, monographs, sermons, poems, children's drawings, videos, souvenirs, photographs, civic decor, proverbs, musical compositions, conversations in bars, newspaper articles, cartoons, advertising, liturgical objects, house decoration, costume, impromptu performances, miniature and neighborhood performances, festivals modeled on the Patum, and festivals created in antithesis to and parody of the Patum. Through these inscriptions, which I could examine more or less at my leisure, I could map local interpretation according to historical period, social class, gender, political affiliation, age, native and outsider identity, or whatever other social categories emerged from the study. And there was surely a contest of interpretations: I could look at the rhetorical tactics used to gain adherents to a particular interpretive community and the influence of power relations on interpretive hegemony. Finally, by comparing interpretations at a deep-structural level, I could perhaps understand something about the constraints placed on interpretation by the form of the event.

This strategy, I realized, would be biased toward elite productions, and I would have to take that into account; popular interpretation of the Patum was no doubt found in the performance itself. For this I would observe styles of participation and perhaps collect taped narratives of festival experience. But I would be dealing primarily with information in the public domain, things that anyone could discover merely by looking. I would not be intruding in anyone's life. Nor would I presume, I thought, to say what the Patum itself was or meant; I would not risk oversimplifying. I would address the event only through its inscriptions.

But turn it around: I would enter into their thoughts without entering into their feelings. It sounds heartless and superficial—even if it had been possible. I would attend not to the central event but to the texts that were its epiphenomena. Is not aura more than this? The Berguedans thought so: when I expected them to speak of symbols in the Patum, they spoke of bodily states and emotions. "It's a feeling—a brotherhood—" said Rossendo of the devils when I asked what they did down there under City Hall all that time. "How can I express it?" "I can't explain the Patum to you," said Ramon Forés, the bartender at the Casino, where I lived that first year. "When you do a *salt de plens*, and they kneel you down to dress you, it's a feeling like, a feeling—I can't explain it to you."

Mossèn Armengou's assertions had seemed overblown. "The Patum is the baptism of our citizenship . . ."; "The Patum is the miracle which Berga has known how to make and perpetuate . . ."; and on and on. But it came from all sides: the Patum was considered not only with humor, pride, and possessiveness but with passion. University students postponed their exams by a year when they coincided with Corpus Christi: there are always exams, but only one Patum. One man told me of a friend who had gone AWOL from his military service so that he could say he'd never missed a Patum. Another one spoke of a Berguedan scientist who'd gone to live in America. She made great efforts to return every year, but on the few occasions when it was not possible she called up friends at City Hall and made them hang the telephone out of the window for an hour at a time, long-distance from the West Coast. Another story was told when I turned off the tape recorder: a man who had cancer and expected to die before another Patum came. He had had a colostomy two weeks before Corpus Christi and was still in the hospital in Barcelona. Could he leave to go up to Berga for the Patum? Out of the question: it would kill him. But sooner that than missing his last Patum. He made himself so miserable, virtually going on a hunger strike, that the hospital and his family found a way: he was borne up to Berga in an ambulance and carried to the balcony of a house on the *plaça*. There he pulled himself up by the railings to see the dancing and collapsed back on the bed during the breaks (the Patum seems to have cured him, for he subsequently recovered and is now alive and well and dressing the *plens*).

The Patum was ineffable: there was no one who did not say this. What it signified was something about Moors and local history—the stories varied and few cared very much—but the important thing was the way it made them feel. The Patum has to be lived. Some people encouraged me to live it; a few politely informed me that my project was useless, for, without having grown up in Berga and lived the Patum all my life, I was incapable of understanding anything about it. The more intellectual allowed that my work could have some utility in clarifying the Patum's history, but the frankest speakers insisted that I was overlooking the heart of things in order to tinker with trivialities.

How was I to get inside the festival, then? My advisor, Roger D. Abrahams, had said to me, "It's Corpus Christi, you know. Isn't the body important?" No, it didn't seem so. And in any case, I thought but did not say, 90 percent of the academy is working on the body now, and I want to do something different. But it was out of my hands. I asked a man so anticlerical and profane that he is nicknamed "The Priest" about how the Patum had changed after the 1971 suppression of the Corpus Christi procession. He said it was a pity, that the procession had been a lot of fun, and what was especially sad was that the Patum didn't smell right anymore because the hazelnut branches used to decorate houses for the procession were no longer there to break off and wave away sparks with. The *olor de Patum*, they all said: it's not the same, but you'll smell it anyway. The odor of Patum! How on earth was I to talk about it?

Here it was—the body—and for the Berguedans it was straightforward enough. Like many peoples who have known poverty in the not too distant past, they tend to be philosophical realists. There was no great epistemological gulf fixed between them and me. The Patum is known by participation; I had but to participate as they did. I could have their experience by living in their bodies, and I could do this by eating what they ate, dancing what they danced, and, in general, by spending time with them: acquiring a history in common with them.

Eating and drinking turned out to be central to my assimilation.

Community in Berga is largely understood through alimentary metaphors, and again, I attribute this to the simplest material cause: the long experience of the threat of hunger. Everyone fed me and everyone was anxious to know how I liked the local food. One old man was gratified but astonished to learn that the change in diet had not injured my health. Several people warned me that the "change of waters" would surely affect me, not because Berguedan water is bad but because the combination of minerals varies from place to place, and everyone becomes accustomed to his or her native mixture. Berguedan bodies have been created by a unique diet formed from a unique ecology, and it was a good sign that I could take it in.

Berguedans are highly self-conscious about the way things are done in Berga, a distinctiveness they attribute to their supposed long isolation as a cul-de-sac in the foothills of the Pyrenees—though the self-consciousness has more to do with their long dependency on external powers. This is how we do it here, they would say, and watch to see if I could follow them. They amused themselves by testing me: can she drink out of a *porró*? I spilled wine all over myself during my first ventures with the narrow-spouted glass pitcher, but mastered it and won approval. Can she drink a *carajillo*? Certainly I can, I said, provoked. I had two—fierce concoctions of espresso and sweet rum—and lay awake all night twitching like a marionette. They laughed at my account the next day, and they laughed even more when I told them that I felt like a monkey in the zoo with children poking things between the bars of my cage to see what I'd do. They made a rendezvous with me at Cal Blasi on the Vall, and I walked up and down the Vall for half an hour. Cal Blasi is not in the phone book, it is a nickname, and the sign above its door says Bar Marc. It never occurred to them to give me an address, and it took me quite a while to ask someone on the street for help.

But they were not just playing with me: there was system in it. I had said I wanted to understand their experience, not impose my perceptions from outside; they had heard me say so on Ràdio Berga my first week in the town. They took me at my word and took it upon themselves to teach me.

It was a job for them to get my body off the balcony and feeling with them. Think what it means to be an urban academic. What has my whole life been but an effort to escape the body? I was a child who was good at reading and bad at games, and books were a refuge from persecution. Later, free of the playground, my life was still spent sitting in libraries or discoursing with friends nearly as unbalanced as I was. Then there was my habitual environment. Philadelphia in the 1980s was constituted of refinery emissions, uncollected garbage, and human effluvia in the heavy air of the Delaware Valley; horns, sirens, boom boxes, quarreling neighbors; trees yellow with blight; sidewalks strewn with broken bottles, fast food trash, cigarette butts, and, as one passed through dark streets, heaps by the curb that suddenly moved and revealed themselves as human. I did not have moral courage enough and tried not to see or hear or smell. I lived in the city by refusing to live in it: numbing my senses, thickening my skin, hardening my heart. Even on the days when the wind blew the miasma away and I was tempted into good humor and physical expansiveness, a remark on the street would remind me of the danger of too much relaxation. I would tighten my lips and freeze my smile, turn my eyes to the pavement, clutch my purse to my side, and stiffen my gait.

For the first three months at least, I walked through Berga at my normal metropolitan pace. "Where are you running off to in such a hurry?" they would ask. The evasions of years caught up with me. I had to learn to slow down and look at people passing, offer myself to the gaze of the community.

The breakthrough in my integration was the Societat Unió Coral Berguedana, one of the innumerable worker's choirs established in Catalonia at the end of the last century. By good fortune, my arrival in Berga coincided with the last rehearsals for the *caramelles*, songs about new life and pretty girls and the farewell to salt cod that are sung in the streets and squares during Easter. I had met Queralt, a music student who conducted the choir, and she was perfectly at ease with my timid suggestion that I might listen in on a rehearsal. The second time she said, "You can come again, but only if you sing!" I came; some people were unabashedly off-key and the music was easy to grasp. So I sang too. The singers were curious and friendly: through the choir's varied membership I gained entrée into many social milieux. And my appearance in the choir after so short a time in the town garnered me a good deal of recognition and good will.

Then came the *sardanes* of Sant Jordi, the feast of the patron of Catalonia on April 23. The *caramelles* had not been so bad, but the prospect of dancing in public brought back all of those humiliating evenings at the Evanston Women's Club, where a crowd of spotty twelve-year-olds were put through the waltz, the cha-cha, and other disciplines judged desirable for the acquisition of gender decorum. With me, left-handed and undergrown, it had left nothing but a determination never to dance again. Now

I was standing behind the dancers in the ring, trying desperately to ascertain which foot went forward first. They kept saying, "Just try it!" as I insisted that I hadn't gotten it down yet. It's Sant Jordi, their looks said; are you with us or aren't you? Queralt took me by the hand and dragged me into the circle; the other dancers gave me encouraging smiles, and Queralt's sister Alba counted the steps for me. On the next occasions I bounced through as best I could, and by the last *sardanes* after the Sunday night Patum I had it almost down. After the last shout of "Visca!" the boy next to me, Jordi, turned to me and said, "Girl, I congratulate you! An American who speaks Catalan and dances sardanes! There are people who've lived here all their lives and never learned to do either." Jordi is the child of Galician immigrants and earned his integration through performance: the Scouts, the town band, political demonstrations, the *sardana*, speaking Catalan. He more than anyone understands the importance of participation.

Beyond that came the Patum and all the coercions of which I have spoken; the insistence that I participate fully and as a Berguedan would. The Berguedans demanded certain kinds of performances from me and offered in exchange true understanding.

The Berguedans do not believe in translation, but in socialization. To know them, they say, you must become one of them. I was not a child, of course, and could not regain the time lost; I would never have the depth of historical experience that they do, through their own and their parents' memories. But they made allowances for this, telling me things, taking me on excursions, and digging through their attics for old programs and pictures to show me. I was allowed enough "research" to repair in part the unavoidable deficiencies of my socialization.

They humbled me too. At the end of my second visit I was sitting with two men who began to talk about an old *patumaire*, now dead, who had been famous for . . . Agustí saw my professional ears prick up and said to me, "You, Dorothy, know many things but you don't know everything yet." "Not by a long shot," I said, to please him. "Not by a long shot," he agreed complacently. Another time Ritxi, the director of the municipal music school, grinned at me and said, "Ah, there's lots that you don't know! I've got old scores from the Patum that you've never seen . . . We'll see if you ever make your way to them."

They wouldn't let me have it all at once, wouldn't let me have it simply to take away and make a book of. They pointed the path I had to follow and left the work up to me. As I acquired a history in common with them, I gained more privileges and also more responsibilities. It began

simply enough, with an increase in social obligations: by the end of my
first visit I was sleeping no more than five hours a night. In the intervals
between my first visits, I wrote endless letters to let them know I hadn't
forgotten them. Leaving town became increasingly difficult. The object
of socialization, after all, is to make you a functioning member of the society; in my case, it was to make me understand the Patum, but understanding and reponsibility are inseparable for them. Right behavior incarnates
right understanding: it is the outward and visible concomitant—or even
more than that. To understand the Patum is to dance it.

I wrote my dissertation in medias res: in the middle of the acquisition of scholarly competence, in the middle of puzzling out Berga and the
Patum, in the fork of the road between becoming a Berguedan and committing myself to the unwelcoming American academy. In Philadelphia,
that last alternative seemed overstated: of course I would stay in America,
and someone would hire me someday. In Berga the choice was not so
clear. It was complicated by their differing expectations of me. My intellectual friends did not want me to go wholly native but to be their American connection and promote Catalonia to the world. For others, my failure
to stay in Berga was proof of my imperfect assimilation. "This feeling we
have here among us," said Pepito at a farewell lunch in the core bar of the
Patum, waving his hand at the table of friends. "Stay for this." "I know,
I do understand," I pleaded. "But I have obligations." "No, you don't
understand," he said. "If you did, you wouldn't leave." Against this logic
I can make no argument. My native notion of understanding has me as
subject and the Patum as object: there can be and in fact ought to be distance between me and it. But for Pepito and his friends, knowing is incorporation. They and the Patum and Berga are an indissoluble whole, one
body. My observer problem is explicitly epistemological and implicitly
moral; their observer problem is simply practical. In a depopulating community desperate for solutions, every onlooker is someone who needs to
be working instead.

For several years afterward, I lived between two worlds and two reali-
ties, a vacillation tolerated by Berguedans (who share the dilemma) but
handicapping me in the less forgiving professional world (as Berguedans
too are handicapped). Now, of course, I have surrendered to what the
louder voices of the latter world assure us is inevitable; the conflict has
been displaced from my life to this book, uneasily incorporating that dissertation written when Berga almost wholly possessed me. I live for my
career, such as it is, and live therefore always in motion, riding an arc toward

an imagined point not just of rest but of incorporation in some loftier state; in the meantime, while I wait for that indistinct brilliance to materialize, my autonomy and mobility are in practice my chiefest goods. My probable future, while it may encompass formal recognitions and abstract incorporations, will be solitary at the level that matters to Berguedans; at best I will be not just an onlooker, but myself an object of the gaze. And yet that other world beats inside me still. Could I bring anything of it to the life I now recognize as primary, or is this fantasy of integration itself part of the Patum's inescapable nostalgia? Written at my present distance, back up in the balcony, the question answers itself.

I would not impose my story upon the reader were it not, mutatis mutandis, a point of entry into the Berguedan predicament. I am somewhat more cheerful about the clash of worlds than many of my Berguedan friends are. After all, I started out in the metropolis; the only game in town is my game too, and I was born to a place at the table and dealt a good hand. But they have a genuine dilemma: they belong to a world that cannot sustain itself and must destroy it to enter the world that can sustain them.

2

The Patum and the Body Politic

A STORY THEY TELL THEMSELVES about themselves? Well, yes, but apparently they don't listen to it. By the fifth day of dancing and drinking, after multiple repetitions of the Patum in the *plaça*, the plebeian mule spins into the royal eagle with no sense of disjuncture or surprise. And even at a distance from the confusions of performance, people are reluctant to talk about meaning directly.

"What does it mean?" is, of course, the classic outsider's question. As a rule, insiders are more immediately interested in what it does, particularly when "it" is a performance repeated annually in the same place by the same people with little scope granted to improvisation. The native Berguedan's relation to the Patum is not typically one of reader and text or audience and performance. The child's first contact with the Patum is not with a distant spectacle but with an enveloping realm: held up to the hand of the giantess, danced on her father's back in the crowd, the child first knows the Patum as something tactile and kinetic, a mass in motion around her and herself in motion within it. She is encouraged to learn the steps and gestures at the same time she is learning to walk; as she grows older, she is allowed and obliged to participate in more and more of the event. It is a great blurry world which she enters by degrees; she finds increasingly familiar clearings from year to year, but she is always aware of surrounding thickets of complexity, some of which she will never penetrate. If she is of an intellectual bent, she may try to mark paths and chart a map, but even so, she knows the Patum by moving through it. It is unlikely that she will ever feel the need to draw back from the Patum, survey it from beginning to end, and declare what it means. What it means was danced into her as she became part of its history and it of hers. The Patum is less an object of analysis than of recognition: an annual return and renewal.

Convivència and Representation

That is the orthodox Berguedan view, and it is true in part—true as an ideal in any case. There are good practical and historical reasons to leave the Patum unexamined—not, as with everyday habit, by declaring it too trivial to merit attention, but rather by making it sacred: superorganic, eternal. In a deeply factionalized community with a history of civil war and a present of economic threat, the incorporation of individuals into active community membership is the primary goal of the Patum, and the history that militates against that incorporation must be overtly silenced and covertly transformed. "For the Patum, all are one." "For the Patum, we Berguedans make a pinecone"—a Catalan idiom used to express solidarity or unity in diversity.

First, the silencing. Catalonia has a language problem, of which the choice of Catalan or Castilian is only the most conspicuous dimension. Unlike, say, postwar Germany, where the Nazi regime was unambiguously defeated and had to be unequivocally repudiated, not least through a cleansing of language, the Spanish transition expelled nothing and no one. Rather, it brought opposing political elements together in a coalition by means of agreement to let bygones be bygones. No idiom was wholly discredited, but neither was any idiom sufficiently unmarked for the voicing of collective aspirations, which had to be reduced to the blandest, emptiest formulas to win assent. The formulation of meanings was relegated from the dangerous public realm to subgroups in which a vocabulary was shared.

Thus *convivència*—a slogan word of the Transition meaning not simply coexistence side-by-side, but getting along together and sharing a social world—became possible. In Catalonia, the challenge of political *convivència* was complicated by that of native and immigrant *convivència* in a region where the proportions were half and half.[1]

Provincial communities such as Berga face the problem more directly: in so small a city, *convivència* is a matter of face-to-face relationships. The poor and the well-off are inescapably visible to each other; political enemies must pass each other daily on the Carrer Major; immigrants live for the most part not in new suburbs outside the city but next door to old Berguedan families.

Like most Catalan mountain towns, Berga has a manufacturing tradition dating from the Middle Ages. Its economy has always been dependent on commerce and industry. It has never been self-sufficient in food production: too cold for vines and olive trees, the terrain irregular, and the soil poor. The ability to eat, for Berguedans, does not depend entirely on their own labors but on their relations with each other and with outsiders.

Physical isolation is a second factor in interdependence. Berga had no great landowners or nobility with extralocal interests. The prosperity of the upper class depends on general Berguedan conditions, and the Berguedan elite has always been provincial with respect to larger Catalan cities. Within Berga, the classes are at no great physical remove from each other and no great cultural distance either. Patron-client and employer-employee relations are affective as well as instrumental and entail a great deal of mutual knowledge and evaluation.

In such a place, the metaphor of the social body is not problematic. For the Berguedans, Berga as a relatively bounded and cohesive entity is not an "imagined community" (Anderson 1991) but a fact of life. This distinguishes it from the hegemonic projects in the form of imagined communities long foisted on the Berguedans: the universal Catholic Church, Franco's "imperial Spain" or the Socialists' "new Spain," the neomedieval Catalonia of the early twentieth century or the "Catalonia-city" of today, to name only a few. All of these require heavy investments in representation, mediatic and political, to compensate for a deficit in lived interaction and succeed in proportion to the intensity of the latter and its compatibility with the former.

Berga's self-representation, the Patum, is also compensatory: not for a lack of interaction but, on the contrary, for its tensions. Differentiation generates interdependence and even desire; it also creates mistrust and resentment. *Convivència* is at once a practical necessity and, in its deeper sense, an ideal recognized as utopian. It is strained by the fact that there is rarely enough to go around—not enough jobs, not enough prestige, not enough money. Although it would be a stretch to suggest that the "idea of limited good" or zero-sum worldview often attributed to peasant cultures holds sway in industrial Berga, it is a commonsense reality there that the gain of one is frequently the loss of another. Competition exists; it is bitter and painful. People are suspicious and factionalized.

Public life therefore vacillates—in tandem with the self-control of Berguedans—between careful avoidances and bitter conflict. Off the Carrer Major, partisan language cultivates itself in innumerable bars, associations, periodicals, and performances. "In Berga everything is double," they said: it has two music schools, two ski clubs, two choirs, two theater groups, two history magazines, two political parties personally opposed and ideologically identical, two of anything you can think of that might profitably be combined to accomplish something worthwhile. Thus, for them, the Patum's contest of interpretations—for me so revelatory, so "democratic"—was so obvious as not to be worth talking about, and it obscured the festival's supreme achievement: wholeness.

It is nonetheless important that the Patum, formed through accretion and negotiation over several centuries, achieves wholeness by a radically different semiotic strategy than that of most political ceremonies created since the transition to democracy.[2] The Patum relies on multivocal pluralism rather than abstract singularities. That is, rather than offering single collective emblems empty enough for a particular content to be projected into them, it provides a heterogeneous ensemble of concrete references allowing multiple points of entry into the whole and multiple stances within it. In Durkheim's terms, rather than a mechanical solidarity in which everyone stands in identical and individual relation to a thinly defined collectivity, the Patum defines an organic solidarity, a true social body that reflects the sense of everyday economic and social interdependence between different positions. These links of the Patum to the lived social world are not merely semiotic but performed in modes of festival interaction that mimic and intensify everyday encounters, as Part II will show. This union of representation and interaction is what gives the Patum its intensity and Berga its reality.

The rest of the chapter will lay out the representational dimensions of the process; but a final point must be made about representation in the political sense. Berga, although geographically it can be seen as isolated, is in no way self-sufficient: it must speak downward to attract clients and upward to attract patrons. Since its emergence in the early seventeenth century, the Patum has been the language through which Berga proclaimed itself to its hinterland; since at least the eighteenth century, when the Patum began to savor of archaism, it has been its most conspicuous cultural capital for trading with the metropolis.

While the peasants who came in for the festival participated in a relatively direct and sustained way, the Patum had to be interpreted to the less accommodating outside forces of church, state, and market. This has been the task of the professional class—clergy, lawyers, and doctors—and later of bureaucrats, entrepreneurs, teachers, and journalists. All of these derive their power from their intermediary position, representing the metropolis to the local and vice versa. But they are doubly dependent as much as doubly powerful. Without the constraint of force or the incentive of resources (and the latter, at least, have been scarce enough in Spain to make even the former difficult to sustain at the local level), their power to impose hegemonic languages upon their constituencies is limited. Instead they must, to some degree, adapt themselves to the population that constitutes their clientele. They can give to the metropolis only what the local has to offer—but in a voice the metropolis is willing and able to hear. They are thus professional interpreters, through whom local interests and cultural models reach the center; they translate, with greater or lesser fidelity according to their ability and the degree of distance, from the restricted code of the local to the elaborated code of the metropolis (Bernstein 1971).[3] Occasionally—and later we will see a prime example in Berga's Mossèn Armengou—a gifted interpreter can succeed in teaching a local model to the metropolis.

There is thus a rich history—dating back at least to 1725, when the bishop complained about disorder on Corpus Christi—of Berguedan explications of the Patum (Farràs i Farràs 1979; Noguera i Canal 1992; Noyes 1992). Such accounts typically provide both an allegorical interpretation of the dances and, since the nineteenth century, an origin narrative. The allegory allows the Patum's combats to be read as the triumph of the current orthodoxy: the Church Triumphant over irrational nature, Carlists over liberals, liberals over Carlists, Catalonia over the Castilian invader, the people over feudalism, Imperial Spain over the infidel reds, democracy over repression, and so forth. The origin narrative places the Patum at the founding moment claimed in the current political master narrative: this has traditionally been medieval and, more recently, pre-Christian.

Both allegory and origin narrative serve a second purpose, especially in periods of political repression. In performing submission to the dominant order, they deflect outside interference. The emphasis on origins as determining factor was especially important during and after the Franco regime as a protective means of "denying coevalness" to the festival (Fabian 1983), which thus makes no controversial commentaries on the present nor threatens to transform it.

There are some popular origin legends too, although they reach us so much colored by their elite transcribers that not much can be made of them. But in general it can be said that elite origin narratives valorize the symbols of order in the festival and view the danced combats as the conquest of the disorderly elements, imagined as both lower-status and external to the community. Conversely, the popular narratives, many of which feature emergence from caves, celebrate these lower elements—the mules and the devils, even the Moors—as indigenous forces able to hold off impositions from above and outside the community. The fundamental story that the community tells itself about itself through the Patum has thus to do with social divisions and what each class fears in the other.

From Corpus Mysticum to Body Politic

Most historians of the Patum have been so urgently imbricated in the dialogue between local and metropolis—the latter primarily Catalanist Barcelona—that their work must be used with enormous caution: where documents have not actually been fabricated to fill the voids left by the frequent burning of the archives in civil war, the reading of them has at least been highly interested. The skepticism fostered by life under Francoist representations encouraged the emergence of a different kind of historian, and the three principal scholars of the Patum—Mossèn Armengou at the end of the Franco regime, Jaume Farràs i Farràs during the Transition, and more recently Josep Noguera i Canal—have been progressively more critical of the historiography and less committed to a given line on the event; this ironic turn, of course, also reflects a change in dominant representations and Berga's relationship to them. Based on their historicizing rereadings of earlier scholarship, their new primary research in local archives, and the comparative data available on Catalan Corpus Christi celebrations in other towns, we can reconstruct the early history of the Patum in its large outlines, and suggest the continuities of meaning over time which give the Patum its depth and richness.[4]

The Patum is an outgrowth of the late medieval Corpus Christi procession, particularly elaborate in Catalonia because when the liturgical feast was made obligatory in 1311, the King of Aragon had just come out of papal interdiction and urgently needed to demonstrate his orthodoxy and that of his subjects. These processions, in the first instance, paid homage to the sacrament of the Eucharist. The consecrated Host was carried in a raised monstrance under a canopy supported by the highest-ranking members of the community, clerical or secular. Around the Body of Christ, the entire Corpus Mysticum of which Christ was the head articulated itself. The various corporations and elements of the local community lined up in much-contested hierarchical order—and the feast thus immediately became an occasion for civic display and competition, both between and within cities. This assembly of the Church Militant, Christ's kingdom on Earth, was complemented, insofar as local resources permitted, by representations of the Church Triumphant: allegorical figures or mobile tableaux of Biblical figures, saints, and all the company of heaven.

These representations, generally sponsored by guilds and confraternities, had to be acted by community members not important enough to be marching in their own persons; and they called upon the performance repertoires of that lower level of the community, sometimes incorporating older genres. As medievalists know, different vernacular traditions emerged from these processions, including both the English mystery plays and the Castilian *autos sacramentales*. In Catalonia, the procession featured *entremesos*, dances with masked performers and/or effigies animated by a carrier. Often these might be the emblem of a saint, such as the Lion of Saint Mark or the Eagle of Saint John, or the supporting figures of a Biblical tableau, such as the ox and the ass of the Nativity.

It took little time for the animal and fantastic figures to become dissociated from their liturgical occasions: for some scholars, an argument for their older and indigenous status. The verifiable contemporary reasons have rather to do with their popularity among festival spectators and the consequent disruptions of the procession's solemnity. Because of the guild sponsorship and the popularity, however, the *entremesos* survived various phases of ecclesiastical repression, gradually moving to the head of the procession as entertainments safely distanced from the culminating Host or separating from the procession entirely and furnishing a parallel, secular celebration, in some cases moving from Corpus Christi to a community's patronal festival.

By the time we have verifiable evidence of what would become the Patum—the first unambiguous document in the municipal archives dates from 1632—this separation has largely taken place. The *entremesos* consist only of the *turcs i cavallets*, the devils and angel, the drum, and the mule—still today the noisiest elements of the Patum—and they constitute a separate entertainment paid for by the city, known as *les bolisies* and later La Bulla—nouns deriving from the verb "to boil" and referring to a noisy, mobile assembly. The elements of the Bulla marched at the head of the procession and then performed separately in the main square of the town, the Plaça Sant Pere.

It seems clear that the Bulla and parallel celebrations of the period represent a popular response to the procession's inadequate representation of the social body: they were born of a desire for inclusion—if necessary, through violent irruption. Both women and the lower classes were excluded from the procession, and its symbolic language was so ethereal, with its gold and silver and solar symbolism, so insistent on transcendence (and on wealth as the means to it), as to provide a very dubious account of humble corporeality—the liturgical point of the festival.[5] The Bulla, with its firecrackers, bells, drum, and reputed provocations to immorality, restored sensuality to the social body.

In the seventeenth century, such festivals were still prestigious means of civic self-assertion in all the cities of Spain. Berguedan records show repeated municipal decisions, despite persistent poverty, "if other communities are dancing, to dance also in the present town" (quoted in Farràs i Farràs 1982, 73). In the eighteenth century, both ecclesiastical pressures and emerging rival forms of display induced festival decay—but not in poor, out-of-the-way Berga, where the bishop had been staved off with a good allegory, where no rival entertainments were available, and where the festival brought the peasants of the surrounding *comarca* to spend their money at the accompanying fair. La Bulla, indeed, expanded with Berga's increasing importance in textile manufacture, acquiring a giant and an eagle during the course of the century. By 1790, the local notary's response to a royal questionnaire identified the festival as distinguishing Berga from other towns and its *entremesos* as notable "antiquities" (Pedrals 1989, 9).

This status as antiquity is the next major construction of the festival for outsiders. In the letter of a soldier quartered in Berga in 1820 we see it as the "*patum patena*, a dance so called that from festivals immemorial is a custom in this town" (quoted in Sales 1962, 212). But contemporary meanings were clearly more important within the town. The word *patum* is onomatopoeic, related phonetically to other words illustrating the sound of a sudden impact: feet striking the ground, a blow struck, projectiles striking their target, and so forth.[6] Notably, the morpheme *pat-* is associated, particularly in this region in the early nineteenth century, with popular disorder and local bands of bandits and irregular troops—the latter not always readily distinguished (Noyes 1992, 347–51).

The nineteenth century completed the partial domestication of the Patum's disorder. New *entremesos* asserting authority and submission—giants, eagle, and dwarfs—were gradually incorporated in order to balance the rebellious performances of mule, Turks, and devils (the Christians and angels being, as they are today, merely nominal victors over the latter two). The town band—such as it was—not only enhanced the appeal of the festival but also set music against the noise of the drum: every *entremes* except for the mule and the devils now had a melody and a choreography to control it. The order of performances was gradually reshaped to highlight the contrasts of order and disorder and, to a certain extent, to contain the latter. The containment was never fully successful, and we may suspect that the Patum's eventual symmetries result rather from the polarizing tensions between public, performers, and city.

In the 1890s, the final *entremesos* of the present Patum were incorporated as part of an attempt to dress up both the festival and the town for potential investors, tourists, and political patrons. The Patum had stabilized the Berguedan social body in representation at least, balancing an orderly upper body with an unruly lower one in an ongoing conflict that, rather than leading to the victory of one side, held the members together—in contrapposto, as it were. The dichotomy was reproduced at several levels of the festival: between procession and Patum, between *entremesos*, and between the elite spectators in the balcony and the working-class participants in the *plaça*. Then as today, the Patum's syntax drew both connections and contrasts:

Turks and Cavallets. A battle turned into a dance, where order triumphs in the choreography as well as in the mimesis.

Àliga. The dance of a hard-surfaced and crowned heraldic bird, which commands attention at the same time it holds the public at a distance.

Old Dwarfs, Giants, and New Dwarfs. A sequence where the climax is framed in miniatures of itself; the claims of the higher social status are

Maces. A battle where the nominal victory of order is belied by the protagonism of the devils, who burn themselves out before St. Michael and the angel dare attack them.

Guites. The improvisatory movement of two cloth-covered farmyard monsters, which scatter the public as they engage with them.

Plens and tirabol. Infernal figures without angels to conquer them, whose music is undermined by the separate rhythms of *tabal* and *fuets*, supported by the emulations of the lower.

followed by a dance "without order or concert" (Armengou 1994, 91) within which symbols of high and low are intermingled. Everyone is still alive at the end.

The *Comparses* and Their Performances

The individual numbers of the Patum comprise effigies or masked figures and a prescribed dance or set of movements. The historical term for these numbers was *entremesos*, in contempory Catalan they are usually called *comparses*, from *comparèixer*, to appear. Each *comparsa* is controlled by a small group of people—overwhelmingly male—and a *cap de colla* (head of the gang), who distribute the *salts* (here, the turns as performer) among themselves and those upon whom they choose to confer the privilege. There are nine *comparses* plus the final *tirabol*, appearing always in the following order even in acts in which not all elements appear:

1. Tabal
2. Turcs i Cavallets
3. Maces
4. Guites
5. Àliga
6. Nans Vells
7. Gegants
8. Nans Nous
9. Plens
10. Tirabol

Apart from the Tabal, which has a framing role, and the final *tirabol*, a hybrid, the *comparses* can be divided into *balls* and *salts*. A *ball* (dance) is choreographed and accompanied by music, hence fixed in time and space. These include the Turcs i Cavallets, the Àliga, the two sets of dwarfs, and the giants. The *salts* or *coses de foc* (things of fire) are the Guites, the Maces, and the Plens: *comparses* accompanied by the Tabal, with music later incorporated in the Plens and the midday Maces. All feature the use of *fuets*, slow-burning firecrackers about one and a half feet long, which trail sparks until the flame hits the charge at the bottom. The effigies, masks, and costumes of these *comparses* are much less well made than those of the dances: they suffer fire damage and require constant repair. Their motion, although it consists of prescribed gestures and movements, is less fixed than that of the *balls*. It is timed not to the music (if there is any), but to the burning of the *fuet*, which takes about three minutes, depending on humidity. The verb used for the motion is *saltar*, which means "to jump" or "to leap" in modern Catalan, but in the Patum retains something of its old Latin sense of disorderly, unholy dancing.[7]

TABAL

The Tabal is a big red bass drum with the shield of Berga emblazoned on its sides, carried by a man in seventeenth-century dress: red velvet slit-sleeved coat over a yellow blouse and red velvet knee breeches, white lace cuffs and collar, yellow sash, white stockings, buckled black shoes, and a broad-brimmed red velvet hat with a white plume. He plays a slow even beat: "PA-TUM," which speeds up slightly to "pa-TUM TUM TUM TUM TUM" before a pause. The Tabal's role is twofold: to announce and open the Patum and to accompany certain other *comparses*. Its sound is penetrating: the verb *atabalar* means "to bewilder someone," so they have *el cap com un bòmbol*, a head like a drum—the older phrase being *un cap com un tabal* (Alcover and Moll 1927–62, entry "tabal").

On the Sunday after Ascension Day, the Tabaler comes out of City Hall and processes through Berga to announce the city council's decision to have Patum. On the Wednesday before Corpus Christi, he leads the giants along the same route: this is the opening of the Patum. On Wednesday and Saturday night he leads the *passacarrers*—or, to speak accurately, opens it up. He foregoes his fancy dress and yields the Tabal to a series of deputies as it passes through the streets, because this is a very long night.

During the Patum in the *plaça* he is located in a small balcony of his own, and accompanies the *coses de foc*: the Maces, the Guites, and the Plens. There is only one *tabaler* at a time, and for the past two hundred years individual families have controlled the role for a few generations each. The present Tabaler is the son and grandson of the last two, and will leave it to his younger brother.

Figure 2. The tabal at the head of the Corpus Christi procession on the Carrer Major, ca. 1960, followed by turcs i cavallets, maces, and Guita Grossa. Photo by Luigi, Berga.

Turcs i Cavallets

Literally, Turks and little horses. This is a simple variant of the Moors-and-Christians dances common in southern Europe; on the Catalan coast in the early modern period the Turks were the relevant threat and the *entremes* seems to have travelled inland.[8] The *turcs* wear no masks but show their identity by turbaned helmets and wooden scimitars. They wear flowered

Figure 3. The Maces in the Plaça Sant Pere in the first decade of the twentieth century. "Els pagesos a la barana": the countrypeople seek safety and a good view behind the *barana*. Photo from *Arxiu Luigi*, Berga.

jackets and loose, full, red knee breeches, with white stockings and *espardenyes de set vetes*, the rope-soled cloth shoes laced to the knee traditionally worn by Catalan mountain people.

The *cavallets* are the variety of hobbyhorse known in French as *chevaux-jupons* (horse-skirts). The brown horse, girded for battle in approximately late-medieval fashion with a red and yellow fringe, is made out of papier-mâché reinforced with plaster and suspended from the carrier's shoulders at waist level. Tiny legs make the carrier appear to be riding in the saddle. The rider wears a helmet and is dressed like the *turc* with inverse colors. He carries a straight sword in his right hand and a flat wooden block strapped to his left palm.

The Turcs i Cavallets appear only in the Patum in the *plaça* and are its first number. Their dance begins with a bright brassy march: they gallop out of City Hall, turn around, line up in two rows, and bow to the city council in the balcony. Then the music turns to a slower 2/4 time. The Turcs form an inner circle, the Cavallets an outer circle, and they skip clockwise, the last *cavallet* spinning on his axis. When the music reaches its cadence, each *turc* strikes the wooden block in the hand of the nearest cavallet with his scimitar. The melody and the blow are repeated three times. On the last repetition, the Cavallets strike the Turcs instead, and the latter kneel in a sign of submission.[9]

The Turcs i Cavallets are a relatively open *comparsa*, and a few young women dance as *turcs*.

MACES

The "maces" are masked and horned devils in heavy red or green felt suits. Each carries a *maça*, a red-and-green pole topped with a metal drum full of pebbles that rattle when it is bounced. A painted devil's face decorates the drum, and a *fuet* is affixed to the top. In addition to its connotations as a weapon, the *maça* is a convenient way of carrying pyrotechnia, and the bouncing motion helps to keep the *fuet* alight in the often-rainy season of Corpus: the *salts* have thus a technical as well as a symbolic raison d'être.

The Maces perform with music and a semblance of choreography at the noon Patum in the *plaça*: this music was not added until the 1950s, in yet another municipal moment of revitalizing and domesticating the Patum. During the night Patum, the *passacarrers*, and the Quatre Fuets (see below), they *salt* to the accompaniment of the Tabal alone. The four of them (eight at noon) stand in a long rectangle, two at each end. Their *fuets* are lit, and they begin to skip toward the opposite end of the rectangle, bouncing the *maça* up and down so that the sparks falling in the air describe thick arabesques, a favorite subject of Berguedan photographers. They move back and forth along the rectangle until a *fuet* explodes: then the devil falls to the ground.

During the Patum in the *plaça*, there are two angels, Saint Michael and a smaller helper, who skip across the middle of the rectangle after each passing of the devils. When a devil falls, Saint Michael steps over him and, with his lance, gives him the coup de grâce, the angel helping with his short sword. The number is thus understood as a battle.

The angels are called a separate *comparsa*, since it would be unseemly to group them with the devils, but because there are only two of them and their role is very minor, they don't really count. They are generally played by pubescent boys or by women. They dress like the angels of the old Holy Week processions, winged medieval knights. Both wear blond curly wigs, Saint Michael with a silver helmet and the angel with a wreath of flowers. They have red velvet capes over white tunics embroidered with gold and the usual white stockings and *espardenyes*.

The Maces are theoretically the same *comparsa* as the Plens, and there is significant overlap between those who *salt* the *maces* and those who dress the Plens. The Maces are somewhat fluid, dividing *salts* between themselves, and there are women among them. In the evening *passacarrers* and also during the Quatre Fuets, the official Maces begin the *salt* and then let other people take a turn, exchanging the *maça* after each crossing of the rectangle over and back.

GUITES

The *guita* or "kicker," from an adjective applied to mules, is one of the *mulasses* or mule effigies common in Catalonia: these, in turn, are one local subgroup of the festival effigies we may call tarasques from the better-known Provençal example. Widespread in Languedoc and formerly in Castile, these creatures share several features: an appearance indeterminate between dragon and domestic animal; aggressive behavior (especially

Figure 4. The two Guites on either side of the *barana* during the calmer daytime Patum. The musicians' balcony against the church and the Bar La Barana can be seen in the background. Photo by Luigi, Berga.

in relation to women) often enhanced by fireworks and snapping jaws; and legendary association with the origins of the city, stressing either agricultural fertility or defense against invasion (Dumont 1951; Very 1962, 51–76; Fabre and Camberogue 1977; Le Goff 1980; Gilmore 2002).

Berguedans often speak of the Guita in the singular, although since 1890 there have been two, because the second is in a sense a redoubling: both number and gender are indeterminate. Its body is a metal frame with wooden slats in the form of a half-barrel, with a light wooden rim which rides on the shoulders of the carriers. A long wooden neck, distinct to Berga and more proper to a giraffe than a mule, is held in a leather holster around the waist of a man under the front of the half-barrel; behind him, another man inside supports a transverse bar. Body and neck are covered with green canvas, with the shield of Berga emblazoned on each side. The head is a grinning green papier-mâché mule's head of sorts, with ears and a short horsehair mane. Inside its jaws is a metal support for three *fuets*, and a bell hangs just below the head.

The small *guita* needs at least eight carriers, the large one more. The *cap de colla* or another responsible person goes in front to lead the animal and direct the man inside, who controls the mobile neck. The weight is mostly supported by the outside carriers, who take the rim on their shoulders.

The *guites* come out for the Wednesday and Saturday passacarrers and for the Patums in the *plaça*, and no one has ever tried to set music to them. They chase the crowd with the fuets in their mouths (one *fuet* for the noon Patum and the *passacarrers*, three for the night Patum), and move through the available space as the spirit of the moment moves them. Each *guita*, however, has its characteristic gestures.

The Guita Grossa (Big Guita) runs through the *plaça*, then lowers its neck and spins so that the surrounding crowd has to fall to the ground to avoid getting hit. It lifts its head to the first-floor balconies and rattles its *fuets* against the metal rails, forcing the spectators back. Its most typical play is against the *barana*, the broad stone barrier rising along the north side of the *plaça*. The *guitaire* in front jumps up on the *barana*, which has crowds of people leaning against it; he takes the neck of the Guita and runs it up and down the length of the *barana*. The crowd ducks down, away from the *fuets*: at the bottom, some brave soul always clings to the lamppost long enough to get burned before jumping down. Some people bring old umbrellas—often full of holes from a previous Patum—to engage the Guita in combat. The Guita draws back as it is about to burst, and after the explosion takes a few humping steps forward, swinging its head back and forth and ringing its bell.

The Guita Xica (Little Guita) is also called the Guita Boja (Mad Guita) because of its greater speed and flexibility. Like the Grossa, the Xica runs and spins in the *plaça*; the crowd chases it and has to react quickly. The Xica's neck is too short for much play with balconies and *barana*. Rather, it specializes in invading inappropriate spaces: it will go behind the *barana*, where the crowd is huddling for protection, or up in the musicians' balcony or inside a bar or up the stairs of City Hall. There is greater scope for improvisation during the *passacarrers*, so the Xica often has more protagonism there than in the *plaça*.

The mule is a richly evocative animal in the Catalan mountains. Stronger, hardier, and more surefooted than a horse, it was of great practical importance in forestry, farming, hauling, and even mining. At the same time, its obstinacy and temper were proverbial. It was associated with disruptive, nonreproductive female sexuality in a host of proverbs: "Do not trust the back of a mule or the front of a woman" (Amades 1950–69, 2, 1200); its uneasy presence in the farmyard was like that of the young wife in the household. Several *blasons populaires* advise the prudent man not to get a wife or a mule from certain villages: they were foreign elements that had to be introduced with great case. In early-modern elite culture in Catalonia, it was the most common simile for manual laborers, who required a strong hand to be kept obedient (Amelang 1986, 150–51). Its particular untrustworthiness was that of workers and women, whose apparent domestication could not be counted on: "a meek mule kills its master" (Gomis 1910, 162). Catalan landowners could not maintain their estates without workers, wives, or mules, but each was felt to threaten the precariously enclosed order and to require repression accordingly. The name change of Berga's Guita—unique among Catalan mules—from *mulassa* to *mulaguita* and finally, by the early twentieth century, simply *guita*—highlights the mule's disruptive qualities.

The *guitaires* are divided into two comparses of about twenty young men each, but dress the same, in black smocks with red felt fringe, and battered shapeless hats to protect themselves from the sparks. These smocks or *bates* are workmen's clothing, and distinguish the *guitaires* from all other comparsa members.

Àliga

The Àliga (eagle) is a papier-mâché and plaster effigy on a wooden arma-
ture with a grille in its breast for its carrier, concealed to the legs, to see
through. It is painted a dark greenish brown and is meticulously sculpted,
with an elegant curve to its head and neck, scalelike "feathers," and a
long, straight tail. It wears a crown—at present that of the Counts of
Barcelona rather than the Kings of Spain—and carries carnations or boxwood tied with Catalan-flag ribbon in its beak; in the old days it carried a
live dove. The three *aligots*—the carrier and the two men who dance on
either side of him—wear blouses and loose flowered knee-breeches with
kerchiefs of the same material, and the standard espardenyes. Tight around
each waist is the *faixa*, a broad wool sash once worn by peasants, which supports the back under the great weight of the eagle.

The Àliga dances only for the Patum in the *plaça*. Its dance begins
with the Àliga in the middle and the two *aligots* on either side mimicking
its steps. It bows to the parish church and to City Hall, and the music begins in a slow 2/4. The dancers do a *punteig* (pointing, or lacing), each
marking a square around himself on the stones of the *plaça* with the tips
of his toes. When the music changes to a faster 6/8, the eagle starts to
sway and then skip from side to side, each time increasing the breadth of
the movement. The two *aligots* are now assisting the eagle from without,
helping the carrier to keep his balance. With another accelerando in the
music, the eagle breaks out of position and skips in a larger circle, the
crowd following the tail, and the *aligots* helping it to turn. At the end of
the dance the Àliga spins quickly on itself, *aligots* and crowd dropping to
the ground to avoid a blow from the hard tail, which is reputed to have
killed a soldier once. The *aligots* help the dizzy dancer to stop, and the eagle bows once more to the church and the Ajuntament before retiring.

The Àliga is the most jealously guarded *comparsa*: to dance the eagle
requires great strength and balance, and there has never been any question of letting a woman do it. There are only three *aligots* at a given time,
who take turns at dancing the eagle itself.

Unique to the Països Catalans, the *àliga* is historically an *entremes*
with special privileges, dancing alone inside the church or in front of the
Sacrament in the Corpus Christi procession. Though its original processional role may have been as the emblem of Saint John, its heraldic associations soon added another resonance, and its primary significance in Catalan

Figure 5. The Àliga bowing. Photo by Luigi, Berga.

processions has been as a civic symbol, the predominant interpretation in Berga. In any case, if not a two-headed eagle, it is on excellent terms with both Church and State. It was a prestige *entremes*, expensive to make and maintain, belonging only to important populations, and the balance of the evidence suggests that it was not a stable part of the Patum until the late eighteenth century, when the city's increasing importance as a textile center both enhanced its prosperity and encouraged its ambitions.

Like mules, eagles have proverbial status in the Catalan Pyrenees, embodying not humility but the opposite extreme. The local varieties of eagle are the "royal" and the "imperial," and the eagle is familiar as the king of birds (as in the internationally known "Cant dels Ocells," the Carol of the Birds). The eagle is conscious of its station and dignity: "the eagle does not chase flies" (Gomis 1910). Like royalty and like the Host before which it walked in the procession, the eagle is associated with light and sun and the gaze. "To see more than an eagle" is to have superlative sight; the eagle is said to be the only animal able to look directly into the sun (Gomis 1910). Flying higher than any other bird, the eagle has the omniscient gaze of power, seeing the world as God sees it, and in turn is visible to the admiring gaze of the earthbound, like the elite in the festival balcony. Not that those below will always admire: to take down a pretentious person is "to throw the eagle to the ground" (Gomis 1910). But eagles must be treated with care, as their anger is redoubtable: to abandon oneself to rage is "to give oneself up to the eagles"—sometimes "to give oneself up to the devils." The Berguedan eagle shares the gesture of the threatening spin with its antithesis, the Guita, and the tender live dove it once carried in its curved beak is a nice emblem of the ambiguities of power.

Nans Vells

The Old Dwarfs belong to the common Iberian genre known as *nans* or *capgrossos* (bigheads) in Catalonia and *cabezudos* (bigheads) in Spain. A *nan* is a papier-mâché and plaster head worn over the head of the dancer, who sees through the open mouth. Very well-made, the dwarfs are caricatures rather than idealized figures. The four Nans Vells are all male, with long noses, melancholy eyes, black tricorn hats, and yellow wigs with eighteenth-century pigtails. The dancers wear red tunics trimmed with gold, reminiscent of the *gramalla* worn by municipal councillors in Catalonia before

1714. They first appear in municipal records in 1855 (Farràs i Farràs 1979, 215), probably in imitation of other mountain cities such as Olot or Vic. They were easily damaged and repaired as the city could afford it, and were not considered essential to the Patum until the early twentieth century (Armengou [1968, 1971]1994, 108).

The dance of the Nans Vells imitates that of the giants and shares their tunes: it is a simple waltz with some changing of partners and exchange of positions, and the dancers play castanets in the first section. The second section is a faster 4/4 time with the same movements. The inner circle of the crowd helps to guide the dancers, who can see very little and, imbalanced by the heavy heads, are prone to vertigo. At the end, each *nan* spins in place.

GEGANTS

There are two pairs of giants, tall effigies on wooden armatures with a carrier hidden in the skirts.[10] Head and hands are beautifully sculpted out of fortified papier-mâché, and they wear natural wigs which must be coiffed every year by hairdressers. The clothes are rich and expensive, in varying tones of red and green with gold trim; the giantesses wear jewelry. In late nineteenth-century Barcelona, the costume of the giantess announced the summer fashions; Berga was too poor to dress its giantesses anew every year, but their coiffures served the same purpose.

The Gegants Vells (Old Giants) are tan in complexion, and the male is dressed as a Moor, with a turbaned helmet and a scimitar in his belt. He wears a moustache, and brown hair curled below his ears, and a red jacket with a paler tunic beneath. He carries a mace in his right hand, resting on his shoulder. The *geganta*, slightly fairer, is dressed as a queen with a tiara and a green veil over her brown hair; she carries a bouquet in her lifted right hand. The Moorish dress does not make the giant alien in popular eyes: in the first known drawing of the Patum, from 1838 in the middle of the first Carlist War, he is shown wearing the emblematic beret of Carlist Berga.

The Gegants Nous (New Giants), from 1891, are usually known as the Gegants Negres or Black Giants because of their complexions. They are, however, dressed as Christians, and their blackness dates from the turn of the century, when the black Madonna of Montserrat was being promoted as the national patron: it is associated with the chthonic rather than the foreign. They are among the tallest giants in Catalonia and re-

Figure 6. The Gegants begin their spin. Photo by Luigi, Berga.

quire exceptional strength to dance. The giantess is very handsome; like her sister, she wears a tiara, back veil, and earrings. Her ample skirts are green with yellow trim, and her left hand holds a bouquet. The Black Giant, with his black beard, silver helmet, huge mace, and imposing figure, is the cynosure of all eyes when his crimson velvet cloak spins in the *plaça*; he is the object of numerous erotic fantasies on the part of both sexes, and it is the *cap de colla* and his intimates who have the privilege of dancing him.

The giants process, waltz, and spin. In the Wednesday noon passada through the streets and the Wednesday and Saturday night *passacarrers* (in which only the two Old Giants participate), the giants are walked by the *geganters*, who take turns; according to the energy of the carriers and the visibility of the place, they dance instead of processing; at the stops in the route they do a full dance. In the Patum of the *plaça* they dance to the same waltz tunes used for the *nans vells*. Their movements are limited by their size, and in the night Patums the crossovers between pairs are eliminated. The faster section and especially the final spin are tests of prowess among the *geganters* and the high point of the middle section of the Patum for the public. In the *tirabols* at the end of the Patum the two Gegants Vells are spun in a corner, with the *geganters* taking turns and defying each other to resist vertigo the longest.

Most major cities in Catalonia kept their giants as the last remnant of the early modern *entremesos*, so festival giants are familiar sights and widely invoked in popular idiom to comment on both social inequality and state administration. "If everyone were equal, who would carry the giants?" asks one proverb, and a 1929 protest song from the textile factories near Berga repeats the theme:

> *Els burgesos ens volien fer la por*
> *però els obrers del Llobregat no en tenim, no*
> *Que no es pensin que encara és com abans*
> *que pertot allà on passaven ens fèien ballar els gegants.*

> The bourgeois wanted to frighten us
> but the workers of the Llobregat aren't afraid, no
> They'd better not think that it's still like before
> when everywhere they passed they made us dance the giants.
> (Ramon Vilardaga, personal communication)

In fact, up through the 1950s the heavy *entremesos* of the Patum were danced by lower-class men given both a cash payment and a new pair of *espardenyes* by the Ajuntament.

The Ajuntament's expenditures also feature in giant idiom. When city officials are observed to be conspicuously consuming resources it's not clear they possess, then the giantess pays: *paga la geganta*. Those people fortunate enough to have bureaucratic sinecures or merely secure, well-paid government positions, such as a schoolteacher or a firefighter, *cobren de la geganta* (are paid by the giantess) or, more pointedly, *mamen de la geganta*, suckle her.

The *geganters* are a large *comparsa* of perhaps twenty men: unlike the more fluid *turcs i cavallets* or *nans*, in which only those doing the immediate *salt* are costumed, all the *geganters* are marked by their red shirts, white trousers, and a *faixa* for support. Those not dancing the giants are supporting and guiding them from outside. Except within the single dances of the Patum in the *plaça*, the *geganters* have to take frequent turns because the effigies are so heavy.

NANS NOUS

Introduced in 1890, when the Patum was being dressed up for summer visitors, the New Dwarfs represent two couples, an old one and a young one. The old man scowls slightly and wears a brimless black hat with gold braid. Because of the ambiguous hat, he is sometimes called "the priest;" he is also known as "the notary" or "the ugly one." The old woman wears a cloth bonnet; the young one has a sculpted pink hat with an upturned brim. The young male is the most difficult to dance because of his heavy broadbrimmed light blue hat, for which he is known as *el barret blau*. Their general effect was best characterized by Xavier Fàbregas: "sundayed up . . . like the commercial petty bourgeosie who want to show off to their neighbors, and distinguish themselves in every possible detail from the country people" (1976, 140).

These dwarfs have the most complex dance steps of the Patum, involving hand clappings, skips in place, and spins between couples. The two *comparses* of *nans* are fairly open to female participation. The *caps de colla* of both Old and New Dwarfs are in their thirties, and the dancers tend to be in their teens or twenties because it is quickness and agility

Figure 7. The crowds of the 1980s dance with the Nans Nous. Photo by Luigi, Berga.

rather than strength that are required. They are often recruited directly from the Children's Patum.

In Catalonia as elsewhere in Spain, dwarfs always appear in relation to giants, and each takes meaning from the other: often as parents and children, or as graceful upper class and clumsy lower class (Amades 1934, 110; Brandes 1980, 27–32). Entering the festival in the nineteenth century, the dwarfs are always seen by Catalan scholars as an indicator of democratic tendencies: "the common people incorporating themselves into the traditional mythology" (Armengou [1968, 1971]1994, 109). But in truth the configuration is more complex, and especially in the Patum: the common people were already there, in devils and *guita*. Unlike these, the dwarfs are controlled; they do not *salt* upwards, but dance in place; they emulate the giants in dress and motion, flattering them by the very clumsiness of the imitation. The dwarfs are the orderly lower class that trusts to the hegemonic promise. They do not make their own meanings or direct their own action.

PLENS

The "full ones" or full devils wear the same heavy felt costume as the Maces, red with green trim or vice versa, and the same masks with horns. Three *fuets* are affixed to each horn, and two more are tied to the tail; the head is protected with a leather hood, and a wreath of *Clematis vidalba*, a green vine that grows along the streams above town, prevents sparks from falling down the neck of the costume; more *vidalba* at head and tail reduces the impact of the *fuets*. About seventy come out in a given *salt*.[11]

Each *ple* dances with an *acompanyant*, an uncostumed friend whose job it is to light the *ple* and lead him or her safely through the *plaça*. The *salt de plens* is the climax of the Patum in the *plaça*, done only at night. For it, the lights are turned off and the *plens* come out slowly and distribute themselves in the crowd. When an *acompanyant* stationed at the lamppost lights his *bengala*, a thick sparkler, all the *plens* are lighted up and the music, fast and repetitious, begins, the Tabal also playing to a rhythm of its own. The *plens* and the entire crowd *salt* counterclockwise around the *plaça*, hopping from foot to foot. The crowd is a rolling black mass with thick flames dancing above it. The *fuets* begin to burst, a few scattered, and then all at once: a long complex ferocious explosion like multiple orgasm (as the Berguedans explain in their cups—*a salt de plens* has a double

Figure 8. The Plens wait for their masks below city hall. Photo by Luigi, Berga.

meaning in Berga). The smoke pushes up from the *plaça* as from a chimney, and the spectators on the balcony are blackened with it. The music repeats itself until the last *fuets* have exploded and the tension subsides.

The Plens are nominally the same comparsa as the Maces, and in the early Bulla this connection was more obvious: "the devils go full" in their second sortie. Although today they are considered the most primitive element of the festival, widely supposed to be pre-Christian and tied to vegetative spirits, it is not clear that the present profusion of vines and green is more than a century old, and the "infernal orgy" of fire is an effect of the great increase in the number of *plens* since 1960, when there were still only sixteen of them. Nonetheless, devils are chthonic figures in the Catalan mountains, associated with caves and water—as are the black Madonnas and the mules—and, like the Moors, credited with responsibility for otherwise inexplicable constructions in the landscape.

TIRABOL

The *tirabol* is not a comparsa, but the final dance or salt—it is both—of each night of the Patum. The meaning of the name is uncertain: sometimes in older texts it appears as *tirabou* (pull the ox) and seems to have been a kind of crack-the-whip dance when the numbers were smaller. Today the usage is most often plural, as the *tirabols* have burgeoned in number. They are in effect a continuation of the Plens, who lift their masks and keep dancing, with the entire crowd *salt*-ing counterclockwise in the *plaça*, in small arm-in-arm groups, to any of three lively melodies used: one in 6/8, a waltz-jota, and an inauthentic but much-loved *pas-doble*.[12] The Gegants Vells spin in place in the corner of the *plaça* by Cal Quimserra, the *geganters* competing with each other against vertigo and exhaustion. The two *guites* dance through the *plaça* with a long loping gait, and friends are given rides on the back. The Tabal accompanies the *guites*: if the *fuets* have not yet exploded at the end of the dance, the *guites* and the Tabal keep going. Four or five *tirabols* are played after the noonday Patum and twenty or more at the end of the night Patum. For the *passacarrers* there are *tirabols* in the Plaça Sant Joan—usually three—and another dozen or more in the Plaça Sant Pere at the end.

Apart from the *comparses*, the Patum has its dignitaries and functionaries. Above all, it requires a public, large and actively participating, for its success. This has not been a problem for the past thirty years: rather, the overcrowding of the *plaça* has interfered with the *comparses*, who do not have enough room to dance comfortably. The public, insofar as its years and energies permit, *salts* along with the *comparses* or behind them in the *passacarrers*, hopping from foot to foot to permit the maximum of motion in the minimum of space. Other personnel essential to the event include:

Musicians

The Patum music is played by two town bands, the Banda de l'Escola Municipal de Música and the Cobla Pirineu, who alternate days in the Patum. The students of the Escola Municipal play for the children's Patum. The musicians are placed on a scaffolding next to the church steps and wear no special costume. As well as playing for the Patum in the *plaça*, they accompany the giants on the Wednesday *passada* and the Wednesday and Saturday night *passacarrers*.

Autoritats

The "authorities" include the Ajuntament or city council, the commandant of the local army post, the captain of the local Guardia Civil, the heads of local institutions such as the hospital and the Red Cross, and by extension the dignitaries and celebrities invited by the Ajuntament for the occasion. They sit in the balcony of City Hall during the Patum in the *plaça*, and walk in the *passacarrers* in front of the musicians. They also attend the daily masses and attend and give receptions. Their Patum is one of good clothes and good food and drink inside City Hall's ceremonial rooms; guests move back and forth between the balcony and the inside, and in the years of democracy, some celebrated Barcelonans have left Berga with celebrated hangovers.

Administradors

The "administrators" were formerly wealthy residents of Berga's four quarters, entrusted with collecting money and putting on the neighborhood festivals of the Octave of Corpus Christi.[13] Since the suppression of the Octave in the twentieth century, and since the emptying of the four quarters in favor of more modern housing on the periphery of the old town, the administrators have become a purely ceremonial role, representing the community among the authorities. They are now four couples married within the previous year, and being administrators is in theory part of their rite of passage to full community membership. (In fact many couples deeply integrated in public life forego the opportunity because of the tedium it entails.) They sit with the authorities in the balcony and at mass, the men in black suits and the women in black dresses with comb and mantilla, an Andalusian borrowing from the end of the last century. Each couple is attended by little girls in their first communion regalia, one carrying a *palma,* a stalk of artificial flowers and ribbons representing one of the four old quarters.

The Syntax of Events

Corpus Christi is a movable feast sixty days after Easter, falling always on Thursday. May 21 is the earliest possible date, June 24 the latest.

PRELIMINARIES

At 11 A.M. on the Sunday after Ascension Day, three weeks before Corpus, the Ajuntament holds an extraordinary plenary session with only one question on the agenda: Will there be Patum? There is a unanimous "yes," except in time of war or famine; not since 1938 has a Patum been cancelled. The band stands below in the *plaça,* and just before twelve o'clock, plays the Ball de l'Aliga. On the stroke of twelve, the tabaler, who has been waiting in the portal of City Hall, steps out and hits the first Pa-tum! of the season. The tabaler steps out and, playing all the while, goes across the *plaça,* up through the Casc Antic, down through the lower part of the city to the Passeig de la Pau, and out along the Carrer del Roser to the old city limits. There he stops for a drink while the children who have been following take possession of the Tabal. When he comes out, he turns back to the old city and down the Carrer Major. Back in the Plaça Sant Pere, he plays his final pa-tums.

Sunday before Corpus is the Quatre Fuets (Four Firecrackers), a ceremonial testing to see if they explode loud enough. They say this was necessary in the days when the *fuets* were of local artisanal manufacture; now it's just because people are eager. Four *maces* are dressed and, led by the Tabaler, march out of City Hall down to the Vall. There the crowd delineates a rectangle; the *fuets* are lit, and the *maces* begin to *salt*. People stand in line to take a turn: the four original *maces* yield their places. After the *fuets* burst—there is always a competition to make one last longest— the crowd cheers. Tabaler and maces go back up to City Hall, crossing paths with the Tabaler, eight *maces*, and two angels of the Children's Patum, who repeat the ceremony with their own smaller *fuets*.

THE PATUM PROPER

WEDNESDAY	THURSDAY (CORPUS)	FRIDAY	SATURDAY	SUNDAY
12:00 *Passada dels Gegants*	12:00 Patum de Lluïment	12:00 Patum Infantil de Lluïment		12:00 Patum de Lluïment
		5:00 Complete Patum Infantil	7:30 *Passacarrers*	
8:00 *Passacarrers*				
	9:30 Complete Patum			9:30 Complete Patum

PASSADA DELS GEGANTS

The "passing of the giants" is the beginning of the five days that constitute the *festes de Corpus*. Again at noon, the tabal comes out of City Hall, this time followed by the four giants and the band. The giants waltz in the *plaça*, then, following the same route as the tabal, process through the streets of Berga, dancing most of the time. The band plays the "Marxa del Patumaire," an amalgam of the music of Turcs i Cavallets and Plens, alternating it with the popular *pas-doble* of the *tirabols*. The public follow, the young *salt*-ing throughout.

PASSACARRERS

The "passing the streets" is a procession of the Tabaler, Maces, Guites, and Old Giants to do honorific *salts* for the authorities on Wednesday and Saturday nights. The route is an elaborated version of the one used in the *passades* and takes at least six hours to cover. At each *plaça*, Maces, Guites, and Gegants perform, in that order. On Wednesday night, *salts* are done before the dwellings of municipal councillors and the mayor and in front of the Red Cross, the courthouse, the convents, the army post, and the Guardia Civil.[14] On Saturday night, the *salts* are performed for the *administradors*.

There are numerous pauses in the *passacarrers*: you can abandon it to have dinner and find it again two streets further down. Although the official route is from authority to authority, the subterranean geography is from bar to bar, and the Guita Xica in particular tends to disappear during these stops. This is its night to show off: bursting into bars, riding on the back of a dump truck, sneaking into a house on an upper street and out the back door on a lower one, reemerging at the head of the procession.

The climax of the *passacarrers* is its return through the old city. In the Plaça Sant Joan, after the *salts*, the band plays the first *tirabols* of the night and, on Wednesday, of the season. Then, tight as forcemeat in a sausage, *comparses* and crowd push themselves up the narrow Carrer Major. The band plays "Ella s'ho pensa," a long-lined, chromatic march never played at any other time. The melody is too broad for the street and makes the crowd strain against its walls: when at last they burst out in the Plaça Sant Pere, they fling themselves straight into the release of more *tirabols*.

PATUM DE LLUÏMENT

The Patum of "Display" or "Brilliance" is the short noon Patum, to which people come in their Sunday clothes. Toward the end of the Mass, the *comparses* of the Patum line up along the church steps and below, forming a corridor from the church to City Hall. As the band plays the hymn of the city (a lugubrious nineteenth-century march), the Ajuntament, other authorities, Administradors, and little girls file out of the church and follow this corridor; they go up to the balcony to preside over the Patum. The *comparses* go back to their places—the Guites on the edges of the *plaça*, the Tabaler in his balcony, and the others under City Hall. Then there is a full *tanda*—the official word—or *salt*—the popular one—of Patum; that is, one performance of each dance in sequence, minus the Plens. A few *tirabols* round off the event.

PATUM COMPLETA

The complete Patum is done at night. It is much longer, more crowded, and less polished than the Patum de Lluïment. There are four *tandes* instead of one, and the Plens are done after the second and fourth. At the end, the *tirabols* go on for another hour or more. Even the Ajuntament is dressed more comfortably; the Tabaler has abandoned his hot heavy velvet; the giants do a simpler choreography; and the Maces, now only four instead of the noontime eight, go without music.

MINOR ACTS

A variety of religious, municipal, and commercial events surround the Patum. At ten o'clock each morning from Thursday to Sunday, a rocket is shot off to announce the beginning of the festival acts. The band escorts the Administradors to the parish church for daily Mass. On Thursday, Corpus Christi Day, it is a High Mass sung by the Orfeó Berguedà, with Ajuntament and authorities in attendance, and the two angels, Saint Michael and his deputy, at the front of the nave. The rector—who is not from Berga—takes advantage of the unusual crowd to give a common post–Vatican II festival sermon: we must celebrate and defend our local traditions, which are the marks of our faith, but always remember that the celebration is occasioned by a liturgical festival, which itself serves only to call to mind things we should bear always in our hearts; it is to be wished that the devotion shown during the festival were part of our daily routine; and so forth.

The Ajuntament holds several ceremonies to integrate itself in the festival, including cocktail receptions for the Administradors on Friday and for Berguedans living outside the city on Saturday—this latter providing a valued occasion to address a population of long-standing importance to the local economy. On Saturday there is a ceremony to award *títols de patumaire*, certificates of ten and twenty-five years' participation in the Patum, as well as the prizes for the annual poster and children's drawing competitions.

Until the 1960s, the Patum was augmented, like any provincial *festa major*, by a variety of entertainments not otherwise available locally, intended to increase the number of visitors and intensify the appeal of the festival. Today the Patum is considered sufficient attraction; however, a few extra acts survive to fill the empty hours and serve the overflow crowds. In addition to the carnival attractions stationed at the end of the Vall, a Barcelona company offers a recent success in the Municipal Theater on Friday night. In the late 1980s, with the rise of the new Catalan rock music and increasing festival hooliganism in the region, a concert in the sports pavilion was instituted to get the young off the streets in the traditionally explosive hours of early Sunday morning. Earlier on Saturday evening there is a fireworks display to create closure for families with young children on the wildest night of the festival. On Sunday afternoon there is a competition of *sardanes*, with visiting *sardana* societies.

The *sardana* has special status as the national dance and a symbol of fraternity, so *sardanes* punctuate the entire festival. One or two *cobles* (traditional wind bands) from outside the city are hired to play in the Vall after each act of Patum. Many people still have the strength to dance. The final *sardana* at night is always "Corpus a Berga," composed by a local priest and incorporating melodies from the Patum.

The *Comparses* as Political Models

When I was still new, I asked several people, "Who organizes the Patum?"

Eh? They looked at me as if I were mad.

Well, who makes sure that everybody's in their proper place, who keeps things going, who runs it?

A sigh of ostentatious patience. Nobody organizes it, we've all been doing it since we were children, it organizes itself. You'll see.

But some explained, Well, you know, each *comparsa* has its own head, and he decides who's in and who's out. The giants have a tendency to boss the other groups around—they're strong, big men. They make order in the *plaça*, they make the circle for the other groups to dance in. Massana is the head of the giants, he's *tot un personatge*. (The phrase doesn't translate, as it would seem to, into "a real character": rather, a "personage" is someone of more distinction than other people.)

"Massana is the mayor of the Patum," some said. But *els de la guita* fight with the *geganters*, they don't like being pushed around by people with no right to give them orders. Mixo put the whole Patum on strike one year. Mixo said "no Patum" and there was no Patum until he got what he wanted.

Don't you know Sobrevias? said a girl to me incredulously before the whole thing started. But Sobrevias gives the orders. If he says you're out of the Patum, you're out. The head of the Plens!

When questions of power come up in the Patum, three groups and three men are regularly cited: Massana, Mixo, and Sobrevias, the *caps de colla* of the Giants, the Guita Grossa, and the Plens respectively. These are the three *comparses* that matter, the *plats forts* (strong dishes) of the Patum. Most Berguedans perceive the three groups as embodying competing models of political authority in contemporary Berga.

Leonil.la Boixader, the librarian, was reminiscing one day about Estanislau, the man who danced the Àliga when she was a child. He was a friend of her father's, a big man, with snowy white hair and an enormous moustache. "He inspired me with so much respect," she said. "I felt such respect for him that when he came out of the eagle I used to look at him as if he were—God!"

The authority of the men who carry the *comparses* stems in the first instance from their imposing physique. A big man is a big man, for starters.[15] It is clearest in the case of Massana, the *cap de colla* of the *geganters*. Massana is himself a giant: not abnormally tall, but big and solid and handsome. His expression is mild; he is slow to speak and slow to smile, so that the gesture is doubly effective. His whole demeanor bespeaks measure and *seny*. He is a family man and a prosperous craftsman, and his background is romantic: his uncle was a hero of the anti-Francoist *maquis*, of whom stories are told throughout north-central Catalonia. One has a sense of strength held back: like Estanislau, he inspires *respecte*.

Mixo, the *cap de colla* of the Guita Grossa, is another matter. He is a big man in a different way: broad and squat, suggesting brute strength rather than Massana's *equilibri* (the quality needed above all to dance the giants). "Mixo is *molt de pagès*," they told me, "very peasant. Don't try to interview him—he'll just grunt at you." He worked in the mines and is a *pagès de secà*, a dry farmer: one who pulls food up from the earth by main force, without benefit of irrigation or modern machinery. He lives on the road up to Queralt and is seldom seen in Berga. Once a year he descends, like the spirit of the mountains, and becomes a protagonist. For the Patum he drinks—the rest of the year he consumes camomile tea during his infrequent appearances in town—and on Sunday night for the last *tirabols* he sometimes rides on the back of the guita, waving his arms in time to the music, his fly conspicuously undone. One year he stood up—and in due course fell off, banging his head hard against the stones of the *plaça*, to no apparent ill effect. "If ever I've seen the image of perfect happiness," said the town archivist, "it was Mixo on the back of the Guita." To Mossèn Ballarín, the priest of Queralt, Mixo in the *tirabols* sums up the Patum as Harvey Cox's "feast of fools" (Ballarín 1990; Cox 1969).

Even more than Massana or Mixo, Sobrevias has the charisma of scarcity. Massana gains it by breaking out of his everyday restraint during Corpus, Mixo by his sudden prominence, but Sobrevias is less embodied: his is the hand below City Hall pulling invisible strings. His outward demeanor gives nothing away. He is a small, old man with thick glasses, not very communicative even at the long table of the Bar La Barana with his friends. He spends the entire Patum below the Ajuntament with the dressers. Because of this he is not as well known and not as individuated a figure as the other two: the twenty dressers are more frequently spoken of as *aquells*, those guys.

The *geganters* are the Patum's visible embodiment of traditional authority, edging, like Berga itself, into electoral democracy. As in all the *comparses*, but better known to the public, the *geganters* have an internal hierarchy. The Black Giant is danced at the most important points of the festival by the current *cap de colla*, and the lesser giants and lesser moments are apportioned in descending order. But there is a sort of shadow cabinet, a group of long-standing *geganters* with ties to the other dominant party. This second group controls the Geganta Negra. It is also understood that the *geganters* are in closer communication with the Ajuntament than the other *comparses* during the Patum itself—the identity of the *geganter* liaison depending on the party in power—and given de facto responsibility for maintaining order.

Estanis of the Guita Xica drew the distinction of his *comparsa* from the giants thus. "We of the Guita are not the *machos*, but the *muchos*."[16]

The *guitaires* play the opposition to the *geganters*: one year after a dispute when the *geganters* tried to end the *tirabols* too early, Mixo declared, "This year there'll be a change of Ajuntaments!" (Rafart 1989a). But more specifically, the *guites* are associated with popular resistance, each *guita* with a different style. The *comparsa* of the Guita Grossa is largely constituted of young working-class men marginal to the mainstream associative life of Berga, with several from the isolated immigrant quarter of Santa Eulàlia. Like Mixo, they are touched with otherness. This, however, is on the surface: there are family connections between guitaires and the men of the Àliga, and the structure of authority in the comparsa is as present as in the *geganters*. The Grossa is not antistructural, but asserts traditional working-class order. One year a mayor's wife, known for her imposing physique and her social arrogance, was in the foyer of the Ajuntament during an altercation. When she expressed her distaste, Mixo said to her, "Woman, go home and wash dishes!" The Guita Grossa's machismo is less domesticated than that of the *geganters*, who after all dance their giants in couples; it bears some of the resentment of the miners and the long-enforced submissions of working-class men under the Franco regime.

The Guita Xica is more consciously inversive, wittier, more middle class, and more explicitly political. Its carriers are better known as personalities, more visible on the Carrer Major. Succession in the Guita Xica is collective: an adolescent peer group takes it on, keeps it up until a majority are married and having children, then retires in a body, with one or two hanging on to instruct the next generation. The rest move up to the Plens or even the Giants. They are political Catalanists, some of a militant character, especially during the Transition. Where the Guita Grossa has had more face-to-face confrontations with the Berguedan authorities, as in 1978 when Mixo put the Guita on strike in mid-Patum or in the lesser incident with the mayor's wife, the Guita Xica has focused more on symbolic action, transgressing spaces such as the Guardia Civil barracks or City Hall, attacking Spanish flags before 1979 and wearing Catalan ones afterward. Today it inverts other norms in conspicuous performances, such as the annual run of women up the Carrer Major during the *passacarrers*, and it improvises conspicuously also, wearing new decorations or coming out dressed in blue.

The giants and the mule summed up the old lines of power and opposition in traditional Berga. Today, with democracy, the Plens have assumed equal importance. Their numbers in the *plaça* and their indistinct identities suggest mass, not hierarchy, and the numbers have allowed the widest participation of any *comparsa* in the Patum: with, say, seventy *plens* per *salt*, and four *salts* in a given year's Patum, in theory 280 people can participate, and these can be women or ungainly men—the *plens* require no special strength or talent. And there is strong normative pressure to do a *salt de plens*, "the baptism of Berguedan citizenship," at least once. This then is the *comparsa* of the new democratic order.

Except that not just anyone can *salt*. You have to "have a *salt*," and this is obtained in the same way as a *salt* in any other *comparsa*. It comes through a personal connection: it is inherited from family or given in friendship. Some people have more *salts* than they can use, others—including members of the same long-established families—claim they cannot get one. Uniquely in the Patum, the members of the *comparsa* are not the *plens* who dance in the *plaça*, but the dressers—twenty men who spend the festival underneath City Hall preparing the costumes and dressing the actual *plens*. Each dresser controls access to a number of *salts*, the distribution of which is both traditional and contested. The great majority of the *salts* are retained from year to year by both the dressers and the *plens* who get them.

There is widespread confusion and disagreement about how this works, and, like everyone else who wins the friendship of a few dressers, I declined to investigate the conditions of my good fortune. From the insider perspective, indeed, there is nothing to investigate. The ownership of a *salt* is part of the reciprocities of any social network, and this is a particularly large and complex network, crossing class boundaries though centered in "popular" families of long standing in Berga. Children grow up and inherit *salts* from their parents; they might hang out and help the dressers with the preparatory work and so gradually earn the right of presence and eventually a *salt*. As an outsider, I performed the same task of self-insinuation, becoming a habituée of the bar where Sobrevias and friends spend their time. At the end of my first field stay in 1989, Sobrevias, who had paid me little overt attention until then, theatrically kissed me goodbye and, in an act of conspicuous patronage, whispered audibly enough for everyone around to hear, "Next year I'll give you a *salt*!"—a promise he remembered and kept.

The extraordinary character of this gift and the obligation incurred by it are viewed with suspicion by those outside the network, who tend to translate gift as exchange. At best, they speak of bottles of cognac presented to dressers on their saint's days and other forms of mild bribery; but there are widespread rumors of cash payments. Sometimes one hears that as much as $300 is paid for a *salt*; in some versions it is the Ajuntament that acts as mediator with the dressers, or, more mildly and plausibly, the Ajuntament is said to retain some *salts* of its own to grant as favors.

It is true that old patron-client relationships facilitated the entry of upper-class participants in the Plens, and some *salts* are held by members of the Berguedan elite whose families traditionally give employment to some of the dressers, for example. To see this as a quid pro quo is to over-simplify: there are more general reciprocities and genuine, though not egalitarian, personal relationships involved. This is simply how things have always worked in Berga. But from the new standpoint of democracy and its sudden promise of equal access, the old way of distributing resources looks sinister: now it is corruption, trafficking in influences. The dressers are widely referred to as "the Mafia."

In the 1980s and early 1990s, there were frequent public complaints and more than one formal petition to the Ajuntament demanding transparency and sometimes the "democratization" of the process via a lottery. The Ajuntament routinely denies any power to act in the matter and says that the Plens are a *comparsa* like any other. Someone let off a canister of tear gas during the first *salt de plens* of the 1989 Patum: the name was not released "for fear of a lynching," I was told, and it was said that the first identification of an outside hooligan was a mistake: it was a disgruntled local.

On the whole, though, Berguedans have greater faith in the old personalism than they do in the abstract logics of the new state, not least because they have never seen the latter put honestly into practice. Seen from Berga, political corruption in the new Spain is not greatly different from the old *caciquisme* of the nineteenth century, which also wore the dress of liberal democracy; nor has the Catalan hinterland done notably better under the new system than under the old. The Plens sum up everyone's understanding of the system: a show of mass participation concealing an oligarchy that controls access to resources. In the Plens as in government, power has not truly changed hands; in the Plens as in government, position is obtained through money and influence rather than merit. The dressers, in the basement of City Hall, literally undermine democracy.

Màrius Lucas, the *cap* of the New Dwarfs, was standing in a bar on the Carrer Pietat having a drink with a teenage boy during the Patum. "This is my secretary," he said, introducing us. "This is the one who will take over when I quit. This is not a democracy, this is dictatorship." He smiled.

"I decide who gets in, I decide everything." "Look," said Pep Camprubí of the Guita Xica. "I'm one of the Mafia. That's just the way it is."

"I never had a godfather," insisted one prominent *patumaire* to me. "I did it all myself." But he does have older relatives, and today his son has assumed his own coveted position. "The ones who complain are the ones who can't get in," said one member of the *patumaire* elite, which seems to imitate the modus operandi of the sociopolitical elite. "These are the things that we used to say shouldn't happen," said one Berguedan intellectual, smiling ruefully as a mutual friend called the editor of a Barcelona newspaper to ensure a prominent place for a story on a local event. In the Patum as in scarce-resource Berga as a whole, no one can be high-minded enough to refuse a preferred connection.

A postscript: the ambiguous call for democratization led in the late 1990s to an ambiguous solution, still acutely debated as of 2002. A Patronat de la Patum has been established, a foundation intended "to administer, preserve, and coordinate the development of the Festival of the Patum, as well as all the activities derived from it and strictly related to the performance of the *comparses* and their members" (Article 1, Estatuts del Patronat). It was declared that the Patronat would open up the Patum to wider and more democratic participation. Although I have been unable to observe the Patronat and its consequences directly, its composition gives one pause: it has a Junta General, an executive commission, a president, and a manager. Only a few *caps de colla* belong, though some younger *geganters* active in municipal politics are enthusiastic promoters of the Patronat and its activities. Many people see the Patronat as necessary to sustain the Patum in a more complex world. Others believe that the political class is reclaiming the only area of public life that was under working-class control; they see the Patronat as a rival mafia to that of the *comparses*. This is, certainly, democracy as many local people have experienced it. Not incidentally, the word *patronat* also means the employer class, and the Patronat has recently appropriated an insider phrase to apply to Patum *comparsa* members: the *plantilla*, or workforce (Pedrals 2000).

PART II

PERSONIFICATION
AND INCORPORATION

3

The Gaze and the Touch: Personhood and Belonging in Everyday Life

De lluny me miro l'amor,   I gaze at my love from afar,
que de prop no goso gaire   for up close I hardly dare
—Berguedan folksong

ON ONE OF MY FIRST EVENINGS IN BERGA, I was out with the municipal music school *colla* after a rehearsal. They asked why I wanted to study the Patum, and I tried delicately to explain, without overt references to class or politics. I said I wanted to know how the people who did it felt about it. I proclaimed that understanding was shaped by everyone's own circumstances and experience rather than some universalizing "meaning" attributed to it from outside; I was not after *the* Patum, but Patums. Queralt, a twenty-year-old university student, became impatient as I stumbled over my prepared phrases. "Look," she said. "You want to know what the Patum means to me? I'll tell you. It's personal liberation. It's a time when I can forget everything, all my obligations—Well, for example, I can dress however I like. In Berga, you always have to follow the fashion. People are always watching to see what you come out with on Sunday, and they make commentaries—if it's old, if it's always the same. It's only during the Patum that I can dress for me and be comfortable. That's really all there is to it. *Alliberament personal.*"

She said it with great firmness and I was silenced but not convinced: I wanted symbols, not side effects. It was an article of my folklorist's faith that people are conscious performers. Was I going to be disillusioned? Nonetheless, I heard a great deal of the same sort of thing in the next few weeks. Ramon, a manager in an insurance company, said, "Just imagine if I were seen drunk in the street on a normal evening. The next day in the

office everyone would know about it, everybody would be whispering behind their hands. It's only during the Patum that nobody watches you—
of course, they're all drunk themselves." Lluís, an office worker, commented,
"I sit at a desk all year long, I never do anything. I go to work and I come
home again. The Patum is the only time I do anything physical, I can un-
leash." And the day before the Patum, one of the more obstreperous local
politicians declared to the newspaper and again to me, "For the Patum I
can be drunk in the daytime, I can yell at my wife . . ."

In those first weeks I heard little but these remarks about unwinding
and the equally endless insistence that the Patum was a time of unity and
brotherhood. The first assertion seemed trivial, the second disingenuous;
together, surely, they were contradictory?

But of course they are closely related and both, up to a point, exact.
Individuals in Berga live under powerful social constraints that act upon
the body to make visible the distinctions within the social structure. The
Patum releases the individual from these constraints by equally powerful
manipulations of the body, which blur social distinctions. In this part of
the book I describe Berguedan *convivència*, the uneasy balance between
personhood and collectivity, as it is worked out in everyday life and intensified in the Patum. More generally, I describe the reciprocal incorporation of Berga into individuals and individuals into Berga—the purposeful,
never final constitution of a Berguedan social body.[1]

The Middle-Class Need to Be Seen

It took me a long time to understand the constraints people were talking
about. But the issue of dress forced itself upon my notice at Easter. I had
gone out on Saturday evening with the *caramelles* choir, the group that
goes from *plaça* to *plaça* singing about springtime. I had dressed up
slightly, putting on my one white blouse, on which I had promptly spilled
red wine as they tried to teach me to drink from a *porró* which someone
had brought out from a house to refresh the singers. Evidently singing in
the street was an informal activity. On Sunday morning I came out to join
the choir in jeans and a black sweater, only to find myself surrounded by
suited men and women in pastel linen dresses with eyelet collars.

I realized then that not merely Easter but every Sunday brought the
middle class out in their best clothes. They were clothes I would never
dream of wearing, always white or starched or pleated or ruffled, calling

for plenty of labor in the maintaining and plenty of care in the wearing: clothes for standing up straight, not for drinking wine or eating lunch or embracing.

As I began to go out on the Saturday night supper and bar-hopping routine of the unmarried middle class, I was further perplexed and intimidated by women's clothes. At the time, I almost always wore jeans and sweaters without jewelry; I don't know how to apply makeup, and I last entered a beauty parlor at the age of seven. On Saturday night in Berga I was hardly classifiable as female.[2] Other women my age were rather heavily made-up and bejeweled and wore outfits darker and more alluring but every bit as troublesome as the Sunday clothes.

The norms of behavior are particularly difficult in times of transition, when rules tend to multiply rather than replace each other. Today, unmarried young women must observe not only the traditional respectability of Sunday afternoon but also the newly mandated sexiness of Saturday night. But rules have always been context dependent. Having become anxious about the likely effect on my liver of living six months in Berga, I was astonished to hear Ramon, a member of the professional class, remark that drunkenness was the most scandalous vice in provincial towns such as Berga. I had been introduced to Ramon in a bar and had spent innumerable evenings with him and his friends over long and well-irrigated dinners (*ben regat*, as they say in Berga) and hours in bars "doing *copes*" afterward. I was certain that I was not the only person affected by our imbibings.

That was it, of course: that I was not the only person. Drinking in a group is acceptable, because the whole group alters: the perception of the group changes to match the changes in behavior. The scandal is the drunk person who is alone, the person seen weaving down the street by others in a state of cold sobriety.

To be seen—this is at once the need and the fear that constrains everyday life in Berga. Folk speech bears out its importance: a practice or person can be *mal vist*, badly seen, or, less commonly, *ben vist*, well seen. Visual apprehension is translated into verbal commentary—gossip—by *males llengües*, evil tongues. One never hears of good tongues, although of course many people are well spoken of. But the natural tendency of the eye is to catch imperfections, the natural tendency of the tongue to criticize. Against these dispositions one must protect oneself, put up the armor of an impenetrable surface. The eyes of the community exact a heavy tribute: all those expensive clothes, all that ironing, and extreme self-control. Never to be exalted or upset while people are watching, always to conceal one's weaknesses with a show of serenity: these are disciplines learned young.

There is, as I suggested, one primary occasion that ritualizes the need to see and be seen: the Sunday afternoon promenade down the Carrer Major. Then the habitual vigilance of every day becomes a more conscious display, with fine clothes the outward and visible signs of an orderly life.

The Carrer Major, Berga's narrow medieval main street, does not dominate commerce the way it used to, but as an *escenari*, a social setting, it is still preeminent. Walking down it, I was always amazed that so small a city could have such crowded streets, until I noticed that the rest of the streets were empty. If I walked to the post office and back along La Canya, the bypass below the old city, the trip took me twenty minutes. If I took the Carrer Major—the more direct route—I had to plan for at least an hour, because I always ran into people: I would chat with one, duck into a bar for a coffee with another, and so forth. An older woman who returns to Berga for the summers confessed to me that she no longer shops on the Carrer Major because she doesn't have the energy for the social interactions it forces on her.

The street's attraction holds even when no one is on it. Once I was leaving a bar at about 2 A.M., walking with Quirze, who also lives on the Vall. I started to turn to the bypass, the quickest way home, as we were not in search of social encounters. But my companion looked at me as if I were mad. "Let's go by the Carrer Major, no?" So we took an extra ten minutes and walked along the cool stone street. Quirze pointed out its beauty to me, rather censoriously, and I acquiesced; in the silence, it was unreal as an abandoned stage set. New streets on the edges of the old city offer better shopping and far more efficient communications, but they are purely functional. Social identity is enacted on the Carrer Major, and even the empty street retains the echo of its inhabited power.

The traditional Sunday afternoon *donar la volta* (taking the turn) on the Carrer Major can be a matter of two hours to make the two-minute trip from the Plaça Sant Joan down to the Placeta de la Ciutat and back again. The street is packed with people and they keep to the right—as on a road—so that forward motion, however slow, can be accomplished. Families come out together, and the children split off to find their contemporaries; everyone still wears the Mass-going clothes of the morning.[3] Adults greet each other, nod at some, notice even those to whom they do not speak. Alliances and interactions are observed: three weeks' company during the promenade marked a couple as engaged as late as the 1970s

(Farràs i Farràs 1979, 30). New clothes, as Queralt pointed out, are noted as well as one's state of health and the appearance of family amity or lack of it. Who greets—or fails to greet—whom is always of interest, and the street is testing ground, even battlefield, for the quarrelsome Berguedans: the Carrer Major ritual makes it impossible to avoid one's enemies. One could walk more comfortably under the trees along the Vall, where there is fresh air and room to spread out, but that is not the point of the exercise. One must be seen.[4]

Working-class Bodies

For working-class people and institutions, other practices dominate interaction. I have another set of friendships in Berga centering on the *popular* bar, La Barana, a favorite local for central *patumaires*. There the simplicity of my wardrobe does not impede gallantry or gender deference. Relatively few women frequent the bar, but those who do are well integrated into the bar's network.[5] Unlike middle-class contexts, where friendship goes by peer groups and tends to diminish in closeness after marriage, the bar mingles all ages in friendship: unrelated sixty-year-old and thirty-year-old men seek out each other's company, and even teenagers participate freely in the bar's social life—though not many of them are inclined to do so.

Instead of the careful surfaces and distances maintained in the Carrer Major promenade, social life in the bar is directed toward establishing and maintaining connections, to performing a solidarity embodied in tactile contact. In the bar there are no booths or even stools: we lean on the counter to talk to Pere, the owner, or huddle in shifting groups. The dining room has long tables, where people are wedged together as best as possible. We jostle elbows, pass plates and bottles, and change tables to have our coffee with another group if our companions have to leave. *Bon profit* (bon appetit) is wished to every table as one walks in or out. Pere and Carme, the *mestressa*, come out to have their own lunch later, and talk, like salt, is passed from table to table. Talk differs in emphasis from middle-class encounters: more of it is joking indexical to the immediate situation and participants, and less is gossip. What goes on in the bar is eminently "phatic communion," as Malinowski called it: "each utterance is an act serving the direct aim of binding hearer to speaker" ([1923]1972, 315). A Berguedan idiom, *fer petar la xerrada*, expresses this. A *xerrada* is a session of chat, and *petar* means "to burst or pass wind"—the word also used for the Patum firecrackers. What is said is of no importance: it's the act of speaking together that matters. And talk is not the most important channel of phatic communion.

There is a great deal of physical horseplay in the bar. Back slappings, pinchings, and play wrestling are the ordinary accompaniments to aperitifs and even to meals. The soda-water siphon is used to spray people. My hair was once braided into the beaded ropes of the doorway while I looked another way. A middle-aged truckdriver and dresser of the Plens named Pepito, nicknamed *la fera* (the wild beast) by Agustí, another regular, is perhaps the chief provocateur of community in the bar: he initiates much of the teasing and roughhousing, and he also arranges more peaceful encounters, such as excursions to restaurants in the mountains above town. The two kinds of action have the same effect: extending and intensifying relationships in the bar. One week Pepito began to steal the flan of Pep Xino. When the flan arrived, he would snatch it away, and begin spooning it into all of our mouths, regardless of the course we were eating. "One for the little girl," he would say. "One for the little boy. One for—" "My flan!" cried the hapless Xino, wincing and grinning at once. "You ask for it, I think," said Pep Escobet. "Why do you keep sitting next to him?"

It was a kind of communion, and the people in the bar are not unconscious of the parallels, though they are rarely made explicit. *Preneu i beveu*, said Agustí one day as he was pouring out champagne. "Take; drink; this is my blood which is shed for you . . ." On Holy Saturday morning 1991 I was sitting at the long table in back having breakfast with the usuals. Ritxi from the music school came in and saw me at the foot of the table between Pepito and Agustí. "Sitting there, Dorry," he said, "you know who you look like? Jesus Christ between two thieves." Pepito and Agustí, at whom this was directed, got up in the ritual response to verbal teasing—simulated physical aggression—and grabbed Ritxi by each arm, pretending to rain blows on him. "Now! Now," Ritxi cried, "I'm Jesus Christ and this is the Flagellation!" "No, no," somebody in the middle of the table said. "This is the Last Supper." This image satisfied them, and everyone sat down again.

For the Bar La Barana regulars, the Saturday morning breakfast, which is substantial and long, is a ritual comparable to the Carrer Major promenade. Sitting down at table and eating together—and especially drinking together—is a means to social integration that was vital to my own acceptance in the bar. My popularity began with an appreciation of my excellent appetite: my eagerness to incorporate "the good things of here," as Pere calls the food and drink they serve, made them eager to incorporate me. They even used my embracing of native habits to tease each other. "Your face should fall with shame!" said Agustí, the defender of Berguedan authenticity, one morning to a man resting his liver with Coca-Cola. "Dorothy, who's not even from here, is drinking champagne. But look at you!"[6]

When my parents came to visit Berga in 1990, I received a proof of the importance of commensality, and of drinking in particular. I had brought them to lunch at La Barana on a couple of weekdays, and they had met most of the *colla* either there or on the street. On the Saturday morning they were to leave, I came to breakfast alone: because my parents could not converse, I reasoned, there was no point in bringing them. But Pepito started scolding me at once and demanded that I go and fetch them. "We've hardly met them. Go get them. Now! Just so we can spend a little time together."

In the next hour and a half, my mother made an excellent impression by accepting three glasses of champagne, asking for some cheese and ham to "make herself a cushion," as they say in Berga, and taking an interest in everyone else's imbibings—the language barrier impeded more complex topics. My father, however, had to drive to Montserrat on a sunny highway and it was before noon: he preferred to keep his head clear. All the blandishments of Pepito—whose obstinacy is legendary and with whom none of the rest of us even bother to argue—were not enough to convince him to add a little cognac to his coffee: he kept smiling but resisted the joking attempt to splash it in the cup. "Your father is a very serious person," observed Pep Escobet. Because he was a foreigner and my father, they let it pass at last, but they were clearly as uncomfortable with his refusal as he was with their insistence. When my brother came the following year, they had their revenge on the men of my family: he was barely able to stagger out of the bar by the time Pere had finished inundating him with Berguedan hospitality.

I've learned not to ask for a small portion or to refuse seconds: it leads to Pere spooning out a double helping and Pepito standing over me like an irate parent: "You're going to finish that, now!" There is no refusing food without refusing them, for feeding someone is an act of love:

given Berga's history of poverty, it once represented real self-sacrifice and still signals a willingness to share one's substance. "No et quedis amb gana!" Pere will say as he loads my plate with twice what he's giving the men or his wife. "Don't be left hungry! If you go home thinner, they'll think we don't take care of you." He is teasing me: he knows that by American standards I am quite fat enough. But he is serious too: he means me to go home fatter, full of Berga. That's what eating means. When Berguedans wanted to praise my willing assimilation, the more intellectual remarked on my improved Catalan, but most people just congratulated me on the weight I'd gained.

The Popular and the Respectable

Rituals of seeing and rituals of sharing—the promenade and gatherings in bars being one example of each—are complementary in most people's lives. However, they are clearly marked by social class habitus, now increasingly recoded and reshaping itself as individual choice.

The fundamental social distinction in Berga today is between the *popular* and the respectable. *Popular* is an acknowledged euphemism for "working class," but it really denotes a lifestyle, and many middle-class people have chosen to affiliate themselves with it.[7] It entails informality, egalitarianism, public sociability, and active participation in local tradition. As well as being a class label, *popular* also implies popularity in the ordinary English sense of the word; and, above all, it means being common property, belonging to the people. A *personatge popular* in Berga is a working-class person who lives in the public eye and is thus known by everybody; someone of whom anecdotes are told, who becomes part of local tradition.[8]

The opposite complex of middle- and upper-class attributes—observance of the forms, respect for hierarchy and the established order (which includes a deference to external influences), a value for privacy, and more controlled participation in public life—is variously named: I give it the umbrella term of *respectability*. Respectable behavior is called *educació* (upbringing, politeness); it inspires *respecte*: deference that keeps its distance. The phrase *fa respecte* (it makes respect) is a not infrequent euphemism for something feared. One shows respect for one's social superiors by keeping one's distance; men observe respect toward women by not making sexual advances to them (the phrase for an improper approach is *faltar de respecte*, to lack respect). *Respecte* is a concept akin to taboo: it is applied to something hedged about with rules and approached with caution, after special dispensation is given.

Both popularity and respectability inhere in the judgment of others, what the eye sees and the tongue declares. The sphere of definition is thus itself middle class and respectable: at the *popular* level there is not such an overt interest in social classification. The upper classes may be blunt in private, as when a judge complained to his son, "You make yourself too *popular*," specifying that he should spend less time in bars and be charier of his company, then divided among too large an acquaintance.

The people who most inspire *respecte* are variously known as the *gent de bé*, the *gent de missa*, the *gent d'ordre* . . . the names trail off in embarrassment because the current political dispensation does not favor the clear delineation of social classes. But the association of respectability, virtue, and wealth (implying the product of generations of labor and frugality) is clear in a phrase such as *la gent de bé*: the people of good, the people of goods. *Gent de missa*, the Mass-goers, reminds us that the official church rituals are historically rites of *respecte* in this part of the world. *Gent d'ordre*, people of order, is a phrase used facetiously but rather often by certain respectable people I know. Such-and-such a town votes for Convergència (the center-right Catalanist party): "Of course, they're *gent d'ordre*!" A bureaucrat meets an old friend in a Hawaiian shirt: "I couldn't go around like that, I'm *d'ordre*!" Or a young teacher declares that he doesn't go to bars, smiling: "We're *gent d'ordre*. The church, the bookstores, and that's it."

The concept of order is historically weighted in the Catalan interior: it was central to the conservative Catholic Catalanism elaborated in the region after the fracas of the Carlist wars (cf. Fradera 1983, 1990; Terradas i Saborit 1987), with which the current dominance of Convergència is historically continuous. A clear picture of this valorization of order may be found in a short story by Martí Genís i Aguilar ([1904]1988). In "La llum blava" (The Will-o'-the-Wisp), the rural heroine's "instinct for order" is embodied in hard work, sexual virtue, and affection for her family. The corrupt young heir who pursues her and who is at last recalled to "the life of order" fritters his time and inheritance away at taverns and festivals and resists his mother's urging to marry, instead pursuing a variety of women. The villain enlisted by the young man to entangle the girl's family in debt is defined by his refusal to be placed in the categories of order: a "mixture of peasant and city artisan," he has no trade, no land, and no family to situate him (Genís i Aguilar [1904]1988, 25).

Genís makes clear the economic advantage of respectability over popularity for those with property to protect. Public sociability at bars and festivals causes its participants to waste money and neglect work; it threatens sexual morality, thus endangering the stability of the family essential to the accumulation and transmission of property. It creates dangerous unequal friendships, allowing the lower classes to rise out of their proper places and acquire influence over their superiors. Genís here puts forth the values common to shopkeepers and landowners that still persist in cities such as Berga, though democratic norms inhibit their explicit expression.

Popularity and respectability have, then, clear historical roots in social class and are still fairly closely aligned with class defined in economic terms.[9] But as the traditional middle class sinks in status with economic change and as more industrial workers move into service jobs, Berga has an increasing population in an ill-defined center. Office workers and shopkeepers are ambiguously positioned and are able to choose their lifestyles to a certain extent. Many people, especially men, bridge the divide or oscillate: they are *popular* with their friends and respectable with their families, or respectable at work and *popular* on their own time. There are genteel shopkeepers forced into the business by the hardships of the postwar years, who still are considered to belong to the "good families." There are successful entrepreneurs who come out of *popular* families and prefer the Bar La Barana to the more elegant La Tosca. The young middle class practices *popular* manners among its peers and becomes more reserved as it grows older.[10]

How does one declare respectability or popularity? Habits of dress and behavior and the frequency and intensity of sociability are indicators. But the cues in such matters are subtle, and individuals vary among and within themselves. Ideological affiliations of left and right codify certain aspects of popularity and respectability, but the alignment is imperfect given the complexity of Catalan political history; local politics is played out at a more face-to-face level of alliances and rivalries. A disposition to one or the other manner is writ large in social location: one sees it in the relatively permanent selections of *local* and of residence.

A *local* (site) is simply a place for an activity: a hall for a voluntary organization or political party, for example. Berga has many *locals* for specific sociable purposes: the Casino for playing cards or billiards, the

Ateneu for ballroom dancing on Wednesday nights, and so forth. But in more specific vernacular usage, a *local* is a "hangout": the bar one chooses for one's habitual coffee and aperitif.

Certain bars, like the Bar La Barana and Cal Blasi, are unequivocally *popular*. Others have mixed use: Cal Negre, an old *popular* bar, has become the preferred bar of the young middle class, more gregarious and more informal than their elders, and was recently remodeled with some deference to the tastes of the new public. Its central location has made it more or less neutral ground, as is the outside of Cal Blasi due to its enticing situation under the arcades of the Vall. "Respectable" bars and restaurants are more specialized: La Tosca gets the newspapers early and is where professionals breakfast; the Restaurant Sala is where one goes for a business lunch or for social dinners on special occasions; L'Erich is for after dinner on Friday and Saturday nights—that is, it is jammed from 11 P.M. to 2 A.M. and close to empty at all other times; Martin's, La General, and Menfis are for dancing; and so forth.

Respectable bars divide up time and also people: they are designed for privacy, with soft lighting, booths, and fixed stools. Recent bars have become lighter and, following Barcelona, more "designerly," but preserve the spatial segregation. In contrast, the *popular* bar has the same harsh functional light at all hours—bright or dim depending on the place but never "atmospheric"; long tables that can accommodate large parties and demand the integration of single diners; and no stools in the bar so that more people can fit in.

Equally, choice of residence marks *popular* or respectable affiliations. If you are *popular* you live or once lived in an old house with a nickname in the old part of the city, the Casc Antic, preferably in the *barri* that rises along the Carrer Buxadé and the Carrer de la Pietat to the Porta Santa Magdalena, the one surviving medieval gate. One or two of the old noble houses along the Carrer Buxadé have been restored, but the majority are still dark, inconvenient, unheated, and primitive in their plumbing; some are seriously degraded. In the 1960s, many families moved out to new blocks of modern flats, subsidized by the Caixa de Pensions savings bank. The families that remain are unambiguously *popular* in orientation: they prefer continuity and the intimate sociability of the neighborhood to modern comforts. And indeed, the *popular* life is not lived inside the home but on the street and in the bars. Choice of both residence and *local* is obviously subject to important economic determinants, but not entirely. Many *popular* people do not lack money for vacations abroad or for

frequent dining out with friends: they prefer this sort of discretionary expenditure to the home improvements of the middle class. A recent development is for younger and well-off *populars* who want more space to buy
decrepit *cases de pagès* (farmhouses) on the outskirts of Berga. They spend
time restoring these houses, plant a vegetable garden, and often keep
horses or donkeys for the July festival of the Elois. They come back to the
bars and the old neighborhood virtually every day and have *costellades*
(barbecues) at their country houses for their friends. The new house thus
enables an extension of the old sociability, not a curtailing of it. And an
extension of traditional lifeways: most of these people have roots in the
countryside as well as on the Carrer Buxadé, and the country excursion
for a meal cooked outside among friends is documented from at least the
mid-nineteenth century as a common popular entertainment.

While a part of the working class was moving into subsidized modern flats in the 1960s, the middle class was also leaving the Casc Antic.[11]
They went off to new luxury flats along the Vall and the Passeig de la Pau,
or to the *xalets*—detached single-family houses along the Serra de Casampons or the Passeig de les Estaselles, the northwest and southeast extremes of the city. The new flats have buzzers and private terraces in back
rather than public balconies in front, their rooms are large, their bath-
rooms are modern, and they have washing machines instead of the old *safareig*, a dank, chipped, stone washtub at the back of the house.[12] The
xalets have front gardens with showy roses and backyards with terraces.
Built on high ground and off of thoroughfares, they are isolated from the
noise of traffic and commerce. Both flats and *xalets* favor family privacy,
easy control over small children, and domestic convenience.

Insiders and Outsiders

Berga has one population that is neither *popular* nor respectable: the
unassimilated non-Catalan immigrants. These are the people who are neither touched nor looked at, who have no relationships and so no social
identity in Berguedan categories. Residential isolation is the key to their
invisibility.

After the influx of Spanish immigrants to the mines and textile factories in the 1960s, a new *barri* of inexpensive blocks of flats was put up in
the low southeast outskirts of the city below the hill leading to the *xalets*
of Casampons.[13] The *barri* was named Santa Eulàlia, after the patron

saint of Berga, but it is known to many Berguedans as "Hollywood" and is cut off ethnically (in their view) and linguistically as well as physically. The people who live here participate in the Patum but generally in little else: Santa Eulàlia has many festivals, a library, a commmunity center, and shops of its own. In all my visits of fieldwork along the Carrer Buxadé-Carrer Major-*xalets* axis, I have met very few people from Santa Eulàlia (most of them children) and no one I know has ever suggested going there for any social event. My relationships in Berga have multiplied into a network stretching to almost every town of the Berguedà and beyond to Solsona, Manresa, Olot, Barcelona, London, and California, but never once to Santa Eulàlia. It is a Spanish island in a Catalan sea.[14] Many Berguedans are happy to keep it this way: they associate the influx of Spanish-speaking immigrants with the dictatorship's efforts to undermine Catalan identity and fear the contamination of their culture with foreign influences, just as they consider the language to have been contaminated with Castilian loanwords.

But there were Spanish immigrants before the 1960s and after who moved into the Casc Antic. Despite the repression of the Catalan language under the dictatorship, all of these children and many of these adults learned Catalan on the street; they went to the old *popular* bars and participated in neighborhood sociability. Many of their children carry Catalan names and identify themselves as independentist Catalans. They may not have as much of a social presence as the *popular* families of long tradition, but they are accepted and active and they intermarry.

Higher-status immigrants have integrated through marriage and by means of participation in neighborhood associations, parents' organizations, and even electoral politics. The local leader of Iniciativa per Catalunya in the time I was there, who is Valencian by birth and speaks the sometimes ridiculed Valencian dialect of Catalan, is widely respected, despite the small vote his party receives, for his seriousness and dedication to the improvement of the quality of life in Berga.[15] At the middle-class level, residence is not as important for integration. Sociability in public space is less central to middle-class life, but speaking Catalan is vital: this is the outward and audible sign of personal identification with Berga and Catalonia. Foreigners are not expected to know Catalan but are encouraged to learn and rewarded for doing so.

I was introduced to Ràdio Berga and the municipal music school—my first contacts—by Lou Hevly, an American jazz clarinetist who lives in nearby Manresa. He became known in Berga as a street musician: at that time he made his living touring European arts festivals with a guitar-playing robot, and between trips he played in Catalan town centers. His versions of Cab Calloway songs are much appreciated in Berga, but he is equally liked for having learned Catalan, which he speaks fluently with an accent they find charming, and for participating actively in local culture, including the band of the Patum.

When I arrived already speaking Catalan, it was an event. For the middle class, it was important enough to obviate my shabby grad-student clothes: it was the principal reason for their acceptance of and interest in me. The praise lavished on me for this accomplishment took no account of the clear fieldwork advantage I gained by it or my possible intellectual or professional motives for mastering the language: speaking Catalan was considered a show of solidarity and a courtesy to them, *una delicadesa*— another concept associated with respectability.

For the working class, language is important as a facilitator to communication, but it is bodily coexistence and commensality, common lifestyle and life in common, that is exacted of the outsider: the treatment of my parents at La Barana is a case in point.[16] Speaking Catalan gave me immediate access to many middle-class people, but the regulars at La Barana were slow to take me in. I went first to the bar with intermediaries, but the important step was when I began to go by myself. I went every day for lunch; I went at other hours when my courage was high. Because they knew that I had other acquaintances and could be in other places, they were able to read my continuing presence as evidence of identification with them. And I learned, gradually, to put away my notebook, to stop introducing myself, and to stop asking questions. From tolerating my presence, they became used to me, then friendly, and at last affectionate. Of course, La Barana, like the Carrer Major, is a public space: I was not so far in during 1989 and 1990 that I was routinely invited to private functions, such as celebrations during the Patum or excursions. But a regular presence in the bar meant a firm social identity and rights to participation in *popular* Berga.

To complete the process—to get all the way in and be one of them— I would have had to have stayed in Berga and either brought my partner along or married one of the *colla*. As the number and length of my visits has diminished since the mid-1990s, my position has inevitably weakened. In earlier years, however, each return strengthened it: few people apparently believed I would come back after the first visit, and they were pleasantly surprised when I did. For a long time, not everyone trusted me to return. Each year it became more difficult to leave. In 1989, I did not become intimate with the La Barana people until after the Patum. The day before I was to leave, Agustí, one of the philosophers of the *popular*, said to me, "You can't leave now. You've only just gotten down among the people." The next two years were worse: it was a betrayal on my part, having been admitted among them, to be able to contemplate another lifestyle and another home. Every year I assured them of my love and pleaded economics, and they said nonsense! You can live with us, we'll find you a job. They'd gotten used to me, was the brunt of it, and nothing people get used to is given up willingly: this is the attachment to tradition of the *popular*. Or, as the proverb people kept repeating to me goes, *Berga té mala entrada i mala sortida* (Berga has a difficult entrance and a difficult exit).

It is anything but mindless traditionalism. The wholeness of the community is at stake: what it has taken in must stay in. Where it has expended resources, it must reap the profit from them. At my farewell lunch at La Barana in September 1991, marked by a cake inscribed "Bon voyage but we'd like you not to leave," Pepito said, "I like this kind of celebration, but it depresses me. Now we're all here together, but she's going, and for the Patum this year she wasn't there, and for the Elois she wasn't there, and we missed her." To miss, in Catalan, is *enyorar* for me: the person who has left "longs" or "pines" for Berga. But for them, it is *trobar a faltar*: they "find me lacking," an absent presence, a piece missing. Berguedans try to compensate for their necessary absences: when Pepito is off driving his truck, he calls La Barana every day at lunch time, not only to speak to his son, whom he could call at home, but to Pere and others. He is as present as he can be. *Populars* who leave to live elsewhere are routinely and mercilessly teased on their return as *pixapins* (pine-pissers, the term for Barcelona tourists).[17] Berguedans fear permeable community boundaries as the beginnings of dissolution. The loss of one member threatens the security of the whole: in a community plagued by the necessity of emigration, each departure seems to set the example for more. But, by the same token, Berguedans cannot afford to eliminate these people from commensality or from participation in festival life: there are too many of them. They do not become nonpersons, forgotten and invisible; rather, the teasing reincorporates them into the community while it punishes them for their departure.

Disengagement can be as threatening as departure. Occasionally they need to remind me of this. There are a few reflective types at the Saturday

breakfast who take a dangerous interest in the outside world and sometimes ask me questions about American culture or politics. Enjoying the
rare opportunity to harangue—for most of them have little interest in my
views—I lose touch with the table around me as I hold forth to my neighbor. This sometimes meets with open rebuke: once when it happened
during Corpus, Massana, the leader of the giants and a man whose physique
and calm manner inspire *respecte*, called over from the next table, "Hey
you two, today we talk Patum!" More often, though, it is halted by teasing: suddenly I notice that my purse is being disembowelled at the other
end of the table or my plate has been emptied or refilled or my hair has
been tied to my chair. Sometimes Pepito just sneaks up behind me and
grabs me by the throat.

All kinds of disengagement are corrected in this way. One day after
lunch Carme was passing out some candies she'd been given at a baptism,
and Pepito, who has lost a few teeth, interrogated her at some length about
which ones were sticky; they even had me translate the English-language
labels. But Pepet, who is getting old and has few real teeth left, was day-
dreaming. Carme gave him the chewiest candy there was. As he burst out
swearing, she smiled and said, "But Pepet, we've been talking about that
caramel for the past half-hour!"

Leaving the common table can no more be tolerated than distraction
at it. Once Ritxi came into the bar with his new wife, and the two of them
went to sit by themselves. Through their meal they had to endure shouts
across the room of "Separatistes!" The political joke is double-edged: as
Catalanists, they all sympathize with separatism and the desire for autonomy, but, living in a factionalized, fragile community and socialized under
the Franco regime, they have a certain sense that unity must be imposed
if the collectivity is to prosper.

A final instance made me understand more fully that this insistence
on engagement has to do with the conservation of the community's human capital. There was a widower in his sixties, a former miner living on a
small pension who had taken the death of his wife hard, spending most of
his days lingering in bars. One year he took to La Barana, where he played
the clown, wearing flowers in his hair and eating his dinner out of order,
taking bites of flan between mouthfuls of stew: it was clear that he was
skirting mental illness. Gradually I realized that Pere and especially Carme
were working to bring him back to normal engagement. They talked to
him as if to a child, scolding him for making a mess or behaving improp-
erly, and Carme gave him little jobs to do, such as setting the tables.

While they showed no respect for his autonomy, their treatment was remarkably successful: he was increasingly cooperative, and after a few months was eating quietly at the table with us, able to carry on sustained conversations.

The members of the community belong to it regardless of the esteem in which they are held: the simple fact of ongoing interaction gives them the right and then the duty of belonging. Massana, who has always been reserved toward me, said after my Easter trip of 1991, "You should stay. You know, you've put on this show now for a couple of years, of coming for the Patum and having everyone make a fuss over you, and if you don't come now, something will be missing from the Patum." The preceding year, when I had come in to Agustí's family house on the Carrer Buxadé for champagne during the *passacarrers*, Massana had seen me and said, "My God, we can't get rid of her! You turn up everywhere!" Remembering this, I said to Massana, "Yes, you know what my strategy is, don't you? I just stick my nose in everywhere until people have to pay attention to me." He smiled and nodded in agreement.

What I did in La Barana is essentially what the successfully integrated immigrants have done; it is what adolescents do who want to get into a Patum *comparsa*. I had, to be sure, the advantage of exotic origins and a high social position, but for La Barana these are dubious recommendations. I was told and shown repeatedly that it was my willingness to live in the Berguedan manner that brought me acceptance, and among the middle class, where outsiders are better-liked, this willingness consolidated the general good will shown me as a foreigner. "You're more Berguedan than a lot of Berguedans are," they told me. Whether it was speaking Catalan with the middle class or drinking wine with the *populars*, this was the crux: willingness, identification. It is what matters with immigrants too, as other studies have noted.[18] In Berga many people told me, "The ones who don't integrate, it's because they don't want to." I have to keep reminding myself and them of the real political, economic, and social barriers to integration. Still, in Berga the situation is a good deal less bleak than in the large cities: copresence has led to interaction and to acceptance.[19] But in Berga—as is not the case in Barcelona—the outsider must adapt and surrender to the demands of the community: the city will not stretch itself to accept the ways of *forasters*.

Fire and Ice

"I'm going to fold up next year," you hear during the week after Corpus from men in dark glasses with headaches. "I've had enough. It's too much work and too much bickering over nothing at all. Next year I'll just go to the *plaça* and enjoy myself. No more dancing the eagle/dressing the *plens*/playing in the band. I'm *cremat*."

Berguedans declare themselves "burned" with a certain frequency. The usual state of political life in Berga is *crispació*, a twitching of the nerves, but to be *cremat* is more extreme: it means you are scarred by a conflict and presumably intend to withdraw from it. In practice, withdrawal is very difficult. You cannot avoid your antagonists in Berga. You meet them every day on the Carrer Major under the eyes of the community. If you do not receive at least the tribute of a greeting, it's very painful, one antagonist observed to me. The forms of *respecte* are the guarantors of one's personhood, preserving a balance between freedom and recognition. The denied greeting, however, is worse than the other extreme of conflict, which transgresses polite barriers to leave battle scars. Berguedans fear the fire less than the cold.

The day my husband arrived in Berga for the first time in 1992, I brought him to Sunday breakfast at La Barana. Across the drama of his initiation—a "rubbing of the ears" from Pepito, marital advice from some of the younger men, a testing of his capacities for eating and drinking, and so forth—there developed an encounter between Pepito and a young man named Jordi that seemed to teeter dangerously on the boundary between teasing and offense. They began amicably by commiserating over their hangovers and reviewing the early part of the previous evening, which they had spent together. Then Pepito began to question Jordi about a girl with whom he'd been seen in a doorway later. Jordi brushed him off with increasing irritation as his questions persisted; at last came the explosion, with Jordi getting up and shouting, "*En serio* (I mean it)! I'm going to get angry if you stay on this topic. *En serio*, now!" Pepito took one more dig, just to come off the victor, and Jordi left soon after. This time, I thought, Pepito had gone too far.

Later when we came back to the bar for lunch, Jordi was there, a little bleary-eyed but peacefully sipping a beer. He turned to Mike, the newcomer, to explain. "I got home at four this morning, but I got up at eight-thirty on purpose to have breakfast at La Barana. It's like an adventure, every week, you never know what will happen." He shrugged his shoulders and smiled. "Today it was my turn."

Pepito is widely agreed to "go a bit too far," but, as Pep Escobet pointed out, people keep on sitting next to him. La Barana would certainly be less animated without him. He's like the Guita, which people chase in the expectation of it turning on them: the fun is in knowing when to draw back.

The fights keep life interesting, relieve the monotony inevitable in a small community where, as they say, "we're always the same." But they do more than furnish entertainment: they suggest that Berga is important enough to be fought over. "In Berga everything is double," they say and bewail the futility of two music schools, two magazines, two ski clubs, two children's Patums, two theatrical groups, and two political parties of identical ideologies, when a unified effort might actually achieve something. And yet, to have two of all those things in a town of fourteen thousand people is a considerable accomplishment; and it may be supposed that if not for the spur of rivalry, Berga would have not one of each but none of any. It's better to have politicians at one another's throats than to have no candidates.

To stay engaged, Berguedans play with fire. It is a dangerous game: you can finish up *cremat* or burn someone else and risk their disengagement. But Berguedans are obstinate, a town of mules, and as often as they threaten to *plegar* (fold up), they always stick around for *la penúltima*. Every year I hear stories like this one: a former mayor, who vowed after his last defeat that he was *cremat* and would never again have anything to do with politics, is negotiating with another party . . .

Open and Closed

The class and nativist dynamics of distance and closeness intersect with one of rural-urban, traditional-modern, local-outsider distinctions. Berguedans told me, "Som molt tancats," we're a very closed people. Outsiders from the region often complained to me of Berguedan chauvinism; recent immigrants told of their loneliness and Berguedan unfriendliness.[20] The Berguedans themselves told me, in so many words: we're mountaineers, peasants, not interested in new people or new ideas. This is "the republic of Berga" and nothing that happens outside of it really matters.[21] The context for such utterances was generally the proclamation of the

speaker's status as a modern and openminded anomaly or of the exception being made for me to a basically inhospitable, suspicious, reserved
rule. People frequently expressed astonishment at their own and Berga's
acceptance of my presence in their lives—an acceptance partly dictated by
the openness of Patum manners, because that was my occasion for being
there. Dictated also, of course, by the willingness of a representative of the
center—an American, a scholar—to explore the claims of the provinces to
importance.

Economic and political dependence have long forced this sort of
openness on the Berguedans. This openness has kept them alive, if not
wealthy. But the question of dependence has become acute since the
opening of the Franco regime to modernizing foreign influences in the
1960s, since the industrial decline of the late 1970s and the consequent
need for new investment, and since the entry into the European Union
and the necessity of competing in world markets. Economic necessity and
the seductions of modernity encourage openness to new influences, but
the loss of autonomy spurs a defensive chauvinism and a desire for closure
against the outside world. For the Berguedans, openness to immigrants
or to investors is felt to be a gamble: the consequence may be fruition or
devastation.

Tancat is a word applied to Berga and also to individuals. More detached participants in Berguedan life remark upon the closed/open contrast as one of bodily disposition, and it's worth remarking that while
popular Berguedans lay great emphasis on the ingestion of Berguedan
things, they worry about threats to their bodily integrity from foreign
sources. The tough Pepito has a terror of injections, and when Carme was
pregnant she took the doctor's vitamin pills with great reluctance. Àngel
the bookseller, whose notorious amorous proclivities made his declaration
not wholly disinterested, once pointed out to me that he, as the child of
immigrants, liked to touch people when he talked to them, male or female, liked to take them by the arm to emphasize his point, and that
Berguedans were frequently taken aback by this. "They're *de pagès* (country people)," he said, "very closed." Barcelona women confirmed my impression of the unusual physical and emotional reserve of many otherwise
modern and cosmopolitan young men from Berga. These reserves are not
universal, of course. They are not *popular*, and they are also less common
among the growing part of the middle class who have spent time in
Barcelona. A *persona oberta*, an open person, one who is approachable and

who deals with everybody, may be either *popular* or cosmopolitan. In contrast, the *persona tancada* most often comes from a rural background—formed on the isolation of the farm rather than in the warmth of the urban street—or from the ambitious, conscientious ambience of the respectable shopkeeping class. One friend explained to me the socialization into such reserve. His mother, whose *popular* but prosperous family had not allowed her to go to Barcelona to study for a teaching degree, kept her two children off of the streets and out of *popular* activities (and eventually got them both to Barcelona, where they earned teaching degrees). "I did everything the others did, but I did it by myself," he said. Like other middle-class children, he studied music, but he had private lessons at home instead of group lessons with his classmates. Social advancement meant social isolation.

Sexual Integration

The balance between the gaze and the touch, the closed and the open body, become crucial in the negotiation of sexual relationships, which in turn are basic to the reproduction of classes within Berga and of Berga as a community. Here the process of integration begins with *respecte* and ends with solidarity.

It is notable at the Bar La Barana that the roughhousing avoids anything that might be interpreted as a sexual touch. Women are either teased in the same manner as men or let alone. Sexual overtures are made from a safe distance, with looks and words. But the sexual gaze has power despite its distance, as any woman there who has been looked up and down or glared at knows, and the gazing relationship between men and women is fraught with all the tensions of *respecte*.[22] In La Barana, I once heard a man in love say to the undecided object of his affections, "Don't look at me like that, you look at me with those eyes and you unman me."[23] He was shifting uneasily in his seat; she reassured him and reestablished normal friendly relations by patting his arm.

As long as the norms of *respecte* hold—prior to sexual contact—the woman has the ostensibly powerful role in the relationship. Her power is embodied in beauty. A common compliment in Berga (and in Spain generally), *Ets guapa com un sol* (you're beautiful as a sun), identifies the woman as something that dazzles, bewilders, burns. Catalan folk speech links feminine beauty to other unattainable objects of desire. The princess and the heiress—only daughters who will inherit the kingdom or the *masia*, but whose powerful fathers keep them shut up at home. The rose, whose beauty is guarded by thorns. The star, out of reach. Gold and silver, locked up in the vaults of the wealthy. The liturgical image, tended by priests.[24]

As with *La llum blava*, another text from the past century may help us to see the complex of associations underlying present-day forms of behavior. One of the best-known Catalan ballads, "La Dama d'Aragó" (Milà i Fontanals 1882, 179–81), once sung in the evenings and now kept alive by revivalist folksingers, strings images together in a paean to the power of feminine beauty. There is a lady in Aragon, beautiful as a sun, whose long blond hair is combed with a golden brush; each hair is a pearl, each pearl a golden ring. Her brother looks at her with an amorous eye and takes her to the fair, where he buys her golden rings, so many that they fall and are scattered on the ground where she walks. She goes to Mass, where, when they see her, the other ladies make a place for her: they are seated on the ground, she in a golden chair (like the monstrance of the Host or a reliquary). The light shining from her turns the church's walls to gold. The priest and altar boys lose their Latin and sing "What a lady I see!" instead of the responses. Who is this lady, who throws off such brilliance? Daughter of the King of France and sister of the King of Aragon, as you may see from her coat of arms.

The song is full of gazing. All eyes are pulled toward the *Dama*'s dazzling light. It is light that confuses, with sexual attractiveness, cosmic power, wealth, holiness, and high birth becoming indistinguishable attributes of the lady. Devotion amorous and religious produces the responses of respect: the offering of gifts, the placement in a high and worthy setting, verbal homage.

In the song, nature and society seem equally to justify the hierarchy wherein the king's daughter is the most beautiful woman in the land. But let us return to consider the singers of such a song—the *popular* classes of Catalonia—and see how social status may shape the apparently natural attribute of beauty.

Beauty is associated with the surface adornments of the body: fine clothes and jewels. It also means good health, size, and bodily integrity: a body unblemished by disease, unmutilated by extremities lost or deformed in work, unbowed by heavy labor, not starved by bad harvests or low wages. The working person's body is open to all of these invasions of experience. But wealth brings in proportion with its possession space and sanitation, adequate diet, doctors, clothes, cosmetics, and freedom from manual labor: insulators, which protect the body's integrity.

We can speak of Berga specifically. Hunger due to the irregular harvests of the Berguedà, to economic inequality, and especially to the wars that have plagued the region was commonplace until the 1960s and has left its mark on working-class bodies malnourished in childhood. Work-related injuries and chronic illnesses are still widespread, given the importance of soft coal mining until the early 1990s. Contagious diseases are under control, but preventive dentistry is relatively new. And fashionable clothes, haircuts, tans, and so forth cost time and money. It is therefore not surprising that physical beauty (as hegemonically conceived) still has underlying associations with high class status and is treated with *respecte*.[25]

But *respecte*, once again, is a function of separation. Like the upper classes, women lose their power as soon as they cease to keep their distance. Courtship is an asymmetrical gazing relationship—the gaze of power meeting the gaze of devotion—but consummation turns man and woman into a couple, a little community of (ideally) equality and solidarity. When the body of the courted woman opens up, she becomes a coworker and companion, no longer an object of homage. The couple's new relationship links the families and friends they already possess and creates more bonds of solidarity within the community, so that the sexual integration of a couple is central to larger societal integration. The sexual bond is an avenue of mobility from the gazing relationship to the intimate one, not only for the couple involved but for their existing intimates. Thus for immigrants in the community, gazing, talking, acting, and eating together are the beginning of integration, but intermarriage is the real test: when the social body of Berga opens itself to a foreign body and takes it in.

Social Attitudes

How shall we tie these threads of Berguedan social relationships together—the gaze and the touch, the respectable and the *popular*, the outsider and the insider, the closed body and the open? First of all we may describe a continuum of interaction styles that creates and maintains both Berguedan personhood and Berguedan social belonging.

The most attenuated relationship is that of the mutual gaze: the glance exchanged, with perhaps a nod, on the Carrer Major. This is to know a person *de vista*, by sight. The talk consequent upon such a gaze and such knowledge is turned laterally: the gossip directed to one's intimates. At the next stage of the relationship, words are exchanged, from the formulaic utterances of greetings and responses to, as confidence increases, loose and improvisatory talk: word play, teasing, nicknames, gossip about others seeking confirmatory judgment, and at last self-revelation. Commensality, the common admission and satisfaction of a common bodily need, follows close upon reciprocal speech: eating and drinking together in a public place and, even more, inside another person's home, is the next advance toward intimacy.[26] Touch, finally, is the seal of solidarity. It may be the kiss on each cheek of middle-class greetings between friends—a kiss often more signified than material; the *popular* horseplay, which expresses affection and cements relationships without risking the sexual implications of the caress; or the decisive touch of the sexual relationship, on which, ultimately, social solidarity depends.

Brown and Gilman, in their classic 1960 article on pronouns of address in Western European languages, note that situational pronoun choice is a guide to the speaker's class status, political attitudes, and transient states of feeling along a continuum of two dimensions: power relations and solidarity. Woolard (1985), synthesizing a range of studies, finds that status and solidarity are central to sociolinguistic variation: more formal styles in a linguistic repertoire are used with the intent of maintaining social distance; more informal ones are used with the intent of collapsing it. I want to extend this sociolinguistic insight to the "interaction rituals" described by Goffman (1967)[27] or to what Schütz called the "mutual tuning-in relationship" (1951). Schütz talks of a bodily process of mutual orientation that precedes and enables communication by placing individuals within a time and space lived in common: creating a "we." But this tuning-in process communicates a meaning of its own, which is often more important than the content of any verbal exchange. There is more than one kind of face-to-face relationship in Berga, more than one kind of "we." The gaze and the touch, I would argue, constitute the poles of a socially stratified continuum of interactional styles, along which variation is socially purposeful.[28] A shopkeeper looking for a higher class of customers may begin to dress up and come out on Sunday; a politician needing the *popular* vote may loosen his tie and clap people on the back during a festival, smiling tenaciously to conceal his discomfort. The denizens of La Barana may offer a curt nod of greeting, then turn their backs on an unwelcome guest to cluster at the other end of the bar. Middle-class people can be *popular* among their intimates; the working class observes *respecte* toward women, strangers, the upper class, and particularly their parents and older relatives. "I know he smokes," said Pepito, when someone jokingly offered his fourteen-year-old son a cigarette. "I know he smokes, I find the packs in the house. But not in front of me! Out of respect for his father, not in front of me."

Berga's interaction styles demand the consensus of participants: if one person is gazing and the other touching, each will consider the other to be transgressing. Any attempt to change the terms of a relationship must therefore be made cautiously. Consider again my father in La Barana. Trying hardest to make him drink was Pepito, the person most interested in maintaining the bar's community. He wanted to draw my father in as part of his general policy, and specifically as a means of binding me still tighter to the bar. But as a stranger and a high-status foreigner, my father was entitled to *respecte*. When he first refused to drink, Pepito scolded him in Catalan—aware that he could understand nothing but the tone of voice—without taking him by the neck and shaking him as he would certainly have done with anyone else. Then Pepito pretended to pour brandy in my father's coffee; that is, he let my father see that he was holding the bottle up and tilting it, giving my father the choice of accepting or of covering his glass and refusing. With someone else, he would have simply poured the brandy in while the other was looking away: I have seen him do such things many times. Pepito was modeling the *popular* without violating the terms of *respecte*, to give my father an opportunity to enter into the more intimate relationship and to force him to declare his intentions one way or the other. An acceptance of Pepito's joke by my father would have led to further teasing proffered by others and finished by incorporating him in the bar's usual horseplay, to which the language barrier is no impediment. But the invitation was clearly refused, and Pepito could not press the matter.

A group's location along the continuum of styles will affect its evaluation of variation in a given situation. It is not to be supposed that the maintenance of distance toward a person of higher status necessarily implies the deference of *respecte*—which is a term that matters most among those wishing to claim it. It may, alternatively, be thought of as coldness or rejection. Similarly, a middle-class person's taking someone by the arm may be considered a show not of solidarity but of *mala educació* (bad manners).

Gaze and touch as ways of knowing have consequences for both the individual and the body social. The gaze of state at citizen, the gaze of man at woman, have received voluminous recent scholarly attention as means of disciplining the body to control the mind (Foucault 1979; Mulvey 1986; and a vast subsequent literature). In Berga, the gaze of the community is unquestionably a means of disciplining the individual: fear of the judgmental eye causes the construction of a surface conforming to the norms of *respecte*.[29] More than that, there is a competition of surfaces so that one may not merely deflect but reverse the power of the gaze, becoming the sun that casts light. But the power of the beautiful woman, for example, is quite illusory: she is controlled and repressed by the gaze that isolates her as an object. She learns to mimic the community's gaze upon her by monitoring herself, her eyes on the mirror standing in for the eyes of others. She looks for cracks in her surface: unbecoming emotions must not emerge nor the contagions of experience enter. To protect herself from these things, she must keep her distance, keep up her guard. Isolation of the self to preserve the body's integral surface is a necessary consequence of the rule of the gaze. The vigilance of the community's eye creates the *persona tancada*, the closed person.

The social body is also affected. As individuals begin to monitor each other so as to rank themselves, they reinforce the mechanism that controls them. Their habit of judgment maintains itself by discovering all kinds of visible signs of status, differentiating ever more finely: reifying social structure. Moreover, by claiming the privileges of *respecte* for themselves, they grant the larger legitimacy of hierarchy. Though individuals may advance along the scale of respectability, the scale itself gains social force from myriad self-presentations, gazes, and acts of judgment.

Touch works on the body in the other direction, to break down the integrity of the person and create a larger belonging. The confusion of boundaries in the multifunctional social space of street or *popular* bar, the physical contacts that force the individual to acknowledge the presence and reality of others, the continual sociable intimacy that invites confidence: all of these open the person to others, prevent excessive attention to the body's surface, and foreground the bodily commonalities that mock the claims of dress. *Popular* conviviality exerts pressure toward equality, toward sharing, and ultimately toward incorporation.

Two kinds of social body are the ideal products—neither ever fully realized—of the two kinds of pressures. One is a hierarchy in which each member has personal autonomy and an appointed place in the structure: a

unity more of concept than of experience. The other is an undifferentiated mass in which all members touch: a unity of feeling not accessible to
analysis. The former model outranks the latter in everyday life, but the
two are in constant dialogue and tension as political ideals. They are
often, too, in physical contest for the possession of public space, as we will
see in Parts III and IV. They are, in fact, Durkheim's organic and mechanical solidarities. In a given context, the ascendant ideal incorporates
the other on its own terms. In everyday social relations, the *popular* stands
as the lower part of a hierarchical social body. In the Patum, which lends
flesh to both conceptions, the respectable body is gradually squashed and
spun into one amorphous whole with its opposite.

4

The Patum Effigies:
Attitudes Personified

RESPECTABILITY AND POPULARITY are balanced and mutually defining in the structure of the Patum: its effigies and dances recapitulate the oppositions of everyday discourse. One conceptual pole is embodied in the beauty, distance, and legible social identities of the giants and eagle. The other is the grotesquery, unboundedness, and ambiguity of *guites* and devils. In the middle are the dwarfs and *turcs i cavallets*, orderly but humble bodies regarded with affection and without awe for their homely charm. Their dances are the less intense interludes, the framing devices, for the *plats forts* (main dishes) of the Patum. The Berguedan *entremesos*, all documented long before the Patum and widely diffused in Catalonia and beyond, have been configured in local thought and practice as a unity in diversity mirroring Berga's own present range of social attitudes. The gaze and the touch, the closed and the open body, the values and political ideals of respectability and solidarity are incarnated in the Patum as both general structuring principles and—the focus of this chapter—embodied social stances, models for individual corporeal engagements with the world. At the level of performance, Berguedans encounter the effigies as other individuals in emotionally charged encounters with a personified sacred.

On Wednesday noon, when the drum and the giants process through the streets to announce the beginning of the festival, I followed along with Ritxi, the director of the municipal music school, and Pep, his second-in-command. When the *geganters* stopped at Cal Tonillo to take a drinking break before turning back toward the Plaça Sant Pere, Ritxi waved a finger at the four giants lined up under the eaves outside. "There's a pretty picture for you," he said. "Go ahead, take it: you won't get another chance to catch them all together in profile." So I took the photograph and we went into another bar to wait. Ritxi turned melancholy, as was sometimes his way between bursts of festival boisterousness. "You can't understand what we feel today, of course," he said to me. "Not even you, Pep, who are younger, feel it the same way—for you it's just a time to have fun. But we—Look at the giants!" He waved his glass toward the door. "Aren't they beautiful? You know, I've seen them come out every year of my life. And they're always the same, always beautiful. You and I grow old, I'm getting bald . . ." He patted his head ruefully. "Those never change."

He gazed into the bottom of his glass while Pep and I gulped down ours to return to the street and the drum. Outside, we met Pep's brother Màrius, who jerked his chin at the giants: *Fan respecte, eh?* (They make respect.) Suddenly I was able to place what Ritxi's emotion called forth in me: my own depression on my twentieth birthday, alone in a wintry Florence, when I went to look at Michelangelo's *David*. So tall, so beautiful, so disdainful; a gaze that would never descend to me and a cold perfection that would never wither. That same day I had gone on to the Brancacci Chapel, where Masaccio's *Expulsion from the Garden* tells the truth about being human: stumpy bodies; Adam's hands over his eyes in a shame that cannot endure the divine gaze; Eve's face distorted in a howl to the heavens, shame already lost in misery. A different kind of art, to be sure, but the Patum speaks in Berga's terms to the same predicament: our contemptibility in the face of power as well as of mortality. The Patum dwarfs, with their distorted faces, their costumes of petty-bourgeois in their Sunday best (cf. Fàbregas and Barceló 1976, 140) show the Berguedans what they are in a comic rather than tragic key: absurd, charming, and not at all intimidating, existing merely to frame and accentuate the majesty of the giants. The giants, though their features are human, are another order of being.

Imposing Bodies

Once again, beauty intimidates. I saw the hairdressers who fix the giants' coiffures each year go about their task with something close to trepidation. Up on a ladder, face to face with the Black Giant, one of them giggled nervously. "His eyes!" she said. "They seem to follow you!"[1] She took a moment to collect her courage before touching his face. Below, the youngest of the three confided to me, with a blush, that she found it hard to get interested in the boys of Berga because they were all insignificant alongside the Black Giant.

The giants, aligned with the upper classes by their height (almost level with the balconies), their serene and level gaze, and their royal dress, are the epitome of incorruptible beauty in Berga. The two Black Giants of 1891 are considered by Berguedans to be the most beautiful in Catalonia, the best made and best balanced but most challenging to carry and dance: the once ninety-kilo Black Giant is a real test of manhood.[2] People often comment on the fineness of the faces, the majesty of the figures, the elegance of the dresses. The coiffure of the Black Giantess, indeed, used to set the style for the summer at the turn of the century. And little girls recognize the giantesses as embodiments of feminine power: a notable subclass of the children's drawings exhibited every year in the weeks after Corpus depicts beautifully adorned giantesses towering over the *plaça* and their male carriers.

Where the giants embody upper-class beauty, the Àliga reinforces the more abstract claims of authority to *respecte*. Defined in Berga as "the symbol of the city," the Àliga too wears a crown. The loudspeakers request silence for its dance, universally qualified as "majestic." Before dancing, it salutes the local representatives of ecclesiastical and civic power with a bow each to the parish church and City Hall. From 1988 to 1992, the municipal corporation returned the acknowledgment by rising from its seats for the Àliga's dance during the noon Patum: this dance has become the single moment of comparative stillness and silence in a now wholly frenetic Patum.

Boundaries between *comparsa* and public are carefully maintained by *geganters* and *aligots*. The giants are always encircled by their red-shirted guardians and protected from flames during the Salt de Plens by sparklers waving the crowd away (the heavy velvet dresses are expensive, the *geganters* explain[3]). The Àliga, with only three dancers of its own, is given space by a common effort of the *patumaires* and by Berguedan taboo ("Watch out for the tail. It killed a soldier once!"). A Manresan woman, resentful of Berga's haughtiness in Patum time, told me that a girlfriend who once ventured to caress the Àliga was actually struck by the *aligot* and told, *l'Àliga no es toca!* (The eagle is not to be touched!). The Àliga does not participate in the structure-dissolving *tirabols* of the end of the Patum (the giants dance in a corner with a little circle protecting them from the crowd) nor in the processions of Wednesday and Saturday. It never leaves the protected space of the Plaça Sant Pere, under the watchful eyes of church and state. Like women and the upper classes, the recipients of *respecte*, giants and Àliga have bodies susceptible to pollution: they must be removed from flames and spectators. Continued vigilance preserves the delicate trimmings of the giants' robes and the eagle's hard smooth surface from the depredations of contact; it preserves their integrity for the wondering gaze of the crowd.

Transgressive Bodies: The "Things of Fire"

The *guites*, on the other hand, are not merely open to the touch, but seek it out, even force it upon the unwilling. The more cumbersome Grossa runs its neck along the *barana* on the side of the *plaça*, forcing the crowd to shrink down. It raises its burning *fuets* to the balconies of the *plaça*, rattling them on the railings and driving well-dressed spectators inside. And it lowers its head and spins in the *plaça*, sending everyone to earth. The Guita Xica or Boja (mad one) has more flexibility. In addition to spinning and chasing, this smaller guita climbs up into the musicians' balcony and rides on the back of dump trucks. It pushes its way inside bars, the more elegant the better, showering sparks until all its carriers are supplied with free drinks. Its invasions of inappropriate spaces often have specifically political implications; always they transgress the boundaries of *respecte*. The *guites'* association with drink (not only does the Xica demand it, but the Grossa distributes it from a leather wineskin around its neck that weighs seventeen kilos when full) and their teasing behavior link them to *popular* strategies of community making, as exemplified in the previous chapter by my friend Pepito.

The *guites* are the most obvious transgressors of the boundaries of inside and outside, high and low, spectator and participant. But they are not alone. The *maces* also let down the barriers by the openness of their participation: except during the more formal midday Patum, people line up to take a turn with the raised flame. The *plens*, by their numbers, have the greatest participation of any *comparsa*, and they force still wider participation, scattering through the crowd so that the entire *plaça* is engulfed in the smoke, nobody knows who is who, and everyone has to dance or be trampled: no one can merely look on. All of these *coses de foc* (things of fire) not only penetrate other spaces and bodies but share the substance of their own, exploding in paper and powder to burn whomever they touch.

The eroticism of the encounter of public and *comparsa* is most evident with the Guita. People chase after it, drawing back when the Guita turns to caress them with its flame. The Guita responds to the provocations of children offering their hats to be burned or of outsiders cowering in a corner; it engages in a coquettish play of advance and retreat with umbrella-wielding tempters near the lantern of the *barana*. Drawing back just before the climax, it celebrates the explosion with a vigorous shake of its long neck and a humping tremor across its green frame.

Touching the Sacred

The comportment of the *comparses* is mirrored by the conduct of the public toward them. The relationships of effigies and public are shaped by the same continuum of attitudes which governs everyday interactions. Giants and eagle must be known by the gaze; devils and *guites* are encountered through touch, desired or not. The principal exception to this rule is notable precisely as an exception and has taken on a ceremonial quality.

The four giants have moments of accessibility on Thursday and Sunday morning before the midday Patum. They are set out in a row under City Hall, a giant in front of each of the four columns supporting the balcony, and left within public reach, the *geganters* nowhere to be seen. This is the great annual occasion for family photographs. All in their best clothes, people line up before the giants, and the photographer makes a group portrait of each family with Berga's "family." Parents bring their children, especially newborns, and hold them up to touch the hand of the Old Giantess or the Black Giant; the parents themselves caress the heavy velvet of their dresses, gaze up into the faces. They line up to approach the giants much as the faithful line up to approach the image and kiss the hand of the local Madonna, the Mare de Déu de Queralt, on feast days.

Even here, the eye's dominance is apparent. Proximity to the prestige of the giants is recorded in photographic testimony. Photographs of the orderly effigies capture knowledge, freeze the gaze. Conventional images have developed in Berga, such as the photo Ritxi told me to take of the four giants in profile under Cal Tonillo. Another is the Àliga in profile against the façade of the church, a picture I've seen in more houses than I can remember. "Look, there you've got a beautiful photograph!" someone said to me, pointing out the Eagle as it lined up with the church. Dutifully, I snapped it, reproducing yet again one of Berga's favorite icons.

If the orderly bodies of the Patum are captured in icons, one might say that the disorderly bodies are captured in stigmata. The *guites* and the two kinds of devils do not separate themselves, but mix with the crowd and share their substance with it. The sign of contact that remains with the receiver is the burn. After my first Patum, my hands and arms were repeatedly seized and examined, my hat surveyed for holes. Then they shook their heads and derided my cowardice. People like to display their Patum scars: one man tried to show me his permanently reddened buttocks from the days when the firecrackers were of artisanal manufacture and exploded harder. Only in his fifties, he had gone mostly deaf from thirty-five years of doing four *salts de plens* per Patum, but it was clearly the world well lost so far as he was concerned. Old hats and sweaters— "more holes than sweater"—are brought out and worn every year, testimonials to participation. Several people recommended that I muddy up my new Patum hat, perhaps even burn it a bit with a cigarette so as not to look like an outsider. And burns when not given are sought: I saw lots of little boys holding their heads under the Guita's flame, and people standing along the *barana* nowadays are clearly asking for it: "if they're at the *barana* they know they're going to get burned." One *guitaire*, observing my intact kerchief on Saturday night the first year, gave me a pitying look. "Give it to me," he said. "I'll bring it back well burned for you." The kerchiefs and shirts are not the only relics of contact: small children pick up the exploded *fuets* and sniff them experimentally, then take them home to keep.

The analogies to icons, stigmata, and relics are not so farfetched. The Patum is closely associated with Berga's only real divinity, the Mare de Déu de Queralt, and itself is a civil religion of much greater depth and complexity than the term generally implies, deeply informed by Catholic traditional form but independent of the church.[4] The Patum elevates the gaze and the touch, modes of ordinary social relationships, to channels of communication with the sacred. The customs of taking pictures, caressing the effigies, and seeking burns are "folk sacramentals" (Hufford 1985, 198): ritual practices giving form to the relationship. More intensely charged than everyday gazings and touchings, they create the special personhood of the effigies.

Images as Persons

To speak of *guites* and giants as persons, much less as sacred, may seem extreme for these clumsy pasteboard figures danced by quite literate people who play video games, go to the doctor, and practice Catholicism as an ethical and social rather than soteriological project (if they practice it at all). But incarnation (and even carnality, as we shall see in Chapter 6) is very much present in Berguedan approaches to their *entremesos*. Rarely is this as explicit as when one of the younger *geganters* said to me, "Some people say the giants are dolls. For me, they're persons." This man is Castilian-born: like many who have had to earn their incorporation, he translates Berguedan habitus into systematic theory (Bourdieu 1990b) and is more eager to demonstrate his participation in it than natives need be. More often, the conception of the effigies as persons is clear from certain avoidances: for this as well as other reasons, most Berguedans strongly resist discussions of the Patum as representation. The Patum *entremesos* do not signify; they are. They have been around too long to be mere stand-ins for ideas or events far more ephemeral than they are. As Armengou says, "after so many centuries of *convivència*, . . . they have become like members of the family" ([1968, 1971]1994, 114). And it is made plain in interaction. The Patum is not a spectacle, remember: one does not stand and contemplate the effigies, but pushes forward to dance with them. They are personalities known all one's life, who act in expected ways and have their quirks and their qualities.

One of the quirks is that they require assistance to act. It is important to understand that the Patum effigies are not masks in the usual sense. The men who carry the giants do not "become" the giants and lose a sense of themselves: on the contrary, the men (and occasional women) of the *comparses* are the most visible and individualized personalities in the Patum. They do not "play" or "act" the effigies as roles. They "go with" the figures or "dance" them or "belong to" them, as companions rather than creators. One may also notice that there is no attempt at concealment or theatrical illusion in the Patum. The giants are carried out of the Ajuntament storeroom in full view of the public, and the *geganter* gets inside without ceremony. A *maça*, once his *fuet* has burst and he has been slain by the angels, will cross his feet, and lie back comfortably on the pavement until the *salt* is over; someone from the sidelines will dash in to lift up his mask so he can breathe easily.

Once, in July, I was walking through the Plaça Sant Pere with a friend and his two-year old son. The little boy tugged at his father's trouser leg and asked, "Daddy, where's the Patum?" His father replied, "The Patum is sleeping," just as an American parent might answer a query about a stuffed animal put away in a drawer. The effigies are comparable to dolls, pets, and especially sacred images, all of which have personhood conferred upon them by the emotional investment of contiguous humans and, more concretely, by interaction—by the gaze, touch, and words of an interlocutor.[5] Although inner states are attributed to the effigies only in exceptional fanciful or literary contexts, they are never denied agency within their sphere. Berguedans make the figures move, but are in turn moved by them.

As the transitional case of domestic animals reminds us, mere animacy is no guarantee of personhood. Nor, of course, is humanity: as is all too well known, the application of what Ruth Benedict called "thing-techniques" to persons easily renders them manipulable entities to whom no face-to-face responsibility is owed (1930). In Berga, we have seen how personhood is socially derived in face-to-face exchanges. The Black Giant is thus a great deal more "real" than the average resident of Santa Eulàlia. The effigies are persons insofar as they participate in Berguedan life by Berga's rules: they interact and communicate with ordinary Berguedans just as Berguedans do with each other, within the same parameters of *respecte* and intimacy. And as among people, the Berguedans distinguish among the figures, everyone finding some more congenial than others. The mobile, episodic, repetitive character of the festival allows individuals to encounter the effigies as individuals also. Active *patumaires* have a variety of brief interactions with each one in the course of a given Patum: they take a turn with a *maça* as it passes through their street, dance behind the Old Dwarfs, duck to escape the Guita's neck when a spin catches them unaware, seek refuge by the giants during the *salt de plens*, and so on. As these encounters accumulate in a personal history, they also become in effect long-term social relationships, which, like human relationships, are sustained in absentia by photographs and reminiscence.

Fetishizing the Social?

The word *sacred*, like *person*, is explicitly applied to the Patum only in unusual moments of metacommentary. Virtually everyone uses it occasionally, but because the Church has so long claimed the concept as its own, the word is most often employed by the forces of *respecte* in their periodic endeavors to transform the Patum from an effervescence into an *ecclesia*. In Patum practice, however, the sacred recovers its experiential hallmarks of fear and desire; it is restored to *respecte* that is not stable at a distance but hopes to advance to incorporation.

In the simplest Durkheimian sense, the effigies are sacred insofar as they are both restricted in access and communal in importance, set off from the everyday world in framed occasions of which they are the focus. They are closely linked to Berga's Marian patron, the Mare de Déu de Queralt, but not of the same stature. She is divine, existing beyond the interactions that bring her into social personhood. The effigies are as good as immortal in relation to individual lifespans, as Ritxi observed, but they are coeval with and dependent on the life of the community in a way that the Madonna is not.[6] "As long as we have Patum, we'll have Berga," said Mossèn Armengou ([1968, 1971]1994, 125), and the converse is also true. Several people have told me over the years that if there were a fire in City Hall the night before Corpus and all the effigies were destroyed, the Patum *es ballaria igual*: it would be danced just the same. *Patumaires* know the weight, dimensions, and motion of the effigies so well that they can bring them to life in absentia (as is done every year in spontaneous "Patums of the Poor"[7]). By the following year, new effigies would be made to restore corporeality to the old companions.

But this confidence was usually expressed in the heat of the festival, when Berga itself seems eternal. Back in the everyday world of faction and economic stress, people imagine with increasing ease a Patum unravelling along with the community.[8] Both are safe just as long as every Berguedan child learns the dance of the New Dwarfs with her first footsteps and every newcomer is "baptized" by the Guita, as I was: safe as long as every Berguedan has a personal tie to every effigy.

What we have in the Patum, then, is a Durkheimian sacred, in which social forces are summed up and projected onto the effigies: in which the sacred presents the profane with an ideal of itself ([1912]1960). Of course it is not so abstract as such a language suggests, given that the effigies dance with Berguedans in the *plaça* and exchange gazes with them on the Carrer Major. Rather, the characteristic social postures, the various moments of the Berguedan "body hexis" (Bourdieu 1977, 82), are hardened and gigantized into effigies, made not just visible but open to encounter:

in the effigies, Berguedans meet their social selves writ large. The Patum is a literal dancing of attitudes (Burke 1957).[9]

In the layerings of the Berguedan sacred over time—the Mare de Déu, deepest; the Patum, most central; and the incipient pantheism of distant, dispersed global objects of devotion—a Marxist could readily mark a historical evolution.[10] The Madonna focalizes natural forces, governing agricultural and human reproduction. Once the object of municipal pilgrimages to avert natural disasters, today she is loved as the landscape is loved, visited as the mountains are visited, and petitioned primarily in relation to childbearing (though new ecological concerns may restore some of her former collective importance). The recent commodity fetishism, like erotic fetishism, exists at a more idiosyncratic level, though its aggregate pressure is already feared to be pushing out more communal devotions, and will surely only increase as Berguedans are drawn further into global economic networks. The Patum reflects the long stage in between: Berga's industrial period, now at its ending. Industrial capitalism developed locally in the context of traditional social relations.[11] The system was paternalistic, governed by personal patron-client relationships, and the labor in mines and factories was collective, so that one's economic survival depended on both respectful links to the local authorities and incorporation in the community of one's equals. Today, when commerce and the state provide most of the viable employment, this continues to be largely true. In living memory, neither nature nor markets have been the primary determinants of individual material security: rather, security depends on social forces in their interactional and more institutionalized political realizations. These, then, are the objects of contemplation, observance, placation: these must be personified so that they can be met face to face and shown respect under the public eye. Personification, like fetishism, gives life to lifeless things and abstractions, but it is a reappropriation of social forces rather than their alienation. Persons have obligations and can be called to account.

The diversity of the effigies is as important as their unity: they embody not a single attitude but the interrelated positions that go to make up Durkheim's "organic solidarity." "For Corpus, all are one," they say, and the verb is a simple copula implying simultaneity rather than dissolution. Conferring sacred personhood on male and female, adult and child, native and foreigner, high and low, respectful and rebellious, even human and animal, the effigies of the Patum represent the community in its entirety.

Difference in Berga is a painful fact of everyday life but can be masked or avoided, at best encompassed in an ethos of pluralism in which principled goodwill struggles against private interest. The Patum takes another tack, making pleasure of pain in a conversion not to an ethical but to an an existential pluralism, not a change of names but a transformed experience. In the festival, individuals are brought up against difference in innumerable physical encounters. Variously threatened, manipulated, and supported by a many-headed collective, they learn to understand themselves as part of a complex whole and to apprehend the variety of libidinal rewards that come with submission to it.

Jane Schneider and James Fernandez have suggested that animist religion fosters an egalitarian "ethic of responsibility" in societies deeply dependent on the natural world (Fernandez 1987; Schneider 1991). By the same token, we may consider the Patum's personification of diverse social stances as similarly reminding the quarrelsome Berguedans of their mutual dependence. To be sure, it is the patrons rather than the clients who most need reminding. Because they have historically witnessed the Patum from the balconies as spectacle and today are present in the *plaça* as guests rather than protagonists, they are best positioned to read one of the festival's clear messages, summed up proverbially as "if everyone were equal, who would carry the giants?" (Amades 1934, 36–37). The Patum has often been a demonstration to local elites that representatives have only the power of what and whom they represent. This means, too, that in the dynamic of the festival as a whole the forces of solidarity ultimately overpower those of respect.

This binarism, as I have suggested, organizes the plural identities of the effigies and, at more global levels of festival structure, is more apprehensible than they are. That is, the Patum is experienced in part, and often articulated, as a series of contrasts between two kinds of performance, synecdochized in two kinds of effigy:

RESPECTABLE EFFIGIES		*CONVIVIAL EFFIGIES*
Balls		*Salts* or *coses de foc*
Àliga	Turcs i Cavallets	Maces
Gegants	Nans	Guites
(high status—low status)		Plens
Closed bodies known by the gaze		Open bodies known by the touch

Respectable conduct to extremes: controlled demeanor, fine clothes, normative family relationships and gender roles[12]	*Popular* conduct to extremes: drinking and physical aggression, working dress, eroticized or ambiguous relationships
Structured time (music and choreography)	Destructured time (drum and free motion)
Structured space (dancing inside a perimeter; clear performer-audience distinction)	Destructured space (*salts* across normal boundaries, loss of performer-audience distinction)
Structured identities (species, social class, and gender clearly legible)	Destructured identities (species and gender confusion)

The sequence of *comparses* in the Patum of the *plaça* is an amplifying oscillation between the poles. The tidy danced battle of the Turcs i Cavallets is followed by the noisy combat of Maces and angels, in which the victory of the latter is merely nominal. The spatial disarray of the Guites is followed by the intense centripetal focus of the Àliga. The humorous dwarfs frame the dance of the beautiful giants on either side, emphasizing the hierarchy internal to the respectable *comparses*, and the Plens and *tirabols* upset this hierarchy in a final dissolution.

Moreover, the sequence of Patum events during the five days of Corpus reiterates the oppositions. The polarities are relative rather than absolute, but consistent. The *Patum de Lluïment* (Patum of show or display) is a much calmer event than the Patum of the night, and people actually come to it in their Sunday clothes after Mass: it was long an occasion to show off one's new summer dress. The night Patum in the *plaça* is a more focused and defined event than the *passacarrers* of Wednesday and Saturday. The Patum Infantil is more controlled and better danced than the adult Patum. And so forth:

RESPECTABLE PATUM	*CONVIVIAL PATUM*
The midday Patum	The night Patum
The Patum in the plaça	The passacarrers
The Patum Infantil	The adult Patum
The official Patum	The "Patum of the Drunks"
Respectable conduct: sobriety,	Popular conduct: drinking, dressing

RESPECTABLE PATUM	*CONVIVIAL PATUM*
dressing up, attendance with family members	down, attendance among friends and the larger community

The Patum, as centuries of popular practice have structured it, maps social relationships in Berga across clear polarities, vividly envisaged. The striking forms of giantesses and *guites* reiterate what everyone knows from daily experience: the rule of the gaze and the community of touch. But Patum practice today upsets the everyday hierarchy of respectable and *popular* as structure is unmoored in performance. Like sexual intercourse, so often invoked as a metaphor for Patum, the festival pulls its participants along the path from the gazing relationship of respect to a mutual incorporation, making union from difference. The next chapter examines this process.

In so doing, it will draw out some of the Durkheimian intimations made here. I've invoked Durkheim several times in this chapter and want simply to point out the effortful cultivation in Berga of everything that in his thought has sometimes been read as a functional given: organic solidarity, the sacred, collective representations, and—our next topic—collective effervescence. Like members of many threatened communities, Berguedans are practical Durkheimians; and although the Patum has been sustained in part by elites seeking arguably to mystify and control, its real energies come from working and middle classes quite aware of what is gained and lost in cultivating the sacred social body. The Patum is a willful collective attempt to create social facts: indeed, to convert them from *factum* to *genitum*, from culture in the mind to nature in the body.

The Techniques of Incorporation

WHEREAS THE PATUM AS REPRESENTATION maps the social divisions of Berga in a way that all can read, the Patum in performance collapses all distinctions into illegibility. The Patum is a forcible communion from which no one can escape without actually leaving the space of *convivèn-cia*. This chapter examines the means (focused and intensified during the last thirty years, toward political ends to be discussed in Parts III and IV) by which Berguedans collaborate to create the sense of oneness that is the universally acknowledged goal of the festival; and by which, to continue the Durkheimian language of the last chapter, collective effervescence is accomplished.

Thickening Ambient

One day in April 1989 I came home to the Casino to find Massana, the legendary *cap de colla* of the *geganters*, sitting at the bar. Dani presented me, and I timidly asked to interview him. "Later," he said, dismissing me. "Later, when there's more *ambient*."

Ambient—ambience, atmosphere—turned out to be an important word. It's usually used in Berga to describe a warm, open, sociable environment proper to certain places and seasons and, in particular, to the *popular*. A bar may have good *ambient*, or a gathering of people; a party that doesn't take off, that remains an atomized assembly of people without its own energy, has no *ambient*. *Ambient* is associated above all with the building up of expectation and the transformation of the social environment in the few weeks before the Patum.

Ambient is bound up with calendrical and local specificities. The Patums out of context long fostered by the Ajuntament, particularly under the Franco regime, have been resented for political reasons, but also because they destroyed the integrity of the *ambient*.[1] This is obvious in the case of Patums taken to other locations. One participant in the 1952 Patum at the Pueblo Español in Barcelona complained that the smell was wrong; similarly, I've heard that the two Patums in Granollers in the 1950s were in too large a *plaça* and the *fuets* had no resonance. *Ambient* is also damaged when the Patum is performed in Berga out of season. Even the 1991 extraordinary Patum in honor of the seventy-fifth anniversary of the canonical coronation of the Mare de Déu de Queralt—a Patum for a local and nominally apolitical cause—was disparaged by many central *patumaires*: "there won't be *ambient*," they said at the Bar La Barana. Only one evening of Patum would be done, without any of the long crescendo that leads up to the Patum in season. "The Patum is for Corpus and in the *plaça* and that's it," say the purists, and this is partly a question of *ambient*. In the first year, I suggested serving *barreja* and *mau-mau*, Patum drinks, for a party I gave before my departure, but Pere told me no: people won't drink it out of season.

The feast of Corpus Christi (simply *Corpus*, in the Catalan vernacular) marks the transition from spring to summer. "Praise to Corpus, which makes the days long," says a proverb (Griera 1930, entry "Corpus"). Leonil.la Boixader, talking to a young friend in the library, remembered her adolescence in the late 1940s. "You've been here for the dry years, Jordi," she said, "but Corpus used to be the time of the change in the weather. We used to *première* our new summer dresses for Corpus and we waited all spring, raining, raining . . ." "For me, the Patum is the beginning of the *bon temps* (good times/good weather)," said Carme, a Manresan aficionada in her thirties. For Corpus or just after, the bars bring out their tables and chairs: afterward it will be warm enough to sit outside every day.

The beginning of summer: a change in the season from cold to warmth, from barrenness to blossom, from work to leisure. Corpus marks a social change consonant with the change in season, from a predominance of *respecte* to a predominance of conviviality. "For the Patum I can relax," they told me.[2]

This is the *ambient* of Corpus: the atmosphere of good fellowship that displaces everyday gossip and competition. It is built up by degrees, by a series of signals that herald the Patum's sensory and social transformation. Each preliminary event adds another ingredient to the mixture.

Sunday after Ascension Day stirs the first tremor of Patum in Berguedans: one feels it somewhere below the diaphragm. The Ajuntament holds an extraordinary plenary session with only one question on the agenda: Will there be Patum? The inevitable *yes* is announced at noon by the Tabaler, who emerges from the Ajuntament to beat the first *pa-tum* of the year, met with cheers. The Tabaler's procession through the streets is followed by a horde of children, all crowding close to touch the great drum with the drumsticks when he stops to take a rest. Behind, the older people follow, filled with sudden gaiety at the sound of the drum, the sight of the Tabaler's red velvet. Everyone goes home to Sunday dinner happier: "There's beginning to be *ambient*."

The beat of the drum, then, is the first element of Patum *ambient*, the one that gives the festival its name (Armengou i Feliu [1968, 1971] 1994, 53). It is the deepest, the decisive element: a Berguedan in exile is supposed to be able to put her ear to the ground at noon on the Sunday after Ascension and hear the sound (this is 6:00 A.M. in my time zone, and the first time I had to miss the Patum I woke up on this day at this hour after dreaming of Berga). The Tabal's emergence from a year of invisibility in City Hall carries civil power out to the street and leaves it there; the drumbeat at the last stroke of twelve usurps the church clock's privilege and takes possession of time.[3]

Odor is the next mark of the Patum, perhaps not as intensely anticipated as the stroke of the Tabal, but lingering longer in memory. After two weeks of impatience, of children tapping their feet and humming in the classrooms, of adults milling in the *plaça* as if waiting for something to happen, come the Quatre Fuets, the Four Firecrackers, of the Sunday before Corpus.[4] The Quatre Fuets bring the first explosion of the Patum, and, most important, the first scent of gunpowder. A rectangle of eager spectators forms itself in the Vall, waiting for the first sight of the thick orange trail of sparks vibrating under the newly green canopy. The first four devils give way to people standing in line behind them for a turn: old men taking the *maça* for what may be the last time, young people who can't contain themselves until Wednesday. The joy of the coming Patum is expressed in extraordinary leaps that seem to go a meter up in the air and just hang there. As the *fuets* burn down, the *salts* become more cautious: canny devils nurse the flame to prolong the pleasure. At last, the explosion, the cheers. "Now we can smell the scent of Patum!" proclaims the next day's newspaper.

No work gets done in offices or classrooms for the next two days. The shopkeepers, on the other hand, are busy putting up metal barriers

against the possible horde of drunken *forasters* while selling Patum kerchiefs, hats, shirts, and souvenirs to the early arrivals. Cassettes of Patum
or *sardanes* blare from every shop. Bartenders clear out everything burn-
able or breakable from their premises and mix endless plastic bottles of
barreja; crate after crate of champagne, beer, and Fanta are wheeled in. A
little boy installs himself in the garden shed outside my window at the
Casino with a comb and a tissue and performs the *pas-doble* of the *tirabols*,
over and over, for hours on end. Miquel of Cal Sala fusses over a pastry
Àliga with a red and green carpet of crudités to be served to the guests of
the Ajuntament. The Red Cross sets up its hospital tent in the Vall in preparation for the inevitable twisted ankles and alcoholic poisonings. The Carrer
Major is fuller than ever of smiling faces, there on no particular errand.
Outside City Hall, children try to peer through the blinds of the storeroom, where the effigies are kept, as members of the *comparses* hurry in
and out to check the preparations. No one can keep still.

At last Wednesday comes, and when the giants come out at noon the
Tabal's beat unleashes "the Patum which beats inside you all year" (Ferrer i
Gàsol 1989, 2). Everyone is beaming with relief and anticipation. Suddenly
all the missing Berguedans have come home, and the air vibrates with
greetings. The Patum has begun; perpetual motion and perpetual noise
have begun. No one living off of the processional route will go home except to shower and steal an hour or two of sleep for the next five days.

As an affirmation of community and its tradition, the practice of the
Patum calls for convivial *popular* manners. And the general motion of
the Patum recapitulates the creation of *ambient*: it moves from coldness
to warmth, hierarchy to solidarity. The effigies embody—in the spirit of
Durkheim once more—the organic solidarity of a differentiated, interrelated community, the *respecte* of mutually recognized personhood. But
Patum practice today creates a solidarity almost literally mechanical, one
based on "keeping together in time" (McNeill 1995). By the time the Patum reaches full speed on Thursday night, divisions are veiled in the haze
of *ambient* and interwound in vertigo.

"Patum i mam"

Before coming to Berga, I had discovered the phrase, "A Berga, Patum i
mam" (in Berga, Patum and booze) in a collection of Catalan *blasons populaires* (Amades 1950–69, 2, 1209). Mossèn Armengou also commented on

the phrase, evincing the social insecurity behind the insistence on *respecte* of the provincial middle class: "The fact that the Patum is a street festival, noisy and reckless at times, has not always been fully understood by outsiders. From this incomprehension was born the puerile slander, 'In Berga, Patum and booze' or 'In Berga, Patum and wine,' with which the envy of other towns insulted us in past times" ([1968,1971]1994, 121, n.67).

So I was surprised when everyone told me, "You know what we say here in Berga, *Patum i mam*! You'll see." "Have you heard what they say, *Patum i mam*? You have to drink with *seny* (good sense), of course. But you have to drink a little." Then they began to explain how to drink. "*Abans* (before), there was none of this *barreja*. It comes from outside. We just drank wine," said Lluís Ferrer, an old *geganter*. "*Barreja* is full of sugar and gives you a headache. Wine doesn't hurt you, you sweat it right out again." Others reiterated: "The drinking doesn't affect you, because you sweat it out all night."

As it turned out, we drank wine, *barreja*, and a great many other things during the course of the festival. *Barreja* (mixture) is the preferred drink of the young and the outsiders, but it also fills the *bóta* of the traditionalist Guita Grossa ("Accept no vulgar substitutes!" they told my husband) and goes down the throats of many who decry its influence on the festival. It is, in truth, not an appealing combination outside of that *ambient*: a sweet and highly alcoholic blend of anise and muscatel. Indeed, when I first came up to Berga with two Manresan friends and they ordered *barreja* at Cal Negre to celebrate my arrival, one of them frowned down in her glass at the sticky yellow stuff after a few sips. "It doesn't taste right without the gunpowder," she pronounced finally.

With the dust of the *fuets* falling on it, however, it is inspiriting and powerful. Thirst forces one to alternate it with other beverages, chiefly beer and champagne: this latter is the most frequent festival drink in Berga and is considered light and thirst-quenching in comparison to other kinds of alcohol. Purists drink red wine cut with *gaseosa*, seltzer flavored with sugar and citric acid. This is a *popular* combination traditionally drunk with meals in the Berguedà. A variation on *vi amb gaseosa* is drunk at the end of the night, while you are sitting at one of the bars along the Vall slowing down. This is *mau-mau*, a mixture of red wine, red vermouth, cognac, and *gaseosa*; after the evening's imbibings, it tastes as innocent as fruit juice.

The local theory of sweating it out seems to work during the Patum, whatever its physiological impossibilities may be. One drinks all night, drinks a great variety of things, and drinks without eating: not how drinking is ordinarily conducted in Catalonia. But I never seemed to suffer the logical consequences, and few people exhibited the familiar symptoms until Monday after the festival, when dark glasses and slowly sipped tisanes signaled the toll of past pleasures. It may be that the *ambient* was too dizzying for me to be conscious of internal turbulence. And I felt that the drink kept me going, fired me to push through to the end.

Patum i mam is not merely a question of drinking. Indeed, even newcomers readily understand its larger meaning. During the rehearsals for the Children's Patum, I saw an immigrant mother instilling spirit into a timid three-year-old. "*Patum i mam*, boy!" she shouted, pushing him out toward the Guita. *Patum i mam* is the battle cry toward a transformed self, an internal fire equal to the circumstances of falling sparks, explosions, and crushing bodies.[5]

But alcohol is a central means of effecting the transformation. The style of drinking is unique to the Patum: drinking to get drunk, drinking without eating and in motion. Whereas ordinary drinking at table is used to enhance sociability and cement relationships within a group, this sort of drinking is less gentle: it is a direct assault on the barriers between persons and groups.

Gregory Bateson considers that alcoholics drink to resolve a painful self-division. Their everyday epistemology is symmetrical and combative: the self in competition with others, the self against the bottle, the self divided from the body, and so forth. Drinking transforms this epistemology to complementarity: the self as part of the whole. Of course I do not wish to suggest that there is anything pathological about Patum drinking, quite the contrary: as I have shown, it is a deliberate break from normal patterns for a specific purpose. And Bateson himself notes that the general purpose of alcoholic consumption in Western cultures is to create community (1972, 329). In Berga, both the individual and the social body suffer from self-division: "all is double." Berguedans live in a continual combat of factions, and the Patum is a relaxation of this as much as of pressures on the individual. Alcohol helps: it dulls the vigilance of one's fellow drinkers as it releases one's own inhibitions, and it takes away factional consciousness by a common process of transformation. Drinking in company is not a social problem, but a social solution—a dissolution of barriers in wine.

Drinking is the paradigmatic and famous technique of the body in the Patum.[6] But it is only one of a whole range. The everyday practices of *popular* sociability, intensified, and special festival devices are combined in the Patum to break down social barriers by robbing the critical eye of its ability to focus and imposing bodily communion upon the participants. The latter effect is the more crucial, for it endures longer. Like everyday commensality—the meals at La Barana from which I was to come home fatter—Patum drinking effects mutual incorporation, bringing the individual into the community interactionally and the community into the individual materially. *Mam* and its associated devices—costume, scent, fire, crowding, noise, centripetal movement, rhythm, and repetition, along with a gradual acceleration toward vertigo—are deployed in the Patum as techniques of incorporation.

DRESSING DOWN

The Patum, as Queralt pointed out in Chapter 3, is a time to dress for one's own convenience. Many men who take the Patum seriously cut their hair very short just before Corpus for the sake of coolness. Everyone, including those who would normally never be seen on the street in jeans, changes after the noon Patums de Lluïment into comfortable and decrepit old clothes never seen during the rest of the year. They are clothes soft with the Patum's embrace, welcoming the wearer after a year of sitting up straight in stiff clothes.

Certain practical considerations are observed. The shirt must be heavy and of natural fiber, because these breathe when you sweat and do not burn as easily. A neckerchief is worn to pull over the face during the *salt de plens* as a protection from the smoke and powder in the air. Among the young and the *pixapins*, these kerchiefs are commercial: black, red, green, or yellow, with an image and the name of the Patum stamped on them. Older or more popular participants use bandanas or *mocadors de fer farcells*, heavy patterned woolen kerchiefs once used for making bundles; their shirts are often of the same material. Hats are likewise important as protection, and they too tend to produce uniformity: black or red cotton, mass-produced for the Patum and its fire-festival imitators.

Like the plain dress of a sect or the habit of a religious order, the costume of the Patum both marks its votaries and reduces differences between them to the terms of the event itself. A shirt full of holes marks a seasoned *patumaire,* and a *comparsa* costume indicates a specific role; teenagers may paint *Patum i mam* on their jeans. But other kinds of difference are lost. In jeans, dark flannel shirts, hats, kerchiefs, and hair either cut off or put up, it is not so easy to identify even the gender and age, much less the social status, of a *patumaire.* The individual is made secure in anonymity, and the social body is leveled by the Patum uniform.

Olor de Patum

The "smell of Patum" is what really defines the intangible of *ambient,* according to locals. In memory and invocation of an absent Patum it is central: when I returned for my second Patum, people said, "Ah, you caught a whiff of something, didn't you?" The scent of gunpowder makes the Quatre Fuets special and makes *barreja* palatable. With the sweat and closeness of the *plens,* the scent of the *vidalba* vines and, better still, the boxwood wreaths is released and blends with the gunpowder of the *fuets* into the charactestic *olor de Patum,* the one tenderly remembered from the past when it was enriched by hazelnut branches used to wave away the sparks and not yet contaminated by the effluvia of intemperate visitors. In the old days of the procession, the *olor de Patum* was enriched with floral carpets on particularly devoted streets. The use of herbs to create a festival *ambient* is traditional in Catalan festivals: the streets are still strewn with thyme, then in flower, for the Pentecost *festa del barri* of the Carrer de la Pietat in Berga, and it used to be a common feature of neighborhood festivals. Incense in religious ritual, Catholic and otherwise, is another parallel: the sense of smell is used there to reinforce a central ritual message.

Fire

Although Corpus falls near the summer solstice, it is not a bonfire festival like so many in Europe. The Catalan bonfire festival is Saint John's Eve, a major festival almost everywhere except for Berga itself, where it falls too close on the heels of the Patum. The Patum uses fire in the form of *fuets,* long-burning firecrackers manufactured especially for the event according to a unique design. The *fuets* are about a foot and a half long, with the explosive charge housed in the reinforced cardboard base. The fuse, sheathed in thinner cardboard, burns with a thick trail of sparks for approximately three minutes (depending on the humidity). In Berga's damp environment the *fuet* needs constant agitation to keep the fuse alight, hence the need for the *salt* and the beautiful waves of sparks left in the air. With three minutes of sparks falling and a burst at the end, the *fuets* combine the two types of fireworks noted by Brandes for Mexico (1988) and common in other Catalan festivals: pyrotechnics and noisemakers (in native terms, *castells de foc* and *petardos*).[7] Both the visual and the sound effects are, however, brought close to the participants by the *fuets*, and the element of touch is added. The flame leaves the trace of the sparks that fall on you, prickling on your shoulders through the flannel, penetrating the sweat on your hands to leave their mark. The light is so intense as to incapacitate the eye, but the sense of touch is constantly stirred by the fire's caress.

There is a progression of intensity in the fire of the Patum. When it first appears with the *maces*, there are only four *fuets*, and their motion is regulated within the rectangle of the *salt*. This is fire to look at: *dibuixos* (drawings) of sparks in the air. The *guites* bring the fire closer. You must be vigilant, for with one turn the Guita is upon you and a shower of sparks descends, the threat of the final explosion looms. With the *plens*, finally, there is no escape: so many *fuets* are distributed on the bodies of devils in the crowd that the fire becomes the enveloping element—the fire of hell, as they call it. Even after the last *fuet* has burst, the *ambient* is more smoke than air, still thickly glowing with refracted light.[8] The word for their bursting, *petar*, recalls the phrase for the phatic communion of La Barana, *fer petar la xerrada*: in each case, there is a diffusion of unifying *ambient* rather than a concrete exchange of substance between discrete parties.

CROWDING

The Patum is generally acknowledged to have too large a public for comfort or safety and certainly for the ease of the *comparses*. Crowding in everyday life—the Carrer Major stroll—creates a sort of moral *convivència* by enforcing the mutual gaze. Patum crowding, like Patum drinking, carries it a level further. The crush of bodies obscures one's view of both the immediate surround and the *entremesos*. And it forces a mutual dependence and cooperation: I was repeatedly warned of the danger of being trampled if I let myself fall or if I tried to change direction or stop moving. Move counterclockwise! the loudspeakers instruct the ignorant, but you don't need to be told: the crowd simply bears you along. At the end of a *tirabol* you may find yourself anywhere, and it takes a few minutes of calm to reorient yourself. During the *tirabol* you lose control over your own motion and also over your bodily surface, usually so carefully guarded. In the most intense moments, when you and your neighbors have danced and sweated into each other, you genuinely lose awareness of where you begin and the others end.

NOISE

The Tabal, the roar of the crowd, the stamp of their feet, and above all, the *fuets* mark the Patum as sensation, not semantics. The burst of the *fuets* carries no content: it is purely phatic, a use of the channel between Patum and people to bind them together. And it claims the channel for its exclusive use: the Patum's noise makes conversation nearly impossible. The critical word is as incapacitated as the critical gaze. The Patum itself is entirely without words, and the few words used by the crowd are sung taunts intended to provoke a bodily response:

Vagos! (Lazy!): chanted when the musicians stop playing.

La Guita Xica no té tita i si la té la té petita! (The Guita Xica has no cock, and if it does it's a little one!): sung to provoke the approach of the Guita Xica or encourage it to greater aggression.

Boti, boti, boti! Espanyol a qui no boti! (Jump, jump, jump—anyone who doesn't jump is a Spaniard!): shouted by the young (especially those not from Berga) as they *salt*. Less common, this was imported to the festival from other crowd contexts such as football matches and protests. It was popularized during the transition to democracy in the 1970s (cf. Mira 1987).

CENTRIPETALITY

The Patum effigies, bright and tall, pull attention toward themselves and away from one's immediate situation within the crowd. The concentration on a focal point pulls the crowd from random motion into oneness, coordinates their attention and their movements. When the Àliga comes out, *fem pinya*, they say: we make a pinecone around it. This is an image frequently used in Berga for the joining of individuals in a common purpose. In the Patum there is a pushing from the periphery toward the center, toward proximity with the effigies. The effigies themselves dance around a center: facing each other, or, in the case of the solitary Àliga and even the vagrant *guites*, turning in on themselves in a spin. Looking over the crowd from a balcony, one sees concentric circles: the *comparsa* dancing in its *rotllana* (round); a still band of people making up their boundary, the ones in front often kneeling to be closer and let others see; and the great undulating mass behind. Above, on balconies, bleachers, and behind the *barana*, a gently rocking crowd bends inward.

RHYTHM

As one Berguedan commentator notes, "The music of the Patum is rather rhythmic than harmonic": he goes on to observe that new orchestrations generally have to be abandoned because, given the noise of the crowd and the imperfect sound system, they are too hard to dance to. In such cases the crowd generally boos until the musicians give up and return to the familiar simple harmonizations they've played for years from memory (Montanyà 1985). The main thing about the music is to be loud and clear. It gives a structure to the *salt*-ing, its simple binary and ternary meters making it easy to move in concert. It is also fast. The speed, the simple meters, and the strong downbeats all contribute to making it the most animating and widely appropriated of Catalan festival musics. In the past hundred years, music has been added to every *salt* but the Guites and the evening Maces, and some people point out that the music facilitates the increasing intensity of the event: the crowd moves as one under the music's mastery.

The *salt* of the crowd is a levelling of choreography, a simple hopping from foot to foot, unless there is room or individual inclination to elaborate. Complex steps only go with the orderly *entremesos,* such as the dwarfs and above all, the eagle; they are not visible to most of the crowd.

Constant motion is the law of the Patum for young people: they begin to salt behind the giants on Wednesday noon and never leave off. Even if you are less determined than the teenagers, you cannot get away from much dancing: the exhortations of your fellows see to that. You dance the Patum into yourself. When at last you're allowed to go to bed, your body quivers and rolls as after a sea voyage, still beating with the *tirabols.* I was jerked out of sleep for a week after the festival by the music pulsing along my spine: I thought I was dancing. A woman working in the municipal archive was rocking in her chair and humming "Ella s'ho pensa" under her breath. My friend Ramon Felipó, at every lag in the conversation on a long car trip one sleepy morning after Corpus, burst into the refrain of the *pas-doble.* A child outside the library beat all that week on an improvised Tabal; left off at the librarian's behest; forgot, and started up again. When the Berguedans say, "We carry the Patum in our blood," they are talking not of heredity but of lived experience.

REPETITION

Repetition works together with rhythm in the cumulative force of the Patum. Patum effigies and events are, as we have seen, polarized in theory between the orderly and the disorderly, but as they occur over and over again the boundaries begin to blur. When the Àliga dances for the fourth time in an evening, it feels much like the Guita. With five days of the Tabal coming out over and over, the Giants coming out over and over, *tirabols* every night, the Children's Patum repeating the big Patum, the big Patum repeating itself, the four *tandes* of the night Patum, the *plaça-*by-*plaça* repetitions of the *passacarrers*, one loses consciousness of specific locations in time and the meaning of particular actions. One experiences the Patum finally as an undifferentiated stream of experience, not as a succession of moments.

In the sum of these experiences—the beauty of the images, the beat of the Tabal, the bursting of the *fuets*, the jostling and burning, the sweet fire of *barreja* in the throat, the inimitable smell of the gunpowder settling over the damp stone streets—we find the congregation of the senses deployed to create con-sensus, as Fernandez describes (1988a): synaesthesia that brings the individual into concord not only with her fellows but within herself. The combinatorial power of these things over someone disposed to receive them inspirits the body and imposes the central goal: the community of the participant with the thousands around her who are practicing the same rite, being instilled with the same purpose.

Mimesis and the Spiral to Vertigo

The deployment of symbols in a specific festival *ambient* that intensifies their message is a commonplace of the scholarly understanding of ritual—ritual manipulations of the senses are said to give perceptual reinforcement to the cognitive goals of the event (Ravicz 1980). But of course it's not as simple as that in practice: the *ambient* can come to control the event, the means transcend the content to give their own message. The Patum of the past thirty years lays out, it is true, a system of symbols known and recognizable to all participants. This is, if you will, the cognitive ground of the festival. But those symbols set in motion transcend themselves, and the Patum lifts its participants off that ground. The Patum's initial showiness—the beauty and spectacularity that make its message memorable—is rapidly veiled in *ambient*, blurred in vertigo. For amid the distinctions of dances and music there is an underlying path to vertigo, a spiraling inward to unity.

The cumulative order of the Patum forces this movement on the participant. There is a crescendo and accelerando of the event as a whole. After the leisurely preliminaries of the tabal after Ascension Day and the Quatre Fuets three weeks later, Wednesday begins a time of constant activity. But Wednesday is still a comparatively quiet and intimate occasion, where few non-Berguedans are present and what matters is recognition: the first sight of the Giants, the first sight of returning friends and family. Thursday still is the crowd on its good behavior, not yet much augmented by outsiders. It is Saturday, with the invasion and the full abandonment of the Berguedans themselves, now wholly warmed up and unconstrained by the schedule of the work week, that achieves the dissolution into rhythm. Saturday into Sunday, almost without a break, is Patum. You begin by noticing and savoring each moment; you end in an ongoing rush of Patum impelled by the *pas-doble* in your pulse, which, when at last the motion stops, finishes literally in vertigo: the Monday morning collapse on a bed that will not stand still.

Within the *passacarrers*, there is a recurrent pattern of acceleration: hopping with the Maces, running with the Guites, dancing with the Giants. The same is true of the Patum in the *plaça*. After the slow beginning of the *turcs i cavallets* (to whom the public used to shout, "Here comes the shit!" because their dance is so long and repetitive), the Maces, and the unmusicked Guites, the structure of each dance is identical.

The Ball de l'Àliga sets the pattern for the dances of giants and dwarfs to follow. It begins with the most "distinguished" melody of the Patum, an adagio in 2/4 time with long holds at the end of each phrase. In this first part, the dancer executes the famous *punteig*, a step that defines the cardinal points of the space beneath the bird. For the held tremolo note at the end of each phrase, the dancer makes the Àliga's body quiver in place. The two *aligots* at either side mimic the step and attend to their feet, facing forward. A faster second section in 6/8 sets Àliga and *aligots* skipping from side to side, widening their *rotllana*, and the crowd, obliged to spread out, begins to *salt*. With another accelerando, the eagle itself begins to describe the circle, the *aligots* turning in to guide it and the closest part of the crowd following behind its tail: a spiral begins to form. The music continues to accelerate and at last the Àliga turns in on itself in a spin, the crowd falling to earth to avoid a blow from the tail, and the *aligots* stepping in to stop the bird and steady the dancer.

The dances of Nans Vells, Gegants, and Nans Nous, have essentially the same two-part structure, although the shifts are less extreme. They begin as allegro waltzes, with the crowd already in a *salt*. With the transition from 3/4 to a presto 2/4 that is a decorated version of the same melody, the crowd leaps higher, and the rapid steps of the dancers toward and away from each other become the focus of interest.[9] At the last held note, *nans* or giants spin—the red cloak of the Black Giant seeming to cover half the *plaça* as it flies out.

The music of the Plens is presto throughout, and the motion of the crowd is a counterclockwise rotation, with individual *plens* being spun from time to time by their "accompanists" to keep the *fuets* alight. The final *tirabols*, presto or prestissimo, are an occasion for the *geganters* in the corner of the *plaça* to dizzy each other spinning the giants. For the *guites*, the lingering devils, and the rest of the crowd, who all dance together "without order or concord" (Armengou i Feliu [1968,1971]1994, 91), the *tirabol* is a collective spin and leaves all breathless: having pulled everyone tightly into the ritual center of the *plaça*, it unleashes them at last on the ludic periphery of the Vall, where, almost literally, they unwind.

Seen from above in slow-motion photographs, the *tirabol* seems to describe a spiral toward the center of the *plaça*.[10] The gunpowder left hanging in the air after the *salt de plens* refracts the light in the *plaça* and gives the *tirabol* a glow of its own, as if from inside. The original dance (judging from less-than-adequate historical accounts) seems to have been a kind of crack-the-whip, a spiral motion of coming together and letting go. And an entry in the 1989 poster competition showing an orange spiral under the words La Patum 1989 was immediately recognized by viewers as a *tirabol*. The circle of the *sardana*, a normative symbol of communitas in Catalonia (cf. Brandes 1990) is not as dynamic an emblem of unity. The spiral captures the pulling, the spinning into union of the Patum: its in-drawing power, its seductive force.

I spoke in Chapter 3 of a linear continuum from gaze to touch, and this is an adequate description of the progress toward intimacy of an everyday dyadic relationship. But for the encounter of the entire commu-nity that takes place during the Patum, the spiraling inward is a better im-age for the same movement. The Patum is not a journey from one point to another through quality space, as so many rituals are imagined (Fer-nandez 1979); neither does it take its participants out to a limen of the set-tled area and the conceptual world to strip them of their social attributes (Turner 1977). The Patum is a dancing in place. It happens in the center of the Berguedan universe and pulls further in.

"The pursuit of vertigo," according to Roger Caillois, "consist(s) of an attempt to momentarily destroy the stability of perception and inflict a kind of voluptuous panic upon an otherwise lucid mind. In all cases, it is a question of surrendering to a kind of spasm, a seizure, or shock which de-stroys reality with sovereign brusqueness" (1979, 23). He claims it is proper to "Dionysiac" or "primitive" societies, where it is found in conjunction with mimesis: an initial act of masking is transformed into reality by ver-tigo, which induces a trance-state in the maskers.

Apart from the thorny question of identifying "Dionysiac," much less "primitive" societies, there are many points of this formulation that will not do for our purposes here. The Patum effigies, as I have said, are not masks for their carriers. Nor can we speak of possession or trance, as I will show below. But Caillois's idea of a ritual progression from represen-tation to vertigo is opportune. The Patum begins in representation: per-sonages such as the giants and the *guita* incarnate particular formations of the social body and enact them in extraordinary enlargements of ordinary social performances. But their particularities are increasingly blurred by the acceleration. In confusion there is fusion: the Patum's normative *unió* is achieved less through a Turnerian stripping down to liminality than through mixing, contact, shaking loose—precisely through vertigo.

The Question of Consciousness

As the existence and repetition of the *Patum i mam* blason implies, Berguedans are quite aware of what they are doing in the Patum. Dressing down, crowding together, dancing, touching the fire, and above all, drinking do not accidentally result in communitas but are enlisted with that end in view. "You have to drink with good sense!" Lluís the *aligot* counseled me in the first year as he was refilling my glass for what seemed like the dozenth time. In effect, good sense (*seny*) in Patum time means drinking enough to achieve the desired experience. A recently recovered alcoholic explained to me that he couldn't stand going to the Patum anymore—it was so boring, so long, so repetitive. Other people who have left off drinking tend to disappear for at least a year or two from the festival. Apart from the powerful incitement to drink, the experience is not the same: they cannot lose themselves in the event.

The pressures on me during my first Patum to get rid of the notebook and dance were considerable, and they followed on observation of my demeanor. "You look serious. You're not drinking enough!" was a not infrequent comment. "You're not dancing! Those notes won't tell you anything." "We have plans for you," a musician announced on Friday. "On Saturday night you're coming with us. No more notebook, no camera, no nothing. We have a *bóta* of *barreja* and you're going to dance all night." My attitude—of body and thus for them also of mind—revealed my distance from the event, so they forced me into intimacy with it: pushing me into the *plens*, chasing me with the *guita*, pouring *barreja* down my throat, taking me by both arms and obliging me to *saltar*. It was from this experience that I came to understand the techniques of incorporation as reciprocal: the individual is brought into the Patum, and the Patum is taken into the individual. One's change of attitude is then literal and visible to others.

The Patum's techniques are as normative as the demands of the Sunday afternoon promenade. Another woman's experience showed me that the norms are not relaxed for total strangers. There was an Italian who came for the 1989 Patum, an architect interested in public space and theatricality. She arrived in the *plaça* on Thursday suited and bejeweled and speaking Castilian, and when I got her a space in the musicians' balcony, endeavored to interview the band leader between *salts*; in mid-Patum, she tried to locate the *Regidor* of Urbanism to ask him for bibliography on social space in Berga. Some friends of mine encountered her later in a restaurant, where she had a table to herself and did not invite them to sit down, though space is at a premium during Corpus. When she went off to the ladies' room, they took possession of the table; she returned and scolded them for their want of courtesy. She left Berga appalled with its boorishness, and a year later my friends were still talking about her outrageous behavior. Which was: she had dressed for prestige, not solidarity; she had persevered in rational discourse in a context demanding surrender to noise; and, most incorrect, she had insisted on her autonomy and her right as a woman, a foreigner, and a professional to respectful distance in a time demanding identification and incorporation with the larger community. The Patum may be a time not to judge or to notice, but the eye still sees and judges.

Like their everyday popular equivalents and respectable opposites, drinking, downdressing, and so on are manipulations of the body with intent.[11] They differ from the everyday, however, in their greater degree of self-consciousness and in their ephemeral character: they are operations rather than disciplines. Everyone acknowledges the temporariness of the transformation into communitas. "For Corpus, everyone is equal," declares the old *geganter* Lluís. "The next day, everyone goes back to what he is." "For Corpus, *el senyor* doctor, *el senyor* lawyer come down to the *plaça* and behave like everyone else," notes Gustau, a potter. His wife Sílvia, a teacher, adds: "For Corpus people you haven't spoken to all year come up and embrace you, 'Oh, how have you been, how nice to see you!' " (in a singing voice, throwing open her arms). "The next day, it's, 'oh, how are you' " (in demonstrating, she brings her elbows in close to her waist, flattens her intonation, and tightens her lips).

The ability to turn the techniques off, as well as to articulate them afterward, reminds us that we do not have here a complete loss of self, an entry into a trance state: we must be cautious about introducing the language of ecstatic religion. The Patum's techniques are dedicated to making the body passive and receptive to the experience: the initial loosening up through drink, the placing it into the power of the crowd, and so forth. But the self so painstakingly constructed, the person so imbricated in the body and its comportment, is not lightly or easily abandoned. The techniques of incorporation have to be learned and ingrained just like the techniques of self-control. The judgmental eye, set free from its usual responsibilities, acts by force of habit to ensure that the new set of social obligations is fulfilled: the touch is enforced by the gaze.

A new set of constraints on the body: the Patum is really this, not a sloughing off to release the Patum within. *Et surt de dintre*, they like to say: the Patum surges up inside of you. But *et surt de dintre* only after a lot of manipulation of the surface. In fact, the Patum has to be let in before it can emerge. You take it in through the eyes, the mouth, the skin, and the feet with conscious effort.

The techniques of incorporation can be as fatiguing as the disciplines of everyday life. When propriety and distance are so deeply internalized as to be second nature, then openness and ease may be uncomfortable. And the Patum calls for rather more than openness and ease. The body has a limited tolerance for the alcohol consumption, sleep deprivation, and constant movement demanded by the Patum: five days are probably as much as anyone could stand. The desired social consequences of bodily transformation can be equally exhausting. In a community of notoriously combative tendencies, the Patum norm of bodily "freedom" combined with the social strain of making this freedom mean unity can create explosive tensions. At every Patum, when passions are high and inhibitions lowered, fights break out between political rivals, insiders and outsiders, competing entities. Even more than the social spaces of the Carrer Major or the Bar La Barana, the Patum brings copresence and forces contact between people who could normally avoid each other. The fault lines of social unity are revealed before they are effaced.

The Patum's freedom then, must be rather carefully controlled by the much-invoked imperative of unity. Berguedans account for the fights with the idea of catharsis: the Patum gets it out of one's system on the way toward unity. But unity is the goal: the unity the politicians enjoin upon each other, the unity omnipresent in the Berguedan imaginary but fleeting in Berguedan experience. *Per la Patum, tots som ú* (for the Patum, we are all one) is in some ways a project, not a description. Far from the unconscious, suggestible, hypnotized mass of crowd psychology, we have in the Patum a group of people cooperating through very deliberate strategies—as Caillois also observed (1979, 88, 94)—to achieve a predefined condition. The self is not mislaid in the crowd or sloughed off like a chrysalis. The disciplined body (and no class or culture fails to discipline its bodies in one style or another) cannot afford to lose itself entirely: having surrendered the infant's freedom to the demands of society, it may be nostalgic for what it has left behind but also fears it. The Patum opens a safe space for the indulgence of this nostalgia and begins with a clear vision of structure, so participants know just what they are letting go. The spin into vertigo is an effort that feels like freedom because it is a change: it is a model of what freedom might be like rather than a genuine recovery. The Patum fits Turner's suggestion that ritual works in a subjunctive mood (1988). The individual's vertigo is an "as if" of possession and self-loss for people weighed down with self-consciousness; the con-sensus of fourteen thousand people is an "as if" of communitas for a community articulated by faction. When the earth stops moving, everything is back in its proper place.

PART III

UNDER FRANCO:
THE OEDIPAL PATUM

6

Return to the Womb

IN THE FIRST HALF OF THIS BOOK, I have spoken of the Patum as an articulation of the contemporary Berguedan social body, a role it has performed since its origins in resistance to the exclusions of the Corpus Christi procession. I move now to the more immediate history shaping the event and to the shorter-term historical consciousness of Berguedans in the festival.

A shift of root metaphor—in fact, to a metaphor of roots rather than members—began with nineteenth-century conservative nationalists, who placed the Patum in a threatened past that needed to be protected by the authorities from the dangers of the new. In the twentieth century, the reproduction of the community as a knowable, stable unity became increasingly problematic with class conflict, civil war, cultural repression, and, at last, deindustrialization and integration into a global economy. The Patum transformed itself from social body to maternal womb, aligning itself with the local Madonna and standing for certain aspects of Berguedan life in a larger metaphor of the community as an Oedipal family. In the most intensely conflictual moments of the recent transition to democracy, the Patum became the scene of Oedipal confrontation; today it is lived as regression to the security of a condition before differentiation. In this chapter I begin with that experience. Chapters 7 and 8 reconstruct the history of eroticized conflict under the Franco regime that reshaped the Patum for the next generation.

La Patum pornogràfica

In 1989, the year of my arrival, I was asked to write an article on the Guita for *Regió 7*, the local newspaper. Uncertain of the proprieties, I remarked as discreetly as I knew how on something that had struck me as important: the Guita's "tremor of pleasure satisfied" after the explosion of the *fuets*. This phrase made a sensation. I heard church-going middle-aged women and well-mannered teenagers telling each other, "Did you read what she said? Dorothy says the Guita has an orgasm!" I even had the impression that certain *guitaires* warmed up to me as a consequence of the article, but of this I cannot be certain.

At that point I only knew of the Guita's "orgasm" from the Patum of the Carrer de la Pietat, which is done for Pentecost, two weeks before Corpus. I had seen there, close up, the pubescent carriers conscientiously raising the *guita* a little from their shoulders and shaking it, with a back-to-front humping motion. A thirteen-year-old girl, one rather ambiguously situated in Berguedan gender norms, turned to me and yelled, "Take a photo!" with a conscious smile. As the children seemed so clearly to understand what they were doing, I was surprised when my remark in the newspaper raised such gratification. But I think it was only because such comments had not been made in the press by a scholar before: that Patum of 1989 revealed a wealth of perfectly conscious erotic feeling.

In the week before Corpus, the Ambit de Recerques del Berguedà, a local research organization, presented the premiere of an audiovisual on the Patum with a script by Agustí Ferrer, then the mayor. The section devoted to the *guites* was a love poem in prose, climaxing thus:

Your kiss of fire, Guita Grossa, when you seek me at the *barana*, is deep and reposeful. And you stretch out your neck the better to kiss me. And I, touched with love, suck in your perfume and am kindled at your lips.

You come to seek me so quickly, Guita Xica, that I have no time to react. So much passion disconcerts me. And your play is so ardent, your strength so great that, at times, you bewilder me and make my blood boil. Are you seeking me when you lower the bar and your head turns and spins, enamored and fiery?

How beautiful you are when you sprinkle fiery rain over the *plaça*! A happy bridegroom, I can't resist your maddened rhythm and your ingenuous countenance . . . The Giants, venerable parents, approve our courtship. The beating of the Tabal, flasks of wine and laughter of Patum prepare our nuptials. And when your face tells me yes with the explosion of the *fuets*, lights of a thousand colors agitate inside me. I feel more Berguedan than ever, as a hot tear of emotion slips down my cheek. (Ferrer i Gàsol 1989, 4–5)

Ferrer's wife joked, "I'm jealous—Agustí has never said those things about *me* in public!" The reader might think his epithalamion overheated: I did on first hearing. I didn't after Saturday night, when they gave me a ride on the back of the Guita Grossa (a consequence, no doubt, of the article)—after Friday night, really, when I was walking with my friends Ramon and Benigne down the Carrer Major.

It was early—only 2 A.M., perhaps—but we were all tired and heading homeward, this being the one night when such early retirement is possible. But a voice hailed Ramon, and we turned into the bar it came from: one more glass. They were a middle-aged couple of considerable social prominence. They were leaning against the bar for support, and they were in the highest of spirits. Ramon introduced me and, as was inevitable, we began to talk Patum.

"The Patum is unique," said the woman. "For example, what exactly *is* the Guita? Is it male or female? Have you ever thought about it? How does the Guita reproduce? There are two of them! Where did they come from?"

"It's obvious," murmured her husband. "The Guita is hermaphroditic."

"Just think!" she went on. "Just think, if one day you were walking through a desert somewhere and you saw little *guites* running around. The daughters of the Guita! If you were from Berga, your eyes would fill up with tears this big!" Her eyes glisten and she begins to reflect. "You know what I'd like to see, I'd like to see the Guita stripped."

"What are you saying now?" says the husband.

"Yes, just once, to see it come out completely naked. Aren't you curious at all?"

He protests. "Poor beast, what do you want to do to it? It would be too sad!"

But she is obstinate. "Stripped! Hey! What if we did a *Patum pornogràfica*? Everything without anything. The *guites* stripped, the giants nude, everything!"

Benigne, who is not quite as far gone as the rest of us, observes, "Casserres [a local giant-sculptor] would have to make some new pieces . . ."

Now the husband has warmed to the idea. He opens eyes like saucers. "Imagine the balls of the Black Giant! And when they're dancing!"

These are not the only erotic fantasies related to the Patum. The Gegant Negre, as you recall, caused the youngest hairdresser of the three who prepare the giants for the festival to look critically at the boys of Berga. "The Black Giant is very handsome, don't you think?" she said to me, using not the familiar word *maco*, but the more erotically charged Castilianism *guapo*. She laughed and turned pink. "I'm in love with him!"

The overwhelming masculinity of the Gegant Negre, though it spurs desire in both men and women, is perhaps a threat to lesser men. In a 1988 series of prints called *La Patum Fabulosa*, the artist Joan Casas Ortínez and the poet Quirze Grifell imagined a scene in which the Black Giant abducts the Old Giantess, leaving the smaller Old Giant to look on, furious and impotent.

The Old Giantess, fairer and more delicate in figure than the Geganta Negra, is the focus of many male fantasies. Quirze wrote her a love letter for the Patum supplement of *Regió 7* for 1983, expressing all the longing felt for her during his year of military service in Andalusia and imagining her lying by his side in dreams. His friend Jepes was less fortunate in his affection. In the Dream Competition after the second annual Sleeping with Beds in the Street Festival of 1990,[1] Jepes narrated the following encounter:

I was in bed in the *plaça* and I suddenly saw passing by me *una tia molt bona* (a really fine woman). Then I saw it was the Geganta Vella. I invited her to lie down beside me, but she laughed and said, "That little thing of yours is no use to me." I said, "Well, it's big enough for my purposes."[2]

The giants of the Children's Patum, less intimidating, are equally enticing. On the last day of rehearsals for the Patum Infantil they're left out on the playground without adults near. I saw children glancing around for intruders, then gathering around the giants, ducking under the skirts, touching and caressing them. Two little girls reached up to squeeze the breasts of the giantesses with faces of solemn inquiry. The Patum, which introduces children to so much in Berga, is also their initiation to the mysteries of sex and growth.[3]

The giants model the orderly sexuality of the family. They go in couples, and are imagined as a family among themselves: Mossèn Armengou designated the Geganta Negra as the *pubilla* (the heiress in the absence of a son) of the Gegants Vells, the Black Giant's dangerous attractions being reined in by the relatively subordinate role of heiress' husband (1953). Other *entremesos* cultivate a more liberated sexuality, the Guita being the most polymorphously provocative. Feminine in grammatical gender, animated by the touch of men, but stereotypically masculine in its aggressively phallic comportment, the Guita is indeed hermaphroditic:[4] it provides something for everyone. It is also, as the woman pointed out, an *entremes* that has succeeded in reproducing itself: there are two *guites*, and once there were three until politics interfered.[5] The other *entremes* that has been fruitful is the Plens, who have multiplied in thirty years from sixteen to seventy or eighty in each *salt*. In Berguedan idiom, a *salt de plens* is the sexual act. It can be a performed metaphor. At the end of my 1989 stay, when I lived at the Casino, the group of teenage boys who hung out there decided they hadn't impressed me sufficiently. On the night before my departure they put a ladder to my window and burst through carrying bottles of champagne and singing the music to the Plens.[6]

Community Fertility

The authoress of the *Patum pornogràfica* spoke to me the next day to laugh over and excuse her fantastic suggestions. "You know, Agustí [the mayor] writes those things, very serious, very beautiful," she said. "Well, *nosaltres diem en conya* (we say it in fun), but it's the same thing."

They gave Agustí Ferrer a ride on the Guita Grossa that year, the first he (or any mayor) had ever had, in thanks for his special attention. It excited a good deal of comment then, and even more so the following year, when his wife delivered their first nonadoptive child after nearly twenty years of marriage. *Ho sap tothom i és profecia* (everyone knows it and it's a prophecy), said Quirze of the gossip about the pregnancy, quoting a famous Nativity poem by J. V. Foix. The Nativity is the paradigmatic birth in Catalan culture, and in the *garrofes*, the Christmas poems satirizing the year's events in Berga, the local birth was placed within that frame:

Per deixar l'infern confús
allà al Casal de les Flors
neix la nena de Cal Ros
més maca que el Nen Jesus.
Del barri antic ets princesa
i ets tu la flor principal
de totes les del Casal
que de tu senten enveja.
No n'ets filla de Maria
ni cap fuster artesà,
però el teu pare et mantindrà
amb el sou d'una alcaldia.
(Vilà Torner 1991, 3)

In order to leave hell confounded,
there in the Manor of the Flowers
is born the little girl of Cal Ros[7]
prettier than the Baby Jesus.
Of the old quarter you are the princess
and you are the principal flower
of all those of the Manor
who feel envy of you.
You're not the daughter of Mary
or of any artisan carpenter,
but your father will maintain you
with a mayoral salary.

The mayor and his wife are not quite Joseph and Mary or even king and queen, but their procreation was nonetheless jokingly considered to have wider municipal implications. The Carnival poems the next year talked of the general consequences of the birth, enumerating the people who could productively be called in as godparents and future members of the political network, and concluding:

Un acte monumental	A monumental act
Un instant quasi a la glòria,	an instant almost heavenly
un afer municipal	a municipal affair
tot un polvo per la història! . . .	a dusting/a fuck[8] for history! . . .
Agafeu-ne exemple, gent,	Take example from him, people,
el vostre arcalde no para.	your mayor never stops
Quan no ho fa a	When he's not doing it at the
l'Ajuntament	Ajuntament
ho fa a casa a cops de vara! . . .	he's doing it at home with his rod! . . . [9]
De tant que ha fuetejat,	From all the exploding he's been doing,
el batlle se us ha gastat	the mayor has used up
la pòlvora de fer fum..	all your gunpowder for making smoke
i enguany no tindreu Patum! . . .	so this year you'll have no Patum! . . .
Recordeu sempre la dita	Always remember the old saying,
tita jove fa bon caldo	a young cock makes good hot broth
i si és boja com la Guita	and if it's crazy like the Guita
te la pots vendre per saldo.	you can put it out for sale.

("Pregó Carnestoltes 1990" 1991)

One does not invoke the gods without consequences. Berga saw a causal relationship between the mayor's declaration to the Guita and his subsequent fertility. It was expressed *en conya,* "but it's the same thing." Here we see it in one of the 1990 *garrofes*:

El secret de la petita	The secret of the little one
de l'Antònia i l'Agustí	of Antònia and Agustí
va ser aquell sacseig diví	was that divine shakeup
del batlle damunt la Guita.	of the mayor on top of the Guita.

(Royo and Grifell 1991, 8)

And another set of *garrofes* turned the occurrence into a general law:

Quina sort! el batlle explica,	What luck! the mayor explains,
desprès de pujar a la Guita	after climbing on the Guita
vaig poder prenyar la dona,	I was able to impregnate my wife,
i el poble canta i recita:	and the people sing and recite:
'Qui vulgui tenir canalla	'He who wants to have children
i veu que un colló li falla	and sees that his balls are failing him,
que els posi damunt la Guita.'	let him put them on top of the Guita.'
(Vilà Torner 1991, 3)	

By this reading, the Patum reproduces the social body, literally as well as figuratively. Of course, the phallic behavior of the Guita and other tarasca figures has often been read as survivals of the fertility rituals of an agrarian society. But what is important in Berga is how the Patum furthers social reproduction. The Patum is really a communal *polvo per la història*, a collective release in which the community is reborn. The Guita moving in and out of the crowd, the Tabal urging the crowd into its own rhythm, the devils encompassing the *plaça* in a prolonged explosion, all enlarge Berguedan sexuality from its usual restricted sphere of the family and quiet deviations therefrom to the level of the entire community.

This is not the same as Carnival, a time of license and multifocal activity favoring the freedom of the individual. The Patum is not a great occasion for illicit lovemaking. Of course practical problems intervene: people drink too much and there is no place to go, the houses, streets, and mountains all being full of visitors. But the real issue is perhaps that "next to the Gegant Negre, they all look insignificant." While middle-class Berguedans think of the Patum as a time of freedom, it is not freedom conceived along everyday lines of individual autonomy but the freedom to find gratification in multiple and extraordinary ways: riding on the Guita or caressing a giant or being squeezed between a thousand faceless bodies in the *tirabol*. It is a freedom of the imaginary as well as the body. The Patum at first encounter recalls Marcuse's "nonrepressive libidinal order," a utopian vision of sexuality allowed to transcend the merely genital and infuse all kinds of relations and activities with its own energy (1962). In fact it is not so free as it seems: it is the libido rechannelled to as socially useful a purpose as baby production. The Patum's manifold eroticism turns the community itself into the object of desire.

The Plens as Rebirth

The *salt de plens* is not only orgasm but birth in Berguedan understanding. Mossèn Armengou, using the religious analogy he would make characteristic, called it "the baptism of Berguedan citizenship," and later commentators, turning to anthropology, call it "initiation."

The ceremonial aspect of the Plens has changed greatly in the past thirty years. They used to be dressed in the *plaça* without fuss. Now, in a Berguedan phrase, "it's a whole ritual": an infernal descent, a return to the womb, the cave, the Nativity stable, the Cova de Can Maurí, which in legend sheltered the people of Berga from the Moors. Because the *plens* are now so many, and it takes so long to dress them, the *comparsa* of dressers has been given the old stable space at the bottom of the Ajuntament: here the tons of *vidalba*, crawling with snails and striped beetles from the banks of the Riera del Metge, are heaped on the ground, and here on tables in back the endless *fuets* are affixed to endless devil masks. Enclosed in their own mysterious space, the dressers see nothing of the Patum in the *plaça*. The person doing a *salt* must go down to them. The stable is approached by a long narrow stair that descends between two buildings on the *plaça*. A line begins to form there an hour or two before the *salt de plens*, and you approach, step by step, the low door.

Inside, you climb in darkness to the upper level, where a face looks over a half-door—the porter of Hell. He murmurs something to voices behind, and, after a pause, gives you a devil suit and a mask; but the dressers are capricious and he may send you back. If you pass, you go on along the unlit corridor and down more stairs to the lower level, an unfinished dirt floor completely submerged in *vidalba*. You pull on your suit, then kneel down—"it's an emotion I can't express to you," said an old *patumaire*. One of the dressers puts on your boxwood wreath, wraps your ears and forehead tightly in white bandages, then places the mask over your face. Then there is a tying and a tightening, a poking of itchy *vidalba* in all your exposed places, a conferring of voices over your head. When they decide you are adequately protected, they stand you up and your *acompanyant*—who is normally a family member or a lover—takes you to the outer stable, where they tie more *fuets* on your tail and twist it up in *vidalba*. Now, wound about like a corpse or swaddled like a newborn and almost blind inside the mask, you are taken by the arm and led back up the long stair to the plaça. Your *acompanyant* finds a good place to stand, not too close to other *plens*, asks if you can breathe well enough, tells you not to be frightened. At last, when all the *plens* are up and distributed through the *plaça*, Pep of the Minc lights a *bengala*—a thick, slow-burning sparkler—next to the lantern of the *barana*. This is the signal for the accompanist to light his own *bengala*; then he turns to you to light your *fuets*. The music begins, and you begin to jump for your life, the crowd pressing, the sparks falling on your hands and inside your mask. You hear explosions above your head, the texture of the *plaça* changes beneath your feet, and a second of open space and air is too quickly resubmerged in smoke and crowd for you to catch your bearings. Helpless, you follow your *acompanyant* until it's over and he lifts your mask and the lights come up. You gasp for air and gape at the *plaça*, emerging in a place you had forgotten.

In contrast to the general experience of the Patum, with the Plens the first time is the paradigmatic time for Berguedans: its awe, its bewilderment. Birth must have been like this: the long descent in the darkness; the helplessness; the struggle to push up, out, through; the release when the *fuets* explode (the ones on your tail hit you like the doctor's slap to a baby). As you do the *salt* through the years and "learn the *plaça* with your feet," more adult sensations supervene. Now it is the old dance toward an anticipated climax, a familiar pleasure made new in every reenactment. In a single moment, the Plens condense the beginning and the end of generation.

Suckling the Patum

The Patum is the mother of Berga. Rossend of the Plens said to me, "A child that's just been born, its father already carries it to the *plaça* and it touches the Tabal, and it touches the face of a *maça*, and it touches the hand of the Giant. It sucks the breast of its mother and it sucks the Patum." Others repeat: "We suckle the Patum with our mother's milk." The word for suckling, *mamar*, also creates the noun *mam*, used for Patum drinking—*Patum i mam*.

El fill regressa al ventre de la mare, wrote the local priest-poet Climent Forner as he imagined coming home to Berga from his exile in other parishes and being received by the *comparses* of the Patum (*Cinquantenari* . . . 1967, 83). "The son regresses to the belly of his mother." A young printer told me as we followed the drum down the street with an army of children, "Do you know why little kids like the Tabal so much? They say it's the rhythm of the mother's heart in the womb." I never heard this again, but I saw souvenirs for a baby's baptism made in the form of a tiny *tabal*. The Tabal's noise, which frames the event, makes an enclosed space out of the Patum, a realm of nurturance and protection, "this archaic mother who permits us, for a few hours, the primitive anarchy of the time of infancy," as a local politician wrote in the newspaper (Fernandez-Pola Garrido 1987).

The mother is credited with decisive creative powers in Berga. The mother confers community membership: "No one is Berguedan who has not suckled Berguedan milk," said one politician in an indiscreet moment in 1985. One curses "the mother who gave birth" to an offensive person, not the offender himself. Bad temper is known as *mala llet*, bad milk, and a vile person is *malparit*, badly born or aborted. By the same token, in popular speech *ben parit* is a term of the most tender praise. And the mother-child relationship is an intimacy like no other. Once I heard a woman make a declaration to her lover in the company of people unaware of the relationship. "*Nen* (little boy)," she said, "I know you as well as if I'd given you birth."

The orality of the Patum—the Patum as suckling Berguedan milk—is not entirely regressive, although the imagery of return and rebirth is increasingly present. The Patum leaves no possible channel of community incorporation neglected and draws emotional force from every kind of desire. We might remember Freud's concept of the "oceanic feeling," the religious sense of boundlessness or unity of the ego and its surroundings, which he explains as a memory of the child's bodily union with its mother (1961, 11–20). Without seeking to create such an explanatory link, we may recognize the appropriateness of the maternal as metaphor. The mother-child relationship of physical intimacy and shared substance describes the sensation of undifferentiated well-being experienced during the Patum. Just as the Patum raises sexual fulfillment to the collective level, so it satisfies a group hunger, Agape layered upon Eros.

The act of feeding someone is in many ways the central act of love in the community, no less tangible and corporeal than sexual intercourse, and more widely practicable ("Take some more, Dorothy," Pere would say as they heaped up my plate at La Barana. "If you go home thinner, they'll think we don't take care of you"). Between mother and child it exists in its most direct form, without the intervention of tables and utensils. It is nourishment created in answer to the child's need: what, in hungry Berga, could be more miraculous? And Berga was hungry in living memory, had always been hungry. The municipal debates about the expenses of the Patum are marked from the earliest years by considerations of the general poverty. Festivals in Berga were occasions to distribute food to the poor until the mid-twentieth century, and Corpus was the greatest festival. [10] For centuries, the Patum literally fed the community. Now, when the literal feeding is no longer practiced, the metaphoric communion is equally restorative. The commensality shared at a table in La Barana or Cal Blasi is, for once, shared by the entire city. In the Patum, fed by the same mother, the divided Berguedans become kin.

The Marian Shrine

Speaking of mothers obliges us to look at another figure of the sacred in Berga, the only one comparable in universality of appeal to the Patum. This is the local invocation of the Madonna, the Mare de Déu de Queralt. She is a small Gothic statue in wood, not quite black but certainly *moreneta*.[11]

She has one of those slight Gothic smiles made hard by restoration in 1916, but alive in popular memory and imagery. The Christ child sits on her lap, as is the way in such images, but as is the way in Catalan popular devotion, he is insignificant except as a proof of her loving maternity—he is her attribute. The Mare de Déu (Mother of God) bears the name of the locality and receives its devotion; the child has no part in this communication.

Like the Guita and the Plens, the Mare de Déu is associated in legend with the land. She was found by a cowherd from the Vilaformiu farm above Berga when one of his oxen strayed and was discovered kneeling before a little cove in the mountainside. Looking into the cove, the cowherd found a small image of Mary and took it back to the house to show his masters. When he opened his bag, the image had disappeared. Returning to the cove, he found it in the same place, wrapped it tightly in his cloak, and, "with pastoral simplicity," said, "Let's see if she'll get away now!" But once again, she was gone when he opened the cloak. At last he returned to the cove with a group of people, and, finding the image there once more, they decided to build a chapel on the same site (Camós [1657]1949, 459–62).

William A. Christian Jr., analyzing the Catalan legends of Marian images (virtually every Catalan mountain within reach of human settlement

has a Marian sanctuary, and the finding legend is always similar), notes
the implication of the image's refusal: the place, not merely the image, is
holy. On the edge of human habitation, discovered by figures also on the
margins of civilization (the semisavage figure of the cowherd and the
semicivilized figure of the domestic animal), and found in a place of connection (the mountain, between earth and heaven; the cave, between the
surface and the underworld), the Mare de Déu is a mediating figure
between nature and culture, called upon to mitigate the impact of such
terrors as epidemic and drought. Her Christian form marks the Christianization and domestication of the Iberian wilderness, or rather, as Christian
suggests, her attachment to the wilderness marks a repaganization of a
formerly urban and parish-based Christianity; a necessary accommodation
of the new religion to the old sacred landscape and the continuing demands of rural life (1981, 20).

For the Mare de Déu is not exactly the humble *ancilla Domini* of the
church, and only the clergy make a point of calling her virgin.[12] She is
abundantly a fertility figure.[13] The Mare de Déu de Queralt receives an
annual pilgrimage on Saint Mark's Day from the people of Berga in gratitude for her intervention against the dreadful plague of locusts, which ru-
ined the harvests of 1687 and provoked uprising all over Catalonia. She
was also processed in special rogations in times of dryness, and even now
Berguedans assert that "The Mare de Déu brings the rain" with perfect
confidence. I would not dare contradict them, for I was in Berga in late
August 1991 when they brought her down for the seventy-fifth anniversary celebration of her canonical coronation. It had been one of the
hottest and driest summers in memory, with no rain in two months except for one violent storm in the mountains that rushed orange mud into
the municipal water supply. Like everyone else, I was sunburned and miserable and had to wash with muddy water carried up in buckets from the
trickle of the public fountain in my street, the pipes having been dry for
three days. The beautiful boxwood street decorations for the festival were
already brown and shrivelled. Then, on the afternoon when they brought
the Mare de Déu down the mountainside, the clouds began to gather. As
they led her through the streets we heard thunder, and when they
brought her up the parish church steps we felt the first drops in the *plaça*.
As soon as she was through the church door the rain began in earnest. It
rained the entire nine days she was down in the town—they had to
process her under plexiglas, but we had water again. The day they carried
her back up the sun came brilliantly out.[14]

The Mare de Déu is as important to human as to agricultural fertility. Newly married couples traditionally go to Montserrat, the principal Marian shrine of Catalonia, and Queralt as well as other sanctuaries have always been much frequented by infertile women. The sanctuary of Queralt, whether for its beautiful site, the popularity of its unorthodox priest, or for deeper reasons, is the most popular church for weddings in the Berguedà. And newlyweds are advised to place the bed facing Queralt if they want to have children quickly.

The mountain landscape is itself maternal. Three green headlands standing in a row over Avià, just to the west of Queralt, are known as "the Three Marias." One of several sanctuaries of the Madonna of the Milk in the Berguedà and adjacent *comarques* is situated on the Montgrony range, which in popular etymology derives from *mugró* (nipple). Standing on the mountain of Queralt in 1901, the great Renaixença poet Jacint Verdaguer looked out on the two ranges Montserrat and Montseny rising from the plain of the Central Depression, and named them "the breasts of Catalonia." In the Upper Berguedà, the famous divided massif of Pedraforca surges up like "two swelling breasts," as a male acquaintance of mine noted happily; another friend recounted the instance of two German engineers who worked in the Berguedan mines watching a new striptease program on television. "Look!" they shouted. "Pedraforca!" The mines, incidentally, are also female. The galleries opened in the nineteenth century bore mostly women's names: Verge de Queralt and Concepció, but also the more evocative Dalila, Venus, Maria Negra, and Negrita (Noguera 1991, 54, 106). An intoxicated miner once told me that they were named for the mistresses of the owner: not true, but *ben trovato*. Mountains are female in their cavities and their protuberances.

The Mare de Déu's intractability to official male authority begins with her refusal to leave her place for the parish church: like the protesters of the 1970s, she "will not be moved."[15] In iconography, the mountain is a seat for the Mare de Déu; in the early modern triangular vestments that once adorned the image, her own shape became mountainous. Place and image are one. The lower slopes of a mountain are called *les faldes* (the skirts) in Catalan, and they are skirts that over the centuries have sheltered bandits, smugglers, political refugees, and resistance fighters, just as the Madonna of Mercy (another important invocation in Catalonia: Berga had a convent of the Order of la Mercè until the 1830s) shelters sinners under her cloak. Unlike that of the clergy, the Mare de Déu's protection does not depend on the moral worth of the supplicant, but on the existence of a relationship. She rewards those who are devoted to her, as seen in those medieval miracles which so annoyed the clergy, of wayward nuns whose place the Madonna takes in the choir while they are out with their lovers, or pious thieves who escape justice thanks to the Madonna's rescuing hand, or sinners for whom Saint Peter dare not plead saved by the Madonna's influence over her son. All those who recognize her as mother are entitled to her support.

The Berguedan mountains are similarly remote from institutional morality. Over the centuries they have provided refuge to the smugglers so central to the local economy, the bandits so detrimental to it, and political refugees and revolutionaries of a hundred stripes. In recent years the Marian sanctuaries themselves sheltered fugitives from the Franco regime on their way to France and radical priests placed there to be out of the way preached Catalanism in Catalan.

Like the landscape and the Patum, the Mare de Déu persists through all of Berga's instabilities. A friend explained her power this way:

I don't know, but here we're so rural and savage and sentimental, and we like the cold of winter and enjoy it like masochists, and run like lunatics behind the guita for nothing and come back for more, and have an inconfessable platonic love for these blue mountains and the tiled roofs which are always there—and for everything that goes away. It's not strange that we look at that which really does remain forever (even if it's only an old wooden image, but a woman at bottom) with such uncontainable tenderness. (Personal communication, 1991)

Like the Patum, Queralt is a motive of consensus in Berguedan society above all points of dispute. Nonchurchgoers, anticlericals, conservative Catholics who disapprove of the santuary's famously idiosyncratic priest Mossèn Ballarín, fans of the same, are virtually all devoted to the little smiling image and her mountain, rocky and scented with scratchy rosemary on the bright southern slope over Berga, cool and silent under pine woods on the far side. Pere and Carme of La Barana, who never go to church, named their longed-for daughter Maria Queralt and embroidered her bed linens with the image. The older men of the Plens wear medals around their necks and hum under their breath the "Aromes de Queralt," a *sardana* written a hundred years ago to advertise a liqueur made of herbs from the mountain. The liqueur itself, though it is sticky and awful, continues to be made, and we drink it now and then out of loyalty; we sing the *sardana* along with the Patum at the end of convivial lunches. The streets were decorated beyond anyone's expectation for the

1991 seventy-fifth anniversary celebration of the canonical coronation of the image in 1916, despite disagreement over the form of the celebration and irritation with the organizers. The local clergy expressed their gratified astonishment at the level of Marian devotion, then caught themselves and pointed out that decorating the balcony for the Mare de Déu is a very different thing from regular Mass attendance. It is indeed. The Mare de Déu, like the Patum, can be directly encountered without the mediation of priests. All day the sanctuary is left open and empty: one can climb the stair to the balcony over the altar where the image is kept and commune with her for as long as one likes. On feast days one has to wait in line, but she is always there waiting: like the mountain itself, she will not be moved.

Two Faces of the Mother

The emotion raised by the Patum and by the Mare de Déu is similar, although the first is more related to people and the second to landscape: the first uproarious and the second tranquil. They are equally bound to the specificity and continuity of the community, the Madonna assuring the reproduction of nature and the Patum of culture, as you might say. They stand in a synecdochic relationship to one another, and only one is necessary in a given performance of community. The extraordinary Patum celebrated for the seventy-fifth anniversary was disapproved by many *patumaires* as inappropriate and lacking in *ambient*. I and many people felt its mood incongruous with the larger event. But it was Jepes who best articulated the problem. He said that the Patum was superfluous. "The Patum didn't move me because I had already had the emotion when I saw the Mare de Déu coming down the Passeig de la Pau."

That extraordinary Patum was felt by many, not by everyone, as *folklòric*, something taken out of context and thrown in to liven up the celebration. "Don't bother," said my *popular* friends, when at Easter I announced my intention of coming back for the anniversary, "It's just going to be a priests' thing. That Patum will be very cold. Come for Corpus instead." The anniversary was very interesting, particularly in bringing out a section of the community I'd never seen before: the oldest and most respectable, the withdrawn people who generally stay behind doors. But they were right at La Barana about the priestly character of the organized celebrations—apart from the descent of the Mare de Déu, nonchurchgoers were pretty

much left out—and by not coming for Corpus I missed one of the most
deeply felt events of recent years: 1991 was the one hundredth anniversary
of the Black Giants, and the *geganters* decided to walk them up to Queralt for the occasion. They did it on the day of the Quatre Fuets, the Sunday before Corpus, carrying them up in relays over several hours, the
whole town following. Friends wrote me of their emotion at seeing the
dark heads against the new greenery of the plane trees; Pepito saved me a
sheaf of photographs so I could have the experience at least vicariously;
Benigne sent me the video immediately produced by Foto Luigi, which
no doubt sold a few thousand copies. When I came in September, the
people at the bar scolded me effusively for not having been there, and in
truth I had not realized the importance of the event. Once arrived at the
sanctuary, the giants danced three times inside before the altar, something
forbidden in the parish church since the early eighteenth century. The Patum came face to face with the Mare de Déu. The underlying link between Berga's two divinities was at last made explicit: age to age,
blackness to blackness. The cove of Queralt and the cove of Can Maurí
are the doubled womb of the community.

"The fountain in the *plaça* ran wine instead of water, did you know?"
they said to me. Again, it didn't strike me at the time. But then I saw the
video. On the last night of the Patum, a *geganter* spoke a message over
the loudspeakers, a thanks from the Black Giants for the homage shown
them in the course of the week. We offer a gift in return, said the voice,
and we ask you to drink to our health. At the fountain in the corner of the
plaça there was a *geganter* operating the improvised mechanism: the
fountain ran red with wine, and the thousands in the *plaça* lined up and
put their heads down, one by one, to experience the transubstantiation.
Patum i mam: thanks to the Black Giants, the fortunate Berguedans
drank deep at the source, the *fons et origo*.

7

The Eye of the Father

THE PATUM AND THE MARE DE DÉU EMERGED in the period after the Spanish Civil War as both symbols and realms of resistance, each experienced as an all-embracing mother whose love does not distinguish between bastard and legitimate, first-born and younger children whose body is the world and is one's own. The reasons for the maternal invocation are not far to seek. The traditional social structure of Catalonia is invested in the authority of the father: an authority given greater ideological and practical force by the paternalist politics of the Catalan interior since the nineteenth century, by the Franco regime's celebration of masculine control, and by the official "national Catholicism" legitimating and legitimated by the regime.

Pairalisme and Industrial Paternalism

In traditional Catalan social organization, the prosperity of the land was bound up with the power of the father and the distinctions of status between siblings. The eldest son, the *hereu*, received the house and land, never divided up as in the more egalitarian but, in their view, poverty-provoking Castilian system. Younger sons and daughters received an equal share of one-quarter of the total value of the property and a choice between leaving to start life on their own and lifelong maintenance at home, working for the good of the household and under the rule of the senior male.[1] Within the household, the authority of the paternal *cap de casa* (head of the house) was near absolute and lasted to his death. The habits of primogeniture persist in places such as Berga, where the oldest son tends to get the family business and where all the incursions of modernity have not wholly eroded the father's claims to *respecte*.

In the Catalan Renaixença of the second half of the nineteenth century, the ideology of the *casa pairal* (paternal house) became a pillar of Catalan nationalism. It was a mark of Catalan difference, an inheritance structure not shared by the rest of Spain.[2] *Pairalisme* was understood as the basis of Catalan prosperity: agricultural land was neither massed in the hands of negligent landlords, as in the latifundia of Andalusia, nor shredded between too many peasant owners, as in the minifundia of Galicia, but rather held in adequate parcels by watchful patriarchs, who cared for the land and those on it with the same zeal they felt for their own good name, itself defined by their house and land. The cities also benefited from *pairalisme*: early Catalan mercantile and industrial development was said to be the work of the younger sons, sent upon the world to make something of themselves.

Each *casa pairal* is a hierarchical social body ruled by the head, benevolently and absolutely. As in Durkheim's conception of organic solidarity, the division of functions prevents conflict: the senior male rules, and the lower members of women, children, and hired laborers have each a specified role in the household. The name of the house unites all in a common goal and in a bounded entity (Contreras 1989, 15).

In pairalist ideology the patriarchal family serves as model for every corporate structure, naturalizing the household, the church, the state, and the factory. Each of these in turn lends authority back to the father. One commentator wrote in 1901, "Our farmhouses, from the most powerful to the most humble, become little rural monarchies, governed by a single supreme chief, by the head of the house, who is a veritable patriarch or family monarch" (Faus i Condomines, quoted in Roigé i Ventura 1989, 31). Another added, "the house is not a transitory association, but a church with permanent worship, a State with immutable authority, a center of perpetual production" (Santamaria Tous 1901, quoted in Roigé i Ventura 1989, 31).

The ideology of right-wing Catalanism, born out of the collaboration of Barcelona industrialists and priests from the Carlist interior, declared itself conservative from the beginning, intending only to maintain and protect the permanent order of things. Bishop Torras i Bages, the great definer of *la tradició catalana*, declared in 1892 that "regionalism has as its principle not touching things in the place where God has put them" (Viola 1989, 20).

But, as the collaboration of the industrialists might suggest, the ideology of *pairalisme* looked very much toward a future where its model of paternalist authority hand in hand with the church might tranquilize the upheavals of a changing society. Its concerns were not wholly or even primarily nationalistic; rather, the industrialists wanted a way of organizing production. Prat de la Riba, the major ideologue of the conservative Lliga Regionalista, identified the *casa pairal* both with the Roman villa and with the future shape of the factory: "When the lord of the *villa* was converted to Christianity, the temple of Jesus Christ was immediately erected next to the *pretorium*; each *dominum* had its church and its pastor; baptism dignified the slaves; indissoluble matrimony destroyed promiscuity . . . Something very similar must be put in effect today" (1898, quoted in Terradas 1979, 29).

Prat was thinking of the industrial colony, a self-contained community of production that would bring this ideal to life. The colony's walls enclosed the factory, the workers' housing, a school, a store, a public garden, and, rising out of this landscape as the two pillars of authority, the owner's mansion and the church. Inside the colony, both men and women worked in the factory (women for lower wages); the children went to school to learn religion, the alphabet, and sewing until their early teens, when they too went to work. A patch of garden supplemented the family wage, the colony store supplied the family wants, and the priest and sisters supervised the community's morals. The doors were locked at night, and periodicals coming in and out of them were inspected for orthodox Catholic content. As Serra and Viladés observe, the colony was a system of near total control—economic, physical, and ideological (1987, 34). The paternal eye was always watching: "In the Industrial Colony the workers can be surrounded with a completely separate environment, a healthy environment . . . it is a nucleus of population which forms itself before the eyes of the director or master" (Prat de la Riba 1898, quoted in Serra and Viladés 1987, 34).

The system took shape in the 1870s as Barcelona textile manufacturers moved inland to look for a more tranquil workforce. The Berguedà offered several advantages. Its conservative Catholic peasantry could be expected to behave respectfully and the poor quality of the mountain land gave small and tenant farmers an inducement to leave it; moreover, the Llobregat river provided a free power source for the mills. The Berguedà and the lower *comarca* of the Bages became the heart of the *colònia* system, the example of textiles soon inspiring mining and even agricultural colonies. By the turn of the century the Berguedà had sixteen colonies (Miralles et al. 1990, 107).[3] Closed or collectivized during the Spanish

Civil War, they were revived after 1939, and the system persisted through
its peak in 1960, when 20 percent of the *comarca*'s population lived in the
colonies (109), until the crisis of the 1970s.

This "industrial family," as Prat called it (Terradas i Saborit 1979, 31),
was often given less benevolent names. The anarchists of the mines of Fígols above Berga called it "industrial feudalism." Even the liberal periodi-
cal *El Bergadán* vituperated against the "industrial feudalism" of the
colonies in 1890 (Serra and Viladés 1987, 138); and the phrase was widely
used in the Berguedà (35). In fact the owner had total legal control over the
colony. Colonies were not incorporated into municipalities until the 1960s,
and their charters gave the owners complete autonomy: the government
surrendered its claims in the interest of industrial and infrastructural development. The very architecture of the colonies bore out the metaphor:
they were walled like castle keeps, with gates closed at night, "as if to keep
out the Moors," noted a worker (Terradas i Saborit 1979, 6). The *torre*
(country house, literally "tower") of the owner was often built, like the
church, in a more conservative version of Barcelona's medievalizing *modernisme*. In Fígols, the *torre*, built before 1911, has ramparts with crenellations
and is gray and forbidding enough to suggest the presence of dungeons
as well.

Feudalisme persisted as a term of criticism: under Berga's left-wing
Ajuntament of the 1930s, it became the name for all the ceremonies of *respecte* that had to be disentangled from genuinely popular tradition.
Working-class people in Berga still describe certain practices as "feudal."
On the other hand, there were conservative writers who embraced the
identification. Feudalism, after all, was another aspect of the *fet diferencial* of Catalonia: Castile, less European, never had it, and the feudal system
with its heroic lords was part of Catalonia's medieval glory, its golden age.

Although the Berguedà had its strikes, industrial paternalism was
largely successful there in creating a stable system of production, which
continued until the crisis of the 1970s. It did not leave the *comarca* with a
useful infrastructure or an educated workforce: as the historian Josep
Noguera observed bitterly to me, "The profits of the Llobregat went to
build the Eixample" (the *modernista* amplification of bourgeois Barcelona). However, it has its defenders: when I made a negative remark on
the colony system to a quite class-conscious *popular* friend, he told me
that the colonies gave out bread during the starvation years after the civil
war; that the peasants had the first steady income of their lives in the
colony and a cultural life they could never have had on the farm, with

choirs and theatrical groups; and that the mines at Fígols gave a general leave of absence at harvest time.[4] Inside the colonies, the paternalist ethos was often strongly internalized by the workers (Serra and Viladés 1987, 24; Terradas i Saborit 1979, 10). "It's the only factory in Catalonia where the owners vote Socialist and the workers vote Convergència," noted a friend about L'Ametlla today.

Berga's inheritance of *pairalisme* and Carlist traditionalism stood the colony owners in good stead. As the institution of impartible inheritance provided the keystone for an autonomous Catalan juridical tradition, so too it legitimized economic practice in industrial Catalonia. The powerful father rules absolutely, but his rule is justified: he seeks not his own aggrandizement but the well-being of his house and household, and thus the general good, if all are organized under powerful fathers.

The competition of would-be lords and fathers was the dynamic of Berguedan politics in the late nineteenth century. Among the towns with their divisive political battles and vulnerable elected officials, the colony owners on their fiefdoms stood up as men of exceptional power, dependent on no alliance or popular support within their own territory. Their workers voted with them: they were the *caciques* of the Berguedà, to use the political idiom of the period.[5] The Carlist Rosal family of the Colònia Rosal just below Berga, founded in 1858 and thus the oldest colony in Catalonia, intervened more than was customary in the life of the town: they founded a Catholic school and a chapel on Queralt, like benevolent fathers. But they were at odds with the liberal mayor of Berga, Ramon Pujol i Tomàs, and at the end of the nineteenth century their political influence in alliance with that of two other industrialists, Lluís Pons and the Conde de Fígols, got the new railway built, not through Berga, but along the river (Serra and Viladés 1987, 21–23). It was partly for their own profit and convenience, partly out of spite against Berga, and it meant that Pujol's hopes of developing tourism and the industry of the upper Berguedà were largely dashed. Pons and Rosal were political enemies, but would freely collaborate for their shared economic interests against what many perceived as the larger interests of the *comarca*. Even in the heyday of *caciquisme*, the destructiveness of owners warring for supremacy was apparent. By 1930, when popular opinion could speak more freely, the *personalisme* of the system was openly denounced:

In politics this can't go on. Neither the Count of Fígols nor any of his concomitants should ever be able to raise their heads again. No more *caciques* from either side. And no personalisms either. Never again Rosalists and Ponsists. People will have to receive their political baptism by other means, godfathered by ideas, not by men. Neither families nor castes. Parties, and nothing but parties. (*Renaixement Bergadà* 1930, quoted in Noguera i Canal 1991, 112)

In great part, the owners were not truly fathers of *cases pairals* working for the future of their children and land, nor even lords striving to enlarge and preserve their domains, but simple capitalists with no link to the land. They turned the Llobregat black with coal dust and poisoned it with dye residues. When it became more profitable to return to Barcelona, they did so, and after the textile crisis of the 1970s the great majority simply abandoned their mills rather than troubling to reconvert them. A few survive, largely automated, with owners who rarely visit. The beautiful *torre* of the Pons family, a *modernista* construction full of stained glass and murals, which hosted Alfonso XIII on his 1908 visit to the Berguedà, is today a dusty towel factory, with a hole knocked in an outside wall for a concrete chute down to the river and the stone trim flaking into ruin. The crumbling factories along the Llobregat bear witness to the lie of the paternalist promise.

The Francoist Corpus Mysticum

The left-wing local governments of the 1930s tried hard to undermine "feudalism," at least in its symbolic aspects: the walls of the colonies were torn down, the church lost its public power, and the eagle of the Patum lost its crown. But the 1939 defeat brought all of this back in fiercer guise than before. The owners and the walls of the colonies came back; in the towns you had to have a good-conduct letter from the parish priest to get any kind of public employment or assistance; and the eagle of the Patum was obliged to wear not the original crown of the Counts of Barcelona but the crown of the King of Spain. The authority of rulers, priests, bosses, husbands, and fathers regained everything it had lost. The tyranny of the eye triumphed over a community torn by war: no one knew who might denounce them for political indiscretions past or for present illegalities necessary for survival. Private sentiments and identity had to be masked in a public show of submission and uniformity: speaking Spanish, attending Mass, raising the arm in the Falangist salute. With no desire to celebrate or to open themselves to the gaze of the regime, the Berguedans shuttered themselves up and lived inside their houses, behind the mask.

Fear kept the defeated Catalans quiet. Franco's armies summarily shot people of all ages and both sexes on the slightest evidence of leftist affiliation: there were fifty-nine executions in the Berguedà alone, fifteen in Berga (Solé i Sabaté 1985, 168–69). Many more were sent to prison camps. Some had escaped to exile or to the *maquis*, the group of resistance fighters in the mountains. But the surviving Berguedans wanted peace and bread and would raise their arms in a Falangist salute to get them.

I was present once at a violent argument among intellectuals about who did and did not "raise the arm." Everybody did, insisted the historian, recounting a long list of collaborations with the regime on the part of well-known Catalans. Everybody. What choice did they have? It was the bourgeoisie, said the editor, the high bourgeoisie went along with it right away because the country was in ruins. "My people never went to Mass even once!" insisted the journalist, grandchild of anarchist peasants, to the historian's disbelieving remonstrances. "Those who had nothing to lose did not raise the arm . . . In the small towns, the first to raise the arm were the professional class, because they were starving." The lawyer from Berga cited one instance of a Berguedan professional who denounced a competitor's politics in order to obtain his position, but added that there was more than opportunism in the middle-class assent to the regime. So exhausted and hungry by the end of the war, they must "have welcomed Franco's army with tears of joy." And the defeat of the Republic had certain compensations. "They lost Catalonia. But they gained peace, tranquillity, and order."

Mossèn Armengou, probably representative of middle-class Berguedan opinion on the matter, blamed Republican leaders as well as the Nationalists for the war: "Responsibility for the failure of the Republic belonged to everyone. To one side, because instead of the Republic they consented to the installation of disorder as a permanent institution, and to the other, because they began conspiring from the first day" (quoted in Rafart 1990, 82). Armengou insisted that Franco's uprising would have gotten nowhere if only the Catalan leadership had divorced itself from the extremism of the left and secured "internal order" (82). "Order" was the key word for the middle and upper class in Catalonia, who had much to lose from working-class revolution.

In Berga religion was as important as class. Public religious manifestations had been heavily restricted under the Republic; after the revolution of 1936 Catholics were increasingly persecuted and priests were assassinated, thirty-two in the Berguedà alone (Badia i Torres 1988, 19). The clergy fled for their lives, including the not yet ordained Mossèn Armengou, who found himself a reluctant chaplain in Franco's army (Armengou i Feliu 1990). Not a few lay Berguedans also fled to Nationalist territory and fought, as they believed, in defense of the church. Other Catholics remained in Berga and supported the Republic to the end, but treading carefully and dreading another outbreak of antireligious violence.

Ambivalent Berguedans, if they did not exactly welcome the "liberating army" of Franco in January 1939, must at least have felt relief that the years of conflict were over. What was the attitude of the new municipal government, made up of Catholic Berguedans of good family? I do not know much about them and the texture of life in those days: the specifics of the Franco regime in Berga are still a taboo subject. But from the Ajuntament's conduct we can see both the old bitterness of division in the community and the practical need and desire for reconciliation.

With the most radical elements of the community eliminated, the new municipal administration could to a point simply resurrect the old language of paternalism. The tradition of *respecte* had not been undone by a mere eight years of the Republic. Individual patron-client relationships of favors and work exchanged for political support were revived or developed anew. The rightness of hierarchy was emphasized in official ceremonies reestablishing the unity and identity of Berga under the new order and made convincing by elite support for and protection of popular tradition, as I will show below. The population's acceptance of the regime was necessary for normal life to begin again, for industrial and agricultural production to resume, for calm on the streets. The Second World War was not very far away in those first years: many of the *maquis* went off to fight with the French resistance, and many old Republicans assumed that the Americans would come to liberate them as soon as they had defeated Fascism elsewhere. Unfortunately the Americans were indifferent, but the Franco regime still felt vulnerable on the French border and had reason to seek the goodwill of the local population.

Increasingly, as the threat from the *maquis* waned and the dictatorship liberalized, paternalism replaced the overt display of power. Paternalism was the key to the style of Joan Noguera, mayor of Berga from 1958 to the restoration of municipal democracy in 1979, who is remembered as having been *molt berguedà* (very Berguedan) despite his sincere and enthusiastic allegiance to the regime. Noguera would pull strings to allow young men to do their military service in Berga if they and their parents came and asked him, I was told by one who did not choose to ask. Àngel the bookseller recalls that under Noguera clandestine Communist Party meetings were tolerated until they became too noisy: his group was once quietly advised by a policeman to change time and location, since a raid was being planned. "I want to be the mayor of all Berguedans," Noguera used to declare, "without taking account of the ideas of individuals. Everyone who comes to City Hall will find the door open" (quoted in Riba i Soler 1989). A great deal of personal and even collective freedom was acceptable as long as there remained a hierarchy of worlds, from idiosyncrasy through community tradition to church and state control. Contained opposition was permissible: you could think what you liked at home, you could venerate the Mare de Déu de Montserrat instead of the Spanish patroness Pilar, and the guita could even burn Spanish flags in the Patum as long as no serious and permanent challenge was made to Noguera's and to Franco's monopoly of power. An indulgent father permits many vagaries as long as his authority is recognized.

And so popular tradition was not merely tolerated but revived and encouraged under the new order. The first anniversary of the "liberation" of Berga was celebrated in February 1940 not only with military ceremonial but with the Ball de l'Àliga and a *salt de plens*. Catalan *sardanes* were danced on the anniversaries of the liberation. The Mare de Déu de Queralt was reinstalled in her sanctuary as soon as it could be restored from the 1936 burning, and the twenty-fifth anniversary of her canonical coronation was celebrated in 1941 with all the magnificence permitted by the general poverty.

The treatment of the Mare de Déu is exemplary of the general approach to local tradition. She was given her due as patroness of the Berguedà, but she was incorporated hierarchically into the larger structures of "national Catholicism," the regime's identification of civil with religious authority.[6] National Catholicism relied on acts of public worship as occasions of both indoctrination and community effervescence, more or less satisfactorily attained. The exiled Cardinal Archbishop of Tarragona, Vidal i Barraquer, wrote repeatedly to Pope Pius XII to complain of the regime's abuse of religious ritual:

Perhaps it is not exaggerated to say that its Catholicism consists principally in promoting showy acts of Catholicism, pilgrimages to the shrine of Pilar, large processions, enthronements of the Sacred Heart, solemn funerals for the fallen with funeral orations, they organize spectacular attendance at Confirmations and First Communion Masses and above all they open almost all acts of propaganda with an open-air Mass, of which a genuine abuse has been made. External manifestations of worship that more than acts of religious affirmation perhaps constitute a political reaction against the lay persecution from before, of which the religious fruits will be very ephemeral and in exchange they run the peril of making religion hateful to the indifferent and to the supporters of the earlier situation. (Quoted in Anonymous 1973, 447–48)

Vidal prophesied truly for much of the old Republican population, although the quiet resistance to co-option of most of the Catalan clergy kept the Mass-going middle class attached to the church. *Triomfalisme,* as its critics called it, was the style of the period: celebrations of the successful imposition of unanimity.

As part of triumphalism, local religious traditions were invoked to pay homage to "national" devotions: they were treated as part-manifestations of a larger whole. When the Virgin of Fatima was brought to Berga in 1949 as part of her pilgrimage through Spain, the streets were decorated with floral arches, improvised chapels, and streamers saying "Ave Maria" and "Salve Regina"; a banner in the hall where she was received read "Love respect and gratitude to our Superiors." Reproductions of the image of Queralt paid homage to the visitor. In such celebrations the Mare de Déu de Queralt was an authority on her own terrain, but not supreme or unique: there were higher-order divinities who held sway in Berga as elsewhere. From being a power of the earth, she was made a minor figure in the heavenly hierarchy: one of those myriad saints on the sidelines in a composition that builds up to a single Trinity and a single devoted Virgin as its handmaiden.

Another way of framing local tradition and, in particular, the unruly Mare de Déu, was to emphasize the regime as guarantor. This tactic was especially visible in the 1941 celebration of the twenty-fifth anniversary of the Coronation. It was the first large celebration in Berga since the war, an opportunity not to be missed for restating the new order of things in a convincing way.[7]

On the cover of the festival program, a tiny Mare de Déu de Queralt is framed in images of male power and transcendence. Instead of the adoring cowherd and his beast, who ordinarily kneel in the foreground of such images, a standing medieval knight on the left and a standing militiaman of the Falange on the right look toward her. The knight carries a tall lance and a banner with the cross of Saint George, patron of the medieval military aristocracy and, by extension, of Catalonia. The young militia-man carries two Falangist flags and a thick rifle pointing up to and indeed penetrating the penumbra of the image. Old and new hierarchies thus join hands, both militarist and male dominated, but the latter now in clear ascendance: "Concentración del FET i de las JONS" is emblazoned in huge letters across the bottom of the image, giving the gathering of Falangist organizations greater weight in the festival than that of the Mar-ian observances. The Mare de Déu is framed in a sunburst as if she were the Host, but the flags on either side mingle with the rays. The mountain and the shrine, usually central features of the image, are minuscule in the background. This new Mare de Déu is a *dona de respecte*, raised up at a distance, guarded and guaranteed by male authority. Her own powers, her links to the land, are minimalized.

When the Mare de Déu de Queralt was brought down from the sanctuary into the Plaça Sant Pere, the arms of the crowd were raised in a massive Falangist salute: there is a photograph as witness. She was taken not to the church but to the balcony of the Ajuntament, where she was obliged to preside over, among other things, the parade of a "column of honor" consisting of the Falangist youth organization, children in uni-form carrying mock rifles made of wood. Mossèn Armengou described the mood of the celebration: "All of this festival threshed itself out amid the racket of cornets and drums, and stamping of military boots, and parades and reviews of all sorts of military and political organizations" (Armengou i Feliu 1971, 134).

However, Armengou continued, even after the bitter conflict, Quer-alt was as always a motive of unanimity for the community (134). The fes-tival called on all the old forms: there were *sardanes*, there was an extraordinary Patum, there were the Hymn of the Coronation and the *goigs* sung in Catalan. But the organizers of the celebration did not allow the memories of division to die down. The program berated *los sin-Dios y sin-Patria* (those Without-God and Without-Fatherland) (Montanyà 1991, 43) who stole the jewel-laden crown of the Madonna during the civil war.[8] It said nothing, however, of how the anarchist Ramonet Xic and his fellow members of the Berguedan revolutionary committee went to great lengths to save the Mare de Déu herself during the war, collabo-rating with Catholics to do so (Armengou i Feliu 1971, 126–30; Montañà and Rafart 1991, 20–24). In the early years, the local regime said nothing of forgiveness and reconciliation; rather, it emphasized at every turn who had conquered. As *Más allá*, the Berguedan Falangist youth magazine of

the early 1940s, instructed its readers, "the path of Spain is that of imposing its justice and its reasons by the force of guns" (1943, no. 1).

There is another way of looking at paternalist tolerance of dissent,
given the Franco regime's Manichaean view of its rule as a perpetual
struggle against the perpetual encroachment of disorder and corruption.
The existence of opposition is necessary to justify the exercise of power. A
little communism is useful to an authoritarian regime. Catalanist errors
create a reason for the Spanish mission of conquest. The devotion to a local Mare de Déu give the priests something to shape and prescribe. The
lower body's disorder necessitates a head to govern it.

The old image of the Corpus Mysticum was revived in force under
Franco, and Corpus Christi was the favorite festival of the regime, so
dedicated to "Order" and "Hierarchies." Franco borrowed its vocabulary,
wrote himself into its hierarchy (cf. González 1977). *Caudillo por la gra-
cia de Dios*, Leader by the Grace of God, Franco used to walk under the
same kind of canopy that covered the Host in procession on his visits to
local communities; he did so when he visited Berga in 1966, entering the
sanctuary of Queralt "as if he were God," as Quirze bitterly observed
(Grifell 1987). Franco was "anointed" by God; he was carrying out God's
mission on earth by building up a Spanish Catholic empire that would
make him "King among Kings" (*Más allá* 1943, no. 1). Like God the Father, he had created a new and yet eternal world ex nihilo: the new calendar began with *El Año de la Victoria* (the year of victory), as all documents
after April 1939 were dated. Franco's face appeared as the frontispiece of
new books, as both the final author of their content and the condition of
their existence. He was *el Hombre*, the conquering virile force that fa-
thered a new Catalonia, and the *padre supremo* of the *Patria*. He was the
eagle who could look upon the Sun of Justice (a favorite image of the
regime) and who in turn dazzled the weaker eyes of his followers: "we believe in our National Head blindly," the youth of Berga were informed in
Más allá (1943, no. 1). *Más allá* (Beyond) in its very name reiterated the
regime's insistence on transcendence, as did the omnipresent slogan *¡Arriba España!* (Upward, Spain!) and the endless invocations of *destino*.

Tensed toward the future, the regime nonetheless taught its votaries
to have an eye on the present. The gossip column of *Más allá* was entitled
"Sight is what works": it offered darkly humorous criticisms of heterodox
Berguedan conduct such as the visits and gifts of families to their relations
in prison, who did not deserve to live better than those outside (1944, no.

14); or not giving money to the Frente de Juventudes for its Corpus Christi fund drive after having been specifically invited to do so (these latter miscreants had their names published; 1944, no. 16).

The Corpus Christi procession with its cultivation of *respecte* and its offering to the all-controlling eye of God was used by the Catalan Francoist leadership to persuade the populace of the rightness and permanence of the new order. The new president of the Junta Provincial de Cultura spoke in 1939 in the newly reopened Ateneu Barcelonés on "Barcelona in the new Spain": "The revolutionary masses were and meant nothing in the city. The authentic and traditional Barcelona was that of the Nativity scenes, that which scattered flowering broom before the Sacrament during the Corpus Christi procession" (quoted in Anonymous 1973, 287).

This Barcelona would later furnish the setting for a major performance of the new Spanish order, as if to proclaim the consolidation of the regime in the most contested territory. During the week of Corpus Christi of 1952, Barcelona hosted the thirty-fifth International Eucharistic Congress, bringing in the first major influx of foreign visitors since the war. The city's public spaces were restored and illuminated, a touristic infrastructure was laid down, and new low-cost housing, both government and church supported, was built or begun to start to address the desperate need now exacerbated by the new immigration. With an eye to international opinion, food rationing and executions of political prisoners were both brought to an end. The organizers represented the full spectrum of the regime's adherents, including some old militants from the bourgeois Catalanist party, the Lliga, and the events of the celebration portrayed a "limited pluralism" (Linz 1962, 296–97, cited in Hansen 1977, 139): there were even *sardanes* and a Claudel play performed in Catalan. The celebration proclaimed a consolidated regime comfortably incorporating the diversity of its subjects: a national-Catholic organic solidarity, in short. Like the medieval Corpus procession, the Congress also declared local integration in a larger order, in this case international. The Congress marked the end of autarky: the Fiat-funded Seat factory in Barcelona was under construction, the Vatican accord would be signed the following year, and the U.S. fleet was on its way.[9]

In the same way, the revived Patum framed local culture in the new Spanish order, either as microcosm or simply as subordinate. At first, the Falange took over the organization of the festival. The 1939 program was stamped with that entity's yoke and arrows and with *¡Arriba España!*, *¡Franco! ¡Franco! ¡Franco!* and similar exhortations. The Patum was explained as the product of the same crusading spirit which led the "epic sword of the Caudillo" to liberate his people from their "Calvary." This little sermon began with a gratuitous quotation from the Castilian poet Fray Luís de León, as if at once to establish Spanish unity as the context of the Patum's meaning. There would be no more quoting Guimerà, no more Verdaguer, lest the people be deluded into believing that Catalonia still existed. Now there was only Berga, *provincia de Barcelona*, inside *la España Una, Grande, y Libre*. Skimming phrases in the festival program gives a view of this new higher-order whole: Christ the king—aspiration—superior ideal—honor of Spain—supernatural—Imperial Fatherland—great destinies—Spanish army—protomartyr—Hierarchies of the Falange—the sun of peace. This new world was the creation of Franco the Father: "the sons of Berga . . . *españolísimos* in their interior, may live anew by the talent of our Caudillo."

Presiding over all of this uplift were the revived *Autoridades* and the new *Jerarquías* of the Falange, as well as the army. Under the Republic, Berga had hosted a summer fresh-air school for the children of the Barcelona slums, an innovation typical of the progressive Catalan education of that period. The large and comfortable building at the western end of the city had been donated by the government of Sweden (Anonymous 1973, 342). In 1939 this building and its terrains were commandeered by the Spanish army and became a permanent garrison: it still belonged to the army until the mid-1990s, and as one walked down the Carrer Comte Oliba one had the disconcerting experience of passing under the rifle sights of a sentry on the wall. The army became a feature of the Corpus Christi procession—by its size a very prominent feature—and the people saluted its passing with the Falangist raised arm. A military band accompanied the Sacrament. The force that upheld the social order was in no way concealed or mystified.

The native elite internalized this new social body, and produced their own artifact of the new order. One of the earliest postwar initiatives of Berga's Catholics, which one must assume was intended as a gesture of commmunity reintegration, was the construction of a new Custòdia for the procession. Finished in 1943, a time of hunger and hardship, this monstrance was made of solid silver and paid for by public subscription. Designed "in the triumphalist taste of the period" (Montanyà 1983), it depicted the sun of the Host sustained by Santa Eulàlia, patroness of the city, in turn supported by the Baroque columns of the high altar of the parish church, which had been burned in 1936. The façades of Berga's churches adorned the sides of the central support. On the base were arrayed the *comparses* of the Patum, eagle and giants occupying pride of place and the devils trodden underfoot as supports to the whole construction. The Patum was thus admitted to the official symbolism, but internally differentiated and the whole made subordinate first to the local, then to the universal Church. On the back of the monstrance the parallel secular hierarchy was made equally clear, with the engraved names of the Caudillo, the Civil Governor of the province of Barcelona, and the mayor of Berga, their authority forever inscribed on this representation of the community.[10] An unnamed local priest—we may speculate that it was Mossèn Armengou, whose account of the Custòdia in his 1968 book is rather curt—remarked in private that "that cumbersome thing looks like the Custòdia of homage to the Regime with the attendance of the Holy Sacrament" (Montanyà 1983). We can imagine popular anticlerical reaction, given that "the Sun of Justice" (a favorite phrase of Franco for himself) is an idiom used for oppressively hot weather, and "to distribute Hosts" is the usual expression for police brutality—a *hòstia* is a blow. Other people found the Custòdia more convincing, but had to adapt their aesthetic to its own. The priest-poet Mossèn Climent Forner wrote a sonnet about it in baroque, Castilianized style. *Oh Sol, al mig dels nostres dies, dia!* he wrote: "Oh Sun, in midst of our days, day!" Rather too much sun, one might say.

The Patum itself was much divided between sun and darkness in that period. It was once again a battle of Moors and Christians (an allegory de-emphasized under the Republic): the fierceness of the Berguedan fight against Moors was proof of their loyalty to the idea of Spain ("Berga y las fiestas . . ." 1954, 36). The tabaler in a *Más allá* drawing was represented in the uniform of the Frente de Juventudes (1944, no. 15). The eagle, its name Castilianized, was fully incorporated into Francoist mythology: "The 'Aguila' of the 'Patum' is the symbol of flight towards tomorrow, towards the conquest of a destiny which transcends the narrow borders of the earth to seek its goal on the vast oceans of heaven" ("Berga y las fiestas . . ." 1954, 37).

As for the giants, one may note that new pairs being created in Catalonia in the postwar era were almost always named for Ferdinand and Isabella, unifiers of the crowns of Aragon and Castile (Centre de Documentació de la Cultura . . . 1991, 284).

Catalans like to lament the Francoist suppression of popular festivals, of the *sardana*, of Carnival. The full truth is more disturbing. In Berga the local authorities went to considerable trouble to revive the popular festivals—Carnival, it is true, being an exception. They did not have an easy time finding enough people to dance the *comparses* of the Patum in the 1940s and 1950s: photographs show us a Patum of adolescents, with Turks carrying the Guita, and old *patumaires* speak of having to do two or three *comparses* at a time because of the scarcity of dancers. Even in 1960, Mayor Noguera felt it was necessary to offer an incentive: he created the *Títols de Patumaire,* diplomas and plaques for ten and twenty-five years of service in the *comparses*. It was not entirely popular demand that kept the festival alive.

Local traditions could be put to the service of the regime and easily encompass this in their flexibility of meaning. The Patum knows only high and low: it does not name them. The rites of *respecte* could just as easily be dedicated to the *Jerarquías* as to the Republican authorities—indeed, far more easily. There was much ambivalence in this mutual incorporation of Patum and regime: did the regime accommodate itself to local tradition or swallow it up?

For the local regime the Patum was a place to contain disorder, a safety valve. "There was a freedom in Berga for Corpus which existed at no other place and no other time," Josep Noguera remembers.[11] This freedom, it was probably hoped, would take the teeth out of protest. For those temporarily released from the all-judging eye, this freedom was a proof of the municipal government's benevolence: Franco off in Madrid might be a monster, but his local representatives were *molt berguedans* at bottom and one could therefore put up with a bit of Falangist humbug for the sake of appearances. Many Berguedans left it at this. Others took advantage of the occasion to turn the Patum around.

Berguedanisme as Civil Religion

The post-Francoist Patum played midwife to the rebirth of the community: it was imagined as maternal against the dictatorship's cruel Fatherland, as primordial against the losses and betrayals of history, and as unified in an embracing darkness against the divisive gaze of the regime. The combat internal to the Patum was ignored: *guites* and eagle, *plaça* and balcony were no longer opponents but collaborators in their assertion of Berga's continuity in the face of all invaders. Nevertheless, the balcony lost its power: active participation in the *plaça* became the new norm for all classes and both sexes, and the disorderly pole of the festival was newly valorized in this period.

Mossèn Josep Armengou i Feliu (1910–76), a tailor's son who spent his adult life as a priest in Berga, defined the Patum, Berga, Catalonia, and Catholicism for the Berguedan middle and upper class of his generation and the next. His Patum, explicated in articles, clandestine Catalan classes, his *tertúlia ambulant* (walking *salon*) along the Carrer Major, and his notable book of 1968, is *the* Patum for a large sector of the community, and even those who would modify his vision have been shaped by it.

Mossèn Armengou articulated, more forcefully and completely than any previous commentator, an ideology of *berguedanisme*: fidelity to the community and its traditions beyond any particular political or religious loyalty and any cultural seduction of the outside world. *Berguedanisme* had the shadow of Catalanism, then unspeakable, behind it. But it was larger: it was both the precondition and the higher consequence of political Catalanism. Armengou's argument began with the removal of the Patum from a Catholic sphere of meaning.

The transference of the Patum from the ecclesiastical to the civic realm began centuries ago in the struggles between bishops and civil authorities. Then it was the clergy who rejected popular accretions to their own liturgy. But Armengou and his fellow priests—Marià Miró, organist of Sant Pere, who used to wander into the music of the Turcs i Cavallets while improvising during the high Mass of Corpus Christi; Antoni Deig, the noted independentist bishop of Solsona in the 1990s, who as a young priest *salt*-ed in the plaça; Climent Forner, who wrote homesick poems of the Patum when he was exiled to a parish a few kilometers to the south; Josep Maria Ballarín, who celebrated the Patum as a medieval feast of fools—were children of Berga or the region and lovers of the Patum. Each of these found the Patum perfectly compatible with his own version of Catholicism; but each of these was very different from that of the regime. It was the clergy of Berga who abolished the Corpus Christi procession by 1972, removing the last ecclesiastical claim to define the Patum.

The Second Vatican Council of 1962 came none too soon for the Catalan clergy. Ostensibly the Franco regime existed to support the church; in practice, it had been the other way around. The council's exhortations to adapt the liturgy to local language and practice, to open access to the Eucharist, and to de-emphasize outward forms in favor of inner feeling became new weapons against national Catholicism.

The presence of the Spanish army in the Corpus Christi processions was a serious grievance for the local clergy, who wanted the message of the Eucharist to be one of reconciliation. They were also concerned about a severe decline in procession attendance, evidently confirming Vidal i Barraquer's conviction that the triumphalist church would alienate regime opponents from religion itself. The second Sunday procession was suppressed in Berga as early as 1956 (Armengou i Feliu [1968,1971]1994, 75). The Thursday procession was itself suffering: Armengou writes in 1964 that he counted 42 men in the procession, many only because their children were making the first communion, and not enough people to carry the banners. Four years later, Armengou chronicles the long decadence of the procession since the early 1950s and declares:

The Corpus processions, with their basically triumphalist cast, hardly fit the religious mentality of today. Because of this they have been wasting away everywhere. I think we Berguedans should congratulate ourselves for not having wanted to maintain them at all costs as a vulgar tourist attraction. It would be a profanation. ([1968, 1971]1994, 78)

In 1970 the procession was suppressed entirely.[12] At the same time, Catalanist Catholicism was working to make its own style more *popular*, more local and homely. Against the Virgen del Pilar and the elaborate Marian ceremonials of the 1940s, which made Mary a stiffly magnificent Spanish infanta, the Berguedan clergy preached and sang of her as "girl of the village, carpenter's wife."[13] The church-promoted Scouts movement, very strong in Berga and Catalonia as a whole in this period, promoted political Catalanism and practical, spontaneous spirituality. Most remarkably, the Berguedan church decided to speak of itself as a sector of the community, not the whole. The priests of Berga put forth their views in a festival program in 1970, when Berga was the *Ciutat Pubilla de la Sardana* (City Heiress of the Sardana) and thus the cynosure of all conservative Catalanist eyes:

Berga, city of popular festivals that had their root in various devotions . . . has seen how the religious significance of many of the festivals weakened, how the real religious unity of the people disappeared, how being Berguedan and Christian became no longer synonymous . . .

And in the light of the Council, Berguedan religious life, instead of jealously defending this unity, in any case already more apparent than real, has attempted and attempts to grow inward, towards a more lively and more communitarian faith. Between having a town that is Christian in the many beautiful traditions

which conserve a Christian appearance, but are in many cases empty of this meaning; or having it there through the active, working, responsible and efficacious
presence of a few Christian persons inserted in the various places of work, family,
leisure, public insititutions, etc., the second road, not without grief or uncertain-
ties and hesitation, is being chosen. (Equip sacerdotal . . . 1970)

That Christianity did not define the Berguedan social body was an
enormous admission, one that had never been made openly in the nineteenth century during the struggles of Carlists and liberals or even during
the church burnings of 1936. But the local clergy preferred this to the fa-
cade of unity imposed by the regime: they had seen how obligatory Mass
made the idea of Mass hateful. The festivals of Berguedan unity, then,
were freely given over to the civic realm.

But not for that had they lost their meaning and purpose. Mossèn
Armengou refused to view the transfer of control as a surrender of the Patum to the Francoist Ajuntament or as a secularization: indeed, it was no
longer an affair to be negotiated between the priests and the city hall, if it
had ever been, but depended on the will of the people, a more permanent
and—he used the word often—sacred entity.

"We will always have to be grateful to (the Corpus procession) for
having been the venerable mother who engendered the Patum" ([1968,
1971]1994, 78), wrote Armengou, and he follows Curet (1967) and other
historians in seeing the *entremesos* as popular elaborations of the triumph
of the Eucharist. But the Patum came together as a uniquely Berguedan
ensemble. It is maintained by and it maintains a distinctive local spirit.
The Patum is not "a folkloric museum piece" (Armengou i Feliu [1968,
1971]1994, 7), but a living civil religion, an enactment of Berga's unity and
identity. It is another species of the sacred, the Durkheimian kind:

The Patum is the baptism of ritual fire which confers upon him who feels it the
most authentic certificate of Berguedan citizenship. Berga has in the Patum an as-
surance of survival. While we have Patum we'll have Berga. As long as the Giants
and Guites and Eagle and Cavallets are moving around the *plaça* we Berguedans
will move around the world with our own passport. (125)

Armengou had the wit to see that the Corpus Mysticum of the Patum was no larger entity modeled, but the transmutation of Berga itself. The old social body of the procession had been a miniature of the
body of the Church. The popular Bulla had instead pointed to nothing
but grounded its unity in copresence. It was this popular conception that

triumphed now. Christianity, the Falange, and Catalanism were all partial communities defined by their respective ideologies. But Berga was an all-encompassing community defined by participation: the Patum. To be *berguedà* is to participate in local tradition, and in that sense it is open to anyone. I receive a book of Queraltine poems in the mail from Mossèn Climent Forner with the inscription, "So you will feel more Berguedan, if that is possible"; the Francoist mayor Noguera was *molt berguedà* because he supported local festivals. *Berguedanisme* has become a merit in itself: local foods and local poets are good because they are ours. At times this develops into an unthinking chauvinism, nutritionally and otherwise unhealthy. But it is also because to be Berguedan, unlike being Christian or Catalanist, is to belong to everybody. Shared tradition should create unproblematic community.

Of course Berga is the least peaceful of communities, and its traditions provoke as much dispute as anything. But the fact of community is indeed unproblematic: if you participate in Berguedan public life, you are by definition part of Berga. And Berguedan identity has a stability that others lack and that is comforting in a country of such frequent and bloody upheavals. Ideologies come and go, fashions in elite culture come and go, but the Patum has been there forever.

Tradition is an anchor, and the Berguedans are conscious of the advantages and the sacrifices of having one. Ramon Vilardaga expressed some of the ambivalences of *berguedanisme* to me during the Queralt anniversary of 1991:

They say we're a closed people, and it's not true. It's that we have good things here—the proof is that people come from outside. We have the Patum, this Mare de Déu, and with that we have enough, because otherwise we'd have to go running all over the place, off to the Mercè [the flashy Festa Major of Barcelona]—If you don't have your own symbols you're lost in the world. Now to Tarragona to that festival, now to Girona . . . Our hymns, they might not be the Boys' Choir of Montserrat, but they're ours, no one else has them. Our [traditions] may not be the best, but they're the ones we can use.

It is no doubt true that Armengou spoke in part of Berga and *berguedanisme* because he could not speak of Catalonia and Catalanism. His clandestine political writings were important in the formation of the ideology of Convergència (*Mn. Josep Armengou, avui* 1986), the conservative and generally Catholic nationalist party, which has governed the Generalitat and the majority of municipal governments since 1979. In Berga he taught Catalan literacy in secret to the children of the middle class, and his sermons were, by all accounts, masterpieces of veiled political allusion. His Patum cannot help being an allegory of national death and resurrection. The much-quoted end of his book describes the *plaça* on Monday after Corpus, silent but redolent of the most evocative odor known to the Berguedan nose: gunpowder mingled with trampled *vidalba*. The *plaça* bears both memory and the promise of a future: "Like a battlefield after a combat, where the spirit of a people unwilling to die has achieved one more victory" ([1968, 1971]1994, 126).

But the outsiders of the 1970s who saw the Patum as a demonstration against the regime were overreading. Armengou had seen the dangers of politicization to community under the Republic as well as Franco, and he felt that the underlying reality of Catalonia could not survive without being independent of even a Catalanist regime. So his Patum, although at the given historical moment it stimulated a spirit of resistance, was not itself political. *La Patum no és política*, the Berguedans say today, because even ideologies of democracy and Catalanism are divisive and will no doubt prove as ephemeral as every other. A political allegiance, good or bad, endangers the Patum's permanence. Armengou's giants insist: "Nobody makes us dance, neither politics nor interest. We serve more sacred interests" (1953, 57).

They serve *berguedanisme*, an ideology that—like other conservative ideologies—asserts its freedom from ideology and its ability to embrace contradictions. Left and right are equally Berguedan, and Berga's key symbols and rituals—the Patum and Queralt[14]—belong to everyone. They are above politics. This meant that nationalist *patumaires* and the Francoist administration alike collaborated in preventing a demonstration of the Assemblea de Catalunya during the Patum in 1975.[15] *Berguedanisme* was not the "anecdotal" product of a given historical conjuncture, but the continuity of the Corpus Mysticum through its incarnation in the Patum.

Armengou was a priest and proponent of order: he had fled the Republic in justified fear of his life and served, reluctantly, as a chaplain with the Francoist troops. He was no anarchist and did not simply reverse the old allegory of the Patum, with the fiery popular symbols chasing out the giants. His Patum substituted an indigenous order for the regime's equation of Franco with order and Catalonia with chaos held down by force. In Armengou's Patum, avenging Christians do not subjugate Moors; rather, each *entremes* is part and necessary, another piece of the whole paying homage to the whole—not now the Eucharist, but Berga.[16] His attempt to dissociate the idea of order from the current ruling class is most apparent in his celebration of the Àliga.

The crowned and elegant eagle had already been singled out as a symbol of order by earlier Catholic interpreters, who decorated the iron railings of the Cove of Queralt with eagle's heads and used the Àliga's music as a melodic source for the Hymn of the Coronation of 1916. Mossèn Armengou disambiguated the eagle: for him it was not Saint John the Evangelist, but a symbol of the city. This interpretation has predominated, is justified with allusions to the inconclusive scholarship, and has led to all kinds of ceremonial uses. The Ball de l'Àliga is played at the funeral of prominent Berguedans; the eagle's head is sculpted on the medal of the city; the loudspeakers ask for silence during the eagle's dance; and in the late 1980s, the administration of Agustí Ferrer would stand up on the mayor's balcony for the dance during the Patum de Lluïment.[17] Eminent visitors to the Patum have learned to say that the part of the Patum that moves them most is the Ball de l'Àliga, and children, when they reach the age of reason, begin to substitute the eagle for the *guites*, whose primordial energies animate their first drawings of the Patum.

There was a quiet national allegory in Armengou's eagle, following a turn-of the-century interpretation of the Patum as a commemoration of the city's liberation from feudal rule:

Solemnly it points a delicate play of feet, all filigree, like an imprisoned princess who embroiders with hope the banner of her liberation; all at once it begins to pull, uncontainable, from side to side, until, its chains broken, it takes broad flight for the serene sky of liberty.—This is the traditional interpretation. We would be wary of saying that it is really the original motive of the dance—. The notable melody that accompanies this dance is as ample and majestic as the ambitions of a whole people. ([1968, 1971]1994, 87)

This is one of the most famous passages of Armengou's book. It is quoted and plagiarized annually in the local media without the reservations Armengou made, the product of his skepticism regarding Renaixença origin narratives but also, I suspect, of an underlying ambivalence of his own. His simile is curiously feminine and gentle, and although it mimics the widening circle, the accelerando of the eagle's dance, it does not capture the cruel curve of that beak, the hard spin of the tail that killed a soldier once. Armengou is both caught up by and mistrustful of the eagle's energy.

Nobody ever remarks upon it, but when during the Patum of the Franco period you looked over at the Àliga at rest by City Hall, you saw it in close proximity to another eagle: the eagle of the arms of the Falange, appliquéed on yellow damask and hanging magnificently from the balcony (Figure 9). People spoke resentfully of that eagle, but it never was equated with Berga's own: it was simply excised from the "intertextual encyclopedia" (Eco 1986, 68–73) of the Patum.

Armengou's imprisoned princess is as far as the Àliga can very well get from the fierce far-seeing eagle of the regime; if the image is strained, that is surely the reason. He is also careful to stress that the eagle originally wore a "counts' crown," meaning a Catalan rather than a Spanish one. The Àliga had to be redeemed and celebrated as a symbol of nonrepressive order, free of any aggressive connotations. Armengou makes it not a conqueror but a self-liberating victim.

Armengou's Guita is humorous, childlike in its primitive ferocity. "Fierce as it is, it's of an ingenuousness which robs your heart" ([1968, 1971]1994, 106). The Guita in the practice of the period was sometimes less innocent, attacking things and people with intent. Apart from the flag-burning, it entered the barracks of the Guardia Civil and, though it was driven out, achieved the closing of the Guardia's doors and the removal of the wooden *Todo para la Patria* sign for future Patums (Farràs i Farràs 1979, 328). The Guita Xica was in the hands of militant indepentists during the Transition, one of whom belonged to an organization committed to armed struggle and was imprisoned by the regime as a terrorist. Then there was the famous *guitaires'* strike of 1978, when the mayor's drunken secretary threatened Mixo with a pistol, but Mixo ultimately forced the mayor to come down to the *plaça* and bring the Guita Grossa its *fuets* with his own hands. The Guita was the clearest anti-Francoist element of the Patum, and outsiders recognized it as such: when the exiled president of the Generalitat, Tarradellas, went off to Madrid to negotiate in 1977, a Barcelona cartoonist pictured his head on the body of a *guita* (Figure 10).

The Plens also slipped from Armengou's hands. Armengou had pointed out that the Plens defined the Patum as Berguedan. He quoted the best authorities to prove them unique: "Joan Amades says that nowhere in Europe is known anything equal or similar to our *salt de plens*" ([1968, 1971]1994, 50). The Plens were thus a kind of objective correlative of *berguedanisme*. While Armengou himself seems to have stood back a little from the "infernal orgy of devils full of fire"—he does acknowledge

Figure 9. The royal visit in 1976: Berga's eagle below the eagle of the Falange. Photo by Luigi, Berga.

Figure 10. Josep Tarradellas, president-in-exile of the Catalan government, seen as a *guita*. Cartoon by Joan J. Guillén, from the newspaper *Tele/eXprès* (Barcelona), June 1977.

them as an astonishing creation of the medieval imaginary (114)—young Berguedans hurried to put *berguedanisme* into performance.

The Plens were an opportunity for popular participation unique in the Patum. The Ball de l'Àliga allows only three men to participate: all have to be very strong and good dancers. Every other *comparsa* requires either strength or a minimum of grace, or is simply limited in number. The Plens are the one *comparsa* divided into dressers, the experts; and those who *salt*, who have only to let themselves be led. Anyone could do it, and the anonymity of thick costume and mask encouraged many to try. The Salt de Plens became the point of entry into the Patum for women, whose participation had always been clandestine and anecdotal, and for the upper classes, beginning with two Berguedan doctors. The *plens* increased in numbers from sixteen on extraordinary occasions in the 1950s, to about forty in the later 1960s (100), to sixty, seventy, eighty; some say ninety in the early 1980s. Pep Sobrevias, the present *cap de colla*, declares that no more than seventy *salt* today: it feels like more. In any case, the little *plaça* became jammed with *plens* and with people dancing among them.

Now the *gent de respecte* wanted to be in the *plaça* among the *comparses*, and their numbers were increased by a great influx of outsiders, who saw the Patum, that one of so few surviving festivals of fire and the street, as the last outpost of the Catalan spirit: they came to fire themselves up to resist the regime. Mossèn Armengou had imagined a balanced Patum with room for order and disorder, the completion of the Corpus Mysticum divided by early modern elites:

> Not everything is melody, nor is it riot. It is not all rhythm, nor all swirling of people. Nor is it exactly a spectacle to be attended. It is something more complex. It has moments of a heart-catching primitivism in which one shouts, runs, even whistles, that is to say, everyone who is in the *plaça* does the Patum. Suddenly the thing is transformed, uplifted: everything is symbolism. The shouts have become melody and the racket has become ceremonial rhythm. (18)

But Armengou's Patum was disappearing even as he preached it. The calmer rhythms of *respecte* struggled to be heard against the beating feet of the multitude; symbolism was dissolved in motion. The new Patum was Dionysiac.

8

The New Generation

Quina folga, en nit de glaça	What a release, in night of ice,
Sortir amb noies al carrer	To go out with girls on the street
I darrere la mulassa	And behind the *mulassa*
Córrer pel bosc carboner,	To run through the charcoal forest;
I si el clergue fa ganyotes	And if the clergy grimace,
Cobrir-nos amb les carotes	To cover ourselves with the masks
De pelussa de mesquer	Of musk-deer's pelt

—J. V. Foix, "Balada dels primers mesos de l'any"

WHEN MIXO OF THE GUITA GROSSA, a young peasant in a grimy black smock, challenged the white-haired, white-uniformed Francoist mayor and won, a new generation seemed to have come to power. Armengou had proposed a softening of the patriarchal order, balancing paternal authority with maternal inclusiveness in a synthesis exemplified by the Patum's balance of *balls* and *salts*. Mixo's victory pointed rather to violent overthrow and the definitive triumph of the *coses de foc*. The younger generation, tensed between continuity and rupture, played the part of Oedipus during the transition, confronting the father, embracing the mother so long kept from them, ultimately uncertain about whether to move forward or backward in history and so ever intensifying and prolonging the present.

The Body in the *Plaça*

Part of the Franco regime's general approach to repression of disorder was sexual puritanism. Complete gender segregation was reintroduced in the schools under Franco, and women were once again taught that their destiny was in the home.[1] Prostitution, long an accepted and, under Franco

until 1956 (Caballero 1977, 139–40), a semi-legal institution in Catalonia,
continued to afford men an outlet that forestalled more disruptive forms
of sexual expression (the strategy of contained disorder once again).[2] Women
were forced into good conduct and approved roles—celibacy, marriage, or
prostitution—by the unavailability of contraception. Strict censorship did
what it could to control popular fantasy, and the standard escape for married couples was minimal: they could go for the weekend across the border to Perpignan, a city that surely made a fortune in adult movie houses
in the 1960s and 1970s.

The first visible result of change in Spain after the death of Franco
was the flooding of newsstands with pornographic literature. Liberation
had to begin at the ground level, in repressed individual bodies, before a
new social body could be conceived. In Berga sex education classes were
organized at the Carmelite school. A group of literary young men left
home and set up "the first bachelor flat" in Berga. They called themselves
"The Factory"—a name owing to Berga as well as Warhol—and engaged
in various forms of cultural and social agitation, including the celebration
of the "Days of Sex and Love in the Mountains." I imagine these to have
been in practice a moderately ribald camping trip, but the declaration was
liberating enough.

Sexual resistance was part of political resistance. A Berguedan man
who came of age in the 1970s wrote:

I think that the fact of coming from a dictatorship excited in our generation an
exaggerated desire for liberty, which materialized sometimes simply in doing the
opposite of what we'd been "ordered" to do until then. Since the official "good
conduct" was to be Catholic, faithful, married, and Mass-going, it was vital to become atheo-communist, liberal and permissive, promiscuous, and against priests
and Masses. (Personal communication, 1989)

I would add the insight of Kenneth Burke that "people try to combat alienation by immediacy, such as the senses alone provide" (1984,
218). Still, small-town, respectful Berga was not the ideal environment for
an erotic free-for-all. The Patum was as close as one could get. In everyone's life it had been the first occasion of freedom from family constraints, when the adolescent was allowed to go off alone with a latchkey,
permitting a discreet return in the small hours, and it never lost this savor
of forbidden fruit. Beyond the doors of the house, out in the freedom of
the street was the place to imagine social and sexual relations not ordered
by the father.

For many years women had stayed out of the *plaça* during the Patum: going in was *mal vist* and led to well-known consequences. "When the lights were about to go out before the Plens," remembers an old *patumaire*, "all the men in the *plaça* clustered around the women there. When the lights went out, ui! When I got married, it was right before Corpus. My wife wanted to be in the *plaça* with me. I warned her, but she wouldn't listen. Afterwards, was she mad! You know, one of the men was my best friend. It's just the way things were then." "It was the only place you could ever get next to a woman," said Àngel the bookseller, an adolescent in the 1960s. "That's why we went. Sometimes a lady would turn around and slap me and it wasn't even me who did it." A Berguedan priest insists that an old widow once told him, "I love the Patum. There's always some shameless fellow who gooses you."[3]

In these years under Franco and in the first years of freedom, sexuality was often described as a destructive force, part of the necessary undoing of all that had been done. Gropings in the *plaça* were assaults upon *respecte*, a taking possession of forbidden territory. Women did not take part in this discourse of liberation: they were only the prize of the struggle. Even today in Berga, Carnival license is imagined and preached in metaphors of war and conquest; the sexual liberation of the 1970s did not do much toward freeing women and did not override the dominant popular male understanding of eroticism as phallic aggression. *Fotem un clau!* (Let's drive a nail/fuck) is the refrain of one protest song of the period: the many political and religious objects of aggression enumerated in its verses are all attained through the bodies of women (Stegmann 1979, 93). The discourse has become more metaphorical since the days when the Radical leader Lerroux famously urged the Barcelona mob to "tear off the veils of the novices and elevate them to the category of mothers" (Mitchell 1998, 61), but there is still an identification of freedom with transgression that makes women the victims not only of the ideology of *respecte* but of its overturning.

It is in the Patum alone (apart, one hopes, from private life) that a more creative, nonviolent sexuality was eventually imagined in Berga. The attack on *respecte* seems to have dissipated as the respectable abandoned their isolation. When women began to come down from the balconies in numbers, they were left alone. Increasingly, too, with the growth in participation it became impossible to single out women in the thickness of the crowd. But now there was a different kind of freedom, unknown in a world where other large public assemblies were outlawed. The body

could relax into other bodies, touch others without having to concern itself with who was being touched where by whom. The fear of contamination from foreign bodies, so omnipresent under the Franco regime, was
of necessity abandoned. I have seen some cases of extreme physical reserve in Berguedans brought up to *respecte*, and I can well imagine how
terrifying and liberating the shapeless crowd in the *plaça* must have felt.
Gratification in the new Patum came not from the long-delayed achievement of a forbidden goal but from the very casualness, purposelessness,
and multiplicity of contacts.

Just as the battles of good and evil or *plaça* and balcony gave way by
the end of the Franco period to the mixing of the community in the
plaça, so it became possible to imagine the freedom of the *plaça* not
as transgressive invasion but as the abolition of boundaries. The Patum
became not merely a means of overthrowing and replacing the father-
invader of the motherland: it taught its practitioners to question the patriarchal practice of enclosing territories.

Primordialism

The Berguedans knew the danger of preaching anarchism, and it was not
what most of them were after. They had been through a war, they had
wanted the restoration of order, and they did not wish to open it all up
again. It is partly for this that the world of free erotic incorporation in the
Patum, which one might see as a future utopian project (as Marcuse did,
1962), was relegated to the realm of origins.

I have already talked of the maternal symbolism in the Patum and
will simply point out again the reasons for its increasing presence as reaction to the Franco regime. Living under the burning eye of the Sun of
Justice, shelter in the dark folds of the Madonna's cloak was all the more
inviting; judged by the Father, one sought the mother's uncritical acceptance. The priestly ceremony of the Eucharist divided the community into
worthy and unworthy communicants, but the Mare de Déu was not interested in the politics of her devotees.

The use of feminine symbolism to evoke an ethos of humility and
equality is familiar from radical religious movements such as Franciscan-
ism and Quakerism (Mack 1987), and some echoes of this may be found
in democratic Catalanism. But it is also important in our case to consider
the mother's specificity against the father's abstraction. This is rooted in

biology—maternity, they used to say, is a fact and paternity is a rumor—and in custom: the mother is the caretaker and the father an imposing occasional visitor from the world outside the house. It is embodied in the forms of the sacred as well.

Christ's body, never seen, is equated with the body of the Church, another thing never seen except in the careful construct of the Corpus Christi procession. But the Mare de Déu is very close: you can go see her and touch her in her sanctuary. She is many: in Berga, the Mare de Déu de Queralt as distinct from Solsona's Mare de Déu del Claustre and Olot's Mare de Déu del Tura. For a long time, believers had to speak to God in his own language, Latin. But the Mare de Déu adapted herself to the local vernacular. And, whereas the Trinity is only understood by theologians, anyone can see how the Mother and her child are two bodies in one: they are literally "of the same wood," as you might say metaphorically of two Berguedans. She and Berga are also of the same wood, the pines and beech growing on the mountainside.

Natural community is born of the mother, growing up out of the land and the body. The communities of church and state are born, like Athena, from the head of the father. The father makes community by fiat, looking down from the sky to draw boundaries: here Catholic, here Protestant; here Spain, here France. In thinking of the two kinds of creator-divinity, we can usefully recollect Marta Weigle's reflections on creation and procreation and distinguish the mother goddess' embeddedness in the world from the father god's foreign, otherworldly nature—the *ganz Andere*, as Rudolf Otto defined the holy (Weigle 1989, xi; Otto 1923).

The Mare de Déu de Queralt and the Patum are of Berga alone: longer-lived than any individual and any political formulation, they are the oldest members and spaces of community. They are the first motions, the first memories teaching the community to children. They belong to the time before separation, before the father gives the orders so difficult of accomplishment, before the child goes out to seek its fortune, before the siblings begin to quarrel.

In the local divinities of Berga, the primordial of ontogeny is bound up with the primordial of phyllogeny: the maternal with the primitive. The idea that the Catalan black madonnas are survivals of pre-Christian Mediterranean earth-mother goddesses has gained fairly wide popular acceptance and even spurred a new ecological movement in Catalan Catholicism (Dalmau 1990). The Patum's pre-Christian origins are taken for granted to a certain extent among scholars and to a great extent among Berguedans.

Survivalism is of course not a new paradigm in Catalonia or elsewhere. The medieval church's definition of superstition depended on the notion of folk religious practices as pagan survivals (Schmitt 1983, 15–27). The idea of survival ·was revitalized with late nineteenth-century anthropology and contended in Catalan folklore studies with a more Christian historicist view: although festival *entremesos* were typically classed as medieval, the noted art historian Josep Pijoan discussed the Berguedan Guita and other Catalan tarasca figures in a volume on European prehistoric art (Pijoán 1934, 7–13). Primitivism was often a left-wing response to conservative Catalanist history, with its celebration of the Middle Ages and the rural *casa pairal*.

With the social agitations of the late nineteenth century, the coercions inherent in industrial paternalism's celebration of "nature" and "order" became apparent. Tyrannical fathers began to disturb the Catalan rural novel, which as it overtly celebrated *pairalisme*, covertly examined the emotional damage wreaked on the dominated (McDonogh 1988, 45; Viola 1989). While anarchists denounced "industrial feudalism," poets explored the violence of father-capitalists, set in a mountain landscape at once legendary and contemporary, and prophesied the contrary violence of worker-sons, now at the "emptied breast" of the land their mother (Maragall 1960, 90; Marfany 1974). The child's rage was the focus of the next generation's primitivism: he became the "Young Barbarian" of Alejandro Lerroux's Radical Party. The first third of the twentieth century, a time of terrorism, strikes, and uprisings on the part of Barcelona's working class and of repression and instability on the part of government, was also the time of the avant-garde agitations of Cubism and Surrealism.[4] With the rise of international modernism in Barcelona, a primitivism imagined not of the mountains but of Africa spoke to the savagery of contemporary class and gender relations.[5] This second Catalan primitivism is exemplified by Picasso's *Les demoiselles d'Avignon* of 1907, which envisions the prostitutes of Barcelona's Carrer d'Avinyó as fierce African masks.[6]

The Barcelonan poet J. V. Foix, a friend of Dalí and Miró, invoked the modernist primitive to write of social upheavals. While his initial references were avant-garde and cosmopolitan, his later poems returned to the Pyrenees of his ancestors to find the primordial energies from which Catalonia would have to be reborn. After 1939 this voyage of rediscovery gained in urgency, in his poetry as in Catalonia at large. I have taken this chapter's epigraph from the largely untranslatable Foix because he captures, like no other writer, the double focus of Catalan primitivism as it was also felt in the late Francoist Patum: a lost whole recalled with longing and a violent upsurge of something kept down by force.

Primitivism lost much of its ambivalence under the Franco regime. Then, when "order" was only too firmly established, the fear of the primitive was overcome by the desire for it; then it was not the incursion of the other, but the realization of the self. *D'un roig encès voldria el món/I dir les coses tal com són* wrote the protest singer Raimon in 1969 in a tribute to Miró's primary colors: "I would like the world a burning red/And to tell things the way they are" (Stegmann 1979, 97). The blank and rigid envelope of the Francoist body contained a self beating for freedom; the empty ceremony of the everyday spurred a longing for authentic, unformed expression. The vivid memory of fratricide and betrayal filled all factions with a yearning back to innocent community. But what Golden Age could be restored? History was all tainted. The roots of the Civil War were in the divisions of the Second Republic—no, in the never resolved questions of the Carlist Wars—no, in the loss of Catalan liberties in 1714— no, in the structures of feudalism—in short, recorded history offered no instance of unproblematic community. But memory seemed to, and evolutionary anthropology suggested a historical correlate to autobiographical nostalgias. Berguedans knew that their mountains were inhabited long before the Romans; many had seen the bones in the Cova de Can Maurí. There, among the primitive Berguedans, the Patum must have taken shape.

Catalan scholars put forth the survivalist theory in the 1970s. Xavier Fàbregas, the great historian of the Catalan theater, looked to festival traditions as a source for its revitalization, producing many important books on the folk culture of "ancestral Catalonia" (e.g. 1979, 1983; Fàbregas and Barceló 1976). For him, the forms of traditional expression attest to a persistent national identity, revitalized in performance. The renewing and destroying power of fire was his preferred image. Pre-Christian solstice rituals were the source he claimed for Christmas and Corpus Christi-Sant Joan, the two central Catalan festival seasons. Needless to say, the Patum was one of his prime examples.

A central Catalan with Berguedan connections and a student of the sociology of religion at the Sorbonne, Jaume Farràs i Farràs articulated the "ethnological" Patum in his 1979 dissertation and the general-audience book in Catalan that came out in 1986, with a second edition in 1992. He spoke of the Christianization of antique agrarian rituals as the origin of the festival, and he was the first to say as a scholar something long obvious to *patumaires*, that the Patum's ritual efficacy was enabled by wine. Only a few years after Mossèn Armengou had died, lamenting the decline of the Patum into drunken, thoughtless hedonism, Farràs wrote:

On the contrary, we are fully convinced that the day the Patum definitively loses this drunkenness, this excess, and this orgiastic character, the community of Berguedans will fall into ruins because it will have lost its soul, because it will have no more vital and sacred energy to circulate. (1979, 270)

He wrote too of the crowding as producing "compenetration" of the community (304), and of the centrality of physical participation to the event. Going beyond Armengou, he spoke of ritual rather than spectacle, action rather than symbolism. This sensitivity to the Patum in performance kept him from drawing the logical conclusion of his own documentary researches as to the relatively late origins of the Patum. The Patum *felt* primitive.

Just as Armengou and the public for which he spoke celebrated the eagle, the younger nationalists, among whom Fàbregas and Farràs moved, celebrated the Plens. "The Patum would be just another traditional festival if it weren't for the Salt de Plens," the future mayor Agustí Ferrer told one of the many Spanish and Catalan reporters who came to see what the fuss was about (Obiach 1987, 50). In my own initial focus on *plaça* and balcony, *guita* and giants, I failed to see the Plens' centrality, but was soon corrected. Lluís Cuadra told me, "You've written about two ways of doing the Patum. There are three. Down at the bottom of everything where they dress them. It's a ceremonial, a rite . . . it's the most primitive thing of all. People who see that hallucinate."

In fact, I'd thought of the stable under City Hall as a backstage space, mere preparation for the *plaça*. It was only after people's accounts of doing the *salt* and my own friendship with the dressers that I realized that the descent was the focus of the "initiation" ritual. It is so recent, the descent and the dressing in secret, but it feels like "the most primitive thing of all." Fàbregas caught the double time of the Plens: "one is conscious of attending a *happening*[7] which has emerged straight from prehistory" (Fàbregas and Barceló 1976, 153). His theatrical instinct catches the contemporaneity; his ideology demands the survivalist explanation. "The

Plens," he declares, "are assuredly the oldest personages of all the throng which inhabit the Patum" (Fàbregas 1979, 255), and he speculates that they are wild men incompletely Christianized into devils, the only Catalan devils to remain thus half-transformed and so "the prehominids of the devil, the Australopitheci of hell" (78).

I think it happened the other way around: the wild man of today is a repaganization of the devils. The wild man appears, named as such, in many medieval Catalan festivals, usually of an aristocratic nature; he seems more erudite than popular. The early Patum commentaries never mention *homens selvatges,* and the Plens did not exist as a quasi-separate entity until the late nineteenth century. Although the graphic evidence is not conclusive, it is possible that the enfolding green of the *vidalba* around the head of the *ple* is a twentieth-century innovation. In short, while I cannot answer for prehistory, the contemporary Plens are just that: contemporary. Their rise or, if you prefer, their resurgence from the dark places of Berguedan memory accompanies the rise of wine, of noise, of motion, of all the techniques of incorporation called in to put Berga back together again.

Primordialism in the Patum was not simply the triumph of disorder and opposition: it was an invocation of a time before order had divided the community. As Torgovnick writes of modernist primitivism, it is born out of a "yearning for the dissolution of hierarchies and of the binary categories so deeply embedded in Western thought and culture" (1990, 253). Berga's own binarism of *respecte* and the *popular* was not to be abolished by a victory of either term: it could only be shaken off by delving deeper. It was no good to declare a Carlist Patum when a liberal one would replace it a year later;, no use to have a Republican Patum when a Francoist Patum would so soon cancel it out. But on the chaos that preceded order no power could inscribe itself.

If primordialism abolished the boundaries within Berga, it did not abolish the boundaries around it. Primordialism is part of *berguedanisme* and is invoked in all sorts of folk explanations of the local character. Josep Carreras, an archaeologist and one of the most vigorous defenders of Berguedan uniqueness, likes to cite Livy's reference to the Bergistani—a Pyrenean tribe presumed to be Berguedan ancestors—as "a ferocious people."[8] Ramon Vilardaga, self-proclaimed graduate of the "University of Pedret,"[9] insists that the Berguedans are not like other Catalans: hardworking, parsimonious, serious. He suggests that the Bergistani were related to the Basques, stereotyped in Berga as fellow primitives: hard drinkers, free spenders, and ferocious celebrators whose diversions include throwing large stones at each other.

The language of anthropological primitivism is increasingly heard, both positively and negatively, in Berga's self-image today. "We're primitive, you know," they say to me with a grin. "This is a *ritus*." By this word, they mean the sort of thing they imagine to be done in Africa. Africa has been invoked rather often in relation to Berguedan festivals. A story is told of a Carnival in the 1920s during which the mayor was being serenaded by a group of drunken citizens. *Això sembla l'Africa!* (This is just like Africa!), he cried and, in one version, is reported to have thrown an old wardrobe out of the window to get rid of the unwelcome visitors. Nowadays Africa is startlingly represented at Cal Negre, the bar that has had that nickname for at least a hundred years, perhaps for the smoky walls, perhaps because in Berga everything old and good is black. But in the 1990 redecoration of the bar—which is gaining an increasingly younger clientele—the owners decided to make Negre mean Negro. The new logo of the bar, reproduced on its outside sign, its advertisements, and inside the bar, is a grinning cannibal with thick white lips. "Cal Racista," one American visitor rechristened the bar, but until the 1990s the African was almost as remote a figure in contemporary Berga as the Turk in the seventeenth century. The logo is merely humorous to the majority of Berguedans, and on a deeper level it represents an invitation: here is a space of festival, not control—come here and be primitive.

My presence has foregrounded their revived ambivalence. Now that there is no Franco to protest, the primitive has ceased once more to be an unmixed virtue, and the Berguedans invoke it to puzzle out their provincialism in relation to Barcelona. "You're anthropological!" Ramon Felipó teases any friend who says something unusually Berguedan. Benigne writes me the news and concludes, "All Berga is an immense doctoral thesis." "Look, our *animalades* are famous all over the world!" says one Berguedan to another. "We've even got anthropologists studying us!" The Manresa newspaper noted my presence and that of a group of foreign students in the summer of 1990: "What is Berga," they write, "some kind of Indian reservation?" The *reserva d'indis* is a rueful metaphor in Berga and Catalonia as well for the paradoxes of a "persistent people" (Spicer 1971).

The Purifying Fire

The perception of the Patum fire as a survival of primitive rituals has not destroyed its infernal or diabolic character. This was part of the conservative Catholic allegory: the Plens represented the fires of hell. But hellfire was transvalued and its affect changed under Francoism, when everyone was obliged to live in a simulacrum of heaven. "We like to live in hell," said Ramon Vilardaga to me one day in 1989. "Heaven"—he waved his hand up to the Carrer Pinsania, a neighborhood of good Catholics perched above the city toward Queralt—"is nothing but praying and . . . All the interesting people go to hell." A few weeks later I heard a ten-year old boy say the same thing, as if repeating something he'd heard from an adult: "It's better to be in hell, because heaven is just priests and rules, but hell is where they have all the wine and the women."[10] "Fire and vice!" said Agustí of the Guita Xica, teasing Massana the *geganter* one morning at La Barana. "The Patum is fire, *mam*, and vice."

They wanted to be in hell. A teacher born in 1950, the same man who spoke of the necessity of doing the opposite of what was ordered, wrote of the feeling of the Patum of late Francoism:

The Patum transformed itself into one of the few tribal, warlike, frenetic, primitive, and heartening dances that remain in Europe. The ecstasy of abandonment to the night and the fire of the plens . . . the exaltation of hell and being an outlaw (the law of the inquisitorial church and the humiliating dictator), the perception of absolute freedom in the pain of the fire and the conquest of fear . . . would be the culminating moment. (Personal communication)

As for medieval Christians, the forces of hell for Berguedans were identified with the older gods. When the law was an imposition, to be outside the law was to precede the law. But they were not such would-be "pagans" as to renounce the idea of law altogether, and it is important to note the mention of pain and fear in this passage. There is danger in the Plens, after all; and if burns and sprains do not seem like much, we must also consider the understanding of Patum participation as resistance: to defy the regime, even symbolically, took courage.

The *fuets* are not only release, but punishment and purgation. "This is the purifying fire we all have to suffer," said Agustí after the Guita chased me around the Carrer Pietat at my first Patum, and that phrase,

el foc purificador, is much-repeated. Why should the defeated Berguedans seek redemption in suffering? Was it not the regime that deserved
punishment?

But the invader from without was really an enemy within. The Civil
War was fratricidal and local, not a united Catalan resistance to foreign
domination. The structures of *respecte* and repression existed long before
Franco came. And afterward, who had not "raised the arm" in pursuit of
his own well-being? The corruption was in ourselves, to be burned out of
us. As Mossèn Armengou said, the recovery of Catalonia had to begin
with "the reconquest of oneself" ([1958]1996, 198).

How strange it had been, after all, to do a *salt de plens* in January
1940 to celebrate the Liberation—that is, the Defeat; how strange must
have been the Patum in 1939. There had been no Patum since 1936, and in
a way it was a return to normalcy. But after so much explosion with anger,
did the Berguedans want to explode with joy? It was surely a cathartic
moment when the *fuets* mimicked the shots and shells of battle, the shots
of execution frequent and feared by many in 1939. The conjunction of Patum and war had happened before in 1873, during the third Carlist war;
Berga being then held by liberals, the Patum was done in the *plaça* while
Carlists occupied the castle, and gunshots from snipers rang over the
fuets, if we are to believe Sansalvador (1916, 118–19). Here was one way to
make light of fears, to triumph over the gunfire by turning it into harmless *pets*.[11] The Franco regime stood, finally, by the threat of force. In the
Patum, both the resistance and the violent response were played out
mimetically. Is it possible that the experience of the Patum gave young
Catalans the courage to mount the mass demonstrations of the 1970s, to
endure the beatings of the police?

The Patum in Catalanist Performance

The Patum's impact certainly moved beyond the Plaça Sant Pere during the
period. Its repetitive, rhythmic tunes gave energy and crowd appeal to the
Catalan rock music formed in the 1970s, most famously in an instrumental suite by the band Elèctrica Dharma.[12] In the theater, a new generation
of critics and generations saw the Patum not only as a testament to Catalan identity but as a bridge to the European avant-garde. It was street
theater—and being nonverbal, it gave the Catalan theater a model that
could both evade language choice in the local context and move out

easily to international audiences. Hermann Bonnín, like Xavier Fàbregas a leading figure in the Catalan theatrical revival, wrote an account of the Patum for *La Vanguardia* in 1973, comparing it to the experiments of Artaud. The Patum had never been seen in such company as this:

The new paratheatrical forms of participation—*"happening,"* intermedia, *"events,"* *"environment,"* etc.—are an unequivocal symptom of a revalorization of the spontaneity of the festival that has its philosophical roots in the thought of Nietzsche. (Bonnín 1973)

Soon the Patum furnished the model for one of the most successful performances of the company Els Comediants. *Dimonis* (Devils), performed in an open space, was premiered for Carnival in Venice in 1981, and has since been performed in Avignon, Madrid, Mexico City, and Chicago, with a revisiting in the closing ceremonies of the Barcelona Olympics in 1992. From their beginnings in 1971, Els Comediants sought to recover the participatory energy of Catalan popular festivals, and all their productions have incorporated *entremesos* of giants, dwarfs and even "guites." The Patum is one of four or five festivals they cite as prototypes; it certainly showed them what might be done with a crowd.[13]

Music and theater were only the most formalized of the many performative appropriations of the Patum in the period. At the end of the Franco regime, activists struggling for the restoration of democracy and Catalan autonomy faced the task of creating practical consensus among individuals of widely divergent backgrounds and ideological orientations. To mobilize the general population, they resorted to nonverbal means of collective organization, invoking the lowest common denominator of the body repressed by dictatorship. As we've seen, the liberation of the body was understood as both the precondition of more institutional freedoms and the necessary preparation for demanding them. The Patum offered a ready-made mechanism for this liberation and the subsequent transformation of individuals into members of a collectivity; its evident antiquity and autochthony helped to label that collectivity in a way that naturalized rather than imposed Catalonia.

Mossèn Armengou's *Berguedanisme* was writ large in the strategies of the activists, the rank and file of whom had grown up in the small cities that had never lost touch with Catalan traditional culture. This was their raw material in creating myriad cultural and political initiatives to restore Catalonia to nationhood. Nationhood, for them, was realized in collective

performance, and *catalanitat* was something assimilated through practice, the embodied memory of performing Catalonia.

Rhythm outweighed discourse as a tool of mass mobilization during
the Transition. The reasons are not far to seek. The need for deniability
under censorship is the most obvious. But more broadly, the long-standing
imposition of a Spanish-language public transcript (Scott 1990), in which
even one's own name on the national identity card was estranged from
everyday usage, had contributed to a general alienation of language. It
was not simply that Castilian was imposed and one could recover authentic
sign-signifier relations by recovering Catalan. After a hundred years of competing hegemonic projects with their attendant sociolinguistic complexities,
all language use was partial and contingent; any language was inflected
toward worldmaking, poised toward a desired future rather than transpar-
ently expressing any aspect of the present. Few people in Catalonia succeeded in inhabiting a single linguistic world, or escaping self-consciousness.

If, then, language could not articulate a nonexistent coherent self,
still less could it be used to articulate the fragments of Catalan society into
a collectivity. Too many efforts had been made to contain the empirical
inhabitants of Catalonia inside the imagined community of one or another of those discourses. Those histories of imposition lived inside each
language and discredited each project.

In the twentieth century, a common reaction to the propaganda of
war or totalitarian regimes, and even to too triumphalist a master narrative, has been the search for a virgin language, a clean slate of pure reference. For Catalonia, semiotic cleansing was not a viable option. There was
no strong external pressure or internal consensus for the wholesale rejection of the previous regime. More importantly, there was a living memory
of the divisions of the Second Spanish Republic, when every aspect of
everyday life was politicized and every utterance declared an ideological
stance. The refrain of Raimon's song to Miró, "I'd like the world a burning red/And to say things as they are" bore the memory of that time—
intentionally or not—in a period that was becoming just as intensely
politicized. The dedication to the painter and the conditional tense might
suggest that primary colors can only safely be realized in the realm of art:
a virgin language can only grow on scorched earth.

They say that three Catalans on a desert island immediately organize
two political parties and a dissident faction. This was no less true of the
clandestine political organizations of the 1970s than of the openly frag-
mented left of the 1930s.[14] Activists were well aware that the same conclu-

sion threatened: internecine struggles would allow the triumph of the outsiders. Scholars have noted the virtual absence of Republican reference in the political rhetoric of the Transition in favor of earlier historical symbols for a purely Catalanist audience (Pi-Sunyer 1985) and abstractions as free as possible of any historical referent for the general public: reconciliation, a new beginning, democracy, *convivència* (Edles 1998). The Assemblea de Catalunya, an umbrella organization formed to enable collective action among all the factions of Catalan political opinion, limited its explicit agenda to the three items abstract enough to be agreed upon: "Liberty, Amnesty, Statute of Autonomy."

"Amnesty" meant more in this context than just the release of political prisoners. The nonviolent resistance movement Pax Christi described it as "reciprocal forgetting" (Colom i Colom 1977, 19). The regime had to erase its dossiers of suspects, but native Catalans also had to forgive the regime, for the regime was in them: to the propertied classes it had come almost as a relief after the years of civil war and left-wing revolution. Many had actively collaborated with it, more grown up inside it, and almost no one could claim never to have "raised the arm" in the Falangist salute. Discussions of amnesty in the period acknowledged that resentments of the recent past, both Republic and dictatorship, had to be forgotten for Catalans to cooperate in the move to democracy.

"Liberty" also implied something more foundational than freedom of speech or the right to vote. Activists restored a sense of collective agency in the immanence of performance. The organizers of a nonviolent march across Catalonia in the summer of 1976 debated its title for some time: should it be the March of or for Liberty? "Some said . . . that it had to be the March 'of liberty,' because in it we would already be putting liberty into practice, in it we would exercise those rights that are not yet recognized. Others supported the second option, because the March was to help us achieve liberty. Finally we all agreed to give it the title of the 'March of Liberty' because with this march we wanted to empower its exercise right away and from now on" (18). When the Guardia Civil began to interfere, the marchers announced, "They've outlawed walking!" (13), echoing a parable of the regime from a protest song that became an icon of the period:

Siset, que no veus l'estaca	Siset, don't you see the stake
on estem tots lligats?	that we're all tied to?
Si no podem desfer-nos-en	If we can't get rid of it
mai no podrem caminar!	we'll never be able to walk!

> . . . *Si tu t'estires cap per aquí,*   . . . If you pull this way,
> *i jo m'estiro cap per allà,*   and I pull that way,
> *segur que tomba, tomba, tomba,* it's sure to fall, fall, fall,
> *i ens podrem alliberar.*   and we'll be able to free ourselves.
> (Lluís Llach, "L'estaca," 1968; reprinted in Stegmann 1979)

The March of Liberty converted the song to a performative metaphor: one that not only dramatized but achieved its goal in the act itself. Action was liberty.

"The Assembly of Catalonia cannot be put into prison because it is in the street!" proclaimed the slogans. By 1977, the Catalan nation was almost literally in the street. The Independence Day demonstration that preceded the first parliamentary elections since the war brought out one million people, over a sixth of the population and, by some estimates, the largest public assembly in Europe since VE Day (Pi-Sunyer 1985, 113).[15]

The protests had been rehearsed for years under less threatening names: concert, excursion, football game, Patum. The few genres of public assembly permitted by the regime came to bear the full intensity of Catalanist desire for self-expression. Events designed as spectacles became participatory and performative. A Catalan New Song recital, nominally one performer on a podium, became an occasion for the audience to lock arms, sway together, light candles in the darkness, join in the chorus, and fill in the texts that the singer had to omit for fear of the censor. Climbing a mountain to see the view became climbing a mountain to deposit a Catalan flag, preferably situated in a position visible from below and too dangerous to be reached by the Guardia Civil. Cheering in the stands for the Barcelona Football Club became a way to wave flags, sing hymns, and chant slogans, their real referent Catalonia. The Patum, as the traditional festival with the most antistructural content of any tolerated by the regime, attracted huge numbers to dance on the side of darkness and brave the *fuets* that taught them how to face the clubs and rubber bullets of the police. The police, to be sure, understood the political agenda beneath all such events, hindering and harassing them as much as possible (and one advantage of the Patum was that under the paternalist Ajuntament such interference was minimal). But the presence of the waiting police also intensified the collective experience; the confrontation provided an occasion for unleashing the emotions cultivated in such assemblies.

As with the Patum, in all these events the great majority of the symbolism was abstract enough for a political significance to be deniable and for Catholics and Marxists, working class and upper class, native and immigrant to identify with some dimension of the event and participate actively. As with the Patum, the focus was rather on "muscular bonding" (McNeill 1995), encouraged by techniques of incorporation drawing the individual into the community and the community into the individual. Shared among the genres of collective performance (the Patum was both donor and recipient), these techniques included dances, marching patterns, gestures, crowding, sleep deprivation, percussion, songs, chants and more general rhythmic patterns and melodic formulas. Some came from Paris in May 1968, others from the American civil rights and antiwar movements, and others from Cuba and the Soviet Union. Most powerful in inducing general participation were those drawn from Catalan tradition, not simply because of their discursive associations but because long practice had already assimilated them "in the blood."

Take, for example, the simple melodic gesture of a falling minor third, sol-mi. Known to musicologists as the "children's interval," it shapes taunts and singing games in Catalonia as in the United States and elsewhere in Europe. From children's lore it moves into other contexts, as when the weather rhyme

Plou i fa sol,	It's raining and the sun is out,
les bruixes es pentinen.	the witches are combing their hair.
Plou i fa sol,	It's raining and the sun is out,
les bruixes porten dol.	the witches are in mourning.

lends its melody to tavern song:

El senyor Ramon	Mr. Ramon
enganya les criades	wrongs the servant girls
El senyor Ramon	Mr. Ramon
enganya tot el món.	wrongs the whole world.
Les pobres criades,	The poor servant girls
quan ja estan al llit	when they're in bed
Tururut! tururut!	Tururut! tururut!
qui gemega ja ha rebut.	the one who whines is in for it.

The continuing popularity of this tavern song is complex. The men who habitually sing in taverns might be seen as celebrating the transgressive and tricky Senyor Ramon, and that might also be the case for those Catalan males reclaiming their virility in songs such as "Fotem un clau!" But conquered Catalonia under Franco easily saw itself as an abused woman, and "El rossinyol," the lament of a woman married against her will, was another favorite song of the period. "The one who whines is in for it" became the title of an anonymous reportage on police brutality during the Transition (*Qui jamega . . .* 1981). The same melody moved into protest chant, as in:

No volem ser	We don't want to be
una regió d'Espanya,	a region of Spain,
No volem ser	We don't want to be
un país dominat.	a dominated country.
Volem volem volem	We want we want we want
volem independència,	we want independence,
Volem volem volem	We want we want we want
Països Catalans.	the Catalan Countries.[16]

The same falling minor third is prominent in many traditional dances, notably many of the giants' tunes in the Patum, and the Patum's music was borrowed for many other local festivals and sung and played at innumerable protest marches. It may still be heard today at the Independence Day demonstrations in Barcelona, for example. As a simple taunt—sol-mi-la-sol-mi—the interval moved from the playground to the festival (e.g. in the chant *la Guita no té tita i si la té la té petita*), the football stadium, and the demonstration. Invoking early memories of unproblematic community, the making of the group through the expulsion of an outsider, the taunt and its related tunes were immediately singable and recognizable, immediately called forth a tapping of the foot. To such rhythms, protesters could march in unison; such melodies induced bystanders to sing along. Coordinating the senses of individuals, they produced consensus (Fernandez 1988a).[17]

Such intense formalization did not just create dialogic resonances to other contexts of consensus, however deep in the body, or simply lend to one public event the momentum of its predecessors. The techniques of incorporation worked to suppress intertextual gaps almost entirely: to induce generic collapse, so that all collective performances felt alike.[18] The Patum, the Barça matches, the concerts, and the Marxa de la Llibertat reinforced each other and were reaffirmed in the intervals between them by the endless singing of mountain excursions and group dinners. From performance to performance, a historical continuity was gained for both the group and the individual, an ongoing bodily disposition now working out to its "natural" consequences of democratic nationalist revolt.

"In the Blood": Identity as Embodied Memory

What made those consequences natural? How could the labels of democracy and Catalonia become attached to performances so carefully avoiding the taint of ideology? As we have seen, explicit linguistic memory was surrendered in the interests of amnesty in the broader sense. Democracy and Catalonia carried extensive resonances of their own: how could they be exempted from the general erasure?

Democracy was much the easier of the two, in part because ideological resistance to it came from relatively small minorities isolated on the extreme left and right. More importantly, it was intuitive to identify democracy with performance. The "natural symbol" of the human body (Douglas [1973]1982) facilitated the elision of the Assemblea's primordial "Liberty" of physical action with more complex liberties of conscience and political action. The mass assembly of bodies in public space without a leader figure or focal image already dramatized equality and cooperation, suggesting a parliamentary assembly.

Catalonia was the more problematic of the two labels. Mossèn Armengou had tried to naturalize it in the same way he did Berga, arguing that language and "mentality" provided a common framework for differences of opinion: "All ideas divide us except for one: the idea of Catalonia . . . Catalonia is the single immaculate name that can make us brothers after the profound divisions occasioned by the Spain of the Civil War . . . Catalonia did not make the war. *Catalonia is the name of reconciliation*" ([1958] 1996, 175). But certainly that was not the Francoist opinion, and, within Catalonia, as Armengou himself admitted, the first Catalanism had failed to confront the social conflicts of the early twentieth century and lapsed into a class-based ideology (182–83). This divisive inheritance proved impossible to shake off completely during the Transition. In the Assemblea's slogan, *Llibertat! Amnistia! Estatut d'Autonomia!*, it took the consensual power of the first two terms and the overarching rhythm of the whole to carry the third. This combination of semantic ambiguity and the techniques of incorporation had to be used to get Catalonia across to a mass audience, and it was helpful even in encouraging the native middle class.

Performances were designed to make Catalonia emerge as a kind of after-effect.

All communities are imagined, but some are more imagined than others. The naturalization typical of the nation-state had already taken place. Catalonia was a linguistic, cultural, social, and economic unity with relatively clear boundaries and reasonable internal homogeneity; it was a territorial political unit sufficiently inscribed in various forms of memory and practice to suggest an identity among its empirical inhabitants. Performance provided a different basis for lived experience to lend reality to imaginings. Catalanist political content rode on the back of present effervescences and remembered childhood solidarities, both concrete, finite, empirical, and thus readily envisioned as a collectivity and credited with substance.

The Patum offered something more, with its inclusive symbolism and its techniques of incorporation. Given the visible antiquity of the festival, Berga's Catalan past was the evident donor of these present resources for community making. It was recognized by scholars of the Transition that (despite the narratives of Berguedan scholars presenting it as unique) the Patum was an ensemble of *entremesos* once found throughout Catalonia, a near-lone survival of what had been a common patrimony. In this sense, the Patum opened the door to everyone's past. And Berguedanism, as inculcated in the Patum, provided a more concrete model for Catalanism. Berga—Pyrenean, medieval, Catalan-speaking—was easily identified with Catalonia as a whole, particularly by Barcelonans with little experience of the hinterland. As Armengou insisted, Berga was deeper than ideology (and for outsiders its seemingly archaic vocabulary suggested no present political labels); Berguedanism was a kind of primordial Catalanism. Most importantly, the Patum's primitivism offered something unique: its slippage between ontogeny and phyllogeny allowed individuals to assume the national past as their own. Furthermore, its techniques of incorporation were powerful enough that a performance first experienced in adulthood could come to feel "in the blood" as if one had participated since infancy. Rebirth in the Plens allowed the individual biography to be encompassed in the space of performance and the primordial to become retroactive.

The Patum was thus an effective means for attaching the label "Catalonia" to a powerful experience of individual liberation and collective strength: for creating, in short, a collective identity. And the Transition came to define collective identity not as state-defined classification or ethnic inheritance but as the traces of performance in embodied memory—the tune that wouldn't get out of one's head.

The activist intellectuals of Berga (and of the other provincial towns that fed the Catalanist parties) had learned a great deal from the popular classes whence many of them came and by whose permission they had entered deep into the *comparses* of the Patum. Like the *populars* of the Bar La Barana, they trusted in the efficacy of ingestion, but now in the metaphoric sense, more generalizable than the literal. They believed that Catalans were made through assimilating "the things of Catalonia." Catalans were not born but made in acts of participation. Afterward, "they feel our traditions," and from then on participation and feeling, collective performance and embodied memory would reinforce each other in a continuous loop. Initial participation would be voluntary, but the traces of performance left in memory were objective and inalienable, becoming more so with each repetition.

In the last chapter, we saw Mossèn Armengou's thoughts on the integrating role of the Patum. The younger generation, informed by *popular* conceptions, spoke more clearly on the means by which this was accomplished. In Berga in late 1985, during an argument over popular representation in the Ajuntament, one of the most conservative of the Convergència councillors made the imprudent declaration, *No pot ser berguedà qui no hagi mamat llet berguedana.* No one can be Berguedan who has not suckled Berguedan milk. Denials and apologies issued at once from City Hall, for the immigrant vote is not insignificant in municipal elections. But the remark was much discussed and debated. And the following February, in the first celebration of Carnival in Berga since the Civil War, La Bauma dels Encantats, a band of young intellectuals engaged in various initiatives to revitalize local culture, placed a papier-mâché cow in the *plaça*. On its side, it advertised Berguedan Milk. Anyone who came up to bend down and drink from its rubber-glove teats was presented by the organizers with a Certificate of Authentic Berguedanism. I need hardly add that the udders were filled with Patum *barreja*.

This is a sufficiently explicit statement of the prevailing generational theory, for Berga or for Catalonia. Its implications for the immigrant population—including, mutatis mutandis, people like me—are evident. A local origin is helpful, for the more milk drunk, the more Berguedan one becomes, but one can make up time and compensate for late arrival by the energy of one's participation. The show of thirst itself grants the right to inclusion. By the same token, the gesture must be made—one has to bend oneself to drink.

Such a definition of identity served multiple purposes. It was good political pedagogy, encouraging activism among native Catalans. It provided a solution to the problem of the immigrant population. And it made Catalan identity at once voluntary and inalienable.

In most of the opinion polls since the death of the dictator, native Catalans have tended to value "feeling Catalan" and participation—linguistic especially—over place of origin as determinants of Catalan identity (Woolard 1989, 39–41; O'Donnell 1995; Vann 1995).[19] The ranking of the two criteria is evident in an observation that was often directed to me and to other outsiders who had decided to submit to the customs of the place: "You are more Catalan than many Catalans," or "more Berguedan than many Berguedans." In the 1970s and 1980s identity evidently had to be understood as active commitment, performative rather than essential. Passive identification was not enough: feeling Catalan in silence would not restore Catalonia. Businessmen and politicians of Catalan origin who had identified with the regime to protect their interests could not be considered true Catalans, because their complicity had facilitated the erosion of the culture. Mossèn Armengou was particularly worried about this "freerider" problem (cf. Hardin 1968): "In the hour of temptation, the Catalan convinces himself that, for the time being, Catalonia can do without him, and that without him Catalanism will manage to pull itself along. This is a self-interested error. We have to convince ourselves that each of us is necessary to the motherland in every one of the twenty-four hours of the day" (Armengou i Feliu [1958]1996, 178). The young activists had a more immediate version of this worry: they needed people not just to restore *catalanitat* to everyday life but to take concrete risks by participating in both demonstrations and clandestine forms of political action. Identity would be conferred as a reward, not granted beforehand.

Immigrants, then, could earn identity as well as the native born. The larger native Catalan population had mixed feelings on the matter of immigrant integration. Against it was a mix of class prejudice, nationalist anxiety, resentment of Franco's attempt to dilute Catalan identity, and some racist feeling. But Catalonia's economy had always drawn immigrants, Catalan nationalism had perforce been imagined from the beginning as inclusive, and the current demographic facts were unavoidable: half the population was immigrant and now rooted in Catalonia. Gunther, Sani, and Shabad note that the Catalanist parties, like those of the Basques, had no choice in the short term but to "formulate their appeals more on the basis of a voluntarist identification with the 'nation' and less on the basis of 'primordial' attachments to language and place of birth" (1988, 315). For the long term, just as Catalanists had had to call upon the primordial to awaken voluntarism in native Catalans, so they hoped to use immigrant voluntarism to instill the primordial. Immigrants, in short, had to be incorporated.

As so often, Mossèn Armengou was representative of middle-class provincial Catalanist opinion and anticipated Convergència orthodoxy in his views on immigration. For the sake of a *convivència* that would protect both Catalonia's integrity and the immigrant's claim to social recognition ([1958]1996, 251), the immigrant must become Catalan. And this was indeed a reward as well as an obligation. Catalonia and the Basques were distinguished from the rest of Spain by their active, hardworking mentality, not having profited by the labor of others, as did Castile first with the American empire and then from its industrial periphery. Still earlier, Castile had surrendered its own local democracy to the Spanish monarchy, still Visigothic in spirit according to Armengou (36–37). Through this historical evolution, the Castilians had acquired a spiritual, passive mentality, and the Catalans a dynamic one. In today's terms, Armengou would define Castilian identity as essentialist and Catalan as performative.

The immigrant could thus become Catalan by performing, and activism per se was already Catalan. Armengou notes that, although the immigrants will have to learn the things of Catalonia bit by bit, "In the end they are Catalan, because the majority of them in coming to Catalonia made an initial act of will: they came disposed to become Catalans. Because many of them thank Catalonia, not just for a standard of living higher than the one they had at their point of origin, but also for a higher conception of man.—'I said to myself: I want to be a man, I'm going to Catalonia,' exact quote—. Because they live and work in Catalonia and because their children will live and work there. They are of our kind" (251).[20]

The line about working and living, as well as the role of the children, lived on in the slogans put out by the Generalitat in the early years of restored autonomy: "Everyone who lives and works in Catalonia is Catalan," "We are Catalan because our children will be," and many others. The slogans elided territoriality and voluntarism, striving for the most inclusive vision of collectivity. But beneath the government's discourse were its own techniques of incorporation designed to bring immigrants into appropriate performance. An intense campaign of cultural Catalanization began. Strong economic and social incentives to use the language supplemented an educational policy that could not afford to be coercive. More to our purpose, the incorporating power of sport, music, and festival was mobilized to induce voluntary participation. Schools and municipal governments in particular devoted considerable resources to collective performance throughout the 1980s, and the festival became an important pedagogical tool in the classroom as well as in the *plaça*.

The Patum reconciled voluntarism and primordiality, performance and essence, in the complex amalgam better defined as desire, that impulse toward incorporation into a whole that seems to have always been there. Such acts of seduction by performance seemed to offer a solution to the democratic challenge of realizing the nation without imposing it by force. But immigrants could see another side to this, for of course a performative notion of identity is more coercive than an essentialist one. If you are given the opportunity to become Catalan, there is considerable pressure on you to do so: Armengou declared those who did not wish to assimilate invaders and enemies (248). In Berga and other parts of the *comarques*, both the opportunity and the rewards were sufficiently present that many immigrants not only assimilated, but became more Catholic than the Pope. This at least is the general perception among Catalanists (though we must remember Berga's neighborhood of Santa Eulàlia): it is frequently remarked that many of the most militant independentists of central Catalonia have Castilian surnames. In Barcelona, residential separation, higher immigrant concentrations, and greater closeness to the centers of Francoist power decreased both the opportunities and the incentives to assimilate. In the same surveys in which native Catalans declare identity voluntarist, immigrant Catalans place more weight on the ascriptive factor of birth (Vann 1995; O'Donnell 1995), which gives them the right not to transform themselves.

Although often resisting pressures to perform as Catalan, immigrants have also taken a hint from the Catalanists as to the potency of performance as a political tool and begun to organize their own. Andalusian festivals in particular sprung up and gained vigor in the 1980s and 1990s: the massive attendance at the Fira Andalusa (or rather Feria de Andalucía!) in Santa Coloma de Gramenet today exceeds any public event in Catalonia. Along with the Andalusian fraternal organizations and civic associations, every political party erects a tent offering flamenco, food, *fino* sherry, and a space for dancing. When I attended in 1995, the Socialist tent had live music and was overflowing. Convergència was gamely playing music on a loudspeaker and attempting to animate its volunteers to dance. Even Esquerra Republicana Catalana was there, with a tent empty of all but policy leaflets and a few disconsolate party militants. Some native Catalans are unperturbed by this move toward an American-style multiculturalism. Others, the political heirs of Armengou and his pupils, fear the consequences of competing performances.

A few veterans of the Transition wonder whether fascist and centralist agendas are not slowly resurfacing beneath the forms of communitas more generally. Sometimes it is not hard to see, as in the skinhead groups who turn up on Independence Day. These are such a minority as to cause little alarm. More disturbing for some were the massive street protests in the summer of 1997 after ETA's kidnapping of a Basque local councillor. In Barcelona as in Madrid, the streets were full, and the universally acknowledged name for the assembly was solidarity against terrorism. But when Raimon, the voice of the Transition in both Barcelona and Madrid, went to sing in Madrid in a concert for peace, the crowd booed him for singing in Catalan. For some of my friends this incident tainted the meaning of the crowds in Barcelona: they felt Spanish centralism creeping back in the guise of democratic solidarity.

This, however, was less unsettling than suspecting their own performances, as the subtle thinkers among them have been obliged to do. The avoidance of interpretation and the inalienability of embodied memory in the Transition's identity strategy made it both effective and unstable.

In June 1989, I went to a barbecue in the mountains of the upper Berguedà at the summer house of two Barcelona professors, both active in the student movements of the 1970s. The guests, from Berga and Barcelona, all belonged to this generation and reminisced at length during the "well-irrigated" meal. When the cognac came out, we began to sing "Blowin' in the Wind," "The Red River Valley," "Auld Lang Syne," a verse or two of "Kumbayah," and "Puff the Magic Dragon," all in Catalan translation. We sang the Patum, we sang traditional ballads in 1970s revival versions, we sang the hymns to the Mare de Déu de Queralt, we sang the "Internationale" and "Avanti Popolo," we sang the hymn of the Barcelona football club, and we sang the anthems of various Catalan-speaking regions and of the Basque Country. Attempting to participate appropriately, I began to sing "Els Segadors," the once-prohibited national anthem that recounts Catalan grievances against Spain and urges uprising. "Not now," whispered the friend next to me, "it's too serious." In fact no one seconded me, so I broke off. Later, at a pause, when the repertoire was beginning to exhaust itself, I turned to the host and said casually, "You know, I've never heard 'Cara al Sol' "—the Falangist anthem, which they all had to sing in school every morning. Instantly, he jumped to his feet, stood erect and lifted his chin, assumed a serious schoolboy face and raised his arm in the Falangist salute. Two of the others, who had been at school with him, joined in. The three sang the anthem with vigor as the rest roared with laughter. The children came down and stood on the stairs with their mouths open. After the second verse, the hostess looked nervously out of the window into the woods: "Hush! The Guardia Civil!" There was an instant of panic on the faces around the table and then everyone remembered and laughed again; but the table broke up, and very soon we went home.

Although they were in a farmhouse well out of earshot of the nearest neighbor in a near-abandoned municipality a half hour's ride from a paved highway, the hostess' joking warning flashed the guests back fifteen years to an urban world of clandestine gatherings and surveillance, followed by public demonstrations that ended with the charge of police on horseback and often clubbings and arrests. For half a second they were ready to get up and run.

But almost at once they remembered where and when they were, and the reference to the Guardia Civil showed them the near-reversal of the historical situation. Now "Cara al Sol," if not actually illegal, was as heavily stigmatized as their Catalan anthems had been twenty years earlier. "Els Segadors," in turn, though now fully legitimate, was still too sacred to play with, awakening violent emotions now better repressed in this moment of political accommodation: it makes explicit what ambiguous performances such as the Patum leave unsaid. This circumstance pointed to a more disturbing reversibility between the songs. They had to acknowledge that "Cara al Sol" was to the enemy what "Els Segadors" was to them. Behind that acknowledgment lay a disturbing question. Is strong collective feeling compatible with the assumption of adult responsibility in democracy?

Still more alarmingly, singing "Cara al Sol" obliged them to recognize the already heterogenous constitution of their own repertoire and to realize that "Puff the Magic Dragon," "The Internationale," and the highly localist hymn to the Madonna of Queralt all felt the same in performance. These are disparate enough, but in fact "Cara al Sol" slid easily into the sequence. To be sure, they sang it with a considerably heavier measure of irony than they had the others. But now, in their maturity, all of the songs remote from any present political necessity, they had sung them all with a bit of a smile. The emotional distance was different in degree but not, perhaps, in kind; so too the nostalgia. Indeed, "Cara al Sol" was deeper in embodied memory than everything but the Patum. They remembered it perfectly: there was no struggling for the words and, above all, not the slightest hesitation in leaping up to assume the posture of their school days and bellow out the too-familiar tune.

Only in retrospect was I struck by the obscenity of hearing three fervent Catalanists, all with an honorable past of struggle against the regime, all currently working for the institutions of autonomous Catalonia, singing the hymn of the enemy. To be sure, it wasn't for the first time. The performance had something of the uncanny quality described by Freud as the effect of something secretly familiar when first exposed to the light.[21] I've never had the courage to ask, but I wonder whether any of the Catalans present felt just a little of the same shock of freedom that struck in 1975 when their silenced history first poured forth in public performances of "Els Segadors."

This barbecue has been recalled among my friends ever since as "the day we sang the 'Cara al Sol,' " assimilated into the repertoire of anecdotes of their more daring days. As all of these stories retreat into memory, their Francoist childhood, their adolescence in the transition, and their early adulthood under democracy take on an indistinct nostalgic haze.

Not every activist in the Transition took so many years to suspect a Fascist political unconscious beneath the surface of Catalanist performance. The Valencian anthropologist Joan Francesc Mira wrote a magazine column in 1976 about a chant commonly heard at Catalan public events: *Boti boti boti! Feixista a qui no boti!* "Jump, jump, jump! It's a fascist who won't jump!" The chant was, of course, accompanied by rhythmic hopping on the part of the crowd—the same as the *saltar* of the Patum—and could go on for quite a long time. Today it is still widely practiced—mostly by teenagers—at public events of all kinds, including the Patum, though the one who does not jump is now called a Spaniard instead of a fascist. Mira complained,

I can understand that folklore has its place in the pre-political, the pre-freedom, the pre-revolution . . . and all that, because folklore is absolutely necessary to humans and because 'there is no revolution without songs,' etc. etc. Fine. But that we all get up and jump under that threat of "jump, jump, jump, it's a fascist who won't jump," is harder for me to swallow . . . It seems to me that this is exactly the opposite of spontaneity, liberty, the festival and the joy of the shout, of solidary protest, or whatever it's supposed to be . . . With all due respect, I do not jump: I'd have the strange sensation of being an imbecile. Or worse: that of participating in a delayed manifestation of the children's "last one in is a rotten egg!" and, there we go, everyone gets up and runs. If it's in this ovinocoactive fashion that we have to express ourselves every time a few hundred or thousand progressives get together, we've really had it.

So, not to keep silent, I ask: would it be so hard for us to shake off the bad habits imposed on us, and the unconscious effects of those bad habits, of psychic underdevelopment, of perpetual adolescence and mental terrorism . . . ? (1987, 82–83)

Alas, you can make yourself Catalan, but you can't unmake yourself Francoist: what's taken into the body stays there. Embodied memory cannot be lost, though you can crowd it round, try to drown it out with stronger messages. But the language of the body does not differentiate: all similar motion provokes similar emotion. Recollected in tranquillity, it produces the same nostalgia.

Freud defined the uncanny as the irruption into consciousness of infantile desires or primitive belief, alike repressed in the course of the civilizing process (1958). As we have seen, the Catalanist performances of the transition and the Patum in particular made a similar identification of individual and collective historical process, invoking both the primitive community and the womb in their cultivation of the "oceanic feeling."

Such a formulation made inevitable a fall into history, into language, into civilization and its discontents. The Catalans of the Transition console themselves for their present squabbles and obstacles with periodic regressions—the Patum, Independence Day, the football game, the concert tour of the protest singer who would really rather sing something else now, the occasional nostalgic lunch in the mountains. The techniques of embodied memory successfully created a collective past as well as immanent engagement in the present: what is not clear is whether they have succeeded in creating a democratic future.

PART IV

THE MASS AND
THE OUTSIDE:
"THE PATUM WILL BE
OURS NO LONGER"

9

Consumption and the Limits of Metaphor

THE POST-FRANCOIST PATUM began as opposition and became an alternative—began as symbol and became sensation. It began by fighting the regime on its own terms and ended in the rejection of those terms. Is this a more radical form of resistance or an abandoning of the struggle? The Berguedans who lived through the Franco period are divided in their evaluations of what has come since. Many would willingly embrace the "primitive" Patum if there were but room in the *plaça* to enjoy it. Others feel the strictures of Mossèn Armengou to be more necessary than ever. For almost everyone the principal point of anxiety is the tension between *berguedanisme* in the blood and the conflicting reality claims of the external world, felt in the presence of outsiders at the festival, the incursion of outsider habits of consumerism and cosmopolitanism, and the economic and political domination of Berga by outsiders. In this last part of the book I explore the local relationship to these increasing external pressures: first, the triumph of consumption as the primary mode of relatedness with the external world, then, the attempts to reproduce and extend the Patum as community reproduction becomes increasingly problematic. In the last chapter, I draw back to look at Berga as a case of local transformation in the transition from the nation-state to the global order.

From Oedipus to Narcissus

Just as the deliberate silences of the Transition deferred the problem of the political and cultural reproduction of Catalonia, so in Berga the Patum has allowed a temporary bracketing of its more urgent problems of economic and demographic reproduction. Within its own intense present, the Patum seems to offer a way out of the Oedipal bind into Marcuse's open libidinal

order in which all can freely mingle (1962). But how does a nongenital order reproduce itself? Time presses on the aging *patumaires*.

To continue to speak of the collective as a family acknowledges as
real both the affective content of paternalism and the authority of the father. It also posits the reality and inescapability of relationship, a filiation
and a history not to be denied—despite the Transition's temporary silencing of memory, which at the local level is thus partially countered. While
the social body metaphor also naturalizes social relations, the family
metaphor places them in history, offering a vocabulary for thinking about
the past and the future.

The Oedipal language is, of course, anything but unique to Catalonia in the 1970s: through the history of modern Europe it has been a
widespread symbolic resource in transitions out of authoritarian regimes
(e.g., Hunt 1992; Paulson 1983). It articulates a double recovery: of virility
(and thus of power over other men) and of access to the denied mother—
to everything from which authority had shut out the disempowered. And,
as Hunt demonstrates in her study of the French Revolution, it forecasts a
reproduction of patriarchy, when the sons will in turn become the fathers.

Despite the moment of *Fotem un clau!*, this option was rejected by
the majority of young Catalans, not least because so many of the activists
were female. There were strong historical reasons as well. As we have
seen, the language of Oedipal revolt in Catalan culture is long established.
Remembering the escalation from the workers' revolts at the turn of the
century through the full-scale social breakdown of the Civil War, the generation of the Transition knew the unanticipated consequences of the
Oedipal metaphor: how male violence too would reproduce itself and the
cycle of repression and revolt grow ever fiercer. The great majority of
Catalans did not want this, and despite much talk of it, there was no revolution, but a peaceful transition to democracy in which both the local and
the larger Spanish family consented to a somewhat more equitable distribution of power in exchange for ongoing *convivència*.[1]

But Berga, in part from the very richness, cohesiveness, and shared
character of its public imagery, got stuck in the Oedipal metaphor. For if
one rejected the repressive father and refused to become the rebel son,
the only term left was the mother, and in the Freudian understanding of
the real world as it is, that meant continued infantilism and social dependency. To escape the cycle of conflict and violence, Berguedans retreated,
in Lacanian terms, from the symbolic order to the imaginary; that is, from
language and all the male-coded attempts to wrest it to monologic mean-

ing to the space before language and thus before differentation. The act of naming, for some Berguedans, has itself become an act of violent alienation from this sheltered space. "The Patum cannot be put into words."

In fact, the language of narcissism has typically played counterpoint to that of Oedipal revolt, as Paulson notes of the French Revolution (1983, 8); certainly it did in the 1968-vintage social theory that came to permeate the Patum of the Transition. In Marcuse's optimistic pages, the integration of "the narcissistic ego with the objective world" could dissolve oppressive differentiations, promoting contemplation and environmental consciousness; the paradox of "withdrawal from reality and oneness with the universe . . . may generate a comprehensive existential order" (147–156; 153). Rejecting the "genital tyranny" characteristic of capitalist domination through the "free eros" of events such as the Patum opened the way to a libidinal reordering of society in which the freedom of play might come to infuse even labor.

Freud, of course, would declare this part of the illusion of omnipotence that, in narcissism, coexists with the reality of total dependence. Adult narcissism dresses itself, as in the Patum, in the language of the infant's "oceanic feeling," but it is in reality an unhealthy withdrawal of libido from the external world in response to frustration. The realm of play and symbol furnish substitutes for the lost sense of wholeness (Adams 1995, 80), and religion especially plays this role: the animism of which we have spoken in Chapter 4 as fostering precisely the environmental consciousness Marcuse anticipates, is for Freud the first step out of narcissism into the real world—but at the price of delusion regarding the latter (Freud [1912–13]1946). Freud's ambivalence about symbolic activity is shared by the Berguedans, who increasingly cannot see the Patum as civilization-building, merely as compensation for impending loss. Freud says that to "cease to be a child and become a member of the social community" is to accept genital sexuality and to find a new love object (1966, 337). And according to the "realism" preached by elites since the Transition, both Catalanist politics and the Spanish economy must likewise acknowledge the end of history, the only game in town, the master narrative. But if adulthood means either the feminine acceptance of what the outside world forces on you or the masculine exercise of power over others (a role hardly available to the undercapitalized Berguedans), and if in either case the new love object is unlikely to reciprocate, then there is something to be said for regression and polymorphous perversity.

Doubly trapped in metaphors that offer no future and in material circumstances that increasingly break with the past, Berguedans feel the loss of the metonymic or indexical links that for so long made the Patum "good to think with" (Lévi-Strauss 1962). In particular, the connections that related the Patum to the world of work are dissolving. But a new and more problematic set of connections is in fact emerging, and it defines precisely what many deem the unsustainable character of the present. The narcissistic bent of the contemporary Patum coincides with a shift in the defining character of everyday life in Berga from production to consumption.

Neither shift happened overnight, of course: consumption is the underside of productive capitalism just as narcissism is of Oedipal conflict, and in that sense it makes sense to situate this dynamic as taking off in the Berguedà in the late nineteenth century. But consumption became the primary term first as a result of the opening of the Franco regime in the late 1950s, then as Berga's traditional industries collapsed in the 1970s. When local cultural expression was severely constrained, and political action was still out of the question, foreign goods and entertainments provided the most important avenue of escape from the claustrophobic Francoist "family." The economic expansion of the 1960s encouraged Catalans to develop consumerist habits, giving some hope of the eventual convergence of desire and possibility. But the oil crisis and increasing international competition crushed this hope for Berguedans. In the 1970s almost all the textile factories closed and the mines began their long decline amid intense labor conflict. While all of Spain was waiting for Franco to die in October and November 1975, Berga was occupied with a different death: that of twenty-seven miners in an accident attributed to the negligence of the outsider owners (Mau Branco 2000; Oliver 2000, 86–89). To local understandings, then, the outside world offered a vision of fulfillment only to steal away the means of attaining it. The frustrations of the economic transition created a new dependence on the political transition— quite literally in that the new democratic administrations provided the best available jobs—but the common sayings "to suckle the giantess" and "let the giantess pay for it" recognize the fragility of this faith.

The Loss of Differentiation

Berguedan consumerism is understood as problematic in that it distracts the community from the vital challenges of production and reproduction.

Even more seriously, it fosters a slippage between communion and consumption, putting in jeopardy the very substance of the community to be reproduced. Narcissism surrenders the boundaries between world and self: it is eager to incorporate the world into the self (cf. Kilgour 1990) and in its desire to regain the "oceanic feeling" does not attend to the details of the surround. This loss of differentiation was cultivated by the Catalans of the Transition and by Berguedans over the longer term as a necessary risk for the achievement of *convivència*. Today, however, it exceeds the community boundary, and Berguedans are forced to recall that infantile omnipotence is a delusion masking real dependence.

In this context, another language of the social body has taken on prominence in Berga. Looking at the ectoplasmic flow of the crowd in the streets, Berguedans speak of this corporeal mass in relation to the "massification" of the event. Despite the fact that the increase in festival attendance coincided with the democratic mobilization, their use of the word is not left-wing optimism, celebrating the revolutionary strength of the masses: rather, it derives from the language of mass production and the Frankfurt School tradition—circulating among Berguedan intellectuals in the wake of 1968—that criticized the pacification of the working class through entertainment and its resultant alienation from its own authentic cultural sources (cf. Williams 1983, 193–37).[2] The discourse of massification undoubtedly expresses covert anxiety over the Fascist political unconscious inherent in large public events (cf. Chapter 8).[3] But it also responds to more strictly economic and, thus, simply existential concerns about the threats posed by outsiders to the community.

Berguedan protests against the Patum's massification began in earlier elite denunciations of the vulgarization of the event—the violation of boundaries laying it open to corruption by loss of the *fet diferencial*. Turn-of-the century writers such as Sansalvador (1916) and Huch i Guixer (1955), promoting the Patum as an allegory of the Catalan racial spirit, criticized its adulteration by urban and Spanish amusements, especially injurious to the young: here the consumption metaphor was already in full operation. In the 1940s and 1950s the young Falangistas of Berga condemned aspects of Patum celebration out of keeping with the festival's "religious and traditional" character. But a more persuasive jeremiad came from Mossèn Armengou: the "Open Letter from the Old Giantess" of 1953, published in the Catholic and quietly Catalanist local monthly *Queralt*.

I am like a mother full of experience, and I have the right to scold you . . . I cannot say that I am flesh of your flesh and blood of your blood, but I tell you that you are cardboard of my cardboard and wood of my wood. I suspect that you are a generation of cardboard and wood (56).

In the name of her "corporation," the giantess rebukes the Berguedans for abandoning the Patum and Queralt—the native spirituality of Berga—for ephemeral material attractions from outside.

It seems as if you are sorry to be a city. Don't worry: soon you won't be. You've undertaken the sure road to denaturalization. Soon you will be a big vulgar suburb, but without physiognomy. You will be strangers to your ex-fatherland . . .
   We are History and you are anecdote. (56)

What dreadful betrayal were the Berguedans committing? This was before the era of mass drunkenness. But it was a time when the week of Corpus was filled up, like a typical summer *festa major*, with cinema, football matches, dance bands, and visiting "folkloric spectacles" of "regional dances." "You have disfigured our Corpus and converted it to a *festa menor* where all the trivialities fit, but we do not," complained the giantess. Corpus was not leisure time, but sacred time. All the world could excel Berga in such amusements, but "no one in the world except you knows how to do the Patum." They were sacrificing the unique for the general.
   Armengou's other major grievance was that in this period the giants, and sometimes the entire Patum, were occasionally transported to other towns for competitions of giants and festivals, often of a specifically Francoist cast. The practice of traveling the Patum was not in fact an innovation of the Franco period: the Republican administration had done it as often as its finances allowed, but Armengou saw it as putting the giants in the service of the regime. More deeply, however, it was equating the Patum, once again, with *una vulgar festa major qualsevol* (any vulgar *festa major*), as the much-repeated phrase goes, and with the traffic in leisure. The Giantess denounced the petty commercial spirit threatening to subjugate the Corpus Mysticum of Berga:

You've taken us for a fair attraction and, like gypsies with a dancing bear, you've dragged us out of Berga to show off your dishonor, which transpires through the holes in our ragged clothes. We are dignity, and were born to celebrate liberty, but you, slaves of other slaves, plucked eagles, have wanted to decorate the tails of other birds with your own plumes.

Peddlers in the insipid folkloristic commerce which has become the fashion, you've carried us all over the place to beauty contests, us who are most singular, to be one of many in the servile *comparseria* of non-Berguedan festivals. You have taken from us the pride of being able to say, "The giants of Berga—like all of the Patum—never leave home." If you follow on this path, you'll soon be using my daughter [i.e., the Black Giantess] to advertise cosmetics . . . (57)

Degradation comes from turning the sacred of the festival into the leisure of the fair and from introducing the Patum to circuits of festival exchange, reducing it to one commodity in competition with others. Armengou's vigorous campaign convinced Noguera's administration to pass a resolution never again to move the Patum out of Berga and made the practice out of the question for the democratic Ajuntaments after 1979. It also "cleansed" the Patum itself of many accretions. The fair attractions are still there to occupy the children and visitors—and adult Berguedans themselves, if truth be told, politicians of all stripes being notorious for altercations on the fairground—but the cinema, the dance tent, the folk dance troupes, and the football game are all gone. Citizen efforts in the 1980s and 1990s to create a sort of arts festival, giving the visitors something to do besides drink and making more room for Berguedans in the *plaça* itself, met with the Armengou-derived insistence that this would trivialize the Patum by acknowledging it as one tourist attraction among many.

Armengou understood Patum drinking as a part of the vulgarization; as he grew older and the Patum wilder he increasingly criticized the "savagery, every year in crescendo" (1964, 5) of the festival. He did not recognize the full meaning of young Berguedans' eager embrace of the primitive and could only see it as the destruction of *respecte*:

It is impossible that the majority of the youth of today, dis-educated by all kinds of advertising techniques and by easy and degrading spectacle, nonchalant, without problems or ideals; whom we have obstinately taught not to think, should look with respect upon the things of their ancestors; should look upon them with the respect with which we looked upon them. (5)

Armengou himself had preached participation but had not foreseen the logical conclusion of the denial of spectacle. Opposing *selvatgisme* to *respecte,* he set up the new terms of Berguedan debate: the *popular* is lost between them, just as many Berguedans felt that their own moderate exercise of liberty was being swallowed up in general festival abandon. Writing under Franco, Armengou concluded that nothing could be done to remedy the education of the young Berguedan—*un bàrbar amb batxillerat* (a barbarian with baccalaureat) (5). Rather, the routes of the *passacarrers* should be shortened to contain the disorder. But this was no real solution. How, he asked, do you reconcile a Patum created in a time of a few thousand Berguedans with a population at ten thousand and growing?

The Outsiders: From Patum to *Mam*

Although Armengou felt that Berguedans themselves were endangering the Patum, he conceived of the negative influences as external and increasingly posed the problem of outside people as well as outside amusements. Later in the 1970s, with a still greater increase in numbers, Berguedans tended to project the disorder on the outsiders alone: not without reason, as these were the participants not socialized into the framework of *berguedanisme*.

It is still a great preoccupation. The first thing anyone said to me about the Patum was that the *forasters* had changed it irrevocably, that they did not know how to do it, that they came only to do the *animalades* they wouldn't dare do at home. "Be careful," said one. "They come up here to drug themselves." "Make sure you're with someone!" they said. "Those *forasters*, they see a girl and think that everything is permitted." "If any outsider bothers you, you just come find a *geganter*," said one to me. "We'll take care of him for you." "They lie in wait for us sometimes," said a *guitaire*. "They have broken bottles or sticks and want to pick a fight with *els de la guita*."

Having prepared myself for Berga to transform itself into an urban gangland overnight, I found the reality less dreadful. The crowd was certainly immense and young and not sober, but harmless enough. On the Saturday night of 1990, going home early because I was unwell, I saw more of the Patum of the outsiders. Far away from the *passacarrers*, all along the Carrer Major and especially on the bars and side streets of the Plaça Maragall, the pavement was lined with teenagers, some in solitary stupor, many in happy coupled oblivion, some in groups of boys looking on and making unpleasant remarks as I passed. The pavement was not the sea of effluvia that had been described to me, but smelled of stronger things than gunpowder and *vidalba*.

Nowadays these people do not really bother anyone apart from the cleaning up afterward. The excesses they committed in the 1970s and early 1980s have been largely eliminated today by the discreet use of police and other precautions. Shops protect their doors and windows with heavy metal screens. Bars use only paper cups and sell *barreja*, the fierce Patum drink, in plastic bottles only. In 1989 the Ajuntament added the further refinement that *barreja* should not be chilled, so that drinkers would be induced to quench their thirst with something less potent. Those who come to raise hell are more or less under control. The real problem is the crowding in the *plaça*.

The Patum I described in Part II, in which the techniques of incorporation work upon the individual to bring her into oneness with the crowd, is somewhat idealized: it is a goal not always achieved. Everyone has had the experience, and some people manage it almost every time, but there is also the experience of being drowned in the crowd: struggling to keep your footing, elbow jabs in tender spots, faces looking angrily back at you to see who's pushing, and your own unreasoned wrath rising against your neighbors.

Some Berguedans say the crowd is so bad it has driven them out of the *plaça*, and in the worst years of the late 1970s there was real and general alarm. People quite in favor of the Dionysiac Patum for themselves were concerned enough about the outsiders to inaugurate a "Save the Patum" campaign. In 1978 and 1979 the Catalan-language Barcelona daily *Avui* carried anguished Corpus editorials with headlines such as *Salvem la Patum!* and *Respecteu Berga!* Banners were posted on the entry to the Carrer Major and on the Vall: *Respecteu la Patum. Respecteu Berga* (Respect the Patum. Respect Berga) and *La Patum és més que una festa. Respectem-la* (The Patum is more than a festival. Let's respect it). A "Service of Order" was initiated, with an information booth along the Vall and personnel dispersed through the *plaça* to oversee the smooth unfolding of the Patum. Visitors were given hand programs explaining, in Armengou's words, the significance of each *comparsa* and requesting silence during the Ball de l'Àliga; there was also a full sheet of instructions explaining what to do during the Plens. A loudspeaker from City Hall repeated these instructions before the first *salt*, as still happens today.

The Berguedan Corpus Mysticum was not wholly compatible with the Patum as Catalanist celebration and source of local pride. They could not keep the Patum for themselves and still make it the basis of their claims to consideration in the new Catalonia. Besides, they needed the money brought in. The *forasters* had to be tolerated. The solution was to

educate them: make them Berguedans for a day. Most Berguedans will
dutifully admit that there are many good and serious outsiders who come
to make Patum, not *merder* (mess). Only a minority insist that outsiders,
good or bad, are outsiders and should stay at home. But everyone of a
certain age resents the loss of *la intimitat*: they remember a Patum *de
casa* with room to embrace a friend who crossed their path in the middle
of a *tirabol*. They complain that young Berguedans are no longer learning
the Patum's special gestures because they are surrounded by strangers;
they do not cry *Pega!* (Strike) when the Turks hit the Cavallets; they
chant *Vagos!* after the *tirabol* with an inauthentic melody imported from
the matches of the Barcelona Football Club. Barça matches and independentist demonstrations furnish the Patum with other foreign cries and
gestures. It cannot be wholly avoided: it is the inevitable slow agony of
the Patum, say the most pessimistic. It is just the Patum adapting itself to
the age as it has always done, say others; but they too sometimes fantasize
about sealing off the entries to the town.

Extensification and Intensification

The Patum expanded externally and internally in this period to fill out the
available time. The traditional structure of events could not be changed,
but they became more crammed with Patum. The Ajuntament curtailed
the route of the Wednesday and Saturday night *passacarrers* in 1984 because it took so long to go through the new sections of town, notably
Santa Eulàlia.[4] But the *patumaires* just took longer to go the shorter distance: only when the weather is really bad will the *passacarrers* get back to
the Plaça Sant Pere before two in the morning. After that there is a "Patum of the Drunks" in the *plaça* for those who haven't had enough: a
performance of the full sequence of *salts* without effigies, band, or *fuets*,
only bodies and voices.

On Thursday and Sunday nights the Patum of the *plaça* has gone
from two repetitions at the beginning of the century to three under
Franco to four under democracy. The Plens, central to the Patum of democracy, have multiplied from twelve in the second salt in the 1950s to
sixty, seventy, even eighty or ninety per *salt*: they exceed the comfortable
capacity of the *plaça*. There were once two or three *tirabols* at the end of
each night of Patum. In the period of massification, the two bands began
to compete with each other to play longest and the *geganters* to compete

with the band to see who would give in first. At the climax, probably about the mid-1980s, there were as many as thirty *tirabols*. I think the numbers are declining slightly, but I generally lose count after twenty. The Escola Municipal de Música band has figured out a tactic to finish: they come down from the bandstand to the *plaça* to play the last *tirabols*, three or four at such a tempo that the crowd, not the band, has to beg for mercy.

Even the Patum de Lluïment has acquired a few *tirabols*. The crowd *salt*-ing in the Patum, as I've said, has overflowed its bounds and now affects all the *entremesos*, not just the *coses de foc*. The giants' walk on Wednesday noon is hopped from start to finish by the young. The Patum of order and contemplation is a thing sometimes glimpsed, more often remembered. Now the *plats forts*, the strong dishes, are the whole meal.

The alimentary metaphor is not arbitrary: it ties the Patum of communion to the Patum of consumption. Increasing prosperity after the 1950s, the opening of Spain to modern influences and consumer goods in the 1960s, and the relaxation of religious and social sanctions on leisure behavior in the 1970s allowed Berguedans to pursue their pleasures more freely. Food and drink were perhaps the easiest of attainment.

Somebody once told me that Berguedans have the highest cholesterol and rates of cirrhosis in Catalonia. I haven't verified this, or noticed that other Catalans are any more abstemious, but I passed the remark along to Berguedan friends to see what they would say.

We're peasants and it's peasant food, said one friend. Those breakfasts of wine and sausage and potatoes, they needed all that when they had to work in the fields or in the mine. Now they don't work so hard but they keep eating the food because they're used to it.

Naturally cholesterol is high, said one family, it's an industrial *comarca*. Look at what they eat here, it's all *embotits* (dried sausages), because when the mother works in the factory she doesn't have time to cook. There used to be cooked food shops all up and down the Carrer Major: you went in and bought chickpeas one day, lentils the next, white beans the next, and you had that with sausage cut up in it for your lunch. We used to do it.

It was a professional family telling me this, and the mother had never worked; they themselves were very fond of *embotits*. A miner's son explained instead that people can afford more meat now than they used to. Those big heavy dishes, that's what people like, and they can eat them every day now. That's why they're getting heart attacks.

I drink champagne on Saturday mornings at La Barana, and people bring it whenever they go to someone's house for dinner. A bottle is ordered to go with dessert when a group of friends goes to a restaurant. Birthdays, holidays, or just the weekend is justification enough. "We used to drink it only for Christmas and Corpus," Benigne told me. "Now it's all the time. Before, there was 'the champagne of the poor': they used to drink beer cut with *gaseosa* (sweetened seltzer) out of a *porró* and that was their champagne."

Sidney Mintz, talking about the rise of sugar use in the English-speaking world in relation to the development of industrial capitalism, has defined the "extensification and intensification" of sugar's original prestige uses. As it became cheap and widely available, its use was ritualized in new ways by new users in everyday contexts—it became a "familiar treat." It was simultaneously "intensified" for ceremonial occasions in emulation of the earlier prestige uses, as in the elaborate confections of life-cycle rituals or the eating of sweet condiments with meats on holidays (1985, 122–23).

Something similar has happened with the preferred foods and drinks of the Berguedà, especially as they become markers of local identity. The "specialties" of the *comarca* were defined in a conference of restaurateurs in 1989 and are now advertised rather than taken for granted in local restaurants. One, *escudella de blat de moro escairat*, a thick meat broth with popped corn, has gone from a Christmas Eve dish to, on the one hand, a frequent winter menu item, and, on the other hand, the "Dish of Peace" as named by Miquel Màrquez, the chef of Cal Sala, for its whiteness and purity: he sent jars of it off to Bush, Gorbachev, the Pope, and other world leaders for Christmas of 1989 in a truly Berguedan vision of international communion. *Patates emmascarades*, potatoes mashed with pigs' blood and fat bacon, are served on huge plates at places like Cal Garretà on the artificial lake of Graugés near Avià, and my friends insist on eating mountains of them even when we go in mid-July. Fresh and dried sausages are eaten at any and every meal.

People eat in restaurants more than they used to for pleasure, for sociability, and also for convenience. Single people (a newly populous category) and people living far from their work often breakfast and lunch out every day; families separate and go out on Fridays and Saturdays. Cooking at home has been much simplified by international-style convenience foods, but the old tastes are also regularly indulged, with less labor than in the old days. I don't know about the old cooked food shops, but two elegant ones opened on the Carrer Major in the early 1990s, specializing on the one hand in miscellaneous international dishes and on the other in the "specialties of the *comarca*." Both stores appear to be doing well. On a more popular level, Carme of La Barana spends the summer in the bar's hot kitchen slaving over plain *escudella i carn d'olla*, the paradigmatic Catalan mountain meal of hot broth followed by the boiled meats. "You know," she says, "people want to eat *escudella* even in August, but they won't make it at home, so I have to do it."

Drinking has been equally affected. Breakfasting and lunching out has a residual festive, sociable quality that encourages consumption: people hospitably encourage each other to have a little more wine or a *carajillo*. And the heavier drinking of festivals such as the Patum and Saint John's Eve has been extensified to leisure drinking, particularly among the young. *Anar de copes* (going for glasses), the Barcelona nighttime ritual of mixed drinks in dark modern bars, is now part of a Berguedan weekend.

My guess is that alcoholism is on the rise. In Berga there is a traditional style of alcoholism similar to that described by Jellinek for rural France (1962): the drinkers are usually underemployed single men for whom the bar substitutes for the home and one kind of *mam* for the other. They drink continually rather than heavily, with a cohort rather than alone, and their condition deteriorates over years rather than all at once. They suffer a constant drag of ill health rather than a spectacular collapse and social marginalization rather than total isolation. This kind of alcoholism probably increased with the closing of the mines and the generous early pensions to the miners. But having acquired the other advantages of the modern world, Berga also acquired modern alcoholism: the solitary combative kind associated with ambition and pressure. In the 1980s this increased among intelligent, upwardly mobile people uncomfortable with Berga's small-town pettiness and conservatism. Patum drinkers seek ritual incorporation; the traditional alcoholics extend the strategy into the everyday; but as Bateson points out, the modern type of alcoholic is also striving for wholeness, conceived of in this case as individual: the two halves of the self (1972). This is the alcoholism of *respecte*, as the other is the alcoholism of the *popular*.

The Patum's expansion can also be seen from this perspective. Like the alcohol with which it is associated, it provides a powerful sensation, and this sensation is increasingly sought. As ritual it has intensified: the climactic fusion of the community in *plens* and *tirabols* has both increased in length and expanded backward into the rest of the *entremesos,* has reproduced itself in "Patums of the Drunks" and children's Patums and spontaneous Patums. The Patum that once uplifted now knocks over.

The Patum has also been "extensified." The specialness of the Patum has restricted the use of its elements in other contexts, but the Dionysiac festival model has been carried over. With the relaxation of restrictions on public assembly after 1979, festivals popped up like mushrooms in Catalonia—I use the simile advisedly in a land of obsessive mushroom-hunters. Berga's own festival calendar was in continual expansion through the 1980s: "The Berguedans will throw themselves into the street on any pretext," they observe proudly or ruefully. Throughout Catalonia, ordinary public gatherings, political or civic, are "animated" with giants or traditional music. Discos hold special nights to coincide with celebrated festivals, such as the Sanfermines of Pamplona. Festival-hopping from town to town is a popular activity among rural youth and even among the disdainful Berguedans.[5] Much as they claim to despise any festival that is not the Patum, they visit not only the more interesting festivals of the region—I saw a dedicated dresser of the Plens hurrying off to the bull running in Cardona one September—but also go on vacation to foreign festivals: the Feria de Abril of Seville or the Palio of Siena. Conservative Berguedans are anxious about this propensity, feeling that it threatens the Patum and its unique spirituality, but it appears irreversible.

We always exaggerate the significance of the transitions we live through: as Raymond Williams has observed, the golden age is generally timed to coincide with a speaker's childhood (1973, 12). And anthropological discussions of modernization are particularly likely to divide community history into an enclosed, timeless "before" and an open, historical present, disregarding the continual flux and movement of people and culture in even the most remote mountain valley (Albera 1988). The Berguedans make this same division between "before" and "now," regardless of a highly developed historical consciousness. They know all about the political reshufflings of 1640, 1714, 1808, 1839, 1868, 1898, 1931, 1939, 1975, and so on, and can distinguish the players far better than the average American can explain our Revolutionary War. But what has mattered in their own lives, even more than the dictatorship and its ending, is the *abans* of relatively hermetic, un-self-conscious, and locally controlled tradition and the *ara* of self-conscious consumer choice among a range of cultural options, a mask of freedom that barely conceals increasing powerlessness in an ever-larger world. "The Patum has changed more in the past ten years than in the whole hundred years before it," a *popular* friend told me. Before, they knew who the enemy was, and the things they feared could be projected onto the conqueror, recognized, resisted. Their souls were their own. Now their complicity is apparent: the Berguedan self is not being invaded from without, but undone from within. The phenomenon is familiar elsewhere: although no one would bring them back, the bad old days of the dictatorship have been nostalgically reconstructed as the good old days of authentic selfhood.

Burning Out

On Tuesday, two days before Corpus in 1990, we were sitting in La Barana's dining room eating breakfast, and Carme came in from the bar trying to hold down a broad smile. "Be quiet and listen to me, everyone!" she said. "Two girls just came in here asking for a certain Sola-Sobre-Sobrevias? They heard that because of the Rolling Stones concert on Thursday there weren't enough people to do the Plens."

We burst into roars of laughter. That anybody in Berga would not know the name of Sobrevias, the *cap de colla* of the dressers, was funny enough. But that *patumaires* serious enough to have a *salt de plens* would run off for the sake of a mere Mick Jagger, was unimaginable—unimaginable, at any rate, to these central *patumaires*, the *populars* of La Barana.

But the story reveals genuine Berguedan fear that the younger generation will slight local culture for the attractions of the metropolis and equate the Patum with other Dionysiac leisure activities. As it happened, the *plaça* was indeed less crowded than usual on Thursday night, and it was not only outsiders who stayed away. Some people I knew showed up only for the final *salt*, having driven at breakneck speed up from the Olympic Stadium in Barcelona. A few did not come at all.

The coincidence of the Patum and the Rolling Stones was not soon forgotten. Mikimoto, a popular music video host on Catalan television, showed a montage the next week of the two: the Guita *salt*-ing to "I Can't Get No Satisfaction" and the Plens to "Sympathy for the Devil," if report is to be believed. When I came back in 1991 there was a rumor that the Stones were using footage from the Patum in the video of that concert tour. This was not the first rumor of its kind: once I heard that flashes of the Patum could be seen in a beer commercial on one of the Spanish channels. Those who repeated such stories were divided between resentment and satisfaction, just as in contemplating the Patum's appearance in an American doctoral thesis.

Whereas the symbolic domain of cuisine has recently celebrated the autochthonous (though in practice home-delivered pizza and even Chinese restaurants made considerable inroads in Berga in the 1990s), the domain of music has long served to express Berguedan anxieties about seduction, as another and less voluntary mode by which foreign influences are incorporated in the body social.[6] In the longest of durées, of course, the concern over Mick Jagger echoes thousands of clerical denunciations dating back to *ibi saltatio, ubi diabolus* (Del Giudice 1990) and, more recently, the oft-reiterated nationalist and conservative fears that the "primitive but not barbarous" Patum will be infected by the "cannibal mambo" ("Berga y las fiestas . . ." 1954, 36).

The tensions between localism and the desire to consume and be consumed by the metropolitan were dramatized in the late 1980s and early 1990s by the emergence of Catalan "agrarian rock," which fed on both the booming discotheques of the provinces and the resentments of the unemployed young against Barcelona, Madrid, Europe, and global capital.[7] The musical sources of such groups were international: mostly heavy metal, punk, and ska. In the early years, most bands depended on the lowest common rock denominator: voice, guitars, bass, and percussion; tonic-dominant-tonic progressions; strophic songs with refrains. The lyrics were another thing. With very few exceptions they were in Catalan—limiting the market a priori—and elaborated on the deliberately uncouth and frequently scatological character of band names: translating some examples approximately, The Farts, Heavy Beans, Ex-Lax, Blood Blister, Fucking Disgusting, Goat Soup, and Berga's own The Brays (Els Brams).[8] Full of local references, the songs aggressively criticized the corruption of the Catalan political class, denounced the neglect of the *comarques*, and preached sex, intoxication, and rural revolt.

A prominent overall theme of the lyrics is the aftermath of consumption. While the old critical tradition is maintained in these songs, most prominently in such anthems as Els Pets' "Qui s'ha llufat?" (Who made the stink?), about the ecological contamination of the Tarragona region in the aftermath of Barcelonan political dealing, they do not simply critique the consumption of others but often assume the voice of the one nauseated as a result of consumption. Typical as an allegory of the rural situation is the end of Sau's early hit, "Deprimit" (Depressed):

És molt dur haver de marxar d'una festa quan tot s'ha acabat.
Quan la clau no et vol obrir i l'alcohol et fa sentir . . .
Deprimit.

It's really hard to have to leave a party/festival when everything is
    finished.
When the key doesn't want to open for you and the alcohol makes
    you feel . . .
Depressed.
(http://www.geocities.com/CapitolHill/Senate/2391/deprimit.txt)

A recent song of Els Brams, "Autoodi" (Self-hatred), further expounds
the paradox of consumerism in the *comarques* through the extended
metaphor of anorexia: the incorporation of metropolitan ideals is starving them.

    The agrarian rock groups and their followers represented the most
politically committed of the younger generation in the 1990s. Many dis-
banded at the end of the decade; others, like Els Brams, continue globalizing themselves from below in collaborations with Basque and Central
American musicians. But the scatological imagery is not unique to those
denouncing consumption: it is simply where the dominant metaphor has
carried the younger generation. One of the more notable recent artistic
representations of the Patum is a pair of pamphlets, the *Manual of the Good
Patumaire* (Escudella i Carn d'Olla 1997) and the *Orientation Guide for
Patumaires* (1998), Numbers 1 and 2 in a purported collection, "The
Berguedan Library of Scatological Studies." Published anonymously, they
were composed by a group of Berguedans in their early twenties, spear-
headed by a cartoonist just then starting to work for Barcelona newspapers.

    The *Manual* brilliantly mocks the fervent prose of Berguedan ac-
counts of the Patum for outsiders, as well as the long-dominant graphic
influence of Berga's notable artist, Josep Maria de Martín. But both pamphlets illustrate a phase in which the apparent loss of differentiation between inside and outside is almost complete. The implicitly generational
community of initiates into which the reader is invited inhabits the geography my friends think of as the Patum of the outsiders, with a heavy emphasis on the fair attractions in the Vall and the areas outside of the *plaça*,
variously specified as the Sex Zone, the Vomit Zone, the Latrine Zone,
and so forth (Escudella i Carn d'Olla 1998). The few strictly local references are not to *popular* Berga, but to the Berga of *respecte*, presented as

hopelessly provincial and absurd—the parents by whom one is embarrassed, in fact. Apart from that exclusion, the Patum of the *Manual* is that of the Transition taken to its logical extreme. A good *patumaire* is defined by conduct, not by origin, and the appropriate conduct consists of the stickiest possible engagement with the stuff of the festival: this is not a visual Patum, but one in which the textures of what goes in and out of the body predominate. The confusion of orifices in interpersonal encounters and the reversibility of drink and piss, food and vomit (relabelled as Berga's signature dish, *patates emmascarades*), are recurrent themes repeating the loss of inside-outside differentation at the corporeal level. The differentiation that does reemerge is that of gender, and much of the male aggression characteristic of the late-Francoist Oedipal Patum is restored here. No doubt it is my age as well as my gender, but I find these productions unremittingly grim, the sexual and alcoholic pleasures promised far outweighed by the subsequent disgust. It is the Patum as binge.[9]

No surprise that the parents in question are worried, along with some of the children themselves. The civil religion of Berga has always inveighed against false gods: a small community has to fight hard to resist absorption. Increasingly, even the Catalonia ruled from Barcelona can seem an imposition. The Berguedan Corpus Mysticum must not be a microcosm of any larger body, but itself alone. Hence the chauvinism of "no one is Berguedan who has not suckled Berguedan milk." The fathers have been legion over the centuries, and at bottom it doesn't matter too much whether they're Carlist or Liberal. The real fear is that Berguedans will wander off to seek foster-mothers.

What if our mother cannot feed us? The children of Berga face this very real problem. Middle-class children are largely unemployable in Berga once they get university degrees, except for the few who can be absorbed as teachers. Working-class children can no longer find employment in mines and textile mills. It is not that, like the savage child of *modernista* poetry, they have satiated themselves on "the emptied breast"; rather, the milk has dried up. Hence the disgust response: as Freud notes, it is the characteristic response to a traumatic weaning (1966, 366).[10] *Munyir la vaca* (to milk the cow), one says in Catalan to mean taking full personal advantage of a situation. Young Berguedans have to find what cows they can.

And perhaps the satisfactions become more instrumental, no longer consummated in that warm milky embrace of mutual love and obligation, but sought and bought and paid for. This is the change that really creates anxiety among Berguedans. It is not just rival goddesses that threaten the Patum, but the total loss of the sacred. Do the drunken children of the Patum find anything more than sensual satisfaction there? Is today's Patum any different from the "cannibal mambo"? Is the Patum just another drug?[11]

I've argued that the late Francoist Patum was a practice ground for forms of more explicit resistance. In thinking of the teenagers of today, apparently so hungry for strong sensation, some Berguedans wonder whether political protest is not just another form of Patum. The new generation has inherited a powerful performative repertoire, but, growing up under democracy, they have no name to resist, no new name by which to organize themselves. Among the educated, demonstrations continue as a routine, often "decaffeinated" form of public expression: after a change of degree requirements at the University of Barcelona in 1993, protesters sang "We Shall Not Be Moved" in four-part harmony and wrote their slogans on sheets so as not to deface the walls of the Faculty. The children of the provinces and the urban working class, hard hit by unemployment, are another matter. These, if inclined to politics, tend to more extremist views, anti-immigrant and either militantly anti-Spanish or militantly anti-Catalanist; more often, cynical about any of those labels so easily changed, they engage in collective performance in what their parents see as an almost nihilist pursuit of temporary gratification.[12]

On September 11, 1991, I was with Berguedan friends in Barcelona for the Independence Day celebration. We had attended the ceremonies in the morning and the demonstrations and speeches in the afternoon. In the evening we walked up the Rambles and through the Plaça Catalunya, where we saw teenagers—several girls there looked no more than fourteen—massing and milling, some murmuring angrily, a few throwing rocks or kicking lampposts, but mostly just waiting. A few police cars approached, their sirens on, and the children tightened their ranks, stepped into the street, and began to run. I and my friends left: the "national" police have a reputation for being indiscriminate with their blows.

We stopped at an outdoor restaurant a few blocks away. As we were having our dinner we heard shouts, sirens, and shots: the police were using rubber bullets to disperse the crowd. I had never seen anything so Ulsterish in Catalonia before and was exclaiming at such measures against children, but my companions, more accustomed, were remarking on the teenagers themselves. "We painted slogans on walls and held demonstrations because we felt we had no choice," said Pep, a militant of the 1970s.

"But we were frightened. These kids, it seems, *want* to run before the police." *Tenir ganes*, he called it—to have a yen or hunger for something. To us, intellectuals headed toward middle age, the children in the *plaça* looked in a state of purely sensual expectancy, like horses tensed for the chase. With the same sort of friends I have seen a fight beginning among drunken sixteen-year-olds outside of a discotheque in Avià; and I have seen the shouts and raised fists of teenage militants, some skinheaded and jackbooted, at the independentist manifestation of the Pine of the Three Branches held above Berga in July, a festival that occasionally ends in blows between factions. In each case the mood felt very much the same, and sometimes I see it in the Patum. No doubt I have listened too much to my own cohort. They went from war to love in the *plaça* as they grew older and their world settled, from phallic contest to ecstatic incorporation to an embracing motherly Patum of happy memories. But the children seem to be making war again: festival violence and vandalism were on the rise throughout central Catalonia in the early 1990s. Though the Patum is now well-policed, the young faces in the *plaça* are often angry. Their parents cannot always see the sources of it: they only know that the dangerous techniques of incorporation were mobilized in the 1970s out of urgent national need. Today, with no need so easily named, the older generation describes the practice of the young with metaphors of addiction. If their future could be resolved would they too settle into a calmer, more comfortable Patum?

In the library or on the bus they seem normal enough, some more optimistic, some more cynical; few seem to aspire to more than the life of the *berguedan moyen sensuel*, no different in this from their elders. But at large gatherings they seem changed from their separate selves and changed from their parents. They are not doing the Patum to transmute the community into a Corpus Mysticum: it is not that fullness they're after. I see them dancing toward transcendence, the purifying flames raised to a height their parents never imagined. They are given only dry husks: what can they do but make a bonfire?

They are always driving: the mother they seek is not Berga in her dual incarnation of Patum and Queralt, but Hecate of the crossroads. How many teenagers have died on the Highway of the Llobregat since I've been going to Berga? The newspaper is full of the accidents; everyone I know knows someone. Look at them going from the disco to the demonstration to the football game to the concert to the festival to the bar. Their rush to exhaust the available pleasures is not sybaritic indulgence, but, sometimes literally, the *via negativa*.

They too long for wholeness, incorporation into something both viable and their own. They cannot find it in contemporary Berga, but the Patum shows them its shadow. Els Brams understand it all better than I do:

L'ULTIM TIRABOL

Era jove, era berguedà,
estava a punt de fer vint-i-tres anys,
s'acostava Corpus, se li veia an els ulls,
encesos com espurnes de Patum.
Mig poble deia que era un bon sagal,
l'altre mig que era un bordegàs,
i la noia que estimava
no li fotia cas.
Dimecres de Patum vem quedar
a la barana, però no s'hi va preentar,
en un revolt, amb el seu cotxe vell
va deixar la pell.
Des d'un racó sentia els gegants;
La música acompanyava
unes llàgrimes galtes avall
quan vaig tornar a la Plaça.
Potser va ser la màgia de la Patum,
o la barreja o la cervesa,
però aquell fet no va ser per a mi
pas una sorpresa.
Em va semblar, veure'l arribar
amb el barret i el mocador nusat
em va dir que Sant Pere té per costum
deixar als berguedans
fer un darrer salt de Patum.
Amb una mirada de complicitat
i un somriure com tenia ell sol,
del bracet agafats vam saltar
l'últim Tirabol.

THE LAST TIRABOL

He was young, he was Berguedan,
he was about to turn twenty-three,
Corpus was coming up, you could see it in his eyes,
lit up like sparks of Patum.
Half the town said he was a good kid,
the other said he was a savage,
and the girl he loved
didn't give a shit for him.
Wednesday of the Patum we had fixed to meet
at the *barana*, but he didn't show up,
at a tight curve, with his old car,
he left his skin behind.
From a corner I heard the giants;
The music accompanied
a few tears down my cheeks
when I came back to the Plaça.
Maybe it was the magic of the Patum,
or the *barreja* or the beer,
but what had happened
was no surprise to me.
It seemed to me I saw him coming
with hat and knotted kerchief
he told me that Saint Peter has the custom
of letting Berguedans
do a last *salt* of Patum.
With a look of complicity,
and a smile that was his alone,
arm in arm we *salt*-ed
the last Tirabol.
(Brams 1992)

IO

Reproduction and Reduction

EVERYONE FEARS "THE LAST *TIRABOL*," and in fact whenever I use the word "last" in Berga (as in "Could we maybe have one last drink and go home to bed?") someone immediately interjects, "No, no, the penultimate!" At times the frenetic cast of the festival suggests that participants are treating the Patum itself as *la penúltima*. But the most committed Berguedans—those who sustain local politics, intellectual life, voluntary associations, and festivals—are working also to sustain the Patum as the keystone of life in Berga, through strategic adaptation to changing circumstances. The strategies are multiple and contradictory, often fragmenting along the lines of the traditional tensions between respectability and conviviality or closure and openness, but increasingly voiced in the idiom of "authenticity." A key arena of both activism and debate is the socialization of children into the festival: here the reproduction of the Patum and the reproduction of the community are most fully identified. Less constrained by *berguedanisme* and more engaged in negotiating extracommunity relationships have been the new Berguedan festivals created between 1986 and 1992. With tourism presenting itself as one of the few plausible options for local economic development, community attitudes toward the outside world vacillate between an assiduous cultivation of networks and a resistance to engagement. Under the real and imagined eyes of outsiders, the rituals of Berguedan identity become flatter and more self-conscious, hardening into the extremes of irony or liturgy.

Children's Patums

Children as young as two years old already play at the Patum. One afternoon at a table in Cal Negre, a little boy held an empty roll of candy in front of his mouth and began to push it at his father, like the *fuets* of the

Guita. Like most Berguedan parents, his father Francesc encourages such play and tries to direct it toward accurate reproduction of the big Patum: he lit a match to affix in the tube, but this frightened the child. "A little too young still," noted an onlooker. Parents take children to look at the Patum from birth: they touch the baby to the hand of the giantess and say "Who's this?" Martí of Cal Negre holds up his small daughter in front of the four giants: "Which is the handsomest?" he asked, pointing her at the Gegant Negre. Teachers and daycare workers bring their charges into the storeroom of City Hall in the days before Corpus to look at the effigies. "Where is the Àliga? What does this one do?" Parents buy tiny Patum hats and kerchiefs for their children, and sometimes full miniature *comparsa* costumes. Children are brought to the Patum de Lluïment and encouraged to conquer their fear of the *fuets*. They soon require no encouragement. "I'm no dancer," one man told me, "but I knew the steps of every dance in the Patum as soon as I could walk." Arnau Pons was given dolls of the giants by his grandparents and played at dancing them every day one summer while he was still barely able to talk. Dozens of families buy an annual Patum videotape from Foto Luigi, since the sometimes daily watching of their children wears it ragged.

The tradition of playing at Patum is no doubt as old as the Patum itself and is documented from at least the beginning of this century. Most people remember playing at the Patum with broomsticks and tomato crates, and some households preserve a *guita*'s head carved by an obliging older relative.[1] Every street had its own children's Patum, say those who grew up before the 1960s, and there were rivalries between them, sometimes stimulated by questions of immigration. Today the Patum is still found in every street where there are children.

Some of these neighborhood Patums have become institutionalized. Apart from the Patum of the special education school, in which both city officials and La Barana *patumaires* collaborate to incorporate the children into full Berguedan personhood, two children's Patums have come to emblematize the debate over the festival's future.

The Patum Infantil is performed on Friday noon and evening during Corpus: it is the Patum to which schoolchildren from all over the *comarca* are bought. But it began as a neighborhood Patum, and the organizers are still predominantly from the Carrer del Pinsania, the high part of the old city, also once known "Little Queralt" from its proximity to the road to the sanctuary. Tightly knit in its devotion to the Mare de Déu, the neighborhood has been perhaps the most active in the three anniversary celebrations of the Coronation.

In 1956, Joan Rafart, owner of a textile factory in the *barri*, noticed children playing Patum on the street and decided to help them with their construction of the comparses. A pair of giants was bought from a commercial studio; Rafart's wife and mother began to sew costumes. Soon afterward the Berguedan carpenter Pere Camps and the painters' society Cau d'Art became involved and gradually constructed the entire *comparseria* of the Patum. In 1958, the Ajuntament sponsored a parade of children's *comparses* during Corpus, of which the Pinsania group was outstanding, and by 1959 the Patum of La Pinsania was in the Plaça Sant Pere. The Ajuntament began to provide *fuets* and ultimately took over the financial responsibility from Rafart. By 1968, the Patum Infantil was "complete and definitive," with *comparses* in near-perfect miniature of the adult Patum (Rafart 1981). Members of the adult *comparses*, many tied to the original neighborhood, others volunteering in order to ensure a steady supply of capable *patumaires* for the future, undertook to rehearse the children.

The rehearsals run from the day the Tabal comes out to just before Corpus. Certain *comparses* require more teaching: while the *guites* are left pretty much to themselves, the *balls* are given a great deal of attention. The *cap de colla* of the New Dwarfs devotes much time to the Patum Infantil because he needs it to recruit the adult *comparsa*. Nans have to be light and agile: they can begin almost just out of the Patum Infantil (whereas the boys who danced the *gegants infantils* have to wait a few years to grow up), and they generally retire by the age of thirty at most. So for many the Patum Infantil serves as what Rafart calls it, a "school of *patumaires*."

"The children dance it better than the grownups!" one often hears. From a choreographic point of view this is true, partly because the children have more space in the *plaça* but also because of the care in rehearsal and the solemn responsibility felt by many of the performers. The Patum Infantil is "a very well-made copy of the Patum, in miniature" (Huch i Camprubí 1982), with those qualities of the miniature pointed out by Susan Stewart: "a diminutive, and thereby manipulatable version of experience, a version which is domesticated and protected from contamination" (1984, 69). Mossèn Armengou was enthusiastic about the Patum Infantil in the face of the Patum's apparent debasement under late Francoism. "A school of initiation to and perfecting of Berguedan tradition" (Obradors 1983, 10), it established a model of ordered transmission now affecting the larger event, as *patumaires* formed in the Patum Infantil have grown up to create the Patronat de la Patum (cf. Chapter 2). Joan Rafart sums up: "The Patum Infantil has furnished a mirror to reflect us, has created a model for the Patum to follow. It has forged, definitively, a valid, impeccable style of doing the Patum which gives hope for the future" (1981).

The Patum Infantil retains the spirit of its founders and of Little Queralt. It is legitimate: it is *the* authorized children's Patum. It is orderly: the men in the blue shirts are the undisputed authorities of the event, and their word goes. Participation is strictly controlled by these men, governed by papers and measures. Parents sign up their children on a given day; *plens* must be under a meter tall or out they go. But, as befits a Berguedan authority, the Patum Infantil is not wholly bureaucratized. The dancers of a prestigious *entremes* are generally the children of prestigious *patumaires*. Old hierarchies, particularly that of gender, have their effect. When Joan Rafart's granddaughter was about eight years old, I asked her what she was going to do in the Patum when she grew up. "Oh, girls can't be in the Patum." "But there's Maria and Fina and Glòria in the *maces*, Queralt in the *turcs*, Griselda in the *nanos*—" I began to enumerate, but she looked at me skeptically. In the Patum Infantil, little girls do the two angels and the *plens*, and that's all.[2] I know a boy kept out because his hair was too long. The Patum Infantil is the Patum of *respecte* and of the old order—but, with the Patronat, of the new order too.

Everything being double in Berga, there is a children's Patum of the *popular* and of the other old order. About the same time as the creation of the Patum Infantil, the Carrer de la Pietat, a *popular* neighborhood above the *plaça* in the old city, began to include a homemade Patum in its neighborhood festival at Pentecost, two weeks before Corpus. The neighbors, once again, made up the *comparses* bit by bit. By the mid-1980s, a group of local men had taken it up, including Miquel Moya, a young pharmacist then known for his collection of military paraphernalia and his taste in dress: hair dyed daffodil, an earring, and a bird of paradise in his *maça* at the Patum de Lluïment. One of the original residents who went off to live in the new *xalets* of Casampons, Miquel took up the Patum as a way of doing something for a street in whose crumbling houses only a handful of families remained—some Castilian-speaking immigrants, and the newest ones Moroccan.

Like the caretakers of the Patum Infantil, the adults train the children in the dances and patch up and restore the *comparses*, year by year. But the Patum of the Carrer de la Pietat has remained a neighborhood Patum and has a very different flavor from the Patum Infantil. It is less well made and more spontaneous; above all, participation is more open. Girls do everything. For me the 1989 *tabaler* who turned out to be a *tabalera* was emblematic of the event: she was a serious tomboy by Berguedan standards and at that time it was no easy matter to guess her gender. The Carrer de la Pietat does not impose fixed identities: kids go from one *comparsa* to another; adolescents are not cast out, but help more and dance less. The adults step in and take a turn when they feel like it. In that intimate space, the boundaries of *comparsa* and public are the most fluid of any Patum: I jumped my first *maça* on the Carrer Pietat, and had my first greeting from its *guita*. There is not only a Patum in the street's tiny *plaça* ("it's like doing the Patum in your dining room," says Quirze), but a long *passacarrers* like that of the big Patum. The Patum Infantil lacks this late-night wandering and has only the morning procession to collect the Administradors and escort them to the church.

The mixings of this Patum are a source of anxiety to many. The Nans Nous are not copies of the big Patum, but mass-production dwarfs, whose likeness can be seen in other cities. The eagle and *guites* of the Carrer Pietat have gone out of Berga to be in exhibitions of Catalan eagles and *mulasses*. Miquel Moya believes in collaborating with new festival groups in other parts of the country. The visit was a source of great annoyance to the then Councillor of Culture, who insists that there is no Patum but *the* Patum: although the Patum cannot leave Berga, still less should anything that is not the Patum and calls itself Patum go out to represent the city. The Patum is *a la plaça i prou* (in the *plaça* and that's it). Economic support has not always been forthcoming from City Hall. There is no need for a second Patum Infantil, so many argue. In 1989 I asked a couple of university students, enthusiastic *patumaires* of "good" families, whether they were going to the Carrer Pietat. "No, we never go there," said the boy, smiling disdainfully. "It's not the Patum, I don't like it," the girl added. "The Patum is in the *plaça*."

Some of the anxiety has to do with the composition of the neighborhood. A few of the children shout in Castilian as they run the *guita* down the narrow street: those who are not from the Carrer de la Pietat come from Santa Eulàlia, the flats built for Andalusian miners and their families.

In 1989 I found myself dancing with a ten-year-old Moroccan girl, although her brothers were standing watchfully by: it had to be said that this Patum was successfully integrating the immigrant population, a virtue Mossèn Armengou liked to see in the big Patum ([1968, 1971]1994, 123–24). But a joke was circulating the next year: "Do you know why the most authentic Patum is the Patum of the Carrer de la Pietat? Because the Turks are real." As with the Patum of the *plaça*, apparently taken over by outsiders, the Patum of the Carrer de la Pietat seems to some to take the tradition out of the hands of true Berguedans.

Which children's Patum is a more genuine manifestation of the *patumaire* spirit? One day there was an argument about it in La Barana. Pep Camprubí of the Guita Xica, then in his early thirties, participated in the Patum Infantil as a child. He is the self-declared "black sheep" of a *família de bé*. He protested, "In the Patum de la Canalla (of the kids) everyone fits. There's no need for another one." Pepito, in his fifties, a lifelong resident of the city's old quarter, was as insistent as always: "No, no, no. Both are neighborhood Patums! The difference is those people up there on the Pinsania had money and on the Carrer Pietat they did it all with tomato crates. But the Carrer Pietat's is older." The Carrer de la Pietat is a threat to unity—so goes the respectable argument. The Patum Infantil is an imposed unity with interest behind it—so goes the *popular*. The fathers of the Carrer Pinsania watch over the reproduction of the Patum, assure and authenticate its transmission to the young; the Carrer de la Pietat has fathers and mothers, and they tend to let nature take its course.

The Patum as Bullfight

Translating from the language of familial reproduction to that of cultural reproduction, we can speak of authenticity rather than legitimacy. The authentic, like the primordial and indeed like the body itself, is dangerously unstable ground, shifting between the personal and the historical, between experience and essence. Regina Bendix has shown the transformation of the concept in European modernity from a Romantic emphasis on spontaneous inner feeling to successive modes of naturalization and reification, as nationalism sought to historicize it and capitalism to commodify it (1997). Inevitably, in a provincial community such as Berga, au-

thenticity is not purely a matter of internal coherence (indeed, Berga is
unusual in its insistence on the Patum that "rises up from inside of you")
but a mode of self-representation to the larger world, privileging the visible surface over the depths.

The *catalanitat* of the Patum did not originate with Mossèn Armengou and the Franco regime, arising from an earlier need more economic
than political. In the late nineteenth century, after the fracas of the three
Carlist Wars, Berga had to compete with better endowed regions in the
Pyrenees for industrial investment and summer tourism from Barcelona.
The former called for a reassuring display of the Catalan national spirit of
industrious patriarchal order (Chapter 7; Fradera 1990). The latter necessitated attractions to compensate for the absence of major historical monuments or high mountain scenery. Performance, and particularly of the
spectacular character of the Patum, could fill both needs. As later during
the Transition, Berga could give Catalonia an occasion to recover itself—
here its glorious medieval integrity rather than its primordial energies—in
performance.

In 1901 Berga held its first Jocs Florals, the poetic tournament in
Gothic dress that was the central ritual of the Catalan Renaixença. The
grand prize went to one Antoni Sansalvador, a young Berguedan just beginning his career as a lawyer in Barcelona, who produced a long paean to
the Patum in lyrical prose. Sansalvador interpreted the danced combats
between Christians and Moors, angels and devils, as allegories of the triumph of the Catalan spirit. The new enemy, clearly, was the spirit of
Spain, embodied in the invasive culture of leisure so troubling to rural
Catalanist intellectuals (Fradera 1990, 62). One much-quoted passage
from Sansalvador defines the Patum against this threat:

The bullfight and the Patum are like two opposite poles, they could not be more
distant. The bullfight is a foreign festival without roots in our land. The Patum a
festival of home, born and conserved in the warmth of love for our country. The
bullfight is a negative expansion, La Patum a positive one; the bullfight a brutaliz-
ing spectacle, La Patum an instructive one. The bullfight represents the closed
and fanatic Muslim spirit; La Patum symbolizes the Catalan spirit, progressive and
practical. The bullfight is the heritage of an old people always buried in the most
numbing nirvana, La Patum the patrimony of a young people, which like the
mythical Antaeus, lifts itself up from the earth where misfortune felled it with
more strength than ever. And in history, the bullfight is a bloody stain, and the
Patum a fortunate moment marking the end of an opprobrious domination.
(Sansalvador 1916, 14)

Sansalvador's Catalanist interpretation of the festival provided the foundations for Armengou, Fàbregas, and all the writers of the Transition. Although the Berguedan compromise with Barcelona Catalanism did not profit them quite enough in the usual sense, Berguedans are still proud of the symbolic capital they accrued and like to describe themselves as the most Catalan of the Catalans—as, in fact, a symbolic capital in the other sense. Imagine, then, their bemusement when the following proclamation appeared in the streets of Berga in February 1989:

The Berguedan authorities, having sought out the true roots of the city of Berga, wish to explain the following discovery to the population:

The millenarian[3] traditional culture of the Berguedà is, without any doubt, that of Al-Andalus, capital Granada. Currently there remain three living symbols of this glorious past, set in the depths of the Bergistan[4] soul: the Muslim moons on the arms of the city of Berga, the combs and mantillas of the *administradores* of Corpus and the paso-doble called Arte Taurino, the most *sentit* [heard/felt] of all the Tirabols.

From this day forward, it will be obligatory to fulfill the following ordinances [a long list, of which I excerpt a sample]:
  1. The citizens of the Berguedà will whitewash the façades of their buildings . . .
  4. The churches of Queralt and Sant Pere will be converted into mosques . . .
  6. Berguedans will place themselves before a mirror three times a day and will do phonetic exercises pronouncing out loud such phrases as "*Ata la jaca a la reja*", "*ni jalem ni jalarem*" or "*jamalají-jamalajà*"[5] . . .
  7. The music schools and sardana clubs will include classes of *sevillanas* and castanet lessons in their programs . . .
  9. Rice and escudella will be replaced by couscous and gazpacho . . .
  13. For the 1989 Patum the Turks will begin to win instead of the Christian Knights. Vengeance is coming! . . .
  17. We will demolish the municipal slaughterhouse, which represents an unworthy death for bulls . . .
  18. Holy Week processions will be restored . . .

This document was the announcement of Carnival, a festival revived three years before (with the Berguedan cow) by a new ludic society called La Bauma dels Encantats. An organization with parallels in every town in Catalonia, La Bauma was created by a group of young intellectuals responsible for many cultural and political initiatives in Berga since democracy. Its name, "The Cave of the Enchanted," was taken from a turn-of-the-century fraternal organization, which in turn drew upon a local toponym. *Encan-*

tats connotes not merely those caught by the fairies, but, more colloqui-
ally, those distracted or "touched," an anticipation of the opprobrium
that often meets activism in provincial towns.[6] And after the years of the
Transition, the name sat particularly well with Berguedan primordialism:
some La Bauma members describe the Barcelona stereotype of Berga as a
kind of tribe frozen in time, unable from their cave to see or communicate with the contemporary world.

During the ten years of its activities, La Bauma avoided direct reference or challenge to the Patum. Some militant *patumaires* resented its
presence, as did some older cultural activists, both out of rivalry and in fidelity to the principles of Mossèn Armengou. But the majority of the
population was happy to have more festival activity in Berga and participated enthusiastically in La Bauma's events. While La Bauma members
were passionate *patumaires* themselves, their activities revealed dissatisfac-
tion with both the civil-religious framing of the Patum and Catalanism as
it had been offered to Berga. La Bauma's mockeries intimated a critique of
what Richard Handler, following Ronald Cohen, has called *entitivity*: the
imagination of the nation (and the festival) as a bounded body, continuous
in time, homogeneous in substance (1988, 7–8).

Official Patum discourse invokes origin as the sufficient and determining explanation of the present, in part to deny the event any subsequent contamination by the centuries of Castilian occupation. A road sign
placed at the bottom of the Passeig de la Pau, at the entry to the town,
dating from the early 1980s, is the reductio ad absurdum of this originary
determinism. It lists Berga's major monuments with their dates: the
church of Sant Quirze de Pedret, seventh century; Sant Pere de Madrona,
twelfth century; Festival of the Patum, fourteenth century; Sanctuary of
Queralt, seventeenth century.

The parodic origin narrative in the Carnival proclamation questions
the inviolate status of the Patum through the same reading of peripheral
details as clues to origin (cf. Ginzburg 1989) that is characteristic of
turn-of-the-century Catalanists desperate to reconstruct their country
out of its fragments. The women in the couples annually selected as festival administrators wear black dresses with combs and lace mantillas,
fashionable formal dress in Catalonia at the end of the last century. The
favorite tune of the *tirabols*, the one which rings in your ears for weeks
after, is a catchy pasodoble entitled "Arte Taurino," the Bullfighter's Art,
incorporated into the Patum in the 1920s. These minor influences on the
Patum signal the major influence of Spain on Catalan culture, economy, and

social structure over several centuries. To deny this influence is to deny history.

We can see here a parallel to the Greek case familiar from Michael Herzfeld's work, with La Bauma using a historicist and realist "Romeic" stance to challenge the essentialist "Hellenizers" (1987). Indeed, La Bauma members did historical research as well as invent festivals, most notably Josep Noguera i Canal, who demonstrated convincingly that the present form of the Patum owes more to the nineteenth century than to the fourteenth, much less to pre-Christian ritual (1992). His views, not surprisingly, have not been assimilated into the civil religion.[7] The performative critique, however, has been less easy to ignore than the scholarly.

La Bauma's use of the shield of Berga as "evidence" for Andalusian/Moorish origins points out that otherness is incorporated in the very heart of Berguedan identity. The city's arms set the four red bars on gold of the counts of Barcelona in opposition to the half-moons of the Moors, giving them equal weight.

The blasphemous equations of the Carnival proclamation point up the Catalanist tendency to define by opposition, to bound the nation in a bundle of cultural isoglosses. The Patum is not a bullfight. The Catalans, the slogan goes, are not Spanish. We speak Catalan, they speak Castilian. We eat mushrooms, they do not. We keep our feet on the ground; they have exalted ideas. We work hard, they, alas, do not. And so forth. We can explain this anxiety for clarity and boundedness by Catalonia's history as a *terra de pas*: its boundaries have so often been violated, its internal reality so often muddled by invasion and immigration. But the definition by opposition creates an overarching structural identity, a mirror-imaging across shared categories that makes the two halves interchangeable (cf. Burke 1957, 50). Hence the ease of substitutions: flamenco for the *sardana*, gazpacho for *escudella*, a mosque for the church, a *romeria* for the indigenous Marian festival—and, as I learned during that lunch in the mountains, "Cara al Sol" for "Els Segadors." Note also that when strict binarism between Us and Them is combined with the historical conflation typical of folk performance, Spain, Andalusia, and the Moors are condensed into a single object and other. La Bauma's Carnival offered an ironic revoicing of the Patum civil religion, equating its essentialist nationalism with the cultural manipulations of the dictatorship.

The climax of the substitutions in the 1989 Carnival was a song sung in pseudo-Andalusian dialect describing the Patum in the language of the bullfight: [8]

COPLISHA DEL ARTE TAURINO

Ezcorteume, zeñora y zeñore,
que lo que vui dirvo é mol impurtán,
i que aluego dezde le he'cole
no inventen hiztorie que no zón verdá.

Que mazcorti tor mon i que zepa
que este festeho que diuen PATU
no lo van inventar lo cristiano,
que ze lo copiaron der duende andalú.

Que ze penzen? que aizó é una fezta
que aquí a Catalunya é mor tradicioná?
No zeñore, que no é ma que una
corria de toro. Zo zí: mu cambiá.

Quan arriba er dia de la fezta
pa donde, mi arma, zen va er perzoná?
Pa la plasa. Iguá que a lo toro,
y digo er matéi de la puntualidá.

Un toreo hasen mu estraño
y en car lló der món lo veureu com aqué.

Listen to me, ladies and gentlemen,
for what I am going to tell you is very important,
so that later in the schools
they don't invent stories which are not true.

Let everyone listen and learn
that this festival they call the PATUM
wasn't invented by the Christians,
but they copied it from Andalusian *duende*.

What do you think? That this is a festival
that's very traditional here in Catalunya?
No sir, this is nothing more than a
bullfight. I admit—much changed.

When the day of the festival arrives
where, my soul, do the people go?
To the *plaça*. Just like for the bulls,
and I say the same of the punctuality.

They do a very strange *toreo*
and nowhere in the world will you see one
like it.
("Coplisha . . . " 1990)

The song goes on for several verses, with each dance of the Patum equated with a sequence of the bullfight, misunderstood or incompetently executed by its Berguedan performers. The Andalusian speaker concludes that however incoherent the Patum may be, it finishes off with a dance so *torero* that there is no better festival in all the world. A confirmation of Berguedan anxieties: it is not in fact necessary to understand the esoteric symbolism of the event or to have "suckled Bergudan milk," to enter into the spirit of the Patum.

Why is Andalusia central to the mockery of Berguedan Catalanism? Andalusia, the southernmost part of a "southern" country, tends metonymically to misrepresent Spain for outsiders, as Fernandez has pointed out (1988b, 22). For the Catalans, it is the most distant part of Spain, the most distinct, the easiest to image in a contrast. But it is also the closest, most strongly embodying the threat to Catalan national identity. It is Andalusian culture that was appropriated in the mass culture of the Francoist state, embodying for Catalans the hollowness of the *folklòric*. Moreover, Andalusian immigrants came to Catalonia in the 1960s in huge numbers to work in its factories, and they were the most visible cultural others in the 1980s. It is generally believed, on good evidence, that this massive immigration was encouraged by the Franco regime to further the erosion of Catalonia's national personality. Andalusians therefore have met with significant Catalan racism, and are pejoratively associated with the Moors, both in their supposed cultural traits and in their status as invaders.

And yet, La Bauma forced Berga to observe, flamenco music isn't bad when you listen to it, and Tio Pepe can be quite pleasant to drink. This was not an easy admission for everyone. The owner of one bar was visibly tense after a few days of *cante jondo* blaring on his tape deck and bearded youths in black mantillas demanding endless glasses of *fino* in grotesquely accented Castilian. When, in midweek, he visited his distributor to pick up more sherry, he pounded his fists on the counter in frustration. "*Un fino, por favor! Un fino!* I'm up to the balls with this *fino* shit!"

Quirze Grifell admitted to me, "A lot of the older people did find it hard to take. Here was all this stuff we'd had forced on us for years, and we were doing it voluntarily! But, you see, for Carnival everything has to be the reverse. And since we're more Catalan than anybody, we had to be Andalusians . . ." He added that the old men of the Patum, the ones most resistant to festival innovation, poked their noses into Cal Negre one night to see what was going on. They stood near the door and nursed their patriotic glasses of *vi bo* in silent suspicion. But soon, he said, they were drinking sherry and dancing with the rest of us. "And I think the Andalusian immigrants really enjoyed it. They were surprised, but they came in and danced too . . ."

Quirze suggests here that ironic and literal interpreters were able to join hands in the dance. I was not present and am a bit skeptical. But his words mark one of La Bauma's serious preoccupations, to expand involvement beyond a limited group of initiates. La Bauma's carnival did what Armengou's strictures forbade the Patum: it comprised a variety of events beyond the central parade, masked balls, and funeral of King Carnival. Lectures, makeup classes, children's events enabled the more reserved, the less prepared, the less acculturated, and the young to participate.

La Bauma mimicked one of the Patum's potentialities in this respect, with a crucial difference. As we have seen, the Patum's power derives from its ability to effect social integration without semiotic integration: its use of multivocal symbols that foreground conflict without defining it too precisely, combined with powerful techniques of the body. After the first shock of resistance, Andalusian folklore is both deep enough and ambivalent enough in Catalonia to serve the same purpose to a lesser degree. But La Bauma has not had centuries to evolve an inclusive vocabulary, and its chosen vehicle of Carnival is vowed to the ephemeral in any case; today, too, the population is invested in a wider range of images. So the global participation in La Bauma's Carnival comes at the price Armengou feared, of fragmentation.

Nor could Armengou have tolerated the irony, which he would have understood as blasphemy; and irony has been La Bauma's constant mode. In fact it is not blasphemy but desacralization, a goal pursued explicitly by some La Bauma members. Desacralization is another price of extending participation, as Fernandez notes in his essay on the self-mocking local images in an Asturian kayak festival in the 1980s (1986, 264–95). Spaniards had learned irony as a means of cognitive and political self-defense under the Franco regime: it allowed them to reproduce the official messages without identifying with them. By the same token, irony permits the circulation of messages to actors who would not be expected to accept them at face value, and certainly Berga in the 1980s was in no position to assert a grand narrative of itself to anyone. Building on Burke's sense of irony's humility ([1945]1969, 513–15), Fernandez suggests that an ironic frame, in which all acknowledge the distance of their pretensions from reality, enables a "transcendent humanization" in which local identities can be tolerated (1986, 288). Certainly this is the best that Berga can hope for.

Similarly, irony permits the reproduction of messages that would otherwise have to be repudiated by the self, as we saw in the "Cara al Sol" incident. It serves the dual purpose of declaring present distance from a dangerous past and preserving that past for possible future need. The members of La Bauma, like festival groups all over Catalonia, paid their tribute of imitation to the Patum's emotional force: the festival is the medium of choice for local revitalization. But living with the Patum, La Bauma is also suspicious of its influence. Just as Sansalvador set the Patum against the bullfight, the Patum of late Francoism set up an alternative orthodoxy to the dictatorship's national Catholicism. Opposing absolutist claims, it made absolutist claims in return. And because it could draw on all the passions repressed in the everyday life of the regime, the Patum developed an intensity to which La Bauma's Carnivals would never pretend. But by the 1980s Berguedans—and Catalans and Spaniards for that matter— were perhaps rather exhausted from strong passions. The historical consciousness of La Bauma led them to mistrust their own as well as other's fervor: perhaps the moment had come to dethrone all gods, imposed or autochthonous, with laughter.

Festival Exchange and the Promise of the Network

Along with the revival of Carnival, La Bauma's first major venture was to make a pair of processional giants in 1987, exciting further cries of blasphemy and fears that La Bauma intended to rival the Patum. Next to the giants of the Patum, Berguedans consider that all other giants in Catalonia look puny and foolish. But La Bauma proposed pluralism in giants as in politics. Their giants commemorated real people: Rafael Penina, a nineteenth-century journalist noted for hard drinking and contentiousness, and La Gosolana, an herbal healer who died in the 1960s. Penina was La Bauma's mocking self-image; La Gosolana was perhaps the first giantess in Catalonia to represent a personality in her own right, not to mention an old peasant woman in lieu of a buxom young bourgeoise. As giants they were unassuming, much smaller than the Patum giants, and light enough to be danced by a tall woman or a slight man. These giants, then, exemplified La Bauma's democratic revision of tradition, as did the women in its membership, a strong contrast to the masculine hierarchies of Patum participation.

The new giants gave La Bauma a means of compensating for what it considered the city's hidebound refusal to let the Patum *comparseria* participate in festival exchanges. "The giants of the Patum never leave home," insisted Armengou's followers. But La Bauma was painfully aware that many other Berguedans had to leave home. Its membership was overwhelmingly drawn from the generation who shared not only the experience of the Transition but the first widespread provincial exposure to university education. With the economic collapse of the *comarca*, most had to choose between underemployment at home—if they were lucky—or a serious pursuit of career in Barcelona. A few members were in fact weekend Berguedans with continuing local allegiances; most were teachers or butchers or drapers who spent their off-hours practicing their true vocation of music or history or journalism. None of them could delude themselves that Berga's relations with Barcelona were purely those of national communion: all were aware of economic dependence.

In this context, not just festival activity but festival exchange took on added importance. Like parallel organizations elsewhere, La Bauma was dedicated to creating *marxa*, movement, in the local community: enhancing cultural life with a view to economic and demographic revival. Throughout the *comarques* of Catalonia in the 1980s, there was a growing movement toward local self-assertion against the top-heavy Barcelonan conception of Catalonia as a city-state with hinterland, *la Catalunya-ciutat*.

The members of La Bauma rejected as a way of belonging to Catalonia the single-stranded relationship of Berga and Barcelona, the Highway of the Llobregat, which stands out so dramatically against the barely paved lateral roads to neighboring *comarques*. They claimed the right to draw the lines of communication themselves, to send messages as well as receive them. Their collaboration with the cities of Olot and Vic produced a satirical newspaper devoted to the promulgation of the Fourth Carlist War, in recollection of the former solidarity of the Catalan interior against the transformations imposed by both the centralism of the Spanish state and the capitalist development of Barcelona.

El Penina and La Gosolana declared this transverse solidarity with their feet. The giants were made in Solsona by a local artisan, Manel Casserres, and the members of La Bauma walked them the forty-five kilometers home to Berga through a depopulated but beautiful landscape. The "translation"—a word normally used only for religious images—was punctuated by receptions at both ends of the trajectory and in each municipality along the way. Mayors made speeches about local cooperation and endless jokes about the giants getting seasick from the condition of the road. The president of the Agrupació de Geganters de Catalunya made a speech at the opening dinner, observing that, because Berguedan feelings about outsiders would prevent him from ever dancing the Patum giants, he was glad to be able to participate in this Berguedan event. In Berga, the giants were greeted at the remaining city gate, the Portal de Santa Magdalena, which leads to the Carrer de la Pietat, by that street's "Mayor," Miquel Moya. The Carrer Pietat's Patum giants were in attendance, along with giants and dwarfs from all over central Catalonia.

The translation of these giants and the sociability that gathered at their feet along the road enlivened links that existed mostly in potentia, pulsing live current along a little-used path. The mayor of Solsona said to the mayor of Berga, "Of course I knew your face from the newspapers." The giants continued to be used for the purpose, traveling to participate in *festes majors* throughout central Catalonia: mutually assisted *marxa* for communities too small to sustain it alone. La Bauma took the giants abroad as well, conscious that local prosperity demanded an international as well as a regional network; where they could not travel themselves, they made intensive use of press releases to diffuse their local initiatives. They were delighted when an account of the Sleeping with Beds in the Street Festival got into a New Delhi newspaper and when Dutch tourists were seen in the Berguedà after the giants visited Amsterdam, arguing that their efforts were doing more for tourism than those of the local government.

La Bauma's focus on exchange to maintain and expand a network builds on a longterm strategy for circumventing Madrid and educating the outside world about Catalonia. *Intercanvis*, or exchanges, occupy a substantial place in the education and leisure activities of any middle-class Catalan in the *comarques*. With the increasing affluence and loosening of restrictions on travel and public assemblies at the end of the Franco regime, junior football clubs, choral societies, bird fanciers, chess players, and folk dance groups began to hold and attend tournaments and conventions, first in Catalonia itself, then across Europe and beyond. Schools cultivated summer-abroad exchanges with England and the United States. Other impetuses to horizontal solidarities are more overtly political, stemming from a long tradition of participation in international workers' and political movements, repaid with the support of the International Brigades in the Spanish Civil War and continuing today in vigorous solidarity campaigns for an impressive variety of causes.

New codes and media have been assiduously pressed into service. In the late nineteenth century, Esperanto clubs were formed in many towns of the *comarques*, enthusiastic about a language that would let them be international without speaking Spanish. Today English is used to the same end. Catalan teenagers are energetic pen pals, and the Internet has been embraced with still more fervor. Weary of the well-beaten single path from hinterland to capital—every kind of capital—many provincial Catalans see genuine liberation in the ethereal self-constituting linkages of the network (cf. Noyes 1997).

It's a question, though, how to develop their own capital to allow them to move in this freer world. Two dangers present themselves: a banalization that will lower the value of Berguedan tradition or a conversion of local culture into heritage that makes Berga into an "Indian reservation."

La Bauma's members acknowledge that the giant exchange quickly got old. One local *festa major* looks much like another, and giants assembled lose their individual impact. In such exchanges the local becomes modular (in the manner of U.S. multicultural representations) and is reduced to superficial emblems of distinctiveness—the local specialties, the giants with their names and attributes, the local Mare de Déu, and so forth. This is precisely the effect Mossèn Armengou feared from the presence of *festa major* attractions in the Patum, and the reason for refusing to circulate the Patum *entremesos*. And the effect is local as well as extramural. In the few years of La Bauma's most intense activity, Berguedans saw El Penina and La Gosolana almost once a month. They were never intended to excite the tremulous awe with which Berguedans approach the Black Giant, but under these circumstances they ceased even to command the collective attention: they were just part of the festival scenery.

If, on the other hand, Berguedans promote themselves as having a unique experience to offer—a unique access to the Catalan or universal primitive—to a limited public granted the privilege of initiation, then they reduce their own present possibilities to the custodial role: the priests of the Patum. Of course to an extent this has been going on since the turn of the nineteenth century, and it has arguably limited Berga's agency. As a reservoir of national essences to serve the city just as their water does, Berga takes on protagonism only in moments of national disaster, as when it relieved the Catalan cultural drought at the end of the Franco regime. Then Berga was both present and a presence. Today the Transition provides just another layer of nostalgia, and the Patum is once more in the past.

The necessity of developing the Patum for tourism places Berguedans in a cruel position. Striving assiduously to participate in modernity, they are always wearing their best clothes for the photograph, always performing for the other in whose eyes they would wish to be an ongoing presence. The Patum is their temporary release from this everyday struggle for *respecte*. But metropolitans have no reason to attend to Berga's modernity, which looks like everyone else's but less so. Rather, they want to penetrate that backstage region (MacCannell 1976, 91–107), which they interpret as the primary and authentic Berga. So Berga's privacy is invaded and becomes a second kind of performance to the outside world. And to succeed with the tourists, it must offer a stable reproducible image to be reconfirmed by each new viewer, joining what Barbara Kirshenblatt-Gimblett calls the 'second life of heritage' and Berguedans condemn as *folklòric*: forms maintained as forms, no longer embedded in the life of the community (Kirshenblatt-Gimblett 1998). But the Patum still has an important job to do in its first life, reconciling Berguedans to their differences, and freezing it will rob it of the power to respond to changing circumstances. Although many Catalan visitors understand this, Berguedans fear that the increasing promotion of the event to international tourism will inevitably turn the event into a museum piece. Many suspect—and the evidence increasingly confirms—that this is exactly what certain local politicians would like to do with this expensive, disorderly event.

Both kinds of Berguedan performance, that of tradition and that of modernity, entail a dissonance of insider and outsider perceptions—each enhancing the ironic or double consciousness of which necessity La Bauma made a virtue. La Bauma tried to place the double dissonance in the best light, arguing in both jest and earnest that Berga had already joined modernity in the best ways, but had to wear the mask for naïve Barcelonans ("Donem la benvinguda . . . " 1990, 4).

Networkers, *Integristes*, and Protagonism

In Berga the classic provincial tension between the yearning to belong and that for individual freedom is nuanced by highly qualified expectations regarding the latter. Freedom without resources is of little use; but, more, freedom has no payoff without *respecte*, one's ongoing existence as a person in the eyes of others. In Berga a person who is overly invested in agency before an audience is blamed for seeking *protagonisme*. More commonly, Berguedans lack the confidence to seek this extreme visibility, or—not surprisingly if one considers the risks of submitting to the gaze—the taste for it.

Collective protagonism permits a pooling of resources for greater visibility and agency at lower personal risk. As Armengou observed of the localist version, *Berguedanisme* redounds upon the individual Berguedan and allows her to move through the world "with her own identity card" ([1968, 1971]1994, 125).

The protagonist of the nineteenth century provincial novel generally attempts to resolve her dilemma of freedom and belonging through transcendence of the local into a less constraining, more exalted order: in the fairy-tale plot against which the novel writes itself, the protagonist is—eventually—incorporated into this higher world. Like other Catalans, Berguedans have always and assiduously sought admission to larger-order wholes, throwing their allegiance in turn to all the ones on offer: the Church Triumphant, Imperial Spain, Catalonia, the international workers' movements and political parties, Europe, the Mediterranean, global markets, and so forth. The problem has been to achieve *respecte*—recognition—within them and the resources that follow. Hence the importance of *intercanvi* and all the passionate efforts so typical of the upwardly mobile to display their competent participation in hegemonic norms.

The formula is clear: Berguedans want to belong to the largest collectivity that is both viable and will grant them full membership rights. They differ in their judgments with respect to the first criterion and their optimism with respect to the second. Some continue to look for the right project of transcendence to pull Berga out of its decline; others have grown skeptical of all large claims and external linkages, citing a history as old as the Patum in which such investments have realized nothing but political domination, economic exploitation, and local division. Most extremists of the first group are middle and upper-middle class, with prospects of some individual upward mobility; the most extreme of the second are middle-class Armengou disciples, but the majority are *popular*. The first group—of which La Bauma is at once the most reflective and the most ambivalent sector—may be called the networkers, an Anglicism of which they are fond; the second are jokingly referred to as the *integristes*, after the reactionary Catholics of the late nineteenth century. We would translate the term as "fundamentalists," but their word rightly emphasizes their concern with wholeness.[9]

In the economic sphere, of course, everyone is a networker, not least some of the most vocal *integristes* in the Bar La Barana. There is no choice. Despite the occasional autarkic fantasy, *integrisme* operates at a purely cultural level. In contrast to La Bauma's approach, *integrisme* is primarily reactive, refusing external cultural attractions rather than itself creating: there is a certain asceticism to it, and in extreme cases it is a kind of *via negativa*, a progressive closing out of the world's distractions to focus on the Berguedan core.

Recall the Berguedan conception of identity: the traces in the body of what you've taken in through performance. The networkers acknowledge that multiple connections result in multiple cultural inputs and a hybrid identity, which is in itself a resource for survival—witness the overall modernity and prosperity of Catalonia, *terra de pas*. *Integristes* argue that only full commitment is enough to sustain a threatened identity like that of Berga—or indeed of Catalonia. At a less articulated level, they know that their purity of feeling must be policed because it is already tainted. Beneath it lies the Franco regime. Outside it the world beckons; and even La Barana's regulars consume international media and take vacations elsewhere. But *integristes* abroad have prophylactic rituals to preserve themselves from seduction. Pere and Carme vacation with their daughter in places such as Egypt, Thailand, and the Dominican Republic. They take a Berguedan sausage and a bottle of good Penedès wine with them for the last night of their holiday, reminding themselves of why they want to go home and back to the arduous labor of the bar. The spontaneous Patums of Berguedans at a distance are a more extreme instance of this: not only displays to the other, but a check to the self, comparable to the self-segregating costume of sectarian religious groups. A group of three boys going off to a summer language course in England once lamented to me that the only thing interfering with their prospects of enjoyment was the absence of a fourth: "we can't dance the dwarfs." Dancing the dwarfs, they protect themselves from ever wanting to be anything else.

Better a dwarf among dwarfs than a dwarf among unheeding giants, the *integristes* retort. And indeed, in Berga one can be a giant among dwarfs in ways that other collectivities do not offer. Berga's rich festival and associative life is common to most towns of comparable size in Catalonia and provides a wide range of opportunities for *respecte* that do not demand a high level of educational or other capital to begin with. The price of admission is the desire to be admitted, and then standing is earned by performance. But on top of that is the Patum, and the chance to be central, a protagonist: for before all is dissolved in smoke, the Patum's exchange of gazes is intense and the Patum makes all its actors visible. Where else but in Berga could Mixo and Pepito be public figures?

Thus the undercapitalized *populars* have a special incentive to think like *integristes* and to censure others for succumbing to outside lures. In Berga you can live in a dim flat with archaic plumbing and still lead a life rich in satisfactions: not only those of incorporation, but those of *respecte*. But if the stage collapses, if, more importantly, the audience trickles away, you lose everything.

The Patum in Spain and the World

No hi ha més ciri del que crema.
There's no more candle than what's burning.
—Catalan and Spanish proverb

The End of Representation

BERGA'S BEST HOPE for a viable cultural future with recognizable links to the past may have been the coalition of La Bauma dels Encantats with the Carrer de la Pietat, the most open sector of *popular* Berga: a reflexive localism willing to make strategic alliances with the outside world in order to sustain itself. But La Bauma fell into desuetude in the mid-1990s. Why was it not sustainable?

La Bauma was in part the victim of its own success. Its Carnival met with such general enthusiasm and grew to such dimensions that responsibility for it was assumed by the Ajuntament. Similarly, various publishing initiatives of the transitional generation were consolidated in the 1990s, in some cases professionalized and in some municipalized. With the "normalization" of the new democratic order, culture became no longer the urgent business of everyone, but could revert to being a specialized product with specialized producers and more passive consumers. The same can be said of the arts in general: although new organizations continue to emerge in Berga, there is not the frenetic activity of the late 1980s and early 1990s, when every weekend saw at least one festival, concert, lecture, exhibition, book presentation, or *trobada*.

The effervescence of the moment soon came up against economic reality. Moreover, participants got tired and older. Berga's intelligentsia of the Transition took an unusually long time to settle down domestically and professionally, for such decisions were not purely personal but necessitated a choice of allegiance to the local or the metropolitan that would have a collective impact. But eventually you have to live for yourself as well as for Berga, and you no longer want to spend every night in bars until 3 A.M. "putting the world in order" or expend your creative energies composing Carnival verses that, however brilliant in their moment, will not outlast it. More than that, you need to start thinking practically—and for most of the university-educated, that meant leaving Berga for better professional opportunities. Many of the people animating Berguedan cultural life at the time of my first fieldwork spend very little time there now. The burden became too heavy on fewer people with less time to spare, and the next, post-Transition generation had not been bred to the motto of *entre tots ho farem tot*: between everyone we will do everything.

Factionalism and "envies" played their part even within La Bauma, and more broadly among the Transition generation. Competition for the scarce resource of protagonism and the scarcer resources of the usual kind led to the typical defensiveness of the haves and suspiciousness of the have-nots—positions exchanged from project to project. Decisions about whether or not to collaborate with the Ajuntament or other official bodies raised long-standing anxieties about the relation of government to civil society and led to painful disputes and personal risk-taking with, in some cases, destructive consequences. Many friendships cooled, and others were broken off. Perhaps the most disheartening aspect of it—coinciding with what seemed like an epidemic of clinical depression among my Berguedan acquaintance in the 1990s—was that factionalism did not lead, as traditionally it has, to more intense engagement, to people "getting burned." Rather, people simply distanced themselves, declared it wasn't worth it; the fire was allowed to burn down.

No one had worked out what was to feed the fire: that has been the great failure of Berguedan democratic politics, and perhaps of the Berguedan imaginary. "The festival is the only thing that works in Berga," said La Bauma's Carnival propaganda one year: "Why not have 364 days of Carnival and one of rest?" On the walk of La Bauma's giants from Solsona to Berga, the mayor of Navès—an exceptionally successful rural municipality—declared that an herbal healer and a journalist seemed like the ideal combination for giants of today. But if the local is this mix—the traditional font of essences and the ironic chronicler—is it sustainable? We are left with the primordial and the postmodern. What happened to Berga's modernity? Where is there an image not of natural reproduction and not of artificial reflection, but of production?

One of the most intelligent members of La Bauma was sitting with some of his cohort during a break in the *passacarrers* on the Saturday of a Patum in the early 1990s. He picked up my notepad and wrote on it, *La Patum és la sort i la desgràcia de Berga* (The Patum is Berga's luck and Berga's misfortune). "You can put that in your book," he said. "We do the Patum so well and so intensely that we never do anything else." He sipped his beer, speculating on the political form his ambitions for Berga might or might not take, and at last stood up. "Well, are we going to go chase the Guita or what?"

Respecte is a three-way process. Each self needs a larger community to serve as the ongoing audience that confers its reality, but both need a material world beneath them, to furnish their representations and sustain the corporeality that allows them to see and incorporate each other. Berguedans need to trust that when they look back at the world it too will still be there: that it too will be stable enough to meet the gaze.

But, as we have seen, the Patum's energies are notoriously untranslatable into any instrumental project, and Berguedan representations have become loosed from their moorings in everyday social reality. The Patum's metaphoric relation to the social body and its innumerable metonymic links to the long-established stuff of Berguedan life and history have traditionally anchored a collective culture so cohesive and rich that almost no gesture is void of resonance. When I first came in 1989, Berguedan public life was perhaps at its highest point: the creative energies of the Transition were supported by the generous cultural budgets of the first years of autonomy, and desire and capacity seemed on the way to convergence.

Today it feels different—and undoubtedly my perspective has changed since that first rapturous immersion, though it has taken a parallel path to that of the Transition activists. Where metaphor and metonymy once anchored Berguedan performances, a fissure is now opening between polarizing interpretive strategies: the ironies of the networkers and the immanence of the *integristes*. Either way, Berga is moving toward the end of representation: the Patum ultimately will stand for nothing or be everything.

Joseba Zulaika, studying another Spanish region with both problematic relations of part to whole and problems of representation more generally, describes the difference in one Basque community between those who approach their culture as metaphor and those who approach it as sacrament (1988). The latter approach makes political violence not only thinkable but necessary: it is ritual action with the power to make the world anew in its image.

Berguedan *integristes* are sacramental thinkers also: the Patum is the body and blood of Berga. Thus far, with a few conspicuous exceptions during the Transition, they have followed what one might call the mystical rather than the activist path of sacramentalism (though we should remember that figures such as Ignatius of Loyola traveled both roads and take nothing for granted). Rather than trying to remake the outside world, they have denied that world's reality. It is Freud a fortiori: Berguedans "cannot subsist on the scanty satisfaction which they can extort from reality" (1966, 372). Freud describes fantasy as a "nature reserve," "withdrawn from the reality principle" and from considerations of utility. As we know, Berguedan networkers, wedded perforce to such considerations, condemn *integrista* Berga as an "Indian reservation." But from within, an ontological inversion is possible, and with the *integrista* conferral of "firstness" on the Patum (Peirce 1991, 188–89), everything else loses reality as it gains in distance: people above all.

One day a Berguedan with one foot in La Bauma and one in La Barana said to me, "You Americans, you know, you all seem to me obsessed with the hunger to triumph, you're all driving yourselves crazy with ambition." A dozen people echoed him in urging me not to leave Berga for the vanities of American academe. "This life, what is it?" said a dresser of *plens*. "We're only here for a moment. What do we need? A good meal, a good friend, a big laugh"—"and ten minutes now and then with a good woman!" interjected the incorrigible Oscar—"that's enough."

The *integristes* have no faith in universals, nor in the particularist but ethereal combinatoria of the Internet, even if they are condemning themselves to live in an archaic geography of centers and peripheries, hierarchies and boundaries. They do all they can to reify, naturalize, and sacralize the face-to-face life of Berga, for hard historical experience has taught them that where the limits of community are clearly defined, its obligations are taken most seriously. Better the devil you know.

One Saturday night in the spring of 1991, very late, I was sitting in a bar with a group of friends—La Bauma members all. We had met for an aperitif perhaps eight hours earlier, had been to a concert or a book presentation—I forget which—had gone out to dinner and eaten long and well and now were having a *copeta*, not the last, of course, but the *penúltima*. As always by the second night of a Berguedan weekend, I was drooping with fatigue. Our faces were pale and our conversation old, but nobody moved to go. Somebody started talking about the extraordinary Patum planned for the seventry-fifth Anniversary of Queralt, and how everyone was sure to go regardless of their stated disapproval of Patums out of season, because everybody always went, and then I began to nod off, but suddenly Quirze turned to me. "You know what, Dorothy?" he said. "This is what you have to put at the end of your book:

POST FESTUM, PESTUM.[1]
AFTER THE PARTY, THE PLAGUE.

Absolutely not, said every reader of the manuscript: what a downer; you can't end the book that way. *Your* Patum might be ending; *the* Patum will go on.

No doubt, a Patum will go forward. But I stand as witness for a certain generation.[2] Let me try, then, in conclusion, to place that generation's anxieties in a larger context: to say something about the position of local culture in the transition between Francoism and—not the "normalization" into national modernity once imagined by Catalanists but global capitalism. For Berga is not the only place in the world to be tossed out of the fire of the state into the frying pan of the market.

Patum/Pactum: Festivals and Constitutions

During the transition to democracy, the Patum was representative in both of the senses I've emphasized in this book. It literally brought the community together: everyone was there, or at least every recognized kind of person. It made people present to each other, mobilizing them for activism. At the same time it depicted and modeled the community, making a statement that had in some ways to be felt as normative.

There is some contradiction between these two modes of representation, felt perhaps more today than at the time. The Patum was activist and dynamic; it liberated bodies and set them in motion to be carried toward unknown destinations. But the Patum was also self-control and self-limitation, as exemplified in the refusal to turn it into an Assemblea de Catalunya rally.

The same tension was felt in the larger society, between the two aspects of the political transition: democracy and constitutionalism. These are old enemies, like the mule and the giants. From the birth of the modern state, notes Jean Blondel, democrats have denounced constitutions as imposed from above, perpetuating elite privilege, whereas constitutionalists fear democracy as the mere rule of the mob, a threat to order (1998).

Pragmatically, however, they are obliged to coexist (and this is what Durkheim failed fully to articulate about organic and mechanical solidarity). "The relationship between the two concepts will therefore continue to be both strong and ambiguous" (85). The *convivència* of the two in both the Patum and the new Spanish state can be described in just such terms. The Patum is a framework in which disorder could be given its place and contained—this is another view of the relationship between constitution and democracy (Wolin 1996, 33)—but also a contest on the ground in which, during the Transition at least, disorder generally had the best of it. I have spoken enough of how this contest fed into the mobilizations for democracy of the Transition; let me now consider further the "constitutionalist" relationship of Patum and Transition—one of deeper historical roots and of longer ultimate impact.

A distinctive feature of both the process leading to the adoption of the 1978 Constitution and the Constitition itself is known as *pactismo* in Castilian, *pactisme* in Catalan; the link, therefore, is one made between Patum and pactum. This is not wholly an opportunistic *figura etimologica* on my part;[3] rather the occasional direct analogies drawn by participants are supported by both formal similarities and, I want to suggest, a transfer of local habits to the larger political realm. The Patum helped to make the Constitution thinkable for the Catalans who had to vote for it in referendum.

Pactisme in the most general sense is the disposition to contract agreements involving mutual concessions with parties of different identities and interests from one's own. *Pactisme* was the practical mechanism enabling political *convivència* across the deep ideological divides in Spanish politics, not to mention across the gulf between the center and the historic regions, and it was also key to labor-capital relations in the period. The famous debate between *reforma* and *ruptura* (Gunther, Sani, and Shabad 1988, 34–36), was suspended in a *reforma pactada* or *ruptura pactada* (depending on which history you read), in which the regime voluntarily surrendered power in a negotiated process leading to the creation of a new Constitution. This consensual process, it has been suggested, contributed to democratic consolidation in Spain insofar as all political groups felt that they had had a hand in creating the Constitution, and the popular referendum validated the work of the elites (Linz, Stepan, and Gunther 1995, 100–101, 117).

At the level of Catalonia, we have seen how prior pacts permitted situational solidarity. The Assemblea de Catalunya was the prime example and set the model throughout the region: for example, a chronicler insists on the "assembly character" of a massive demonstration in support of the Berguedan miners' strike of 1977, in which no single union sought protagonism (Mau Branco 2000, 92). In these situations, where pacts preceded mass demonstrations, rhythmic unanimity offered—as it did in the Patum—a counterweight to felt differences of identity and interests. By analogy, a more foundational solidarity could overcome factionalism at need.

The labor pacts of the Transition, responding not only to the new political situation but to the troubles of aging industries exacerbated by the oil crisis, might also be seen as unity in the face of a common external threat. But it is impossible to speak of solidarity between labor and capital: historical memories were too long, conflict was too entrenched, and worker identities in particular were too bound up with the distinction. These pacts were made of grudging necessity, as regarded the immediate local situation, and—here the utopian dimension was not absent—as an investment in a different future: unions sacrificed not only immediate gains but their own organizational interests in exchange for concessions implementing more democratic procedures in the workplace and in the hope of contributing to the stability of Spanish democracy (Fishman 1990).[4] The class barrier could be crossed but not transcended. In this sense, *pactisme* held conflict in check; it was not strong enough to work towards a common identification.

And this was the point of *pactisme* in the larger Spanish political realm: pacts were formed between the parties with no expectation of or even desire for solidarity, but rather in order to create a structure for regulating conflict. The "era of consensus" (Gunther, Sami, and Shabad 1988, 113) of 1977–79 served first, with the 1977 Pacts of Moncloa, to establish an economic and social policy to mitigate the economic crisis while preserving the social peace necessary to draft and approve the Constitution; next, to attain the necessary cooperation to pass the Constitution and the Basque and Catalan Statutes of Autonomy. *Pactisme* was a necessary evil to achieve "a consensual and possible way out of the dictatorship," a pragmatic response to the "rupturist dream" (Segura 2000, 45), since no party was strong enough either to transform or to preserve the status quo alone. It lasted no longer than necessary to achieve its goals: even the Assemblea, once the first elections were announced, began to fissure along party lines as competition for supporters began (37). *Pactisme* was a practical recognition of irreducible diversity of positions, to be institutionalized in a constitution that would acknowledge that diversity and secure its institutional, geographical, and material base. At the same time, *pactisme* had a visible centripetal effect on all parties, allowing the right to make unexpected concessions and causing the left to soften its discourse and moderate its demands (Gunther, Sami, and Shabad 1988, 68; Segura 2000, 32–33, 37, 45).

Like the Patum with its noise to drown out speech and its multivocal symbols, the constitutional process was understood to depend on silences and ambiguities. Cass Sunstein, writing in the context of U.S. constitutional debates and the new constitutions of South Africa and Eastern Europe, argues that both silence and ambiguity are crucially important to the process in plural societies. What is wholly intractable must sometimes simply be shelved. And constitutions work by abstractions, the "incompletely specified" (2001, 56), leaving room for maneuver in response to new situations. More generally, says Sunstein, cooperation in plural societies tends to succeed in practice through "incompletely theorized agreements," allowing agreement on how to proceed without demanding an impossible consensus on first principles.

Laura Desfor Edles has noted the importance of abstractions (*convivencia*, "a new beginning," etc.) as tools of consensus in the period of the Constitution's framing (1998). The Spanish Constitution itself, strangely absent from Sunstein's discussion, has often been noted for its combination of clearly new and democratic content with much that is "ambiguous, imprecise, and unfinished" (Segura 2000, 48). Both the Constitution and the Catalan Statute of Autonomy were deliberately vague regarding several issues that could not be resolved at the time and today recur in debate: Spain as a not quite federal "state of autonomies"; the definition of nation and its identification with either Spain or the "historic regions" of the Basque Country, Catalonia, and Galicia; the special status of those historic regions as something somehow more than the other autonomies; the definition of culture (Prieto de Pedro 1998, 63); and what it means for a language to be "official" (77).

In addition to such absences of specificity, *pactisme* itself is institutionalized: "the composite Spanish state model places cooperation and loyalty among its essential principles" (74). The "organized pluralism" of the Constitution (Linz, Stepan, and Gunther 1995, 100–101, 117) became itself the locus of such imagined community as the Transition could permit itself, substituting for the historically rooted unitary narrative of the ideal nation-state (cf. Boyd 1997, 306). Like the Patum of the period, the

Spanish state had to make much of collective process in the absence of collective content and to flatter itself that the two might ultimately fuse into something like Durkheim's organic solidarity.

Sunstein talks of constitutions as ideally a means of promoting encounters across enclaves and suggests that the polarization of opinion characteristic when like-minded groups are left to themselves may be averted by the creation and enforcement of opportunities for mutual exposure. The Spanish Constitution is especially attentive to creating such opportunities in the conflictive realm of culture, according to Jesús Prieto de Pedro: Article 149.2 imposes on the state the task of "facilitating cultural communication between the Autonomous Communities, in agreement with them" (quoted in Prieto de Pedro 1998, 71). The creation of parallel competences rather than exclusive ones was intended, according to Prieto, to promote interactions between entities and to create multiple sites for the generation of policy discussion, precisely as Sunstein prescribes—though the Spaniards who have now lived twenty and more years under the system might point out some drawbacks: the reduplication of efforts and so of expenditures, competition over concrete domains resulting in stagnation, and the evasion of final responsibility.[5] And Sunstein, to be sure, notes that imperfectly theorized agreements are generally lesser evils, not devoid of inherent problems.

It appears, in any case, that entities have not much availed themselves of the opportunities constitutionally provided for. "There is no dialogue," I once heard a prominent Catalan linguist complain, lamenting that none of his Catalanist colleagues would agree to read a bestselling book opposing the Generalitat's sociolinguistic policy, even for the sake of refuting it. In Catalonia and Spain at large, the *pactista* phase has given way—as was no doubt anticipated in the constitutional process—to renewed factionalism and mutual distrust, each to his own, rather than to a cross-fertilization of ideas and policies. Now that the constitution and the statutes exist, interaction is no longer necessary. Here, to be sure, the face-to-face community has an advantage over the nation-state. Hitherto, Berguedans have had a sense of being stuck with each other and have been eager to remind one another of their mutual dependence in the absence of much attention from the outside world; nor could complete avoidance be cultivated. In the Spain of the Transition, when the economy was in crisis and membership in Europe was not assured, and when military uprising, worker revolution, and terrorism threatened peace within, most Spaniards also had a general sense of needing each other. Today, with Spain so fully networked in larger political structures and a global economy, this is less the case. Here too, performance has an advantage over text, as Rousseau knew ([1758]1967). The Constitution models Spanish society as the Patum models Berga: but the Patum is a permanent reconstitution, an annual effervescence that founds anew the bases of social coexistence.

The Spanish transition has been seen as "paradigmatic" and often, indeed, as a model for the integration of plurinational states (Linz, Stepan, and Gunther 1995, 77, 87, 90; Morán 1991, 232–41; Dufour 2000). Catalonia rather than the Basque Country provided the successful case in which "complementary multiple political identities" (for example, Catalan and Communist) assisted the reconciliation of national, democratic, and statist needs (Linz, Stepan, and Gunther 1995, 121–22).[6] The Catalan situation was eased in part, Edles suggests, by considerable overlap between mainstream Catalanist symbols and those invoked in the Transition, whereas for the Basques this was not the case: thus Catalan nationalists could participate fully in the Transition without betraying their sense of themselves (1998, 118). Edles does not examine the sources of the symbols she posits, but *pactisme* was emphatically one of them.

Catalans, indeed, considered *pactisme* a tendency peculiarly theirs. Just as their civil society was in many ways post-Francoist long before the rest of Spain (Oliver 2000), so it is possible to see Catalan political processes as setting the pattern for Spain as a whole, the Assemblea and other coalitions serving as the model for the later Platajunta (Segura 2000, 29). Reversing the picture, some see the Catalan habit of compromise as what prevented a true break with the inequities and iniquities of the old regime.

As with the Patum, commentators on *pactisme* mitigate the ambiguities of its contemporaneity by casting it back deep in the past; and like those of the Patum, these origin narratives respond to a present sense that *pactisme* is both *sort* and *desgràcia*, luck and curse.[7] *Pactisme* is what accounts for Catalonia's ambiguous survival as not quite a nation.

The term was first popularized by the great historian, Jaume Vicens Vives, in his 1954 book *Noticia de Cataluña*. Vicens explains this leading "tendency . . . of the national mentality" (1954, 88) as a product of the conditions of feudalism in a frontier setting. Concretely, he defines it as a procuring of political order through a pact with the sovereign power. The Kings of Aragon swore an oath to defend the constitutions of Catalonia,

dating, as Catalan scholars enjoy pointing out, from before Magna Carta
(e.g., Giner 1980, 5), and by the thirteenth century a parliament representing the three estates met regularly; the Catalan Generalitat became
the permanent body representing the Catalan elites in their relations with
royal power (McRoberts 2001, 10–11). The elite and the estates within it
collaborated with the monarchy and with each other without surrendering identity or a certain level of autonomy. These arrangements continued
through the early modern period: royal violation of the pact served as
the legitimation of the 1640 revolt that is now a keystone of Catalanist
memory (Elliott 1963, 286, 549).

Pactisme in this analysis is an alternative to absolutism: by this argument, taken up by mainstream nationalists, Catalans gave up nothing
without concessions in return, making the best of an unequal situation.
Elliott suggests that the longevity of the Spanish monarchy (and, Catalan
thinkers would add, the Spanish state), lay not in its strength but in its
weakness: local elites found it tolerable because they could sabotage its
initiatives at the local level, and often got the best of the bargain (1989,
90–91).

The application of the term was broadened as its usage was generalized. The sociologist Salvador Giner described *pactisme* as characteristic
not just of relations with the sovereign, but of relations between the
classes, and situated both political and socioeconomic *pactisme* in his account of Catalonia's trajectory as a kind of England manqué (Giner 1980,
and cf. McRoberts 2001, 10–11). Mainstream nationalists popularized the
term, claiming that this characteristic allowed Catalonia to flourish and facilitated its more recent success in integrating its immigrants, accommodating politically to Spain, modernizing and globalizing its economy, and
so forth. The term was thus extended from the pact with the center to
pacts within the elite (as those between parties in the Assemblea) and to
the *pacte social* between employers and workers (for which precedents
could hardly be found in more recent Catalan history). Today in the post-
Transition period it has come to mean a general willingness to compromise between interests and, more generally still (the English analogy
again), a kind of Third Way pragmatism allowing Catalans to make sensi-
ble business and political decisions. As a slogan, *pactisme* positions the
Catalan past as a central resource for the Spanish collective present.

For, to be sure, there are other lineages for the phenomenon, most
of a more recent and embarrassing character. After the evidently divisive
extremisms of the Second Republic, the Franco regime was marked by

compromise and mutual accommodation at every level of society, including within the regime's elite itself, which overcame its ideological diversity to preserve its rule. The Catalan bourgeoisie, out of fear, exhaustion, and a desire to preserve its interests, found itself able to accommodate to the regime very well; and local postwar reconciliation, as we have seen, drew upon celebrations such as the Patum as well as on more brutally imposed national-Catholic rituals to restore at least a show of unity. In ludic, ritual, and instrumental forms, Catalans learned to collaborate with and participate in the regime, and this accommodation produced both accommodation from the other side and, in at least some cases, a consensual character to the restored order. While the threat and reality of violence maintained the regime's power, so did its concessions, and in Catalonia compromise was often found preferable to the expense of constant imposition by force, given the impossiblity of ideological incorporation.

It is thus not surprising that the compromises of the Transition created dissent within parties, unions, and other partners to agreements (Gunther, Sami, and Shabad 1988, 396–97; Fishman 1990). Celebrated on one side, *pactisme* is denounced on the other as Catalonia's fatal unwillingness to go all the way. Today, militant nationalists and, in parallel arguments, militant leftists reserve the epithet *pactista* for their fullest contempt, placing in withering alliteration *pragmatisme, possibilisme, i pactisme*.[8] Vicens himself, at the very moment of putting the term forward, expresses his ambivalence. Pactism was "paradoxically beneficial . . . it nourished the illusion of an elected monarchy—and, therefore, one obligated to maintain the pacts and conditions with which they received sovereignty" (Vicens Vives 1954, 85). But, says Vicens, when a foreign dynasty inherited the kingship, Catalonia became vulnerable to those not playing by the same rules. This, precisely, is the drawback judged intolerable by nationalists and leftists, each feeling that the compromises entered into by their respective leaderships have timidly preserved their narrower interests to the prejudice of the group they represent. *Pactisme* becomes associated with another highly ambiguous word, "collaboration."

Pactisme, in the critical view, provokes not merely a loss of power for the period of the contract, but a fatal erosion of identity: Catalans are no longer Catalan and the left is no longer left (an argument not exclusive to Catalonia). This is often seen by outsiders as an advantage of the process: for example, Linz, Stepan, and Gunther note that one consequence of giving security to minority identities is that those identities become more open to change (1995, 92). Today, such widespread adjectives as "lite" or "decaffeinated," applied to everything from linguistic norms to political projects, mark the strategies felt to be adulterations. Alternatively, a meaningless consumerist cultural diversity is cited, facilitated by a civility that is as destructive to dialogue as avoidance. Guillem Martínez, defining post-Transition culture as continuous with the "pop Francoism" of the 1970s, complains that there are no shocks of encounter. Real opinion is rejected as violence, resulting in an "I'll-suck-yours-if-you-suck-mine way of life" with no real pluralism because nothing serious is at stake (2001, 15): difference means mutually tolerant narcissisms. Most widespread is the complaint of loss of identity through enforced amnesia (Morán 1991; Vilarós 1998; Resina 2000, etc.). The "pact of forgetting" of the Transition (Segura 2000, 16) has not simply allowed power to remain in the hands of an elite that changes color with the fashion but left a younger generation ignorant of the repression and so with no burning need to understand what came before it.

We have seen similar anxieties in Berga as the generation of the Transition contemplates the future of the Patum. The Patum, as Berga's living constitution, was the locus of the renegotiation of power relations and modeled the larger situation for participants. In the Patum's organized conflicts, differences are recognized but not resolved; no decisive victory is ever earned, and all parties, however polarized, are still there at the end. Similarly, the reduplications and ambivalences of the constitution and the "period of consensus" are anticipated in the Patum. The multiple overlapping and contradicting selves of the *comparses* reflect not only the local sense that "everything is double," but what would become a national predicament.

The Patum encapsulates a kind of knowledge particular to face-to-face communities from which exit is difficult (cf. Hirschman 1970). There compromise is essential, and some sharing of the public space and the *res publica* must be carried out to ensure the viability of the whole. Elites need to accommodate both to the outside powers whence their authority derives and to the people who are their power base. In Francoist Catalonia, this micropolitical knowledge was formalized and so made transmissible to other contexts in two ways: the symbolic form of Patum and related genres, and the more instrumental form (reinforced, of course, by the symbolic) of voluntary associations such as the Boy Scouts, in which most of the Transition's Catalanist elite received their political education. As a formative symbolic experience for thousands of people from all over

Catalonia who identified themselves as politically active, the Patum provided a matrix for understanding how order and democracy might be seen as compatible and how diverse parts might be integrated into a whole.

There were times when the micro and macro levels were brought together explicitly, as when, using Berga's older language of the body politic, Franco came to Berga to preside over the festival; the new King Juan Carlos did the same in the middle of the Transition. Allusions showing a more widespread use of the analogy can be found in the press of the period, as when in June 1977 *Tele/eXprés* published Joan J. Guillén's cartoon of the returning Catalan President-in-Exile, Josep Tarradellas, as a *guita* charging toward Madrid to negotiate the restoration of the Generalitat. Tarradellas surely did not welcome the analogy: he despised the "folklorism" and "confusion" of the Assemblea's style of politics and favored a more instrumental approach to the restoration of institutions and his own power, a probable reason for his having been chosen by Madrid as the Catalan representative in the first place (Segura 2000). But there is no question that his negotiating power was greatly enhanced by the masses in the street (Segura 2000, 38; Gunther, Sani, and Shabad 1988, 68), and the cartoon made a still stronger claim. Tarradellas is the figurehead of the effigy, and the neck presses forward as if to charge, but beneath the *guita*'s body is a multitude of dancing feet, and heads pressing up against the canvas.[9]

Catalan, Taliban, Caliban? Globalizing Slogans and the Fate of Local Culture

The ambivalence about *pactisme* is not soothed by the global voices praising Catalonia as a kind of model minority. Just as Spain has been seen as a model of democratic transition in a multicultural society, so some prestigious apostles of liberalism have singled out Catalonia as an exemplary stateless nation for its ability to reconcile cultural identity with political accommodation and economic globalization—its third way, if you will. *The Economist*, for example, gave flattering attention to Jordi Pujol throughout his years as President of the Generalitat, and particularly praised his cross-regional initiatives in the European Union; other commentators suggest that Spain offers a model for a "Europe of the regions" (Dufour 2000).

Manuel Castells, sociologist and globalization guru, sees a double evolution in the current "informational revolution" (1997): while the information society becomes increasingly flexible, networked, virtual, based in flows and not in entities, selves become increasingly committed to identities—defensive entrenchments seeking meaning and control. There is thus a felt decoupling of action and meaning. Castells reproduces, in more sophisticated fashion, Benjamin Barber's distinction between McWorld and Jihad: but whereas Barber qualifies Catalan nationalists as "viperous" Jihad adherents, apparently because of their interest in using their own language (1996, 174), Castells (who has multiple connections with the region, beginning with his surname) singles out Catalonia for implicit praise. Catalonia is the purely cultural nation, defined by meaningful historical continuity based in an ongoing sense of separate identity sustained by a fully developed language and thus culture. It has no need for a state, and its voluntarist, participatory notion of identity fosters social inclusion. "The differentiation between cultural identity and the power of the state, between the undisputed sovereignty of apparatuses and the networking of power-sharing institutions . . . seems to relate better than traditional notions of sovereignty to a society based on flexibility and adaptability, to a global economy, to networking of media, to the variation and interpenetration of cultures" (1997, 50).

Bill Clinton gave it a more rhythmic formulation. In late October 2001, he visited Barcelona, sponsored by a group of multinational corporations and consulting firms with offices in the city. In the Palau de Congressos before 2,700 businessmen and politicians, he called for a social dimension to globalization, urging prosperity and tolerance as the best antidotes to terrorism. He had clearly done his homework on Catalonia for the visit. Making a metaphor of Gaudí's unfinished Sagrada Família (like many a Catalan poet before him), he urged a humble recognition of the partial character of our knowledge, turning this into an argument for diversity and the need for plural perspectives. Catalonia, he said, would not enjoy its present prosperity were it not for its long-term commitment to an open society: in support he cited Jordi Pujol's historic singing of a forbidden song in the presence of Franco, the country's present embrace of diversity, and its exercise of rivalry through the healthy channel of sport—as in the forthcoming match of Barça and Real Madrid. Catalonia had had the strength to turn from separatism and terrorism, he said. The world could make the same choice to embrace common humanity through celebrating diversity, or it could choose darkness and isolation. The future, he said, will be Catalan or Taliban.[10]

The editorialists of *Avui*, the Catalan-language newspaper heavily subventioned by the Generalitat, praised the speech and pointed out the difference between Clinton and José Maria Aznar, then calling for a Spanish "patriotism" and denouncing what he termed closed-minded regional "nationalisms" in a discourse widely perceived as capitalizing on the world security situation to make more instrumental assaults on regional autonomy (Simó 2001; Sintes 2001). A wider range of Catalan commentators, fearing globalizers bearing gifts, noted that the admirable Catalan-Taliban soundbite was clearly Clinton's bouquet to his hosts in exchange for his substantial speaking fee (Mira 2001; Pernau 2001; Porcel 2001).

What is Clinton proposing here as the future of local communities under globalization? We could paraphrase it, depressingly, as the choice between tourism and terrorism.[11] But if he were to revise his speech for an audience of literature professors instead of businessmen, he might well expand the options by one. The future will be Catalan, Taliban—or Caliban.

The future will be Catalan: local identities rooted in practices marked off as cultural, compatible with economic and political integration into larger wholes, and tolerant of other such identities similarly framed. The future will be Taliban: warring enclaves policing both their boundaries and their cores, imposing univocality within and separation without. Or the future will be Caliban: subaltern actors speaking hegemonic languages in order to curse, half-tamed, half-tied to the remembered magic of their origins, their local bodily intensity a compensatory move for their larger political impotence.[12]

All of these options have been present in the Patum for a long time, as we have seen, and they have come historically in this order. Provincial places have been undergoing the first form of globalization throughout the long advent of modernity, and since at least the late eighteenth century local elites have been transforming the Patum into a simulacrum of local autonomy and distinctiveness as they work desperately to build ties between Berga and sources of power and capital. Mainstream Catalanism has, after all, its historical roots and its demographic base in the *comarques* and draws on older habits: it is self-provincializing not in its demands but in its accommodations and its longing for recognition.[13]

A moderate form of the Taliban response dates from at least the nineteenth century at the elite level, when we can associate it with the

Carlist movement, and comes to focus on the Patum with Mossèn Armengou and his followers; the current *integristes* among the *patumaires* of La Barana profess a less austere version of this same tendency to vigilant separation. Douglas Holmes notes "integralism" as an orientation spreading throughout Western Europe (2000), and subsequent populist victories and anti-immigrant agitations confirm his view. But two things militate against serious *integrisme* in Berga. One is the long-bred feeling of insufficiency. While many Berguedans might admire the kind of anti-globalism fostered by José Bové, they are likely to see him as a kind of Astérix, a compensatory fantasy—and that in fact is what popular *integrisme* is, something propounded in La Barana at the Saturday breakfast.[14] The other is the memory of the war and the present shadow of Basque terrorism. Frustration and the slow erosion of selfhood is better than living—and dying—in perpetual hatred of the other. *Pactisme* is preferred as both the only viable and the least destructive option.

But there is resentment that cannot abate, since its sources are only growing stronger. Berguedans are *cremats*, neither destroyed by the fire nor free of it. And so the *integrista* desire has metamorphosed into a version of Caliban: from active combat to the curse of the vanquished, and eventually from rejection to simple denial of global power, a withdrawal into body and territory. Recall the primitivism and the physical intensity of the Patum of the young. Caliban has his own Patum: he drinks, and like Berguedans seeking to escape subjection to one ideology through the next one that offers itself, Caliban in the clouded vision of his drunkenness offers his devotion to Stephano and Trinculo, who are neither interested in nor capable of saving him. Both Caliban and the Berguedans awaken (not all of the Berguedans, and only after centuries of painful experience) to recognize the folly of looking for freedom in yet another servitude. But both are too weak for independent revolt: they are prisoners and seek renewed intoxication to forget it. The Berguedans in despair finally make gods of their pasteboard giants and withdraw into their social body, whose sensations provide their escape from mental pain. Like Caliban, they are punished with the body's aging and the disgust of the aftermath.

Post festum pestum, in short. But the Berguedans and I their chronicler are not more apocalyptic than cultural commentators with a wider Spanish view, such as Martínez with his "Franquismo pop" (2001), Resina with his "specter of difference" (2000, 11), or Vilarós, with her account of the Transition as the monkey on Spain's back from the late Francoist addiction to authority, consumption, and compensatory utopias (1998).

The humanists despair of the new Spain and the political scientists delight in it: no surprises there, and no point in arguing with the mules against the giants when both will always be with us and both are, in their fashion, right. However, although this round of *tirabols* is coming to an end and the band has stopped, I still have a bit of *fuet* burning: permit me one final *petar* in the plaça.

Following Morán (1991, 26), Vilarós claims that Spain became post-modern *avant la lettre*, because liberalization arrived in commodity form in the late years of the dictatorship, and globalized too, because modernization arrived through foreign investment and through tourism (1998, 77–78). But she writes with the normative expectation of an autonomy proper to the nation-state and never experienced by much of the world's population. Berga and other provincial communities depended on outside investment and tourism already in the late nineteenth century, if not before.

We are all becoming provincial: Berga's past and present are everyone's future. The developing world will follow its path, and the developed world will collapse back into it. Barcelona post-1992 is acquiring layers that make it a global city like any other:[15] it is no longer the primary source of its own languages for representation. Those things distinct to it are already becoming as *folklòric* and as in need of preservation as the Patum is felt to be. Every place is becoming provincial in relation to a now placeless metropolis, the both omnipresent and slippery global network along which meaning and resources circulate. Everything marked as local—resistant to circulation—is becoming either a museum of itself (Kirshenblatt-Gimblett 1998), a generator of increasingly violent refusal, or a source of temporary and increasingly self-destructive escape: Catalan, Taliban, or Caliban.

What can we learn, then, from the provincial knowledge embodied in the Patum? Certainly not any means of escape from dependence. The Patum tells us we have no choice but *pactisme* between mules and giants. But it offers us something more: the fire in which they merge. Plens and *tirabols* are dangerous (and the giants have ways of sheltering themselves from the impact) but also exhilarating.

By extension, Vicens Vives has a generally positive conclusion about *pactisme*, despite its risks—and one suggesting his own experience in more face-to-face communities. *Pactisme* understood as a habit of thought, he concludes, "is nothing but the refusal of all abstraction, going to the reality of human life and establishing the tightest collective and individual responsibility in dealing with the public good" (1954, 88). What matters, perhaps, is not the consensual aspect of *pactisme*—giving something up is after all inevitable—but the confrontation of meaningful difference. The encounter provides the *pets* and *patratrac!*, the clash and "crunching" that Martínez claims is missing from current Spanish high culture (2001, 15). The pa-tum of the drum and the kick of the Guita make consensus not in the air, through abstraction, but on the ground, through common material being. Berguedans insist on everyone's responsibility for the *res publica* of the Patum, and this obligation of presence offers what Sunstein sees as the mitigation for the necessary evils of compromise in plural societies and, we should add, unequal ones: the necessity of looking the other in the face, of being I and thou to one another. *Pactisme* opens the possibility of organic solidarity.

The diminution of everyday social interaction in Berga does threaten this. When the ritual encounter is not one of friends and enemies, but one of comparative strangers, it necessarily takes on a more abstract character: the sense of mutual belonging and responsibility is not "tight," as Vicens described it. This does not necessarily threaten the reproduction of the Patum as a form. Catalans and Calibans both have an interest in maintaining it: the mules of local resistance will continue to dance it out with the giants of globalization for years to come. Both, to be sure, treat it as exactly what Berguedans spoke of with fear in the late 1980s: "an Indian reservation," cut off from modern, instrumental life.

Catalans and Calibans disagree about the purposes and potential of Indian reservations. For the networker-*pactistes*, such places should remain bounded as national parks, designated heritage sites; spaces of escape and refreshment. For the young, the squatters, the antiglobalization protesters, the neotribals, the Indian reservation can generate an alternative way of life and reach out to other such preserves in pan-indigenist initiatives—bit by bit.

Older, stricter materialists—among whom many of the "Indians" in question count themselves—would turn instead to an ecological metaphor, more appropriate to the region given the ever lower reservoir of La Baells above Berga. The role of the provinces may be just to keep bringing water to the metropolis, and when Berga is finally exhausted, it will be left dry.

But to lodge ourselves in possibly more defensible territory—a new cave of Can Maurí in which Berguedans can hide from the current invasion—we can take refuge in the forms themselves. As long as the effigies are preserved physically and, more importantly, in memory, they can be picked up and reanimated. "The Patum is sleeping," Jepes said to his son looking at the empty plaça. It is now guaranteed—this book among myriad other objectifications ensures it—that Berga will be put to bed as "heritage" even if it burns itself out as a material and human community. Will it wake again?

Recall Durkheim's modeling of organic solidarity on heterosexual marriage. Although the probable reduction of the Patum to heritage will entail a loss of traditional practices of *convivència* (and thus of important collective knowledge), heritage marks the site of loss and thus sustains desire: in the case of the Patum, the desire for integration with the other. Even this is important in the face of individual consumerism and careerism, hostility toward new immigrants, and general political cynicism. Gérard Noiriel suggests that Durkheim's program of organic solidarity was initially formed in rejection of the *intégrisme* of the period (1996, 14–16, cited in Holmes 2000, 15): Durkheim insisted on an ethos that would embrace rather than resist the differentiations of modernity. The Berguedans, from their weaker position, have made a virtue of necessity and infused their dependency with moral and affective meaning. The provincial attachment to the project of organic solidarity offers our best hope against fragmentation into a world of armed camps. What matters now is that the metropolis should keep its promises.[16]

Notes

Introduction

1. See Jay (1984, 27ff.) for one tracing of this lineage. I will discuss the Corpus Mysticum in Chapter 2, but see Rubin (1991, 259–71) and note that the elaboration of the social body metaphor in medieval thought coincides with the reification of social categories in the twelfth century, often seen as the *longue-durée* inception of modernity (Moore 1987). For the early modern social body, see Davis (1981); for nationalism, Dumont (1986, 113–32) and Handler (1988); for Fascism, Gentile (1996); for corporatism and neocorporatism, Rabinow (1989), Fishman (1990), Pérez-Díaz (1993), and Kasmir (1996).

2. The literature on Carnival is, of course, enormous, and here as elsewhere my citations offer only an initial orientation. As examples, see Mintz (1997) and Gilmore (1998) on the subtleties of class, gender, and Carnival in Andalusia; for a fascinating Italian case, Bertolotti (1991). For the relationship between Carnival and other public genres, Da Matta (1991) is illuminating.

3. For some interpretations exploring ethnic and class conflict in folk drama, see Glassie (1975), Abrahams and Bauman (1978), and Green (1980) for the Anglophone mummers' play; Fabre and Camberogue (1977) for Languedoc; Silverman (1985) for central Italy; Ariño (1988) on Moors and Christians in Spain and Harris (2000) for a view extending into Mexico; Danforth (1983) for Greek shadow theater; Hammoudi (1993) for Morocco.

4. This theme has been a less explicit focus in the literature on contemporary festival, but see, for example, Magliocco (1993), Bendix (1985), and Neville (1994). For contemporary civic festival in Europe, see Dundes and Falassi (1975), Fribourg (1980), Gueusquin (1988).

5. Durkheim proposed professional corporations as the basis for a new social organization in the preface to the second edition of *The Division of Labor in Society* ([1893]1984, xxxi–lvii); his later writings also emphasize the continuing importance of religion and national ritual to the creation of solidarity across class boundaries.

6. To be sure, Durkheim's astonishing indifference to the inequality he sees as a necessary concomitant of complementarity ([1893]1984, 17–21) is not shared by Berguedans, and this is for them the principal barrier to organic solidarity.

7. I adapt the phrase from Bakhtin ([1968]1984, 123, quoted in Morson and Emerson 1990, 460).

8. Strictly speaking, the Patum has been constructed over nearly four centuries,

but its basic form was completed and stabilized in the early 1890s; cf. Noguera (1992).

9. Durkheim's frequent use of the phrase *le corps social* reveals the continuity in root metaphors ([1893]1911, xxxi, 26, 38, 72, 75, 85, 475). His interest in corporations—that is, guilds—is one example of his conscious attention to medieval social theory and organization.

10. I am not exempt from this tendency to credit my constructs and theirs with reality. In this book I have often found myself using a Berguedan shorthand, which is in part convenience and part the necessary forgetting that makes culture second nature (cf. Bourdieu 1984, 11). When I say, "The Patum does X," I mean something like, "The thousands of Berguedans who have shaped the Patum over four centuries have contributed to a formation which, according to many Berguedans, has the effect of . . ." Of course this is unsatisfactory—it is also unavoidable.

11. The enormous "critique of ethnography" discussion has established this at length. The line of ethnographic work I find most productive is summarized in Fernandez and Herzfeld (1998) regarding poetics and Fabian (1990, 1994) regarding epistemology.

12. Most important to my thinking over the long term have been Roger D. Abrahams' synthesis of history and cultural performance (e.g., 1992, 1995), and James W. Fernandez's development of the rhetorical line of Kenneth Burke on symbolic forms as the shaping of inchoate situations so that they can be addressed (1986).

13. Extreme instances, which theatricalize powerlessness through the expenditure of self, may be found in such protest genres as hunger strike and self-immolation (e.g., Feldman 1991; Noyes 2000a).

14. In Balzacian terms, every Rastignac leaves a Lucien de Rubempré in his wake. On the importance of both the province and the fairy tale in the bildungsroman, see Moretti (2000).

15. In Flaubertian terms, M. Homais gets his decoration from the government, but Yonville remains Yonville, and Hippolyte loses his leg to science.

16. I have not yet been able to see Jenkins (2003 in press), which apparently makes this argument.

17. Scott's observation on the aesthetic character of high modernism (1998, 195–96) supports the point.

18. Despite the diversity of their imaginings, consider Flaubert's Mme. Bovary, Stendhal's Julien Sorel, Dostoevsky's Raskolnikov, Eliot's Lydgate, James's Isabel Archer and, for a Catalan example, Oller's Gil Foix.

Chapter 2. The Patum and the Body Politic

1. Since the late 1990s, with sharply increasing tensions over extra-European immigration, *convivencia* (the Castilian spelling) has once again become a slogan word and appears daily in the Spanish press. Its use in the Transition drew on

Américo Castro's *España en su historia* (1948), a work that challenged Francoist emblematizing of Spanish history as "crusade" by pointing to the centuries of peaceful coexistence between Christians, Jews, and Muslims in the Middle Ages. In Spanish scholarship as in Spanish festival, Christian-Muslim relations have been the paradigm in which all other social conflicts can be read.

2. To be sure, the interactional strategies, which are more important, have more in common: see Parts II and III.

3. The elaborated code of the metropolis may, moreover, belong to a different "language" than the restricted code of the local.

4. For the full and fascinating story, see Farràs i Farràs (1979) and Farràs (1982) for the earliest documentation and some later points of interest; Noguera i Canal (1992) for a detailed account of the late nineteenth century Catalanist "potentiation" of the festival; Noyes (1992, 213–372) for a more comprehensive overview and bibliography; and Harris (2000) for a fuller comparative account focusing on the connections to Moors-and-Christians plays. I summarize here from Noyes (1992). Important general accounts of Catalan Corpus Christi celebrations include Ariño (1988), Duran i Sanpere (1943), Jack (1923), Very (1962); for Corpus Christi and Eucharistic theology, see Bossy (1983), Devlin (1975), and Rubin (1991). For class relations and civic culture in early modern Catalonia, see Amelang (1986).

5. The Bulla prepared the way for the symbolic reinsertion of the feminine but was of course all male in participation. For women's direct response to their exclusion in the procession, see Noyes (1995). Women's use of the body as a spiritual resource was, to be sure, at the origins of the feast of Corpus Christi: see Bynum (1987) and Rubin (1991, 170–73).

6. Outside of Berga, the word *patum* refers to a celebrity of more noise than substance.

7. Cf. Del Giudice (1990): "ubi saltatio, ibi diabolus." To preserve the distinction between this and ordinary dancing *(ballar)*, I have conjugated *saltar* like an English verb in this text: the connotations of "hop," the only verb suggesting repeated motion, are too childlike.

8. See Harris (2000) for a general history of the *entremes*, with an extensive account of the Patum *turcs i cavallets*.

9. Max Harris has, however, noticed that the last Turk consistently escapes (2003)!

10. For a general account of Catalan giants, to be used with caution, see Amades (1934); for an update, Grau i Martí (1996); for an overview of giants in Europe, Meurant (1979); and for the fullest documentation on Berga's giants, Rumbo i Soler (1995).

11. A hotly disputed figure: estimates range from 60 to 100.

12. In Spanish, *pasodoble*. They are typical of bullfights, a more sinuous transformation of the military march (Mitchell 1991, 147).

13. Costa and Farràs i Farràs (1987) give a richly documented history.

14. For convenience, only the principal councillors are honored; those who do not live in the old city find a location there to receive their *salt*.

15. Invariably a man. None of the three major *comparses* include women. Many women do the *salt de plens*, however—they just don't serve as dressers. Women also serve as angels, dwarfs, and Turcs i Cavallets: these less significant *comparses* are more open, though I do not expect to see a female *cap de colla* any time soon.

16. He put these two words in Castilian to allow the pun.

Chapter 3. The Gaze and the Touch

1. Many of the points I make about Berga will be familiar to readers of the extensive literature on everyday life in Catalonia and Spain. For some illuminating comparisons, see Hansen (1977, 107–33) on the associative and bar life of a larger provincial capital in the 1960s and Collier (1997) on the transformations of subjectivity in an Andalusian village from the 1960s to the 1980s. For a rich treatment of the dynamics of local identity in Old Catalonia, including Berga, in the early 1980s, see Barrera (1985).

2. My divergence from middle-class Berguedan norms facilitated my fieldwork. Although my project required me to spend a great deal of time with other women's men, I was rarely perceived as a threat by the women, and middle-class men did not flirt with me. Dressing up in Berga is a social performance that invites evaluation (cf. Bauman [1977]1984, 11), and one can escape overt evaluation by choosing not to perform.

3. Note that a common word for "dressed up" is *endiumenjat*—"Sundayed." In Berga as elsewhere in Catalonia, the middle class is notably more inclined to attend Mass than the traditionally anticlerical working class, and the initiation into the church is also an initiation into rituals of the gaze. First Communion calls for new adult-style suits on the part of the boys and miniature bridal dresses for the girls. I was with a young mother from an old Republican family one day when her daughter dropped in on her way to catechism class. The mother turned to me with a show of embarrassment and said, "You know, none of us are *gent de missa* (people of the Mass). But she wants to do it because all her friends are doing it. And it drives me crazy: it's all for the sake of the long dress."

4. Compare Del Negro and Berger (2001) on the central Italian *passeggiata*.

5. Whether working or middle class, women are less visible in public life than men, but working-class women traditionally have greater freedom of movement due to their necessary involvement in the working world.

6. *Cava*, Catalan sparkling wine, is a favorite at Saturday breakfast among those not up to cognac or a *carajillo*.

7. In general Catalan usage, *les classes populars* means the peasantry and the urban working class.

8. Popularity in this sense is generally achieved in Berga either by participation in the Patum or by involvement in commerce: for example, women who tend bar or sell fish have the best chance of becoming popular characters. The possession of a nickname is one sign of popular status. Only working-class people are

usually spoken of as *popular*, but their popularity crosses class barriers: they are known by the entire community.

9. For statistics on the structure of employment in Berga since the Civil War see Miralles i Guasch et al. (1990); for class structure in the late nineteenth century, see Noguera i Canal (1989, 27–36). From the late nineteenth century on, we may speak of an industrial working class in Berga—miners and textile workers, largely drawn from and interpenetrated with the small landowners or sharecroppers of the surrounding countryside until the immigration of the postwar era; a middle class of shopkeepers and, increasingly, of public- and private-sector functionaries; an upper class of factory owners and professionals; and a few rentiers from the old petty nobility on top of the pyramid.

10. The social changes since the end of the Franco regime are moving middle-class manners to resemble the *popular* in certain superficial respects, but with important differences: see Parts III and IV.

11. Of the housing existing in Catalonia in 1984, more than half was built during a period of rapid economic growth from 1960–75 (*Valorar la història* 1984, 13). See Map 3 for Berguedan neighborhoods.

12. Many popular households did not even have a *safareig* in 1960 or did not make use of it. Public washhouses still exist in Berga and were used until quite recently. The extra labor necessary to achieve cleanliness had social compensations for women, who were thus enabled to spend time together. In common slang, *safareig* is a word for gossip—but this "gossip" was women's equivalent to the bar, their sociability. Where *malparlar* (bad speaking) is the destructive gossip associated with the tyranny of the eye, *safareig* is sociable chat, gossip in the community-making sense described by Harding (1984, 174–75). *Hem de fer safareig!* (We have to gossip!) is the gleeful exhortation of one of my respectable male friends before a convivial evening.

13. Previous immigrants came primarily from Berga's rural hinterland, and this is still a source of population growth in the city, though there is now not much population left to deplete.

14. There are, however, signs of change in the next generation, now that schooling is in Catalan and the children of Santa Eulàlia have acquired a certain demographic weight: children's Patums (see Chapter 10) give them one means of integration.

15. Iniciativa per Catalunya is a left-wing Catalanist coalition, heir to the old Catalan Communist party, the PSUC.

16. A few working-class people greeted me affectionately on my second trip but had forgotten that I spoke Catalan and addressed me in Castilian. Indeed, a few older people persist in addressing me in Castilian despite my responses in the other language, so deeply have they been socialized by the dictatorship into believing Catalan a local patois.

17. When Barcelonans visit the Berguedà, they tend to be aggressively bucolic in their enthusiasms.

18. A commonplace of commentary on Catalan identity is its "base, more than in ethnic roots, in the absorption, integration, and Catalanization of

outsiders" (Anna Cabré, quoted in García 1991); see also Pi-Sunyer (1971), Barrera (1985), Conversi (1988), Gunther, Sani, and Shabad (1988, 315), Woolard (1989), and Brandes (1990) on voluntaristic definitions of Catalan identity. See Chapter 8 for the political context.

19. This applies to earlier immigration from other parts of Spain; more recent extra-European immigration has met with much more resistance. At the time of my primary fieldwork, Berga had about thirty Moroccans living primarily in the otherwise almost deserted Carrer de la Pietat of the Casc Antic. This is an old *popular* neighborhood with its own Patum (see Chapter 10); a new neighborhood association was formed with Maghrebin participation, and signs of integration include Spanish names for children born here and Catalan language use among the children. Militating against integration are a long-standing prejudice against *moros* and a reportedly conservative local imam; mistrust on both sides has been fortified by the instrumentalization of immigration as an issue in the national and European public spheres, though as yet there has been no anti-immigrant violence in Berga. South Americans, more numerous than Maghrebins in Berga since the mid-1990s, seem to have an easier time in the labor market but to be more transient as a population.

20. An immigrant perception of Catalans as more "closed" than Spaniards seems to be general (Woolard 1989, 62; Barrera 1985, 442); Catalans themselves draw this contrast frequently.

21. The stereotype of mountaineers as *tancats* and urban coastal people as *oberts* is extended even to their linguistic use. The northeastern dialect of Catalan, best preserved in the mountains, is notable for its more closed vowels. Berguedans, conversely, make fun of the Barcelonan's barbaric yawp; they are particularly annoyed when the Barcelona media pronounce Berga (a closed e) as "Bèèèrga," like the bleat of a sheep. A Berguedan mocking a Barcelonan will open her mouth very wide, give equal weight to every syllable, and make every vowel approximate (a).

22. I am prepared to believe that "looks can kill" in Berga. At my last meal in La Barana during my Easter 1991 visit, Pepito, who was upset about my departure and had expended arguments in vain, undertook to glare me into submission: he stopped talking but fixed on me his black eyes, narrow with fury, for the duration of the meal. Under that gaze I was unable to eat or attend to the conversation; no joke of mine could deflect it, and he only left off when the waitress came to take the plates and he saw that mine was still full. He let me alone so I could eat and resumed the stare during dessert. I was shaky for the rest of the day. I've since seen him direct this gaze at other women; never, so far, at a man.

23. Literally, *em deixes acollonit,* "you take my balls away." *Acollonit* is the most common word for "intimidated" in Berga, except in intensely respectable contexts, and can be used by both genders.

24. See Noyes (1995) on the relationship of women to other enclosed objects of value and the challenges from within and without to such enclosure.

25. The working-class ideal is less dependent on dress and artifice than the middle-class one and emphasizes health and adequate nourishment. A full figure is preferred for women, and the men most admired are tall and solidly built. I

knew a woman, an immigrant who had suffered for many years from ill health and economic insecurity; she was nervous, lonely in Berga, and very thin. She confessed to me her attraction to two men, both *geganters*: both were tall, muscular, and fleshy, rather fat by American standards; both had thick hair, regular features, and lovely round, clean-shaven pink cheeks: the picture of well-nourished health. So much hunger yearning to be fed . . .

26. There is an important class difference here. *Populars* rarely entertain at home: they often lack the facilities, and in any case the bar is communal territory. Middle-class people entertain friends at home as well as going out together. There is an element of display involved and a clear statement of willingness to take the guests in: in public places, commensality and intimacy are less easily controlled and so mean less. Sunday lunch, the most important meal of the week, is a family affair for the middle class. But La Barana is always jammed on Sunday afternoons by the many people coming for lunch or at least an aperitif: the solidarity of the middle-class family belongs to the larger community of friends in La Barana.

27. Goffman's work on deference and demeanor describes just such performances as interest me here with far more subtlety than is possible here, but although he notices "relations between ceremonial distance and other kind of sociological distance" (1967, 64), he is primarily interested in the construction of the self and not of the social body. For Berguedans, the challenge of *convivència* goes beyond the individual's relationships with other individuals: explicitly collective performances such as the Carrer Major promenade or the gathering at La Barana or the Patum are important to them.

28. See Labov (1972) for an account of systematic style shifting within a speech community. These interaction styles are not so readily quantifiable as the presence of postvocalic "r," but I am confident that more systematic observation would in fact reveal the structure of variation I describe; more to my present purpose, this variation is culturally recognized in the elaboration of concepts such as *respecte* and the *popular*.

29. For the local sociopolitical context of this, see Part III.

Chapter 4. The Patum Effigies

1. For the importance of the eyes of the image, see Turner (1983, 335) and Freedberg (1990, 51–53).

2. Recent restorations have hollowed out the heads of giants and dwarfs and lightened the frames of giants and *guites*. But the Berguedans would never dream of substituting fiberglass and plastic for plaster and wood, as is now being done in much of Catalonia. The weight of the effigies is part of their power.

3. The new dresses for the centenary of the two Black Giants in 1991 were made by a well-known operatic costumier in Barcelona and cost more than three million *pessetes*, or about thirty thousand dollars.

4. See Part III.

5. Catholic sacred images are distinguished from artistic or "commodity

images" by being culturally defined as persons, which confers effective power upon them. See Scribner (2001, 129–48); Kay Turner on how icons are enlivened and enabled to act by the gaze of a devotee (1983); and David Freedberg's insight that the scholar's and connoisseur's concern to explore the techniques of visual representation can be a way of defusing the closeness of images to "reality," the fact that our fundamental responses to images are to what they represent rather than how (1989). On the animation of toys, see Kuznets (1994).

6. See Chapter 6 for the linkages of Patum and Mare de Déu as autochthonous powers invoked in resistance to external patriarchal authorities.

7. See Chapter 10.

8. See Part IV for fears of the death of the Patum.

9. See Stewart (1984) on gigantism and Young (1999) on postures. For these ideas about gigantized attitudes, I owe much to a conversation with Katharine Young, Rick Livingston, and Brian Rotman.

10. I draw here from Taussig's work on the religious response to economic transformation among colonized indigenous populations in South America (1980).

11. See Chapter 8.

12. Women in the Patum effigies appear only as parts of couples: the giantesses and the female dwarfs never appear without their partners. The Turcs i Cavallets are all male, as befits warriors. The Àliga, like the Guita, is ambiguous in gender: female in grammar and male in conduct. But whereas the Guita is sexually active with the public—polymorphously perverse, indeed, as Chapter 7 will show—the Àliga is sexless, complete in itself, as its in-turning round dance emphasizes. Ageless and immortal, it is the Patum body that most closely approximates an emblem rather than a person.

Chapter 5. The Techniques of Incorporation

1. See Chapter 10 for these Patums.

2. The relaxed atmosphere of the Patum is maintained, in lesser degree, throughout the summertime. A plethora of minor festivals supports the *ambient*—neighborhood festivals, Saint John's Eve, and the Festa dels Elois, when the fires of the Patum are finally cooled in a deluge of water.

3. The Patum is famous as the only event that ever begins on time in Berga. More accurately, it is the only popular, voluntary event to challenge the everyday sonoral-temporal order directly. The two sounds more penetrating and more strictly timed than the Tabal are the church bells and the factory whistle (cf. Ferrer, Piñero, and Serra 1997, 118).

4. Many teachers of my acquaintance virtually give up during this period: they bring in a cassette and dance the Patum in school for a good part of the day.

5. Jaume Farràs was the first Patum scholar openly to acknowledge the importance of drinking in creating the "warrior spirit" of the Patum (1979, 262–64, passim).

6. I take this phrase, of course, from Mauss ([1935]1979). But Mauss is con-

cerned with the use of the body as an instrument, and I speak here of practices that work on the body as the object of transformation. Compare the ascetic techniques described by Bynum, which also "manipulate (the body) . . . for religious goals" (1989, 163). In the Patum the goal is communitas rather than ascesis, but the notion of a body of techniques is equally valid.

7. These types are used peripherally during Corpus. A *castell de focs* was introduced in the twentieth century by the Ajuntament for the benefit of families and visitors on Saturday night: it turns fireworks into spectacle. At the opposite end of the political and pyrotechnical spectrum, children and joking young adults play with *petardos* in Patum time, improving on the proximity and improvisatory quality of the *fuets*.

8. Note that another word used in all contexts for *ambient* is *caliu*, the warm glow of embers.

9. The exception is the dance of the Nans Nous, which goes from 2/4 to 6/8: it was not added until 1890.

10. Compare Fernandez's account (1965, 905–6) of a torch-lit procession in the Fang religion of Bwiti, which spirals into a cluster of people and a single massed flame: "oneheartedness."

11. Intent that may not be wholly explicit or that may be lost as a practice is routinized, but that is clear from the sanctions on deviance among adults and in the importance given to the socialization of children.

Chapter 6. Return to the Womb

1. One of several festivals improvised by La Bauma dels Encantats, a ludic organization created in 1986: see Chapter 10.

2. Even in fantasy, the difference between respectable giants and *popular* Guita is maintained. The giants are desired and unattainable—problems of inequality intervene!—but the Guita readily mixes with its human lovers.

3. Giants and especially giantesses figure more generally in the Catalan erotic imaginary: see for example Grau i Martí (1996, 55–56).

4. The Guita Xica is, however, ritually surrendered at least once during each Patum to a group of women, usually on the narrow final run up the Carrer Major in the *passacarrers*. Agustí Massaguer likes to jump on its back when this happens to ensure the women receive the full benefit of the privilege.

5. In 1891 the Foment Catòlic introduced the first Guita Xica into the Patum as a joke: it was liked, and the organization continued to carry it for the next thirty years. Under the Second Republic it was considered inappropriate for part of the Patum to have a private, Catholic affiliation, so the Ajuntament made a Guita Xica of its own. The first year all three came out; then the Catholic *guita* was suppressed, and its head now sits in the Municipal Museum (Farràs i Farràs 1979, 331–32).

6. Having done which, I hasten to add, they became embarrassed and left in an orderly manner through the door.

7. The Ferrer family house on the Plaça Sant Pere: members of old Berguedan families are often identified by the name of their house.

8. *Polvo* is a Castilianism, but one peculiarly appropriate to the Patum: it means "powder," with a second colloquial sexual meaning, and the dusty explosion of the *pòlvora* (gunpowder) of the *fuets* in the Patum also has a second sexual meaning.

9. The symbol of mayoral office.

10. The *àpats dels pobres* (meals of the poor) at Carnival and other occasions in Catalonia are festive remembrances of this custom.

11. *Morena*, the reader will recall, is derived from "Moor" and associated with low class status and working women touched by the sun; in popular usage the tender diminutive *moreneta* reclaims the dark woman as more loving and sensual than the fair one.

12. Fortunately for women, virginity does not have anywhere near the salience in Catalan culture that it seems to in, say, Andalusia. The control of female sexuality is of course important for the control of property, but they are not obsessed with it. Popular Catalan usage calls Mary "la Mare de Déu" rather than "la Verge" (Auladell 1990, 16; Armengou i Feliu [1958]1996, 107), with the exception of the *goigs* or Marian hymns, usually composed by local clergy.

13. See Camós ([1657]1949) for examples of Marian miracles attested at local shrines, and Prat i Carós (1984, 95–105) for a summary of the work on the Mare de Déu as a fertility figure.

14. To be sure, the calendar of agricultural communities gives special emphasis to important points of articulation in the seasons, changes in the weather pattern among them (cf. Ariño 1988, 152–73). The Patum marks another such calendar transition, to the good summer weather.

15. Translated into Catalan as "No serem moguts," "We shall not be moved" was an important protest song and is still sung after long lunches by nostalgic Catalanists remembering their university days. As for the Mare de Déu, there is a story about Ramonet Xic, a Berguedan anarchist exiled in the Ariège after the civil war. The anarchist lamented that the Mare de Déu de Queralt had to live under Franco when he himself had escaped, and a companion proposed that on their next raid across the border they rescue her. But Ramonet Xic, a good Berguedan who had hidden the statue from his church-burning comrades in 1936, refused to have her moved. The exception that proves the rule, apart from carrying the images down in procession in time of drought or plague, was at Núria, a Catalan shrine second only to Montserrat. In 1967, the image at Núria was to have been canonically crowned amidst a host of government officials by a pro-Franquist papal nuncio and the Spanish bishops named to Catalan seats under the dictatorship. But the statue was stolen a few days beforehand by a group of young Catholic nationalists, with the cooperation of the local clergy, to avoid its profanation in a politicized ceremony. The kidnappers made a series of demands, including the return of the exiled Abbot of Montserrat and the naming of Catalan bishops in Catalan territory without the interference of the Francoist government. The Mare

de Déu was not returned until 1972, when the most important of the conditions had been met (*Le Vatican et la Catalogne* 1971, 256–60; Solé i Sabaté n.d., 257–59).

Chapter 7. The Eye of the Father

1. This is the ideal story, not always realized. For some of the strategic adaptations and changes over time, see Hansen (1977), McDonogh (1988), and Barrera González (1990). For a rich history of one *casa pairal* and the relationship of *pairalisme* to Carlism and regional politics, see Terradas i Saborit (1987).

2. See Prat i Carós (1989) and Contreras (1989) for the extent to which a pattern prevalent in Old Catalonia was generalized for the purposes of this argument: all variation in custom between Catalonia and Castile was hardened into binary oppositions in the formation of Catalan civil law.

3. For an excellent account of the development of the *colònia* system, its ideological foundations, and its relation to similar experiments in England and elsewhere, see Terradas Saborit (1979). Terradas treats the Berguedan colony of L'Ametlla de Merola in some detail; another, Cal Pons, is featured in Serra and Viladés (1987). An important recent survey is Serra and Casals (2000).

4. On the other hand, the mines were obliging in small things because they condemned their workers to an old age of bad health. And the colonies may have given out bread when the bosses were in fear of their lives, but in the 1940s the colony workers were so hungry that the young bishop of Solsona defied the regime and spoke out in protest, earning himself an eighteen-year stay in that tiny and impoverished diocese. Interestingly enough, the ground of the bishop's criticism was that the paternalist ideal was not being realized: a shepherd was required to make sacrifices for the well-being of his flock, he instructed the owners and the Francoist government, and he himself as bishop and therefore another "father and shepherd" was morally obliged to speak "in defence of (his) sons" (Rafart 1989b).

5. *Caciquisme* did not run as rampant in Catalonia as elsewhere in Spain, but in the Berguedà it was very important. For Spain, see Carr (1982, 366–79); for Catalonia, see Vicens i Vives and Llorens (1958, 286–92); for the Berguedà, see Noguera i Canal (1989, 37–42).

6. For the ideology of national Catholicism, see Lannon (1987) and Behar (1990). It is important to recognize that the state, not the church, had the upper hand in this synthesis: a sympathetic Vatican allowed the election of bishops to be more or less dictated by the regime, giving Catalonia a succession of prelates who neither spoke the local language nor had any sympathy with local religious tradition.

7. See the restrained account of Mossèn Armengou, written under the dictatorship (1971, 132–34) and the more critical one of Josep Montanyà (1991, 42–44), which is illustrated.

8. In fact there is no evidence of the identity or political affiliation of the thieves. The treasure of Queralt was removed from the sanctuary by the Ajuntament in 1936; it was then taken by the Generalitat of Catalonia at the beginning of

the war and deposited for safekeeping in a Barcelona bank. In the disorder of the end of the war, it disappeared (Armengou i Feliu 1971, 128–29).

9. I summarize from an excellent series of articles in *La Vanguardia* by Jaume Fabre and others ("50 años del Congreso Eucarístico" 2002).

10. The Custòdia's symbolism is described in Serra (1944); it is now kept in the convent of the Sagramentàries in Berga.

11. The historian Josep Noguera is no relation to the mayor Joan Noguera.

12. A third motive is possible, apart from the concerns that the procession was an empty ceremony and manipulated by the regime. A *popular* Berguedan told me, "Oh, the procession was *el més bo de tot* (the best of all)," with a vibration of remembered glee in his voice. As he explained it, the whole of the Patum walked at the beginning of the procession (cf. Figure 3) and danced and drank without any mind to what came behind. Confirmation can be found in a film made in the late 1950s by Sr. Benet Boixader. Other Berguedans told me they lamented the suppression of the procession because of the loss of the hazelnut branches on the houses and the carpets of flowers. Berguedan folk religion likes outward forms better than the priests do, as I saw again in the Queralt anniversary of 1991—indeed, its religion *is* the outward forms. This is a well-known problem of the implementation of Vatican II in local communities (Brandes 1976; Behar 1990).

13. Note that her divinity is here much weakened: the alternative immanent divinity of the popular Mare de Déu is not explicitly acknowledged by the local church.

14. Armengou and many other writers would add the Pi de les Tres Branques, but this has always been an emblem mobilized in ecclesiastical and political ceremonial, never a popular devotion and key symbol with the depth of the Patum or Queralt (cf. Felipó i Oriol 2003 in press).

15. Certain militants of Berga did not fail to notice the advantage to the conservatives of ostensibly depoliticizing the Patum (Rafart 1989a); their own position was that a demonstration was appropriate during the Corpus festivities, but that it should have stayed out of the Patum itself, merely taking advantage of the proximity of its energies.

16. Note that the democrats of the Second Republic, who were left-wing, did not manage to rehabilitate the symbols of order in the same way. The *Actes Municipals* of the 1930s are full of anxious discussions about traditions associated with *respecte* and religion, with the most left members of the Ajuntament arguing for their abolition as "feudal" and the Catholic members responding that they are traditional and therefore popular, or that they are proper to urban civility. I speak of the homages done to the authorities during the *passacarrers* of the Patum or the pilgrimage to Queralt on Saint Mark's Day: such traditions were generally maintained with public disclaimers and private reservations becuase they were in fact popular, in all senses of the word. The Patum *comparses* themselves were too important as ethnological survivals and too dear to all tendencies for their abolition to be contemplated, but the Àliga's crown was taken off, and after the revolution of 1936 there were rumors that the Patum would be burned like the

churches (Montañà and Rafart 1991, 129). The Republic avoided explaining the Patum's symbolism at all; it was clearly too problematic.

17. The subsequent administration decided that this went too far and sat down again.

Chapter 8. The New Generation

1. As part of a general loss of women's legal rights and social position under the regime (cf. Caballero 1977; Torres 1996).

2. Berga's brothel, Les Quatre Boles, remained open until the early 1960s, and it got an unofficial *salt* during the *passacarrers* of the Patum as an honorary "authority." The brothel of Gironella, down the river, lasted somewhat longer. After that, I am told, it became traditional for provincial men to visit prostitutes on days of football matches, then a primary channel for Catalanist feeling. This was the husband's license to go down to Barcelona. He thus took his holiday from the regime and from the family simultaneously.

3. I cannot recall a woman ever speaking of these intrusions, and they may owe as much to male fantasy as to reality.

4. See Kaplan (1992) for the connections of avant-garde art and working class activism (taking her readings of Catalan language and folk culture with caution). My account of the period is, obviously, drastically simplified for reasons of space. For industrial relations and social imaginaries in Barcelona, see McDonogh (1986); for capitalist mythologies of the mountains, Noyes (2000b) and Sobrer (2000); for a historical account of Lerroux and worker violence, Ullman (1968).

5. Here I mean the international avant-garde, not Catalan Modernisme, an earlier movement parallel to Art Nouveau and Jugendstil (McCully 1986).

6. For the gendering of modernist primitivism, see Torgovnick: her discussion of Freud's "oceanic" (1990, 204–9) is particularly relevant to my argument.

7. In English in the original.

8. For the actual references and their dubious relationship to Berga, see Castany et al. (1990, 222–24).

9. A complex joke. Pedret is the site of the Visigothic church of Sant Quirze, the oldest standing monument in the Berguedà. *Pedra* means "rock"; and when popular Berguedans talk about spending time at the university, they are referring to prison or, by extension, the labor camps where Republican prisoners were sent after the Spanish Civil War. When Ramon contrasts his formation with mine, therefore, he is suggesting an intellectual imprisonment in provincial isolation, an upbringing in "the school of hard knocks" (here, rocks), and yet a rootedness in the land and in history that I cannot match.

10. Women also rejected the restrictions of heaven once they were able: an album by the wonderful Catalan singer Rosa Zaragoza was called "Good Girls Go to Heaven; Bad Girls Go All Over the Place" (Madrid: Saga, 1991).

11. Cf. Warner's interpretation of the Patum in the context of children's ogre lore (1998).

12. Recorded on the 1983 album *Catalluna* (Madrid: Polydor).

13. For the work of Els Comediants see *Comediants 15 años* (1987) and their website (www.comediants.com); for the work of two artists whose work owes much to festival *entremesos*, Joan J. Guillén and Antoni Miralda, see www.esceno grafia.com/ and www.connect-arte.com/miralda/, respectively. On the theater revival in general, see Massip and Noguero (1999); Lane (1996) addresses the problem of "normalizing" a theater of resistance.

14. A manual printed clandestinely in 1974 presented the programs of ten full-scale political parties, and these were only the major ones among those with avowed democratic agendas (*Partits* 1974).

15. Morris Fishman uses the case of the Spanish Transition to argue for the use of public space as a neglected variable in the study of working class power, especially as a compensation for restrictions on formal organization. He notes the utility of mass public strikes as a tool of rapid labor mobilization in the period: their visibility in public space countered press censorship, and their mass character allowed a minimal level of participation in the labor movement among people unable to organize effectively or communicate freely within their own workplaces (1990, 129, 251). He observes that the strikes in Catalonia made especially effective use of performance forms, though worker organizations there were weaker than in Madrid (128–29). Present-day Catalans might find reason for concern in this last point.

16. That is, a federation of the Catalan-speaking regions.

17. See Aiats on the continuity of rhythmic, melodic, and kinesic formulas among children's songs, football songs, and political slogans in Catalonia and France (1997).

18. On the suppression of intertextual gaps, see Briggs (1988, 289–340); Bauman and Briggs (1990).

19. Gunther, Sani, and Shabad, however, provide a more complex account based on survey data from 1979. They found that the general public sense that Catalan nationalism is integrationist where Basque is racialist—based on the historical tradition of each—was belied by survey data in which both native Catalans and immigrants in Catalonia weighted ascriptive criteria more heavily (1988, 317–20). These responses may be shaped in part by some ambiguity over the speaking of Catalan. This appeared as both ascriptive, a cultural inheritance, and voluntaristic, an act of will. As I suggest here, in the activist view a cultural inheritance had to be earned by voluntary participation—the primordial begins with the voluntary.

20. Although there is no doubt that Armengou believed Catalan and Basque the most advanced of all the Peninsular cultures, the socioeconomic context must be considered. Immigrants from parts of rural Andalusia, for example, came from working conditions very close to bondage and living conditions little better than those of the animals they looked after.

20. A colleague told me a similar anecdote of Basque militants singing after dinner and spontaneously breaking into "Cara al Sol" at the end of their own songs; from his description, it sounded like a comparable mix of parody and nostalgia.

Chapter 9. Consumption and the Limits of Metaphor

1. Compare the recent transformation of the *pairal* family of rural Catalonia, in which the father has sacrificed a great deal of authority for the sake of keeping the agricultural household together (Barrera González 1990).

2. In earlier, more conservative Berguedan usages, it probably also partakes of Ortega y Gasset's *La rebelión de las masas* ([1929]1958), with the latter's disdain for the cultural mediocrity imposed by the multitude.

3. It is worth noting that the "mass" is also the uneasy underside of Durkheim's celebration of organic solidarity. While he describes the mass as the most primitive form of social organization—Durkheim translated his perceptions of ritual effervescence in modernity to a primitive background, as indeed Berguedans have long done—his practical prescriptions to remedy the ills of the division of labor revolve around mechanical, not organic solidarity, and certainly twentieth-century technologies of incorporation, owing more to LeBon than to Durkheim, took this course.

4. Santa Eulàlia was understandably resentful at being excluded, arguing that ethnic discrimination was involved. The Ajuntament phrased their justification in terms of aesthetics, saying that the Patum belonged in the old city in which it first took shape.

5. The summer *festa major* circuit was of course long the only amusement available in the provinces and also the best way to meet with the opposite sex. But today the festival experience itself is sought.

6. The provincial girl seduced and abandoned by a metropolitan man with a short attention span is of course a topos of the nineteenth century European novel. This figuration of the provincial condition continues with Fellini's *Amarcord*, in which the openhearted prostitute Gradisca encapsulates the town's openness to Fascism and any other glamorous offering of the center (Lewis 2002, 70–71, 82), and in Joseba Zulaika's account of the Don Juan dynamic through which the Bilbao Guggenheim was built (1997).

7. There were six by my count in Berga and Avià in the early 1990s, all flourishing.

8. In Catalan, Els Pets, Gra Fort, Lax'n'Busto, Sangtraït, Karda Fàstic, Sopa de Cabra, and Els Brams. Sopa de Cabra (Goat Soup) exhibits the same local/ global slippage as the Rolling Stones rumor in Berga: their name, apparently so local and rural, refers to a Stones album. Bands often play on the phonetic relationships between "ska," "Catalan," and perhaps even "scatology," as in the band "Skatalà." For an excellent overview of Catalan *rock agrícola*, see the website of L'Iraultz@-revolta (http://www.geocities.com/CapitolHill/Senate/2391/), a group of politico-musical activists.

9. To be sure, the scatological is prominent in Catalan folklore, often celebrating the leveling effect of biologicial processes ("The king does it, the Pope does it" *Virtuts del Cagar* n.d.). Scatological imagery is especially pronounced at Christmas, related to Nativity scenes set in everyday landscapes. Like Corpus Christi, which comes at the opposite end of the calendar, Christmas is a holiday

celebrating incarnation, but in contrast to the exalted representations of Corpus Christi, the Nativity emphasizes the body's humility. It is logical that a more democratic Patum should accentuate this register of the body (cf. Bakhtin [1968]1984), but the current scatological imagery strikes me as marking not acceptance but rejection. Nor does it recall the other resonance of shit in a peasant culture, as fertilizing the dead earth for rebirth: here it is not cyclical but a dead end.

10. I am reluctant to pursue the metaphoric trajectory, but the anal phase is of course the way out of orality, in which separation is negotiated and some initial autonomy pursued; one might also see the scatological engagement as a symbolic concern with production, so problematic in Berga's current economy, in which its culture appears to be its only resource, but not the ideal one, for development.

11. The same artist produced a slightly less ferocious account of the younger generation's Patum, published in the Patum supplement of the local paper in 2000, depicting the festival in the language of adventure sports and reality TV (KAP 2000).

12. Recall that my ethnographic present precedes both the revival of ETA violence and antiglobalization movements. Both phenomena have been having their effect on the youth of rural Catalonia.

Chapter 10. Reproduction and Reduction

1. For a detailed account of the making of a neighborhood Patum, see Simon (1982).

2. There were some reforms in the late 1990s.

3. 1989 was the year of Catalunya Mil Anys, the celebration of the millenium of the Catalan state.

4. The Bergistani were a warrior tribe mentioned by Livy, locally believed to have inhabited the Berguedà at the time of the Roman invasions.

5. The Castilian *j* does not exist in Catalan.

6. One of La Bauma's favorite strategies for drawing attention to itself was to invent opposition to its activities, for example scattering denunciatory leaflets from a supposed "Association of Shopkeepers and Fathers of Families."

7. Noguera's argument was anticipated in part by Jaume Farràs (1979); my own work along parallel lines (Noyes 1992), circulated in the local media and in conversation since 1989, both drew on Noguera and confirmed him in his efforts.

8. The language is basically Catalan with the insertion of Castilian words and the imitation of Andalusian phonology: final consonants dropped, standard Castilian *s* and *th* reversed, the replacement of *l* by *r*, etc.

9. Douglas Holmes found a parallel tendency among Friulani worker-peasants that he christened "integralism"; he argues that it is found widely in Western Europe today and has fed the new populist and neofascist political movements (2000).

Chapter 11. The Patum in Spain and the World

1. *Sic*, for the Latin.

2. And it is worth noting that the 2002 theme of "FestCat," the Generalitat's summer school for festival practitioners, is precisely "Post Festum, Pestum?" Topics addressed include violence, standardization, the viability of the agrarian festival calendar, and multicultural integration. The organizers, to be sure, belong to the generation of the Transition.

3. There is not, it would seem, a true etymological connection (see Chapter 2 for the actual etymology), though we might note the Italian *pattume*, meaning a squashed mass of disparate stuff—not a bad description of the Patum of the Transition—which does seem to derive from *pactum* (Zingarelli 1970).

4. To be sure, the labor pacts were less consensual than either the activist pacts or the constitutional pacts. The 1977 Pactos de Moncloa, the labor agreement that established the basis of social tranquillity to permit the constitutional process to proceed, was made not by unions but by parties. In particular pacts between unions and management, union leaders tended to play a more accommodating role than the rank and file, and there was always a significant minority of union opinion completely opposed to the making of concessions, as well as more general subsequent regrets (Fishman 1990).

5. The same has been noted of neocorporatism in Spanish industry (Kasmir 1996).

6. DiGiacomo demonstrates, however, that these identities were not so easy to reconcile in local political practice (1986).

7. As with many other elements of Catalanist history, this layer of origin narratives builds upon a late-medieval construction of earlier medieval history, itself manipulating the past to claim greater autonomy in the present: see Giesey (1968) and García Gallo (1975, 1, 746–47).

8. See, e.g., http://www.onas.com/pe/ArticlesHemeroteca/Arola%20i%20 Blancafort.htm). The terms can be sorted out more precisely as a chronological progression: *possibilisme* marks the strategies of late Francoism (Martínez 2001: 41, 56), *pactisme* belongs to the Transition, and *pragmatisme* marks the present of barely disputed Anglo-American hegemony.

9. The cartoonist himself, commenting from the distance of today, shares Tarradellas's doubts about "folkloric politics." Guillén recalls using the Patum as an analogy in many of his political cartoons of the period, "responding to the desire to symbolize through them, something 'big,' 'important,' 'untouchable,' 'sacralized,' and at the same time proper to another period" (personal communication).

10. I do not have an exact quote: his English was variably translated in the press accounts.

11. The succinct formulation of Mary Hufford (personal communication).

12. See Lamming ([1960]1992), Fernández Retamar ([1971]1989), and an enormous additional literature on Caliban as a figure of the colonized subject.

13. Compare Zulaika on the building of the Bilbao Guggenheim, facilitated

by the local longing to see the word "Basque" in world media coupled with anything other than "terrorism" (1997).

14. *The Economist* may have been the first to put the Bové/Astérix analogy in print, noting the commonality of moustache as well as of ideology (Delicious Irony 2002).

15. Such as the Maremagnum development of the port, which is much like Navy Pier in Chicago, Baltimore's Inner Harbor, and every other seaport entertainment area in the world. 1992 was the end of Barcelona's own transition, in a sense: the highly successful Summer Olympic Games, which called upon extraordinary cultural, economic, and social local resources and left them pretty well exhausted, put Barcelona onto the world tourist map for good, at once granting recognition to its distinctiveness and bringing some of that distinctiveness to an end.

16. An account of desire and heritage may be found in Cantwell (1993), and see also Stewart (1988) on nostalgia. Zulaika (1997) uses the metaphor of seduction and betrayal for globalization; Lebow (2003) argues that an ethical framework is as necessary to the strong as to the weak in intergroup relations.

References

Abrahams, Roger D. 1992. *Singing the Master*. New York: Pantheon.

———. 1995. History and Folklore: Luck Visits, House Attacks, and Playing Indian in Early America. In *History and—: Histories Within the Human Sciences*, ed. R. Cohen and M. S. Roth, 268–95. Charlottesville: University Press of Virginia.

Abrahams, Roger D., and Richard Bauman. 1978. Ranges of Festival Behavior. In *The Reversible World*, ed. B. Babcock. Ithaca, N.Y.: Cornell University Press.

Adams, Jeffrey. 1995. Narcissism and Object Relations in Goethe's Creative Imagination. In *Mimetic Desire: Essays on Narcissism in German Literature from Romanticism to Post Modernism*, ed. J. Adams and E. Williams, 64–85. Columbia, S.C.: Camden House.

Aiats i Abeyà, Jaume. 1997. *La Música i l'expressió sonora dels col·lectius a les manifestacions de carrer i als estadis de futbol*. Doctoral thesis, Universitat Autònoma de Barcelona.

Albera, Dionigi. 1988. Open Systems and Closed Minds: The Limitations of Naivety in Social Anthropology—A Native's View. *Man* (n.s.) 23: 435–52.

Alcover, Antoni, and Francesc de B. Moll. 1927–62. *Diccionari català-valencià-balear*. 10 vols. Palma de Mallorca: Alcover.

Amades, Joan. 1934. *Gegants, nans i altres entremesos*. Barcelona: Impremta la Neotípia.

———. 1950–69. *Folklore de Catalunya: Cançoner*. Vol. 2. Barcelona: Selecta.

Amelang, James S. 1986. *Honored Citizens of Barcelona: Patrician Culture and Class Relations, 1490–1714*. Princeton, N.J.: Princeton University Press.

Anderson, Benedict. 1991. *Imagined Communities: Reflections on the Origin and Spread of Nationalism*. 2d ed. London: Verso.

Anonymous. 1973. *Catalunya sota el règim franquista. Informe sobre la persecució de la llengua i la cultura de Catalunya pel règim del General Franco*. Vol. 1. Paris: Edicions Catalanes de París.

Ariño, Antoni. 1988. *Festes, rituals, i creences*. València: Edicions Alfons el Magnànim.

Armengou i Feliu, Josep. 1953. Carta oberta de la geganta vella. *Queralt* 3: 56–58.

———. [1958]1996. *Justificació de Catalunya*. Barcelona: Columna/Albí.

———. [1968, 1971]1994. *La Patum de Berga*. Barcelona and Berga: Columna/Albí.

———. 1964. Crònica de la ciutat. *Queralt* 41: 3–6.

———. 1971. *El santuari de la Mare de Déu de Queralt*. Granollers: Editorial Montblanc.

———. 1990. Petit diari de guerra. In *Armengou, Tuyet, Ballarín. Prosa escollida*, ed. C. Forner. Berga: Edicions de l'Albí.

Auladell, Joaquim. 1990. El misteri de les Mares de Déu negres. *Xarxa* 30: 15–17.

Azevedo, Milton, ed. 1991. *Contemporary Catalonia in Spain and Europe*. Berkeley: Gaspar de Portolà Catalonian Studies Program, University of California at Berkeley.

Badia i Torras, Lluís. 1988. *Martirologi solsoní*. Solsona: Delegació Dicocesana de Mitjans de Cominicació Social, Bisbat de Solsona.

Bakhtin, Mikhail. [1968]1984. *Problems of Dostoevsky's Poetics*. Trans. C. Emerson. Minneapolis: University of Minnesota Press.

―――. [1968]1984. *Rabelais and His World*. Trans. H. Iswolsky. Bloomington: Indiana University Press.

―――. 1981. *The Dialogic Imagination*. Trans. C. Emerson and M. Holquist. Austin: University of Texas Press.

Ballarín, Josep Maria. 1990. La Patum dels folls. *Avui*, July 1.

Barber, Benjamin. 1996. *Jihad vs. McWorld: How Globalism and Tribalism Are Reshaping the World*. New York: Basic Books.

Barrera González, Andrés. 1985. *La dialéctica de la identidad en Cataluña. Un estudio de antropología social*. Madrid: CSIC.

―――. 1990. *Casa, herencia y família en la Cataluña rural*. Madrid: Alianza.

Bateson, Gregory. 1972. The Cybernetics of "Self": A Theory of Alcoholism. In *Steps to an Ecology of Mind*, 309–37. New York: Ballantine.

Bauman, Richard. [1977]1984. *Verbal Art as Performance*. Prospect Heights, Ill.: Waveland.

Bauman, Richard, and Charles L. Briggs. 1990. Poetics and Performance as Critical Perspectives on Language and Social Life. *Annual Review of Anthropology* 19: 59–88.

Behar, Ruth. 1990. The Struggle for the Church: Popular Anticlericalism and Religiosity in Post-Franco Spain. In *Religious Orthodoxy and Popular Faith in European Society*, ed. E. Badone, 76–112. Princeton, N.J.: Princeton University Press.

Bendix, Regina. 1985. *Progress and Nostalgia: Silvesterkläusen in Urnäsch, Switzerland*. Berkeley: University of California Press.

―――. 1997. *In Search of Authenticity: The Formation of Folklore Studies*. Madison: University of Wisconsin Press.

Benedict, Ruth. 1930. Animism. In *Encyclopaedia of the Social Sciences*, ed. E. Seligman, vol. 1, 65–67. New York: Macmillan.

Berga y las fiestas de la Patum. 1954. *El Español*, June 26: 36.

Bernstein, Basil B. 1971. *Class, Codes and Control*. Vol 1. London: Routledge and Kegan Paul.

Bertolotti, Maurizio. 1991. *Carnevale di Massa 1950*. Torino: Einaudi.

Blondel, Jean. 1998. Democracy and Constitutionalism. In *The Changing Nature of Democracy*, ed. T. Inoguchi, E. Newman, and J. Keane. Tokyo: United Nations University Press.

Bonnin, Hermann. 1973. Entre el teatro y la fiesta. "La Patum", supervivencia de un espectaculo excitante. *La Vanguardia Española*, August 14: 45.

Bossy, John. 1983. The Mass as a Social Institution 1200–1700. *Past and Present* 100: 29–61.

Bourdieu, Pierre. 1977. *Outline of a Theory of Practice.* Trans. R. Nice. Cambridge: Cambridge University Press.

———. 1984. *Distinction: A Social Critique of the Judgment of Taste.* Trans. R. Nice. Cambridge: Harvard University Press.

———. 1990a. The Uses of "the People." In *In Other Words: Essays Towards a Reflexive Sociology,* 150–55. Stanford, Calif.: Stanford University Press.

———. 1990b. *The Logic of Practice.* Trans. R. Nice. Stanford, Calif.: Stanford University Press.

Boyd, Carolyn P. 1997. *Historia Patria. Politics, History, and National Identity in Spain, 1875–1975.* Princeton, N.J.: Princeton University Press.

Brams, Els. 1992. *Amb el roc a la faixa* (LP). Barcelona: Audiovisuals de Sarrià.

Brandes, Stanley. 1976. The Priest as Agent of Secularization in Rural Spain. In *Economic Transformations and Steady-State Values: Essays in the Ethnography of Spain,* ed. J. B. Aceves, E. C. Hansen, and G. Levitas. Flushing, N.Y.: Queen's College Press.

———. 1980. *Metaphors of Masculinity: Sex and Status in Andalusian Folklore.* Philadelphia: University of Pennsylvania Press.

———. 1988. *Power and Persuasion: Fiestas and Social Control in Rural Mexico.* Philadelphia: University of Pennsylvania Press.

———. 1990. The Sardana: Catalan Dance and Catalan National Identity. *Journal of American Folklore* 103: 24–41.

Briggs, Charles. 1988. *Competence in Performance: The Creativity of Tradition in Mexicano Folk Art.* Philadelphia: University of Pennsylvania Press.

Brown, Roger, and Albert Gilman. 1960. The Pronouns of Power and Solidarity. In *Style in Language,* ed. T. A. Sebeok, 253–76. Cambridge, Mass.: MIT.

Burke, Kenneth. [1945]1969. *A Grammar of Motives.* Berkeley and Los Angeles: University of California Press.

———. 1957. The Philosophy of Literary Form. In *The Philosophy of Literary Form: Studies in Symbolic Action,* 3–117. New York: Random House.

———. 1984. *Attitudes Toward History.* 3d ed. Berkeley: University of California Press.

Bynum, Caroline Walker. 1987. *Holy Feast and Holy Fast: The Religious Symbolism of Food to Medieval Women.* Berkeley and Los Angeles: University of California Press.

———. 1989. The Female Body and Religious Practice in the Later Middle Ages. *Fragments for a History of the Human Body. Part One,* ed. Michel Feher, 160–218. New York: Zone.

Caballero, Oscar. 1977. *El sexo del franquismo.* Madrid: Cambio 16.

Caillois, Roger. 1979. *Man, Play, and Games.* Trans. M. Barash. New York: Schocken.

Camós, Narcís. [1657]1949. *Jardín de Maria planteado en el principado de Cataluña.* Barcelona: Editorial Orbis.

Cantwell, Robert. 1993. *Ethnomimesis: Folklife and the Representation of Culture.* Chapel Hill: University of North Carolina Press.

Carr, Raymond. 1982. *Spain 1808–1975.* 2d ed. New York: Oxford University Press.

Castany, Josep, Eduard Sánchez, Lluís A. Guerrero, Josep Carreras, Rafael Mora, and Goretti Vila. 1990. *El Berguedà: De la prehistòria a l'antiguitat.* Berga: Ambit de Recerques del Berguedà.

Castells, Manuel. 1997. *The Information Age: Economy, Society, and Culture.* Vol. 2, *The Power of Identity.* Malden, Mass.: Blackwell.

Castro, Américo. 1948. *España en su historia: Cristianos, moros y judíos.* Buenos Aires: Editorial Losada.

Centre de Documentació de la Cultura Tradicional i Popular. 1991. *El món de Joan Amades.* Barcelona: Generalitat de Catalunya.

Christian, William A. 1981. *Apparitions in Late Medieval and Renaissance Spain.* Princeton: Princeton University Press.

50 años del Congreso Eucarístico, un acontecimiento que marcó el rumbo de la ciudad (series of articles). 2002. *La Vanguardia,* May 19–31.

Cinquantenari de la Coronació de la Mare de Déu de Queralt. Els Jocs Florals. Berga, Setembre del 1966.1967. Berga: Ciutat de Berga.

Collier, Jane. 1997. *From Duty to Desire: Remaking Families in a Spanish Village.* Princeton, N.J.: Princeton University Press.

Colom i Colom, Angel. 1977. *La Marxa de la Llibertat.* Barcelona: Edicions Auto-gestionades de "Pax."

Comas i Argemir, Dolors, Iolanda Bodoqué, Sílvia Ferreres, and Jordi Roca. 1990. *Vides de dona: Treball, família i sociabilitat entre les dones de classes populars (1900–1960).* Barcelona: Editorial Alta Fulla.

Comediants 15 años. 1987. *Cuadernos El Publico* 27. Madrid: Centro de Documentación Teatral.

Contreras, Jesús. 1989. La invenció de la família catalana. *L'Avenç* (December): 15–17.

Conversi, Daniele. 1988. L'integrazione degli emigrati a Barcellona. *Studi emigrazione* 25: 67–82.

Coplisha del Arte Taurino. 1990. *El Carallot* 1: 34.

Coser, Lewis. 1984. Introduction to *The Division of Labor in Society,* by Émile Durkheim. New York: Free Press.

Costa, M. Dolors, and Jaume Farràs i Farràs. 1987. *Corpus berguedà i administradors 1619–1987.* Sabadell: by author and Àmbit de Recerques del Berguedà.

Cox, Harvey. 1969. *The Feast of Fools: A Theological Essay on Festivity and Fantasy.* Cambridge: Harvard University Press.

Curet, Francesc. 1967. *Història del teatre català.* Barcelona: Editorial Aedos/Enciclopedia Catalana.

Dalmau, J. 1990. Per què un santuari dedicat a la Mare de Déu de l'Ecologia? *Serra d'Or* 371: 49–50.

Da Matta, Roberto. 1991. *Carnivals, Rogues, and Heroes: An Interpretation of the Brazilian Dilemma.* Notre Dame, Ind.: University of Notre Dame Press.

Danforth, Loring M. 1983. Tradition and Change in Greek Shadow Theater. *JAF* 96: 281–309.

Davis, Natalie Zemon. 1981. The Sacred and the Body Social in Sixteenth-Century Lyon. *Past and Present* 90: 40–70.

Del Giudice, Luisa. 1990. Ubi saltatio ibi diabolus: Dance and Eros in the Italian

Ballad and Dance Song. In *Dona folcloristica: Festgabe für Lütz Röhrich zu seiner Emeritierung. Sonderdruck*, ed. L. Petzoldt and S. Top. Frankfurt am Main: Peter Lang.

Delicious Irony. 2002. *The Economist*, April 27. Online edition.

Del Negro, Giovanna P., and Harris M. Berger. 2001. Character Divination and Kinetic Sculpture in the Central Italian Passeggiata. *Journal of American Folklore* 114: 5–19.

Devlin, Dennis Steel. 1975. *Corpus Christi: A Study in Medieval Eucharistic Theory, Devotion, and Practice*. Doctoral thesis, University of Chicago.

DiGiacomo, Susan. 1986. Images of Class and Ethnicity in Catalan Politics, 1977–1980. In *Conflict in Catalonia: Images of an Urban Society*, ed. Gary Wray McDonogh, 72–91. Gainesville: University of Florida Press.

Donem la benvinguda als pixapins . . . 1990. *El Carallot* 1: 4.

Douglas, Mary. [1973]1982. *Natural Symbols*. New York: Pantheon.

Dufour, Gérard and Jean-François. 2000. *L'Espagne: Un modèle pour l'Europe des régions?* Paris: Gallimard.

Dumont, Louis. 1951. *La Tarasque. Essai de description local d'un point de vue ethnographique*. Paris: Gallimard.

———. 1986. *Essays on Individualism: Modern Ideology in Anthropological Perspective*. Chicago: University of Chicago Press.

Dundes, Alan, and Alessandro Falassi. 1975. *La Terra in Piazza: An Interpretation of the Palio of Siena*. Berkeley: University of California Press.

Duran i Sanpere, Agustí. 1943. *La fiesta del Corpus*. Barcelona: Editorial Aymá.

Durkheim, Émile. [1893]1911. *De la division du travail social*. Paris: Alcan.

———. [1893]1984. *The Division of Labor in Society*, ed. L. Coser. Trans. W. D. Halls. New York: Macmillan.

———. [1912]1960. *Les formes élémentaires de la vie religieuse*. Paris: Presses Universitaires de la France.

Eco, Umberto. 1986. *Semiotics and the Philosophy of Language*. Bloomington: Indiana University Press.

Edles, Laura Desfor. 1998. *Symbol and Ritual in the New Spain*. Cambridge: Cambridge University Press.

Elliott, John H. 1963. *The Revolt of the Catalans*. Cambridge: Cambridge University Press.

———. 1989. *Spain and Its Worlds, 1500–1700*. New Haven, Conn.: Yale University Press.

Equip sacerdotal de Berga. 1970. La vida religiosa de Berga. In *Berga Ciutat Pubilla de la Sardana-1970*. Berga.

Escudella i Carn d'Olla. 1997. *Manual del bon patumaire*. Berga: by authors.

———. 1998. *Guia d'orientació per a patumaires*. Berga: by authors.

Fabian, Johannes. 1983. *Time and the Other: How Anthropology Makes its Object*. New York: Columbia University Press.

———. 1990. *Power and Performance: Ethnographic Explorations Through Proverbial Wisdom and Theater in Shaba, Zaire*. Madison: University of Wisconsin Press.

———. 1994. Ethnographic Objectivity Revisited: From Rigor to Vigor. In *Rethinking Objectivity*, ed. A. Megill. Durham, N.C.: Duke University Press.

Fabre, Daniel, and Charles Camberogue. 1977. *La fête en Languedoc: Regards sur le Carnaval aujourd'hui*. Toulouse: Privat.

Fàbregas, Xavier. 1979. *Tradicions, mites i creences dels catalans: La pervivència de la Catalunya ancestral*. Barcelona: Edicions 62.

———. 1983. *El llibre de les bèsties. Zoologia fantàstica catalana*. Barcelona: Edicions 62.

Fàbregas, Xavier, and Pau Barceló. 1976. *Cavallers, dracs, i dimonis. Itinerari a través de les festes populars*. Barcelona: Abadia de Montserrat.

Farràs i Farràs, Jaume. 1979. *Histoire et sociologie d'une fête populaire auprès d'une festivité religieuse*. Paris: Thèse de IIIe cycle, Ecole de Hautes Etudes en Sciences Sociales.

Farràs, Jaume. 1982. Textos i comentaris sobre les Bullícies de Berga al segle XVII, segons les Actes i Comptes Municipals. In *XXIII Assemblea Intercomarcal d'estudiosos celebrada el juny de 1979 a Berga*. Berga: Ajuntament de Berga.

———. [1986]1992. *La Patum de Berga*. 2d ed. Barcelona: Nou Art Thor.

Feldman, Allen. 1991. *Formations of Violence: The Narrative of the Body and Political Terror in Northern Ireland*. Chicago: University of Chicago Press.

Felipó i Oriol, Ramon. 2003 in press. El Pi de les Tres Branques i Mn. Cinto Verdaguer. *L'Erol* 72.

Fernandez, James. 1965. Symbolic Consensus in a Fang Reformative Cult. *American Anthropologist* 67: 902–27.

———. 1979. On the Notion of Religious Movement. *Social Research* 46: 36–62.

———. 1986 *Persuasions and Performances: The Play of Tropes in Culture*. Bloomington: Indiana University Press.

———. 1987. The Call to the Commons. In *The Question of the Commons*, ed. B. McCay and J. Acheson, 266–89. Tucson: University of Arizona Press.

———. 1988a. Isn't There Anything Out There That We Can All Believe In? The Quest for Cultural Consensus in Anthropology and History. Paper read at the Institute for Advanced Study School of Social Science, Princeton, N.J., December 15.

Fernandez, James W. 1988b. Andalusia on Our Minds. *Cultural Anthropology* 3:21–35.

Fernandez, James W., and Michael Herzfeld. 1998. In Search of Meaningful Methods. In *Handbook of Methods in Cultural Anthropology*, ed. H. R. Bernard. Walnut Creek, Calif.: AltaMira Press.

Fernández Retamar, Roberto. [1971]1989. *Caliban and Other Essays*. Trans. E. Baker. Minneapolis: University of Minnesota Press.

Fernàndez-Pola Garrido, Oscar. 1987. La Patum: Una puntual metamorfosi de Berga. *Regió 7*, June 18.

Ferrer, Llorenç, Jordi Piñero, and Rosa Serra. 1997. *El Llobregat, nervi de Catalunya*. Manresa: Angle Editorial.

Ferrer i Gàsol, Agustí. 1989. *La Patum: Foc i Fantasia* (slide-tape show). Berga: Ambit de Recerques del Berguedà.

Fishman, Robert M. 1990. *Working-Class Organization and the Return to Democracy in Spain*. Ithaca, N.Y.: Cornell University Press.

Foix, Josep Vicenç. 1980. *Antologia poètica*. Barcelona: Edicions 62.

Foucault, Michel. 1979. *Discipline and Punish: The Birth of the Prison*. Trans. A. Sheridan. New York: Vintage.

Fradera, Josep Maria. 1983. Les nocions de 'progrés i 'ordre social' en Balmes. *L'Avenç* 65: 14–20.

———. 1990. Rural Traditionalism and Conservative Nationalism in Catalonia (1865–1900). *Critique of Anthropology* 10: 51–71.

Freedberg, David. 1989. *The Power of Images: Studies in the History and Theory of Response*. Chicago: University of Chicago Press.

Freud, Sigmund. [1912–3]1946. *Totem and Taboo. Resemblances Between the Psychic Lives of Savages and Neurotics*. Trans. A. A. Brill. New York: Knopf.

———. 1958. The "Uncanny." In *On Creativity and the Unconscious*, ed. B. Nelson. New York: Harper and Row.

———. 1961. *Civilization and Its Discontents*. Trans. J. Strachey. New York: W. W. Norton.

———. 1966. *Introductory Lectures on Psychoanalysis*. Trans. J. Strachey. New York: Norton.

Fribourg, Janine. 1980. *Fêtes a Saragosse*. Paris: Musée de l'Homme.

García, Fernando. 1991. Cataluña está amenazada por la falta de inmigración extranjera. *La Vanguardia*, August 8: 18.

García Gallo, Alfonso. 1975. *Manual de historia del derecho español*. 6th rev. ed. Vol. 1. Madrid: Artes Gráficas.

Geertz, Clifford. 1973. Deep Play: Notes on the Balinese Cockfight. In *The Interpretation of Cultures*, 412–53. New York: Basic Books.

Genís i Aguilar, Martí. [1904]1988. *Novel.les vigatanes*. Barcelona: Curial.

Gentile, Emilio. 1996. *The Sacralization of Politics in Fascist Italy*. Cambridge: Harvard University Press.

Giesey, Ralph E. 1968. *If Not, Not: The Oath of the Aragonese and the Legendary Laws of Sobrarbe*. Princeton, N.J.: Princeton University Press.

Gilmore, David D. 1998. *Carnival and Culture: Sex, Symbol, and Status in Spain*. New Haven, Conn.: Yale University Press.

———. 2002. *Monsters: Evil Beings, Mythical Beasts, and All Manner of Imaginary Terrors*. Philadelphia: University of Pennsylvania Press.

Giner, Salvador. 1980. *The Social Structure of Catalonia*. Sheffield, Eng.: The Anglo-Catalan Society.

Ginzburg, Carlo. 1989. *Clues, Myths, and the Historical Method*. Baltimore: Johns Hopkins University Press.

Glassie, Henry. 1975. *All Silver and No Brass: An Irish Christams Mumming*. Philadelphia: Univeristy of Pennsylvania Press.

Goffman, Erving. 1967. *Interaction Ritual: Essays on Face-to-Face Behavior*. New York: Doubleday.

Gomis, Cels. 1910. *Zoologia popular catalana*. Barcelona: L'Avenç.

González, Fernando. 1977. *Litúrgias para un caudillo. Manual de dictadores.* Madrid: Cambio 16.

Grau i Martí, Jan. 1996. *Gegants.* Barcelona: Columna.

Green, Anthony E. 1980. Popular Drama and the Mummers' Play. In *Performance and Politics in Popular Drama,* ed. D. Bradby, 139–66. Cambridge: Cambridge University Press.

Griera, Antoni. 1930. Litúrgia popular. *Butlletí de dialectologia catalana,* gener-març: 1–98.

Grifell, Quirze. 1987. La història des del balcó. *L'Erol* 20: 45–48.

Gueusquin, Marie-France. 1988. Cities, Giants, and Municipal Power: Parody Rituals for the Investiture of Processional Effigial Figures in Northern French Cities. *Ethnologia Europaea* 17: 117–28.

Gunther, Richard, Giacomo Sani, and Goldie Shabad. 1988. *Spain After Franco: The Making of a Competitive Party System. With a New Epilogue.* Berkeley: University of California Press.

Habermas, Jürgen. 1989. *The Structural Transformation of the Public Sphere.* Trans. T. Burger. Cambridge, Mass.: MIT Press.

Hammoudi, Abdellah. 1993. *The Victim and Its Masks. An Essay on Sacrifice and Masquerade in the Maghreb.* Chicago: University of Chicago Press.

Handler, Richard. 1988. *Nationalism and the Politics of Culture in Quebec.* Madison: University of Wisconsin Press.

Hansen, Edward C. 1977. *Rural Catalonia Under the Franco Regime: The Fate of Regional Culture Since the Spanish Civil War.* London: Cambridge University Press.

Hardin, Garrett. 1968. The Tragedy of the Commons. *Science* 162: 1243–48.

Harding, Susan Friend. 1984. *Remaking Ibieca: Rural Life in Aragon under Franco.* Chapel Hill: University of North Carolina Press.

Harris, Max. 2000. *Aztecs, Moors, and Christians: Festivals of Reconquest in Mexico and Spain.* Austin: University of Texas Press.

———. 2003. *Carnival and Other Christian Festivals: Folk Theology and Folk Performance.* Austin: University of Texas Press.

Herzfeld, Michael. 1987. *Anthropology Through the Looking-Glass: Critical Ethnography on the Margins of Europe.* Cambridge: Cambridge University Press.

Hirschman, Albert O. 1970. *Exit, Voice, and Loyalty: Responses to Decline in Firms, Organizations, and States.* Cambridge: Harvard University Press.

Holmes, Douglas. 2000. *Integral Europe: Fast-Capitalism, Multiculturalism, Neofascism.* Princeton, N.J.: Princeton University Press.

Huch i Camprubí, Jaume. 1982. Una còpia molt ben feta de La Patum en petit. *Regió 7,* June 10.

Huch i Guixer, Ramon. 1955. *Notes històriques de la ciutat de Berga.* Berga: Impremta Huch.

Hufford, David. 1985. Ste. Anne de Beaupré: Roman Catholic Pilgrimage and Healing. *Western Folklore* 44: 194–207.

Hunt, Lynn. 1992. *The Family Romance of the French Revolution.* Berkeley: University of California Press.

Jack, William Shaffer. 1923. *The Early Entremes in Spain: The Rise of Dramatic Form*. Philadelphia: University of Pennsylvania Press.

Jay, Martin. 1984. *Marxism and Totality: The Adventures of a Concept from Lukács to Habermas*. Berkeley: University of California Press.

Jellinek, E. M. 1962. Cultural Differences in the Meaning of Alcoholism. In *Society, Culture, and Drinking Patterns*, ed. D. J. Pittman and C. R. Snyder. New York: John Wiley and Sons, Inc.

Jenkins, Jennifer. In press. *Provincial Modernity: Local Culture and Liberal Politics in Fin-de-Siècle Hamburg*. Ithaca, N.Y.: Cornell University Press.

KAP. 2000. La Patum com a esport d'aventura. *Regió 7*, June 22: 26–31.

Kaplan, Temma. 1992. *Red City, Blue Period: Social Movements In Picasso's Barcelona*. Berkeley: University of California Press.

Kasmir, Sharryn. 1996. *The Myth of Mondragón. Cooperatives, Politics, and Working-Class Life in a Basque Town*. Albany: SUNY Press.

Kilgour, Maggie. 1990. *From Communion to Cannibalism: An Anatomy of Metaphors of Incorporation*. Princeton, N.J.: Princeton University Press.

Kirshenblatt-Gimblett, Barbara. 1998. *Destination Culture: Tourism, Museums, and Heritage*. Berkeley: University of California Press.

Kuznets, Lois Rostow. 1994. *When Toys Come Alive: Narratives of Animation, Metamorphosis, and Development*. New Haven, Conn.: Yale University Press.

Labov, William. 1972. *Sociolinguistic Patterns*. Philadelphia: University of Pennsylvania Press.

Lamming, George. [1960]1992. *The Pleasures of Exile*. Ann Arbor: University of Michigan Press.

Lane, Jill. 1996. Albert Boadella and the Comedy of Catalan Cultural Politics. *Journal of Dramatic Theory and Criticism* 11: 81–100.

Lannon, Frances. 1987. *Privilege, Persecution, and Prophecy: The Catholic Church in Spain, 1875–1975*. Oxford: Clarendon Press.

Le Goff, Jacques. 1980. Ecclesiastical Culture and Folklore in the Middle Ages: St. Marcellus of Paris and the Dragon. In *Time, Work, and Culture in the Middle Ages*, 159–88. Chicago: University of Chicago Press.

Lebow, R. Ned. 2003 in press. *Ethics, Interest, and Order: The Tragic Vision of Politics*. Cambridge: Cambridge University Press.

Lévi-Strauss, Claude. 1962. *The Savage Mind*. Chicago: University of Chicago Press.

Lewis, Jenna. 2002. *Reflections on the Second World War: Themes of Memory and Escape in Three Italian Films*. Senior Honors Thesis, Department of English, The Ohio State University.

Linz, Juan, Albert Stepan, and Richard Gunther. 1995. Democratic Transition and Consolidation in Southern Europe, with Reflections on Latin America and Eastern Europe. In *The Politics of Democratic Consolidation: Southern European in Comparative Perspective*, ed. R. Gunther, P. N. Diamandouros, and H.-J. Puhle. Baltimore: Johns Hopkins University Press.

Linz, Juan J. 1962. An Authoritarian Regime: Spain. In *Parties, Cleavages, and Ideologies*, ed. E. Allardt and Y. Littunen. Helsinki: Transactions of the Westermark Society.

Llobera, Josep R. 1990. Family, Class, and Nation in Catalonia. Special issue. *Critique of Anthropology* 10 (2–3).

Lukes, Steven. 1985. *Émile Durkheim: His Life and Work*. 2d ed. Stanford, Calif.: Stanford University Press.

MacCannell, Dean. 1976. *The Tourist: A New Theory of the Leisure Class*. New York: Schocken.

Mack, Phyllis. 1987. Feminine Symbolism and Feminine Behavior in Radical Religious Movements: Franciscans, Quakers, and the Followers of Gandhi. In *Disciplines of Faith: Studies in Religion, Politics, and Patriarchy*, ed. J. Obelkevich, L. Roper, and R. Samuel. London: Routledge and Kegan Paul.

Magliocco, Sabina. 1993. *The Two Madonnas: The Politics of Festival in a Sardinian Community*. New York: Peter Lang.

Malinowski, Bronislaw. [1923]1972. The Problem of Meaning in Primitive Languages. In *The Meaning of Meaning*, ed. C. K. Ogden and I. A. Richards, 297–336. New York: Harcourt, Brace, and World.

Maragall, Joan. 1960. *Obres completes*. Vol. 1. *Obra catalana*. Barcelona: Selecta.

Marcuse, Herbert. 1962. *Eros and Civilization. A Philosophical Inquiry into Freud*. New York: Vintage.

Marfany, Joan-Lluís, ed. 1974. *Joan Maragall. El Comte Arnau*. Barcelona: Edicions 62.

Martínez, Guillermo, ed. 2001. *Almanaque Franquismo Pop*. Barcelona: Mondadori.

Más allá. Boletín del Frente de Juventudes. 1943–45 (bimonthly). Berga: Frente de Juventudes.

Massip, Francesc, and Joaquim Noguero. 1999. The Exportation and International Presence of Catalan Theatre. *Catalan Writing* 16. http://personals.ip.ictonline.es/%2bpencatala/comites/cw16-3.htm. Accessed January 10, 2003.

Mau Branco, Matias O. 2000. *Història de Carbones de Berga, S.A.* Berga: by author.

Mauss, Marcel. [1925]1967. *The Gift: Forms and Functions of Exchange in Archaic Societies*. Trans. I. Cunnison. New York: Norton.

———. [1935]1979. *Sociology and Psychology: Essays*. Trans. B. Brewster. London: Routledge and Kegan Paul.

McCully, Marilyn, ed. 1986. *Homage to Barcelona: The City and Its Art 1888–1936*. London: Thames and Hudson.

McDonogh, Gary Wray, ed. 1986. *Conflict in Catalonia: Images of an Urban Society*. Gainesville: University of Florida Press.

———. 1988. *Good Families of Barcelona: A Social History of Power in the Industrial Era*. Princeton, N.J.: Princeton University Press.

McNeill, William H. 1995. *Keeping Together in Time: Dance and Drill in Human History*. Cambridge: Harvard University Press.

McRoberts, Kenneth. 2001. *Catalonia: Nation Building Without a State*. Oxford: Oxford University Press.

Meurant, René. 1979. *Géants processionnels et de cortège en Europe, en Belgique, en Wallonie*. Brussels: Commission Royale Belge de Folklore.

Milà i Fontanals, Manuel, ed. 1882. *Romancerillo catalán, canciones tradicionales*.

Segunda edición refundida y aumentada. 2d ed. Barcelona: Libreria de D. Alvaro Verdaguer.

Mintz, Jerome. 1997. *Carnival Song and Society: Gossip, Sexuality, and Creativity in Andalusia.* Oxford: Berg.

Mintz, Sidney W. 1985. *Sweetness and Power. The Place of Sugar in Modern History.* Harmondsworth: Penguin.

Mira, Joan Francesc. 1987. "Fascista el que no bote." In *Punt de Mira,* 81–83. Valencia: Tres i Quatre.

———. 2001. Talibans, Catalans. *El País,* Valencian edition. November 1.

Miralles i Guasch, Carme, et al. 1990. *El Berguedà: Una comarca d'industrialització antiga.* Barcelona: Caixa d'Estalvis de Catalunya.

Mitchell, Timothy. 1991. *Blood Sport: A Social History of Spanish Bullfighting.* Philadelphia: University of Pennsylvania Press.

———. 1998. *Betrayal of the Innocents: Desire, Power, and the Catholic Church in Spain.* Philadelphia: University of Pennsylvania Press.

Montañà, Daniel, and Josep Rafart. 1991. *La guerra civil al Berguedà (1936–1939).* Barcelona: Abadia de Montserrat.

Montanyà, Antoni. 1985. Repàs de la història recent de la música patumaire: refilets i desafinaments. *Regió 7,* 4 June.

Montanyà, Josep. 1983. La Patum dels anys posteriors a la Guerra Civil. *Regió 7,* June 3.

———. 1991. Aniversaris de la Coronació: 1941 i 1966. *L'Erol* 34: 42–44.

Moore, R. I. 1987. *The Formation of a Persecuting Society: Power and Deviance in Western Europe, 950–1250.* Oxford: Blackwell.

Morán, Gregorio. 1991. *El precio de la transición.* Barcelona: Planeta.

Moretti, Franco. 2000. *The Way of the World.* London: Verso.

Morson, Gary Saul, and Caryl Emerson. 1990. *Mikhail Bakhtin: Creation of a Prosaics.* Stanford, Calif.: Stanford University Press.

Mossèn Josep Armengou, avui. 1986. Berga: Centre d'Estudis Berguedans.

Mulvey, Laura. 1986. Visual Pleasure and Narrative Cinema. In *Narrative, Apparatus, Ideology: A Film Theory Reader,* ed. P. Rosen. New York: Columbia University Press.

Neville, Gwen Kennedy. 1994. *The Mother Town: Civic Ritual, Symbol, and Experience in the Borders of Scotland.* Oxford: Oxford University Press.

Noguera i Canal, Josep. 1989. *Berga en temps del Canal Industrial.* Berga: Ambit de Recerques del Berguedà.

———. 1991. *La Mineria al Berguedà.* Berga: Ambit de Recerques del Berguedà.

———. 1992. *Visió històrica de la Patum de Berga.* Barcelona: Editorial Dalmau.

Noiriel, Gérard. 1996. *The French Melting Pot: Immigration, Citizenship, and National Identity.* Trans. G. de Laforcade. Minneapolis: University of Minnesota Press.

Noyes, Dorothy. 1992. *The Mule and the Giants: Struggling for the Body Social in a Catalan Corpus Christi Festival.* Doctoral thesis, University of Pennsylvania.

———. 1995. Façade Performances in Catalonia: Display, Respect, Reclamation, Refusal. *Southern Folklore* 52: 97–120.

————. 1997. Reciprocal Tourism and the Fear of the Floating Local: Networkers and Integristes in Contemporary Catalonia. *Performance Research* 2: 54–63.

————. 2000a. Authoring the Social Drama: Suicide, Self, and Narration in a French Political Scandal. *Narrative* 8: 210–31.

————. 2000b. Breaking the Social Contract: *El Comte Arnau*, Violence and Production in the Catalan Mountains at the Turn of the Century. *Catalan Review* 14: 129–58.

Obiach, Xavier. 1987. Angeles contra demonios. *El País Semanal*, June 7.

Obradors, Albert. 1983. La Patum Infantil del Carrer de la Pietat, 23 anys de bullícia a redós de la capella. *Regió 7*, June 3.

O'Donnell, Paul. 1995. "It Depends Who I Marry": Linguistic Recruitment and Defection. *Catalan Review* 9: 163–72.

Oliver, Joan. 2000. *El 20-N a Catalunya. Els catalans i els últims dies del franquisme*. Barcelona: Planeta.

Ortega y Gasset, José. [1929]1958. *La rebelión de las masas*. Madrid: Espasa-Calpe.

Otto, Rudolf. 1923. *The Idea of the Holy. An Inquiry into the Non-Rational Factor in the Idea of the Mind and its Relation to the Rational*. Trans. J. W. Harvey. Oxford: Oxford University Press.

Els partits polítics en la Catalunya d'avui. 1974. Barcelona: Edicions Catalunya.

Paulson, Ronald. 1983. *Representations of Revolution (1789–1820)*. New Haven, Conn.: Yale University Press.

Pedrals, Xavier. 1989. La Patum a finals del XVIII, unes dades per conèixer l'evolució de la festa. *Regió 7*, May 28.

————. 1990. *El Berguedà a través del temps: Resum d'història*. Berga: Centre d'Estudis Berguedans.

————. 2000. Per no oblidar cap patumaire. *Regió 7*, June 22.

Peirce, Charles Sanders. 1991. *Peirce on Signs*. Ed. James Hoopes. Chapel Hill: University of North Carolina Press.

Pérez-Díaz, Victor. 1993. *The Return of Civil Society: The Emergence of Democratic Spain*. Cambridge: Harvard University Press.

Pernau, Josep. 2001. Opus Mei. Un modelo catalán para el mundo. *El Periodico* November 1.

Pijoán, José. 1934. *El arte prehistórico europeo*. Ed. F. Cossío and J. Pijoán. Vol. 6, *Summa Artis. Historia General del Arte*. Madrid: Espasa-Calpe.

Pi-Sunyer, Oriol. 1971. The Maintenance of Ethnic Identity in Catalonia. In *The Limits of Integration: Ethnicity and Nationalism in Modern Europe*, ed. O. Pi-Sunyer, 111–46. Amherst: Department of Anthropology, University of Massachusetts.

Pi-Sunyer, Oriol. 1985. The 1977 Parliamentary Elections in Barcelona: Primordial Symbols in a Time of Change. *Anthropological Quarterly* 58: 108–19.

Porcel, Baltasar. 2001 *Clinton, el primero*. La Vanguardia, November 1.

Prat i Carós, Joan. 1984. *La mitologia i la seva interpretació*. Barcelona: Dopesa.

————. 1989. El pairalisme com a model ideològic. *L'Avenç* 132: 34, 51–57.

Pregó Carnestoltes 1990. 1991. *El Carallot* 2: 38–39.

Prieto de Pedro, Jesús. 1998. Democracy and Cultural Difference in the Spanish Constitution of 1978. In *Democracy and Ethnography: Constructing Identities in Multicultural Liberal States*, ed. C. J. Greenhouse with R. Kheshti, 61–80. Albany: SUNY Press.

. . . *Qui jamega ja ha rebut.*1981. Països Catalans: Comités de la Solidaritat amb els Patriotes Catalans.

Rabinow, Paul. 1989. *French Modern: Norms and Forms of the Social Environment.* Chicago: University of Chicago Press.

Rafart, Benigne. 1989a. Aquella Patum del 1975. *Regió 7*, May 28.

———. 1989b. El bisbe Tarancón ens va deixar fa vint-i-cinc anys. *Regió 7*, March 12.

———. 1990. Els anys de la Segona República i la guerra civil en els escrits de Mn. Josep Armengou i Feliu (Berga, 1910–1976). In *Anuari 1988 de la Societat d'Estudis d'Història Eclesiàstica Moderna i Contemporània de Catalunya*, 75–85. Tarragona: Institut d'Estudis Tarraconenses Ramon Berenguer IV.

Rafart, Joan. 1981. Untitled ms. on the history of the Patum Infantil.

Ravicz, Marilyn Ekdahl. 1980. Ephemeral Art: A Case for the Functions of Aesthetic Stimuli. *Semiotica* 30: 115–34.

Resina, Joan Ramon, ed. 2000. *Disremembering the Dictatorship: The Politics of Memory in the Spanish Transition to Democracy.* Amsterdam: Rodopi.

Riba i Soler, Jaume. 1989. Un home d'ànsies socials. *El Vilatà* 76: 19.

Ricoeur, Paul. 1970. *Freud and Philosophy.* New Haven, Conn.: Yale University Press.

Roigé i Ventura, Xavier. 1989. Els juristes i la família catalana. *L'Avenç* 132: 28–33.

Rousseau, Jean-Jacques. [1758]1967. *Lettre à M. D'Alembert sur son article Genève.* Paris: Garnier Flammarion.

Royo, Jordi, and Quirze Grifell. 1991. Posa me'l . . . per barret! In *XVIII Concurs de "Garrofes" 1990*, 7–10. Berga: Agrupació Teatral La Farsa.

Rubin, Miri. 1991. *Corpus Christi: The Eucharist in Late Medieval Culture.* Cambridge: Cambridge University Press.

Rumbo i Soler, Albert. 1995. *Història dels gegants de Berga.* Berga: Consell Comarcal del Berguedà.

Runciman, W. G. [1966]1971. Relative Deprivation and the Concept of Reference Group. In *Sociological Perspectives*, ed. K. Thompson and J. Tunstall, 299–315. Harmondsworth: Penguin.

Sales, Núria. 1962. *Història dels Mossos d'Esquadra. La dinàstia veciana i la policia catalana el segle XVIII.* Barcelona: Aedos.

Sansalvador, Antoni. 1916. *La Patum.* Barcelona: Antoni Lopez.

Schmitt, Jean-Claude. 1983. *The Holy Greyhound. Guinefort, Healer of Children Since the Thirteenth Century.* Trans. M. Thom. Cambridge: Cambridge University Press.

Schneider, Jane. 1991. Spirits and the Spirit of Capitalism. In *Religious Regimes and State-Formation: Perspectives from European Ethnology*, ed. E. R. Wolf, 24–54. Albany: SUNY Press.

Schütz, Alfred. 1951. Making Music Together. *Social Research* 18: 76–95.

Scott, James C. 1990. *Domination and the Arts of Resistance: Hidden Transcripts.* New Haven, Conn.: Yale University Press.

———. 1998. *Seeing Like a State.* New Haven, Conn.: Yale University Press.

Scribner, Robert W. 2001. *Religion and Culture in Germany (1400–1800).* Leiden: Brill.

Segura, Antoni. 2000. Memòria i història de la Transició. In *Memòria de la transició a Espanya i a Catalunya,* ed. R. Aracil and A. Segura. Barcelona: Edicions de la Universitat de Barcelona/Generalitat de Catalunya.

Serra, José. 1944. *La Custodia Monumental de Berga.* Berga: Impremta Huch.

Serra, Rosa, and Lluís Casals. 2000. *Colònies Tèxtils de Catalunya.* Manresa: Angle Editorial.

Serra, Rosa, and Ramon Viladés. 1987. *La Colònia Pons de Puig-reig (1875–1987).* Berga: Ambit de Recerques del Berguedà.

Silverman, Sydel. 1985. Towards a Political Economy of Italian Competitive Festivals. *Ethnologia Europaea* 15: 95–103.

Simó, Isabel-Clara. 2001. De fil de vint. Patriotes. *Avui,* October 31.

Simon, Jordi. 1982. La meva Patum d'infant. *Regió 7,* June 13.

Sintes, Marçal. 2001. Non stop. Clinton i els catalans. *Avui,* October 31.

Sobrer, Josep-Miquel. 2000. The Moving Mountain: Aporias of Nineteenth-Century Catalan Ideology. *Catalan Review* 14: 173–90.

Sobrer, Josep Miquel, ed. 1992. *Catalonia, a Self-Portrait.* Bloomington: Indiana University Press.

Solé i Sabaté, Josep Maria. 1985. *La repressió franquista a Catalunya, 1938–1953.* Barcelona: Edicions 62.

———. N.d. La desaparición de la "Verge de Núria." In *Cataluña durante el franquismo,* ed. Josep Maria Solé i Sabaté. Barcelona: Biblioteca de la Vanguardia.

Spicer, Edward H. 1971. Persistent Cultural Systems: A Comparative Study of Identity Systems That Can Adapt to Contrasting Environments. *Science* 174: 795–800.

Stegmann, Tilbert D. 1979. *Diguem no-Sagen wir nein! Lieder aus Katalonien.* Berlin: Rotbuch Verlag.

Stewart, Kathleen. 1988. Nostalgia: A Polemic. *Cultural Anthropology* 3: 227–41.

Stewart, Susan. 1984. *On Longing: Narratives of the Miniature, the Gigantic, the Souvenir, the Collection.* Baltimore: Johns Hopkins University Press.

Sunstein, Cass R. 2001. *Designing Democracy: What Constitutions Do.* Oxford: Oxford University Press.

Taussig, Michael. 1980. *The Devil and Commodity Fetishism in Latin America.* Chapel Hill: University of North Carolina Press.

Terradas i Saborit, Ignasi. 1987. *El Cavaller de Vidrà. De l'ordre i el desordre conservadors a la muntanya catalana.* Barcelona: Abadia de Montserrat.

Terradas Saborit, Ignasi. 1979. *La colònia industrial com a particularisme històric: L'Ametlla de Merola.* Barcelona: Editorial Laia.

Tóibín, Colm. 1991. *The South.* New York: Viking.

Torgovnick, Marianne. 1990. *Gone Primitive: Savage Intellects, Modern Lives.* Chicago: University of Chicago Press.

Torres, Rafael. 1996. *La vida amorosa en tiempos de Franco.* Madrid: Temas de Hoy.

Turner, Kay. 1983. The Cultural Semiotics of Religious Icons: La Virgen de San Juan de los Lagos. *Semiotica* 47: 317–61.

Turner, Victor. 1977. *The Ritual Process: Structure and Antistructure.* Ithaca, N.Y.: Cornell University Press.

———. 1988. *The Anthropology of Performance.* New York: PAJ Publications.

Ullman, Joan Connelly. 1968. *The Tragic Week: A Study of Anticlericalism in Spain, 1875–1912.* Cambridge: Harvard University Press.

Valorar la història: Nova vida per a velles ciutats. 1984. Barcelona: Generalitat de Catalunya.

Vann, Robert. 1995. Constructing Catalanism: Motion Verbs, Demonstratives, and Locatives in the Spanish of Barcelona. *Catalan Review* 9: 253–74.

Le Vatican et la Catalogne 1971. 2d ed. Paris: Edicions Catalanes de París.

Very, Francis George. 1962. *The Spanish Corpus Christi Procession. A Literary and Folkloric Study.* Valencia: Tipografia Moderna.

Vicens i Vives, Jaume, and Montserrat Llorens. 1958. *Industrials i polítics del segle XIX.* Barcelona: Editorial Vicens Vives.

Vicens Vives, Jaime. 1954. *Noticia de Cataluña.* Barcelona: Destino.

Vilardaga y Cañellas, Jacinto. 1890. *Historia de Berga.* Barcelona: by author.

Vilarós, Teresa M. 1998. *El mono del desencanto. Una crítica cultural de la transición española (1973–1993).* Madrid: Siglo 21.

Vilà Torner, Antoni. 1991. Olor de garrofa verda. In *XVIII Concurs de "Garrofes" 1990,* 3–6. Berga: Agrupació Teatral La Farsa.

Viola, Andreu. 1989. Raó de família, raó d'estat. *L'Avenç* 132: 18–21.

Virtuts del cagar. N.d. Barcelona: n.p.

Warner, Marina. 1998. *No Go the Bogeyman: Scaring, Lulling, and Making Mock.* London: Chatto and Windus.

Weigle, Marta. 1989. *Creation and Procreation: Feminist Reflections on Mythologies of Cosmogony and Parturition.* Philadelphia: University of Pennsylvania Press.

Williams, Raymond. 1973. *The Country and the City.* Oxford: Oxford University Press.

———. 1983. *Keywords. A Vocabulary of Culture and Society.* Rev. ed. Oxford: Oxford University Press.

Wolin, Sheldon S. 1996. Fugitive Democracy. In *Democracy and Difference: Contesting the Boundaries of the Political,* edited by S. Benhabib, 31–45. Princeton, N.J.: Princeton University Press.

Woolard, Kathryn. 1985. Language Variation and Cultural Hegemony: Toward an Integration of Sociolinguistic and Social Theory. *American Ethnologist* 12: 738–48.

———. 1989. *Double Talk: Bilingualism and the Politics of Ethnicity in Catalonia.* Stanford, Calif.: Stanford University Press.

Young, Katharine. 1999. Memories of the Flesh. Paper presented at the Center for Folklore Studies, The Ohio State University, November 22.

Zingarelli, Nicola. 1970. *Vocabolario della lingua italiana*. Bologna: Zanichelli.

Zulaika, Joseba. 1988. *Violencia vasca: Metáfora y sacramento*. Trans. José Gil Aristo. Madrid: Nerea.

———. 1997. *Crónica de una seducción. El museo Guggenheim Bilbao*. Madrid: Nerea.

Index

Acknowledgments

This book is a small installment on large debts. I have been exceptionally fortunate in my informants, my colleagues, and my institutions, and many more people will see themselves in the text than can be named here.

Most important among those who have waited patiently and impatiently for this book to emerge are my Catalan teachers. In addition to inducting me into the Patum, they fed me, housed me, guided my reading, shared their own scholarship and private archives, showed me the region, criticized my arguments, and gave me their friendship. They were hard to leave, and I never expect to see the match of their collective and individual generosity: the text will show how much I owe them. Special thanks for polymorphous benevolence and wisdom must go to Leonil.la Boixader, Pere Boixader, Lorda Brichs, the late Ricard Cuadra, Àngel Gómez, Jordi Gómez, Quirze Grifell, Lou Hevly, Benigne Rafart, the Roca sisters, Estanislau Salas and Montserrat Santandreu, Carme Serra, Marta Serra i Màjem, the late Josep Tañá, Carme Tor, Ramon Viladomat, and the inexhaustible Ramon Felipó i Oriol.

My enlightenment took place largely in collective settings: the festival itself, bars, institutions, and voluntary associations. I must therefore acknowledge several corporate entities, remembering warmly their communal *ambient* and encompassing in their mention all the individuals who constitute them. My orientation came through Ràdio Berga, the Societat Coral Unió Berguedana, the Casino Berguedà, Comissions Obreres, *Regió 7*, the Àmbit de Recerques del Berguedà, Cal Negre, and Cal Blasi. Most of what I eventually came to understand about Berga was a result of time spent with the Escola Municipal de Música, the Bar La Barana, La Bauma dels Encantats, *El Vilatà*, and above all, of course, the *comparses* of the Patum.

For help of a more individual character in Berga and beyond I'm also indebted to Joaquim Auladell, Jordi Bertran, Benet Boixader, Joan and Josep Casals, Lluís Comellas, the architects of the Direcció General d'Arquitectura i Habitatge of the Generalitat de Catalunya, Manel Escobet, Jaume Farràs i Farràs, the Ferrer family, Mn. Climent Forner, Jaume

Huch, Dolors Llopart, Josep Noguera i Canal, Salvador Palomar, Xavier
Pedrals, Josep Pons i Arcas, Francesc Ribera, Joan Rafart, Josefina Roma,
Jordi Royo, Ramon Sala, Toni Sales, the late Manuel Sistachs, Carles Solà,
Josep Ureña, the Vidal i Puigvert family, and Ramon Vilardaga.

Institutional archives and libraries used include the Arxiu Episcopal
de Solsona; the Arxiu Municipal de Berga; the Biblioteca de la Fundació
de la Caixa de Pensions, Berga; the Biblioteca de Catalunya; the Centre de
Documentació i Recerca de la Cultura Tradicional i Popular, Barcelona;
and the Institut Municipal de la Història, Barcelona.

At the Ohio State University, I have had the happiness of being affili-
ated with the Department of English, the Center for Folklore Studies, the
Institute for Collaborative Research and Public Humanities, and the Mershon Center, each full of provocative colleagues and each under exceptionally supportive and stimulating leadership: James Phelan, Amy Shuman,
Christian Zacher, and Richard Ned Lebow. The Institute and Mershon
provided invaluable time off and research funding, respectively, and I am
grateful as well for support from Ohio State's College of Humanities and,
earlier, the National Endowment for the Humanities and the Andrew W.
Mellon Foundation.

The host of non-Berguedan colleagues obliged to listen to me over
the years have offered insights of all kinds, but some deserve special mention. Roger D. Abrahams has given me most of the good ideas I've ever
had. The University of Pennsylvania's Department of Folklore and Folklife—Roger D. Abrahams, Dan Ben-Amos, Henry Glassie, the late Kenneth S. Goldstein, David Hufford, Dell Hymes, Margaret Mills, John
Roberts, Brian Sutton-Smith, and Don Yoder—and, at a distance, James W.
Fernandez taught me the kind of ethnography I have tried to practice here,
and my colleagues and students at Ohio State have created an equally fer-
tile environment for folklore research. I would also like to thank my colleagues in the Department of English for their generosity to the very odd
bird in their midst. Regina Bendix has been my disciplinary conscience
over the years, and Josep Miquel Sobrer my Catalanist one: happily both
are of a far more festive temperament than the office implies and have
made a constant pleasure of the obligations.

Readers at various stages have urged me forward. Margaret Kruesi,
Emily Socolov, and Bill Westerman got me through the early part. Sabra
Webber and Marge Lynd nudged me through the middle of the present
manuscript, and Ned Lebow and Ted Hopf pushed me to articulate its
comparative implications in ways of which I hope someday to be capable.

Two anonymous readers for the University of Pennsylvania Press gave meticulous, enormously helpful critiques, and Ned provided a final reading of the whole. Max Harris and David Gilmore offered encouragement and generous previews of their own Patum scholarship. Colleagues in the American Folklore Society and at many institutions have given me opportunities to share my work: I am grateful to all, and especially to Lluís Calvo i Calvo in Barcelona, Cristina Sánchez-Carretero, Luís G. Díaz Viana, and Carmen Ortíz García in Madrid, Christian Bromberger in Aix-en-Provence, Renata Jambresic Kirin in Zagreb, and Arzu Öztürkmen in Istanbul for arranging for my participation in transformative international encounters.

Peter Agree's enthusiasm for the project and editorial reassurance brought me through an anxious period. Foto Luigi, Berga, and Joan J. Guillén in Barcelona kindly gave permission to reproduce visual materials, and Francesc Ribera to reprint a lyric of Els Brams. Abhijit Varde made the maps. Ohio State's College of Humanities and the Spanish Ministry of Education and Culture provided important financial assistance for the publication of the volume.

I need not thank my family for undergoing the Berguedan initiation, which they all enjoyed, but rather for their patience, financial and moral support, intellectual nurturance, and generous encouragement of my work over many years. Accustomed to standing on the sidelines on such occasions, my parents, Thomas and Virginia Noyes, and my husband, Michael Krippendorf, will not be surprised to see the people of Berga on the dedication page instead of themselves. Without them, however, I would never have known how to look for Berga, much less have gotten there. This book is theirs too.